SWEAT

The Story of
the Fleshtones,
America's Garage Band

Joe Bonomo

continuum

NEW YORK • LONDON

2007

The Continuum International Publishing Group Inc
80 Maiden Lane, New York, NY 10038

The Continuum International Publishing Group Ltd
The Tower Building, 11 York Road, London SE1 7NX

www.continuumbooks.com

Copyright © 2007 by Joe Bonomo

Printed in Canada on 100% postconsumer waste recycled paper

Library of Congress Cataloging-in-Publication Data

Bonomo, Joe, 1966-
 Sweat : The story of the Fleshtones, America's garage band / Joe Bonomo.
  p. cm.
 Includes bibliographical references (p.   ), discography (p.   ), and index.
 ISBN-13: 978-0-8264-2846-2 (pbk. : alk. paper)
 ISBN-10: 0-8264-2846-0 (pbk. : alk. paper)
 1. Fleshtones (Musical group) 2. Rock musicians--United States. I. Title.

ML421.F58B66 2007
782.42166092'2--dc22
[B]

                                                             2007006479

"Pocketful of Change" by Ken Fox/Keith Streng/Peter Zaremba, published in 1993 by
    Piledriver (BMI)/Busybuddy Music (BMI). Used by permission.
"Right Side of a Good Thing" by P. Zaremba, published in 1983 by My Idea Sounds
    (ASCAP). Used by permission.
"New Scene" by P. Zaremba, published in 1983 by My Idea Sounds (ASCAP). Used by
    permission.
"Screamin' Skull" by K. Streng/P. Zaremba, published in 1983 by My Idea Sounds
    (ASCAP). Used by permission.
"The Return of the Leather Kings" by K. Streng/P. Zaremba, published in 1986 by My
    Idea Sounds (ASCAP). Used by permission.
"We'll Never Forget" by K. Streng/P. Zaremba, published in 1995 by Nascha Music
    (BMI)/Busybuddy Music. Used by permission.
"I'm Not a Sissy" by P. Zaremba, published in 1998 by Busybuddy Music (BMI). Used
    by permission.
"I Want the Answers" by K. Fox, published in 2005 by Smashed-In Music (BMI). Used
    by permission.

Contents

There is hope in honest error, none in the icy perfections of the mere stylist.   —Chas Mackintosh Glasgow

Garage music is not bad, because Christ was born in a manger, which was probably like a garage of that time.
                                                        —Sky Saxon

cult > Latin, cultus, *worship*

For Bill, Marty, & Steve—the original rock & roll gang,

and to the memory of Gordon Spaeth, 1951–2005

Acknowledgments

Sweat took a long time to write. I have lots of people to thank, starting with Keith Streng, Peter Zaremba, Bill Milhizer, Ken Fox, Marek Pakulksi, Lenny Calderon, Robert Warren, and, in memoriam, Gordon Spaeth. I pitched the idea of this book to the Fleshtones in a small, loud bar (surprise) and they were receptive and enthusiastic, and since then they've given much of their personal time. Thanks guys, for allowing me into your homes and onto your roofs. Thanks also to Marilla Palmer, Jean Fox, and especially Anne Streng, whose enthusiasm for the Fleshtones was immeasurably helpful in the form of her decades-worth of press clippings, photos, and memorabilia that got this project off to a roaring start and helped to finish it.

Thanks also to the many folk along the way who allowed me to interview them or to otherwise toss questions their way: Steve Albini; Leslie Aldredge; Betsy Alexander; Jim Ball; Miles Barken; Helaine Berman; Lori Blumenthal; Jay Boberg; John Bruce; Peter Buck; Brian Butterick; Peter Case; Robert Christgau; Mike Costello; Peter Crowley; Jimmy Descant; Jimmy Destri; Glen Dicker; George DuBose; Karen Everson; Dia Farber; Dave Faulkner; Jimmy Ford; Daniel Gilbert; George Gilmore; Anders Goldfarb; Richard Gottehrer; Carlos Grasso; Brett Green; John Guarnieri; Richard Hell; John Holmstrom; Sam

Acknowledgments

James; Paul Johnson; M. Henry Jones; Nick Jones; Hilly Kristal; Alain Lahana; Max Lebreton; Miriam Linna (thanks for the shirt!); Richard Manitoba; Jim Marshall; Richard Mazda; Legs McNeil; Billy Miller; Cathy Nemeth; Terry Ork; April Palmeri; Bruce Patron; Jon Quinn; Jeff Reinholz; Martin Rev; Jason Ringenberg; Ira Robbins; Jules Roinell; Kim Saade; Randy Sadd; Andy Schwartz; Andy Shernoff; Rick Shoor; Robert Singerman; Fred Smith; Marty Thau; Roy Trakin; Eric Weisbard; Jon Weiss; Paul Wexler; Steve Wynn; and Tom Wynbrandt. No thanks to Debby Harry for hanging up on me.

A big thank you to David Barker, Katie Gallof, John Mark Boling, Gabriella Page-Fort, and everyone at Continuum for handling this project so enthusiastically and generously. It isn't surprising to me that David, with his appreciation for the possibilities and the promises in rock & roll, took a chance on telling the Super Rock tale.

Many people over the years offered tangible and intangible support for this book. I'm especially grateful to Phast Phreddie Patterson and Lindsay Hutton for their generous support and help. Thanks also to my family, and to Angie, Glenn, and Marc at YepRoc Records, David Behrel, Violaine Bernard, Blair Buscareno, Louis Bustamante, Jim DeRogatis, Hans Frank, David Fricke, Eric Fusco, Steve Greenfield, Esmond Harmsworth, Larry Higgs, Manfred Jones, Dave Kaplan, Raphael Louviau, Pat Lozito, Nick Maier, Scott McCaughey, Fred Mills, Didier Pasquier, Jean-Marc Rimette, Jean-Pierre Soulignac, Gary Stewart, Tim Tintle, Nick Tosches, and Jeroen Vedder. Thanks to the staff at New York Public Library, Greenpoint Public Library, New York Historical Society, Northern Illinois University Founders Library and Music Library, Film-makers Cooperative (Clocktower Gallery), City of New York Police Department, Legal Bureau, and the YMCA in Greenpoint, Brooklyn.

Thanks to the waitresses at the Triple X diner, and to the many bartenders over the years who offered support, both moral and intoxicating, at the Lakeside Lounge, the International [R.I.P.], Mona's, the Cherry Tavern, Manitoba's, the Greenpoint Tavern, B-Side, and the Parkside Lounge. (And probably elsewhere. . . .)

A special tip of the hat to Steve Coleman, head honcho at the Fleshtones Hall of Fame and longtime fan, whose research, knowledge, and comments during the draft stages of the book were very helpful. His energy, support, and encouragement were great tonics throughout.

Above all thanks to Amy, whose love, patience, and support assured that this book would get done despite the many dark days. *Sweat* wouldn't be here without her.

List of Photos

List of Photos

The Party: Peter, Paris, 1985. (Photo by Jacob Forsell)

Chapter 10: Bill, Music Building, New York City, 1983. (Photo by Anders Goldfarb)

Chapter 11: Backstage, CBGB, New York City, 1980. L-R: Gordon Spaeth, Brian Spaeth, Peter, Bill, Marek, Keith. (Photo by Laura Levine)

Chapter 12: Onstage, Paris, 1985. L-R: Marek, Keith, Peter, Gordon. (Photo by Jacob Forsell)

Chapter 13: Peter, Keith, Marek, O.N. Klub, Los Angeles, California, 1981. (Photo by David Arnoff)

Chapter 14: *Hexbreaker!* promotional photo, 1983. L-R: Keith, Marek, Peter, Gordon, Bill. (Photo by George DuBose)

Chapter 15: Backstage, London, 1983. L-R: Gordon, Bill, Peter. (Photo by Richard Dumas)

Chapter 16: Tompkins Square Park, New York City, 1986. L-R: Marek, Gordon, Peter, Keith, Bill. (Photo by Monica Dee)

Chapter 17: *Fleshtones vs. Reality* promotional photo, 1987. Clockwise from top left: Keith, Bill, Gordon, Peter, Robert Warren.

Chapter 18: Peter and Keith, Brest, France, 2004. (Photo by Herve Le Gall)

The Hangover: Peter, Gibus Club, Paris. (Photo by Richard Dumas)

Chapter 19: Promotional photo, ca. 1989. Clockwise from top left: Fred Smith, Keith, Peter, Bill.

Chapter 20: Ken, Brooklyn, New York, 2006. (Photo by Frederic Mahieu)

Chapter 21: On Keith's roof, Brooklyn, New York, 1992. L-R: Keith, Ken, Peter, Bill. (Photo by Anne Streng)

Chapter 22: Peter and his Farfisa, Coney Island High, New York City, 1997. (Photo by Eric Fusco)

The Remedy: Le Rocksane, Bergerac, France. L-R: Peter, Keith, Ken. (Photo by Lionel Gibaudan)

Chapter 23: Gordon passed out, Martinique, 1985. (Photo by Rick Shoor)

Chapter 24: On Keith's roof, Brooklyn, New York, 1996. L-R: Ken, Keith, Bill, Peter. (Photo by Anne Streng)

Chapter 25: Bill and Keith, 31st Street Pub, Pittsburgh, Pennsylvania, 2003.

Chapter 26: Coney Island shore, New York, 2005. L-R: Ken, Peter, Bill, Keith. (Photo by Anne Streng)

Epilogue: Peter, Keith, Ken, getting into cab in front of Nightingales, New York City, 1996. (Photo by Tom Hosier)

Prologue,
or Maybe I'll Go Back to School
to Find Out Where I Went Wrong

He's somewhere between a song and a shout. Pulling a mock-heroic face, throwing a profile at a half-filled club, graying bangs falling in his face as he moves to a mongrel Jerk, a Frug, moves like he probably moves at home in front of the stereo.

Columbus, Ohio, halfway across the god damn country. A long way from the East Village, anyway. A medallion swings around his neck like a knockoff of a psychedelic relic glinting beneath red and yellow stage lights. At the bar sit a dozen drinkers who aren't really watching, engaged in hunched-over debauchery of their own, snorting powder, flirting skirts, slaying some hours in the din of yet another rock & roll band making noise from a stage.

My dreams are frayed, my dreams and shoes more worn.

He'll take the mike stand and spin it around like a geeky shaman. If you listen closely he might be channeling something, a prism for long-lost 1-4-5 and "Louie Louie" chord changes and beer glasses clinking. He'll hold the mike stand out in front of him and hop over it, his back to the crowd, willing James Brown or Kid Thomas or Jackie Wilson from some poorly lit basement party a hundred years ago in a white concrete garden suburb in Queens, New York. Wail, baby, wail.

An hour earlier he'd wrapped duct tape around that mike, marrying it to the stand with a faraway look in his eyes, the twirling repetition of a nights-old gesture spinning a dreadful dullness that had to be avoided at all costs.

Later, he taped a handwritten sign on the wall near the front door: MERCHANDISE FOR SALE. He tried three times, the damn thing still hung crooked.

One more big night, another bitter dawn.

The song kicks into the chorus now and the singer's eyes light up and he grins crooked, sweat rolling down his face, but now no one can really tell if he's for real or if he's some kind of joke.

Onstage he does something weird: he pulls out the pockets of his pants, scatters some lint on the stage, shrugs his shoulders at no one. He's laughing.

My life's been spent, too late to rearrange.

But I didn't sell my soul.

At least I've nothing for it to show.

Now he grabs a beat-up harmonica from his front pocket, looks down to check his bearings, blows while the guitarist, axe flashing, puts one pointy boot on the stage monitor and wails. The drummer and the bass player keep an impossibly energetic beat going behind the ragged melody that soars over the heads of the club-goers, the drinkers, the cute college-age waitresses, the distracted soundman, the hipsters. The music leaks out the occasionally opening front door onto High Street and the swirl of a grimy late-night avenue and its grimy shadows and the many memories forgotten in those shadows. The song lifts to the rooftops.

But I gave my life away for a few good memories and a pocketful of change.

Hitsburg, U.S.A.

"Just leave 'em alone
and they'll have some fun."

1.
The Most Simple Song Possible

The 1965 Fender Mustang guitar lay in pieces at the bottom of a cardboard box, a mess of twisted wire and wood. The guitar had once been useful, had once hummed in someone's hands, and would find itself one day reborn and spirited away to dozens of countries and rock & roll stages around the globe. But for now it was a reminder of the sorry fate that a beat-up practice guitar suffered in the early-1970s era of Super Groups, smoke machines, and expensive light shows.

Welcome to Rock America.

He was born the only son of second-generation Polish parents in Maspeth, New York, on the sixteenth day of September in 1954, eight weeks after Elvis Presley cut his prophetic tracks in Sun Studio down in faraway Memphis. By his gawky and shy teen years, Peter Michael Zaremba was a six-foot, hood-eyed misfit with a Palooka smile and Warhol bangs living in Flushing, well past the end of the Number 7 train. Queens is a big left-handed fist. Nestled beneath the blue-collar neighborhoods of College Point and Whitestone, Flushing rests at the bottom of the middle finger, and the three burgs threaten to lift that middle finger against the world. The simple houses lining the Queens streets of Peter's youth rested under the burden of unpretentious mobility, and growing blue-collar families filled the houses and their tiny fenced-in yards in civic harmony, a subway or express-way ride from Manhattan but a world away in civility and quiet.

At age three Peter would stand in front of the living room mirror and try on his junior Frank Sinatra hat—the one with the small brim and the little feather and the toddler ear flaps—practicing for hours to get Ol' Blue Eyes' rakish, jaunty-grin-with-the-trembling-lip. When Peter was around the age of ten, Sinatra's "Fly Me to the Moon" was on the radio. Peter's working-class dad—he was also named Peter, but "Sonny" became his familiar name—would arrive home after a day of driving his gasoline delivery truck around the borough, having urged his truck through streets crowded with fin-tail Buick's and wood-paneled station wagons, and relax with a cold beer and the living room radio. Pop, swing, ballads, rock & roll, doo-wop, it all poured through the Zaremba household in the late 1950s and early 1960s. Peter was too little to notice the panting, swooning girls or the breathy cadence of a master like Sinatra. But he knew that that mouth, those lips, that sound stood for something fun in this world. *Fly me to the moon, let me play among the stars*, he heard in his home. *Fill my heart with song, let me sing forever more.*

Agitating in Flushing and in the hearts of teenagers? Tedium common to any suburb, tree-lined streets and backyard barbecues doing little to enliven long adolescent days. The coming years would change the music and the culture, but the posters would remain the same on Peter's bedroom wall. Large-mitted and big-hearted, Peter wanted to learn to play guitar and battle his boredom, to rediscover the simple songs of the Kinks, the Yardbirds, the Troggs, the Music Machine, Mitch Ryder and the Detroit Wheels, the Strangeloves. In the summer of 1970 he'd started working at the outdoor Schaefer Beer Presents music festival concerts in Central Park, a shit job for an acne-scarred fifteen-year-old. He started by setting up the chairs and sweeping after the concerts, but from there went fairly quickly to working backstage doing menial tasks, stocking drinks, writing up the guest lists for the V.I.P. backstage area, letting bands and press people in and out. Sometimes he even did a little security. There were some decent bands that came through: the Byrds, Arthur Lee, NRBQ, the Flamin' Groovies. The gig was okay, worth taking the train out for.

A local kid everyone called Doy was lurking in a service alley in Flushing one afternoon. He found a busted-up Mustang guitar sitting forlornly in a trashcan and after peeling off apple rinds and blowing off coffee grounds he showed it around to anyone who cared to take a second look.

Peter came by his house one day and fell in love with the beat-up instrument, shyly admiring its curves, the long neck, the strings he'd finger and caress to the tunes in his head. Doy sized up the situation: *Here's a sucker.*

"A Mustang's a practice guitar, you know, to learn how to play on," he said dismissively to Peter. "No one would play this on stage. But I'll sell it to you for sixty-five bucks."

That was a good amount of money to Peter, but he really wanted a guitar, and so he earned his dough and he saved his pocket change and he got it. The previous owner, some kid, had tried to repaint the guitar with shellac and it had the resinous, beaded stuff glopped all over it in a crude psychedelic pattern. Peter had a project that slow-moving summer of his sixteenth year: sand the Mustang down, make it his own. He sanded and lost interest, sanded and lost interest. While the radio on the patio next door played the Carpenters' "We've Only Just Begun," Peter sat out on his front porch and sanded a five-year-old practice guitar, dreaming of a stage.

Brian Spaeth, a buddy from nearby College Point, took an interest in Peter's project. He lived in a cramped apartment on 150th Street in Flushing, near Zaremba's house. He was a few years older than Peter, a towering, lanky misfit already mired on the post–Flushing High School treadmill of deadening factory jobs, afternoon drug oblivion, and vanishing expectations. His home had become a local flophouse. He'd often walk through his front door and find fifteen kids drinking wine and smoking pot in his living room, and he wouldn't know any one of them. On one of these ragtag nights Peter wandered in with some friends, looking for kicks, and he took an instant liking to Spaeth's impressive, purist record collection, sensing after a few conversations with Brian that they had a lot in common. On television that night, drunk and sleepless, they watched in agony as a bloated Marc Bolan took ten minutes to end a song, indulgently milking an over-the-top finish for as long as his Glam band could flog it.

Peter turned glumly to Brian, his new like-spirit: "Man, it's the fucking end of the world."

Hopeful enough the next day when the sun came up and the ground was still beneath their feet, the two buddies went on record-buying excursions to Colony Records and Rocks in Your Head, picking up discs like "Talk Talk" and "Little Girl" by the Syndicate of Sound, slabs of lively and snarling, up-tempo and brief rock & roll already fiercely discredited, if not wholly ignored, by the local

Queens crowd. They'd fly back to Spaeth's place, throw themselves on a cheap sofa, and spin the discs all day, the tops of their heads coming off at the sounds that were a few years old but already sounded timeless.

Eventually, Peter and Brian got that Mustang guitar looking pretty good. Peter took it over to Paul Niewierowski, a local hotshot guitarist with a flashy rep whom Peter casually knew from Brooklyn Tech High School. Gripping his trashcan guitar, his voice tightening in frustration, Peter said, "Look, I really just want to learn how to play this guitar, the most simple song possible. 'You Really Got Me' by the Kinks."

Niewierowski stared at him blankly for a moment, then lowered his head and chuckled softly. "You know, you really can't learn how to play the guitar by starting that way. I mean, if you start like that then you won't have the basics and you won't know how to play. What you've got to do is to learn how to play scales."

Scales? So many notes. But Peter tried. He turned off "Everything Is Beautiful" and "Fire and Rain" and "In the Summertime" and whatever else was clogging up Top 100 Light Rock radio that week, and he practiced his scales. And he practiced. And he practiced. His eyes glazed over and his fingers cramped in the rigidity of virtuosity while the sweet ease of Ray Davies seemed increasingly lost in the breezes off of Flushing Bay. Over the next couple of months, Peter approached one or two other local folk and asked them to teach him how to play guitar.

"All I want to learn is how to play 'You Really Got Me,'" he'd say. Everyone looked at him funny. *Bar chords? Mersey Beat? That fuckin' old fashioned shit?* Pretty soon Peter gave up. He thought, *Fuck scales and modes, I'll never learn, I don't even care, this is too hard.* Somewhere in the back of his mind, there was a voice whispering: "It's too hard to learn how to play."

Frustrated, Peter took apart that Mustang, a relic of the *Hullabaloo* and *T.A.M.I. Show* era, threw the pieces in a box, and stuck it on his front porch.

The glittery cover bands at the Coventry in Long Island City always felt and sounded like relics to Peter and his friends. But things are changing. His ear to the ground, Peter can just about make out through the murky, garbage-clogged waters of the East River the distant rumble of disaffection, chaos, and fun emanating from the filthy Bowery in Lower Manhattan. Scruffy bands are playing something called "Street Rock," and they don't look very Glam anymore.

The Most Simple Song Possible

Keith Streng, a small, skinny, borderline juvenile delinquent with a sharp, narrow face and a manic grin, was a year behind Peter at Flushing High School. Keith had mischievously formed a camping group called the Alister Crowley Trail and Ski Club, ostensibly to go on school-financed camping expeditions in upstate New York. It was really just an excuse to take LSD and go mental for a few days. Peter overheard students snorting about the club, and he was curious. He met Keith in the Catskill mountains under a clear night of aligned stars on the Alien Rock Expedition Trip. (They were watching a lot of *Lost in Space* instead of doing homework.) Keith was as charged by rock & roll as Peter, and he'd been fooling around on a guitar in his bedroom on the long nights in his College Point neighborhood, having fun but struggling with a cheap Japanese model. The guitar was outlandish and cool, but cheap and unreliable.

"I need a real guitar," Keith said to Peter one day.

"Man, Keith, I'll sell you mine," Peter said. "It's in a bunch of pieces in a box. Just lemme finish it." Peter dug the box out of the porch, lifted out the forgotten pieces, opened a can of Minwax varnish, and after five years finally gave that guitar the beautiful finish and stain that it deserved.

The Mustang changed hands that day, and it would serve its purpose well: rescued from virtuosity, restored to simplicity.

2.
The Kids Are the Same

Did the song vanish? Were the Gods toying with him?

"So in Love," recorded by the Tymes and released on the Parkway label in 1963, was a gorgeous doo-wop pledge of undying love along a moonlit shore, and a radio hit in the New York metropolitan area. It was the first song that Peter consciously followed up the charts, as another kid might've trailed the ascension of Mickey Mantle's batting average. For a kid too young for girls, discovering the magic of radio, that plastic-and-wire beacon of invisible and unlimited joy, was like discovering a new best friend to lose the afternoons with. Peter dreaded in his young mind that "So in Love" might someday disappear.

Of course, "So in Love" did fall off the charts, in the manner of all Top 100 tunes that burn brightly for a season. Nine-year-old Peter was heartbroken. The words, caressed by the street-corner soul of George Williams—*as we stroll along together holding hands, walking all alone, so in love are we two that we don't know what to do*—were so haunting that Peter might as well have been addressing them to the very song itself. "So in Love" did fade away, but not in mean-spirited bewitchment: what Peter didn't know yet was that he could've found it the next week at the Flushing Woolworth's, still in its crisp, virginal-white sleeve, or years later amidst stacks of cracked

The Kids Are the Same

45s in a Salvation Army somewhere in the East Village. But all Peter knew at the moment was that "So in Love" had disappeared from the radio, had vanished, for good.

A few months later a new sound would burst forth that wouldn't disappear.

Down in Dallas, Texas, the country would change with one bullet, while in Queens something was detonating on the radio: four long-haired guys who looked alike but who sounded like nothing we'd heard before. "It's the Beatles! *Omigod!! It's the Beatles!!*" Sandra Zaremba was screaming in her bedroom, trembling in epileptic Beatlemania. Vibrant, race-free harmonies and a muscular backbeat, high-pitched "ooohhs" and the breathless rush of SOMETHING NEW. Peter flew down the hall to his sister's bedroom and flopped down next to her on the bed. In front of her crowd of teddy bears, the opening harmonica-guitar riff of "Please Please Me," the first Beatles tune to hit big in the New York area, came pouring out of the radio as an irresistible party invitation. Peter could feel in Sandra's sobs the rhythms of something magical. On her bed they listened together to two and a half minutes of pop ecstasy.

Peter's radio was always on, and he was always listening. Elvis Presley seemed like an old-fashioned hoodlum by the mid-sixties, the butt of too many corny jokes about Hollywood, hound dogs, and pink Cadillacs, and the Beach Boys were too West Coast for the boroughs—they sure as hell never surfed the East River. Mostly Peter liked weird stuff, singers like Gary "U.S." Bonds and Freddy "Boom Boom" Cannon, who were yowling something fiercer, wilder, and blacker into their songs. *Shindig!* debuted on channel 7 during the happy afternoon of Peter's tenth birthday, hooking him deeper into the long-haired, squealing exhilaration of rock & roll, an eye-opening present for a kid a year or two away from really digging the lure of caged dancers, go-go boots, and frosted, pouting lips. When Peter became a teenager in 1967, Sandra threw him a party in the attic of their new home in Flushing. As black light bounced off of the groovy posters, big sis presented Peter with a copy of the Rolling Stones' *Big Hits (High Tide and Green Grass)*. The Aeolian roar of Beatlemania had blown open the doors. Wandering in were scraggly mates the Kinks, the Yardbirds, the Animals, and, better yet, all of the young American teenage bands who tried their damnedest to sound just like their rocking U.K. heroes.

A few years later, that gust had dwindled to a breeze. The likes of Yes, Procol Harum, and countless progressive jamming bands could do little with their artful and sophisticated pretense to stir the breeze. By the end of the decade, as Woodstock blew its cannabis zephyr across the landscape, Peter was reduced to buying old Yard-birds records and scouring the sleeves for obscure tracks that he'd yet to hear on the radio or at his friends' homes. There were still some bursts of pure, exciting rock & roll: in the early seventies the radio could offer something as dangerous as the Rolling Stones' "Brown Sugar." Peter dug that filthy tune one night at a Whitestone bar into which he'd snuck with friends. The underage scofflaw accli-mated himself to his smoke-filled second home as the romance and glamour of the seedy place competed with Mick's exciting leer and Charlie Watts' driving and pounding.

At the festival concerts in Central Park, work and play mingled for Peter, but he found precious little that turned him on. The Kinks played the Park a couple of times in August of 1972, and Peter dug Ray Davies, one of his heroes, so he was excited to take the Number 7 train out from Flushing on those late afternoons. He enjoyed the weird asides that the Davies brothers often choreographed, the awk-ward, strange stage mannerisms that signaled Ray as an English out-sider. But what Peter started realizing was that Ray used the same aside every night in the same place in the same song. At the Philhar-monic Hall, Dave Davies, high on God knows what, lost his balance in the middle of a song and stumbled backward into a gigantic bank of high-wattage amps that blew up in a shower of fiery sparks and black smoke. He was nearly killed. Peter was at that show. He was glad that Davies survived, but on the subway ride back home that night, beneath a scribble of graffiti, he had to admit to himself that that moment—so outlandish, so unpredictable, so absurd—really turned him on.

A lot of nights Peter endured anonymous, crowd-pleasing oldies bands and watched as the music he loved trickled out as watered-down souvenirs of a past that seemed far away. And when the Mets were in town, it took a summoning of all the work ethic he had inher-ited from his day-laboring father not to blow off the Park for the park. One muggy night late in the summer, Peter was in the wings doing something menial when an outfit he couldn't have cared less about, Sergio Mendes & Brasil '66, hit the stage. They began with "Mais Que Nada," their glorious, exotic Brazilian pop number.

A minute into the performance, Peter felt something invisible tap him on his shoulder. He turned toward the stage and saw Mendes bent over his piano in a feverish trance, magically channeling a Bossa Nova rhythm in jazz changes. The minor chords only made more mysterious the origins of this sound, a Latin brew of Anglicized jazz wrapped in colorful robes and tossed with a floral, South American half-grin. The band put so much into that song that it seemed like all of midtown stopped to listen. Suddenly Peter felt like dancing and moving, grabbing strangers. Startled into the magic of Mendes, surprised into abandoning his preconceptions about what music can do, Peter paid close attention to that stage.

Central Park sat under a thick haze of marijuana smoke that warm evening as "Mais Que Nada" plunged its South American rhythms into Peter's blood.

Keith Carl Streng was the son and the nephew of no-bullshit New York City cops. Born in Manhattan one year and forty-eight hours after Peter, Keith grew up knowing well the difference between discipline and recklessness, work and play.

Keith's father Robert was a police sergeant in Manhattan. By the time Keith was five, his dad had had it with the clamor of Manhattan and moved his family—his wife, Joan, Keith, and Keith's brother, Rick— over the East River to Whitestone, Queens. A booming, unassuming tree-lined suburban neighborhood, Whitestone jutted out along the East River, bordered on the west by Flushing Bay and the east by Little Neck Bay. The Bronx-Whitestone and Throgs Neck Bridges into the Bronx and northern bedroom communities opened up Whitestone in the midcentury to a great influx of population and steady commerce. By the time the Prussian-descended Strengs arrived, four years before the 1964 World's Fair put Queens, Shea Stadium, and New York suburbia on the map, Whitestone was a comfortable, thriving area, its proximity to the darkness of the Rikers Island Correctional Facility belying the quiet, family-friendly streets and neighborhoods.

The Strengs settled happily in a modest home, but Keith's father was ultimately to be driven out of the borough. Pristine and quiet New England—Maine, especially—called his name. He had longtime vacation friends there, where the most stressful decisions involved "What drink tonight?" and "What lake tomorrow?" After his marriage busted up, Keith's dad would move to Maine for good and become Chief of Police at Booth Bay Harbor, leaving behind the congestion and madness of New York.

Keith endured Flushing High School in a haze of detention and idleness, finishing his homework with a beer. Lunatic-eyed, he peaked at well under six feet, and though hallway lockers towered over him, there was surprising and aggressive strength coiled in his hard, compact frame beneath his long, narrow face and longer bangs. His father was often up in Maine looking for that idyllic house and lifestyle, leaving his two teenage sons to live with their grandmother. Grammy Streng shuttled among Whitestone, Maine, and Long Island, where she suffered a long recuperation from eye surgery, leaving the house in Whitestone without adult supervision. Here was a recipe for fun and relaxation for the two Streng boys. And they followed the recipe to the letter. Nearly every weekend Keith threw booze and LSD parties, funded by his father's weekly allowances, and they were packed with Keith's nutty, deadbeat friends while rock & roll roared on a tiny, beat-up record player.

Like Peter, Keith wasn't pleasantly cooled in the lengthening shadows of popular music. Rock & roll had became rock, and teenagers turned their lusty gazes from honey-thighed *babies* to long-haired *mamas* and started dragging four stacks of keyboards and two kick drums onstage. A dark time dawned. On the prowl for minimal, raw rock & roll, Keith turned to blue-collar cities like Detroit and the crunch-noise and sometimes laughable politics of the MC5, or better yet the mess of Iggy and the Stooges. Also around were the J. Geils Band, Mott the Hoople, Roxy Music, the Move, a couple of other rocking bands. But the two-and-a-half-minute rock & roll record was becoming a seriously scarce commodity.

What had changed Keith early on was hearing the Beatles and the Rolling Stones. He was a scrawny nine-year-old who liked to buy 45s, forty cents apiece with picture sleeves. Shortly after Peter had recognized in a cloud-clearing epiphany that records don't disappear forever, Keith began buying up the seven-inch black vinyl slabs, just about anything he heard on the radio, and soon he had a huge collection. The first full-length album Keith bought was *Meet the Beatles*. And soon after came the Stones. At age ten he heard "(I Can't Get No) Satisfaction" at the Astoria Public Pool while hanging out with his friends, and under the high sun Keith didn't fight the song's hostility and urge. He took it as his own prepubescent call to arms.

The weeks circling Keith's eleventh birthday prove how vital American Top 40 was for kids who dug rock & roll and rhythm & blues, even if they were too young to know what they dug, only that it made them want to dance. 1966 was an *annus mirabilis*. Tune in this on your transistor radio: "Land of 1000 Dances" and "Mustang Sally" by Wilson Pickett, "I'm Not Your Stepping Stone" and "Last Train to Clarkesville" by the Monkees, "96 Tears" by ? and the Mysterians, "Psychotic Reaction" by the Count Five, "Devil with the Blue Dress on/Good Golly Miss Molly" by Mitch Ryder and the Detroit Wheels, "Fa-Fa-Fa-Fa-Fa (Sad Song)" by Otis Redding, "Have You Seen Your Mother Baby, Standing in the Shadow?" by the Rolling

Stones, "I Had Too Much to Dream Last Night" by the Electric Prunes. And that was just fall and winter. A pretty good party. Sure, Keith had to wade through "The Ballad of the Green Berets" and "Winchester Cathedral" and "My Heart's Symphony" and "Georgy Girl." But it was worth the wait when the Troggs' "Wild Thing"— one of the top singles in the summer of 1966—tore through AM radios unable to disguise its foreign language of sexual need. And that was only the national charts: local New York radio also spun regional bands, whose one-off singles were attempts at imitating Mick Jagger, raw, lo-fi replicas hatched in a garage on a Saturday afternoon filtered through frustration, suburban ennui, and teenage hangovers. Peter and Keith were too young yet for such rebellion to make sense to them politically, but they would feel that soon enough. Anyway, the lo-fi snarl of New York-area bands such as Magic Plants or the Groupies translated nicely.

Peter and Keith, like so many young American teens and pre-teens, had a lot to enjoy during those bleached mid-sixties summer afternoons when the radio played all day. They sang along to those songs, and continued to stubbornly a few years later in the hallways of Flushing High School, where few of their long-haired, bell-bottomed classmates would care to remember the dopey words to "Wild Thing." Tastes were shifting: on Peter's sixteenth birthday, England's *Melody Maker* produced a reader's poll asserting that Led Zeppelin had replaced the Beatles as the U.K.'s most popular group. A year later, Pink Floyd become the first rock group to appear at the Classical Music Festival in Montreux, Switzerland. The struggle against rock pomposity was on.

Three hundred sixty miles northeast of New York City sits the bucolic town of Wayne, Maine. The town-that-rhymes rests sublimely in the low mountains along Lake Androscoggin, twenty miles west of Augusta in the center of the state. As the 1960s gave way to the 1970s, the population of tidy Wayne stood at around seven hundred, and held steady. In this craggy, idyllic small town everyone knew everyone else, neighbors helped other neighbors in trying times of need, and the general practitioners made regular house calls.

Jan-Marek Pakulski emerged blinking into the Wayne sun on August 26, 1956. At the cusp of the seventies he was a handsome but gangly fourteen-year-old student bearing the small town's cultural limitations and narrow borders acutely. (His first grammar school had been a one-room schoolhouse.) Teenagers couldn't find a whole lot to do in the summers except to fish, swim, boat, tan, and listen to

Sweat

AM radio. As do Peter and Keith, Marek remembers thrilling to the magic of the Beatles over his small transistor radio, and later to the more curiously and crudely channeled magic of the Stones. *Rubber Soul* was the first record he ever bought, but his sister had gotten *A Hard Day's Night* for a gift the previous Christmas. He played it to death, eventually wearing down the grooves.

Few music trends braved the wild trek up into sunny central Maine. Marek had tried to take piano lessons when he was young, at his parents' insistence, but he couldn't stomach the oppressive atmosphere of his elderly teacher's home, with her doilies and her copies of *Grit* newspapers lying around collecting dust. He started fooling around on a guitar with some high school friends, but he never really took it all that seriously. He played drums—marching snare in grade school—and he had a practice pad at home. He sang a little bit with some guys at school, but young, shy Marek Pakulski was more of an onlooker than a doer. In junior high and high school, he listened to whatever music the other kids were digging, mostly blue-collar rock and gutbucket boogie like Grand Funk Railroad and Black Oak Arkansas. At some point he heard a Moody Blues record, and being an intuitively depressive sort and a geeky gadget-head, cleaved onto their spacey poetry and futuristic melotrons. Later, at boarding school, he fell in noisily with kids from up and down the East Coast and started hearing heavier stuff like Savoy Brown, J. Geils Band, a lot more Stones, and eventually the Stooges' *Fun House*.

The Strengs had met and befriended Marek's parents, John and Ruth, in Maine, and the Pakulskis would often visit New York City and stay with Keith's family in Queens. Despite being a year younger, Marek naturally gravitated to Keith, shyly admiring his misspent style, the way he'd waste afternoons on end searching for fun and kicks. Keith would occasionally come up to Maine with his dad and brother, and he and Marek would hang out together, go swimming, boating, drink booze. Marek came down on his own to visit Whitestone for a couple weeks. He, Keith, and a growing crew of kids hung out together in Whitestone in a very lively scene, with a lot of parties and a lot of unsupervised adolescent fun.

Marek graduated high school in 1973. Wayne was a beautiful place, but Wayne was a beautiful *small* place, with limited options for a boy closing out his reckless teen years. Marek was adrift. He applied to some local art colleges, but didn't really have a clue what he wanted to do, spending a careless summer after high school with a bunch of rough local kids who had committed one of their parents to an insane asylum and spent the inheritance on pot, Jeeps, Land Rovers, and stereo equipment. Marek lost himself in that toasted summer, but was able to clear his head long enough to recognize that he needed to earn some dough.

In the summer of 1973, a regional epidemic of disease among fowl, *lavingo trachiaitis*, an affliction of the larynx and the trachea, ravaged local New England farms. DiCoste Egg Farms in Maine, one of the largest brown-egg producers in the country, was forced to inoculate all of their chickens, and fast. Marek heard from his friends that DiCoste was paying three dollars an hour to local kids to inoculate, which to Marek was a whole lot of money. All of the local kids were going over to DiCoste and signing up, but most of them couldn't last two days doing the numbing, repetitive work. Marek and his cousins bit the bullet—they knew that they had to work or have zero money for the coming year. So Marek vaccinated over a half a million chickens in three months, often dosing himself with cut-rate speed and whipping through the barn armed with a blue eyedropper and a handful of squawking chickens. There were hundreds of thousands of these chickens, and the barns were enormous. Eventually Marek would find himself in a row, look endlessly in either direction, the chickens cackling their white noise as he began hearing people calling his name. But it was purely imaginary, the matrix of sound providing a background for a toxic psychosis. Marek grew terribly ill by the end of the summer, the horrible bacteria tattooing him.

For Marek's eighteenth birthday, Keith came up from Whitestone and he and a couple of other friends took Marek out to a low-rent strip club in Lewiston, twenty-five miles south of Wayne. These trips up to Maine, hanging out and partying with his buddy Marek, were becoming happily routine for Keith. In July of 1975, Keith made the five-hour trip to visit his father. By this point Marek was miserably bored. He'd let his hair and beard grow, and as he and Keith stayed up one night concocting whiskey sours, even those festive and colorful drinks couldn't rouse Marek from his small-town blues. Marek looked to Keith like a drunk, unhappy Christ.

"You know," Keith said to his friend, "this is a real drag working in this fucking chicken farm. What the hell do you got going on up here?"

Marek snorted. *Days of inoculating chickens? Nights of getting stoned?* Pakulski needed to get out of Wayne. "I can't take it up here much more," he confided to Keith.

Keith fixed him a hard stare. "Marek, listen, man, why don't you get out of here if you don't like it? Come with me! Get in the car, man! Take your bag! New York is fucking exciting. There's a music

scene! We party all the time! You should come down!" It took all of
about two hours for Marek to decide to pack a bag and throw it in the
back of Keith's Volkswagen and head down to New York. He said
goodbye to his family, jumped in the car, and before he knew it he
was moved in with Keith in a small basement apartment in Queens.
And the parties continued unabated. But there was one problem: the
fun kept spilling out into the street. Keith and Marek knew they
needed a bigger place.

As a small child, Bill Milhizer looked longingly at old photos on soft
pages in oversized hardcover books, and at the naturalistic paintings
at the local public library of the romantic all-American Troy, New
York, a strong and picturesque river-centered nineteenth-century
town, burgundy and gold in its aspirations to commerce and prosperity. Images entranced him of big, beautiful steam ships carrying
goods, produce, and merchandise up the river from New York. Situ-
ated a hundred and sixty miles north of Manhattan, Troy was a
model, booming, postwar American city, prospering from its benev-
olent and divinely chosen location on the Hudson River.

Troy's population was approximately sixty-five thousand when
Bill was born, the final Milhizer child, on September 21, 1948. He
remembers as a boy the excited bustle of weekend and seasonal
shopping, the city's lively reputation having made it the place to shop
in the Hudson valley, not Schenectady, or Albany across the river.
There was a thriving and competitive Little League Baseball team for
which young Bill, already lengthening toward the lean, six-four
frame he'd carry as an adult, pitched with success. His was the arche-
typical, burnished childhood that lost itself in the lengthening shadows of summer days.

Bill grew up in a lively musical home. Monday through Friday his
father Elmer designed steam turbines for General Electric, a varia-
tion on the very turbines that once powered the river steamers from
a century before, but on the weekends he played trumpet in the
Happy Dean Orchestra, mostly in nightclubs but occasionally in
dance and Legion Halls. Near Troy lies an area of lakes with small
hotels, caverns, and halls, and here tourists would come up from
New York City and nearby regions to spend their summer days listening to the Happy Dean Orchestra.

In the photograph that Bill remembers, Happy Dean didn't look
all that happy—in fact, he sat grim-faced at the piano, the only one in
the band *not* smiling—but Bill's father looked joyful. Partly because
he had the opportunity to play, and partly because Bill's mother

The Kids Are the Same

Helen also made music. She played piano for the Sentimental Dolls, tickling the ivories in song standards of the 1940s and 1950s. The Milhizers usually played separate gigs, but occasionally would magically float down the stairs together decked out in sequined gowns and dinner jackets, perfumed and cologned, and drift out the door together to play in their own dance band.

Eight-year-old Bill watched his parents go from their humdrum life to getting dolled up, a metamorphosis of show business romance right in his own front foyer. He hated those evenings because it meant that the babysitter had to come over: he wanted to go where his parents were going. There was a piano at the house, so he knew what his folks were up to. They weren't playing standards to swaying upstate weekenders strictly for the money—Bill's father's job was secure and well-paying—but for the simple love of making music that they knew and adored. Watching his parents court their weekly flirtation with the golden era of music was to forever charm young Bill.

Before the Beatles splashed down, before Sandra Zaremba's squeals would lure Peter into the thrill of long-haired rock & roll, before Keith cocked a shocked ear to "I Want to Hold You Hand," an oft-maligned era for rock & roll was thriving. The post-Private Elvis and pre-Beatles Top 40 years of the early 1960s hold some great memories for Bill. He absorbed his father's Tommy Dorsey and Harry James records, and noisy garage bands like the Trashmen were also getting radio airplay in upstate New York. It was a joy and a riot for Bill to hear the insane "Surfer Bird" and other one-hit wonders competing with his father's glamorous and decorous Big Band records. Bill and his friends would go down to the local radio stations in Troy, WTRY 980 AM and WABY AM, walk right through the front doors and into the studio. The owners would let them in to watch the DJ behind the booth, spinning records like he was making fire. They were allowed to watch him there for a bit, once in a long while overstaying their welcome, but it was all very informal and welcome. Later, the stations would hand out the playlist to the kids, and Bill loved knowing what was hot each week. He and his friends would sprint home arguing who was better: *The Orlons! The Chiffons! No, The Essex! Bobby Rydel! No, Gene Pitney! Dion!*

Elvis Presley was a shock to nine-year-old Bill, as seminal as the Beatles would be seven years later. One afternoon out at his uncle's house in the country, Bill noticed a copy of *Life* magazine on the sofa, and there was Elvis on the cover with his arms around a teddy bear. None of Bill's relatives out in the country were really sophisticated enough to know that this was a publicity shot, they just saw a big guy with crazy hair. And a teddy bear! *What a sissy*, they whispered, hoping that they were out of range of the children. *I can't wait for him to get off the radio!* Naturally, the adults' shock and raised eyebrows only made Bill that more fascinated. He was too young to fully understand the teenage appeal of Elvis, but when his older brother had his sixteenth birthday party in the Milhizer household, the appeal was made manifest. All of his brother's teenage friends came over, the boys *and* the girls, each clutching a stack of prized 45 singles. They stood around demurely before hormones and curiosity took over and they began pairing off to make out in the corners of the rec room. "All Shook Up" drifted up the stairs to young Bill, who'd snuck out of his bedroom to spy.

In the autumn of 1963, Bill took his first drum lesson. The blue sparkle kits looked so exciting in the music store display windows at night. A football-playing friend of Bill's, Gary Burke, had started playing drums three years earlier, and they used to hang out a lot, talking music, girls, and music. Burke was already playing in bands at high school dances, and so he stood for Bill as a kind of beacon of coolness and teen possibility. They'd see shows together, too, players they admired like the Dave Brubeck Quartet with Joe Morello on drums, and anybody coming to the R.P.I. Fieldhouse, the big venue for music. At that point Burke was so far ahead of everybody in the area that he was quite an influence on Bill. He was so good, and so young.

So Bill wanted to find out about drums. The Saturday afternoon of his first lesson changed him. "It sounds like a cliché," Bill recalls nearly thirty years later. "But I became a man that day."

Paul Buehler was his teacher. The moment when Buehler stood and shook fifteen-year-old Bill's hand was when Bill felt he had entered the world of grownups. *This is what they do*, wide-eyed Bill said to himself. *They're musicians.* He paid $2.50 for a half-hour drum lesson, and his life shifted tectonically. He had no idea how much fun it was going to be, how right it would feel to play drums. He went directly home after that first lesson, got the drum book out and his practice pad, and spent all the rest of that Saturday night playing while his friends held hands and grew rowdy at the high school football game. He improvised around an ironing board, imagining, *Okay, this would be the area for a cymbal.* He couldn't get away from it, and he discovered an entire world in that book full of music. He charged ahead on his own, and when he came back the next weekend he said to Buehler, "I think I've got it right on my own. Can I show you what I did?" Paul Buehler was simply thrilled to have somebody whose parents weren't dragging him in for a lesson and plopping him down.

In the summer of 1964, Bill bought his first drum kit, the same set that he plays now with the Fleshtones. In March of that year the Beatles had completed their infamous assault on North America by holding the top five spots on the *Billboard* singles charts, and now every teenager in Troy wanted drums and guitars. Forget the old accordion players, the soft-shoe horn players, the sequined Big Band dance players (Bill's parents had hung up their own patent leather shoes around this time). Rock & roll and pointy boots were in *and listen to the girls scream!*

Overnight, Buehler had dozens of Beatle wig–wearing students. So he turned to Bill, his best and most serious pupil, and asked him if he could take up some of the slack for the beginning students. Bill was only sixteen but he was capable in getting students off the ground and off to playing a set, because by that time Bill had been out playing with his own band the Charades, named after the popular movie from the previous year starring Cary Grant and Audrey Hepburn. The title tune, a Henry Mancini number, was nominated for an Academy Award for Best Song in 1963, and Bill and his band loved it and played an instrumental version as their theme song. Local desires and circumstances required that the band play and sing *everything* because people in Troy wanted to hear old swing music as well as popular rock & roll. A couple of guys in the band were Polish, and since they played some Polish weddings they had to do polkas, and later they clumsily learned some Latin music because people wanted to do a tipsy cha-cha or samba. And of course they had to do the hits, so every weekend they'd throw in a new Beatles tune. The Charades was a very instructive band to be in.

In April of 1965, the Rolling Stones came to Albany, New York, on their Rolling Stones, Now! tour, and a thrilled Bill went to the afternoon show at the Palace Theater. All of the kids who went came to the theater directly from high school, running *en masse* in a stampede of teenage kicks. The Stones played an indoor theater with great big sound. The house lights went down, a couple hundred Troy kids were plunged into thrilling darkness, and as the curtain opened the Stones threw out the opening riff of "The Last Time." The kids went bananas, and Bill and his friends ran down as the curtains opened fully. Kids in the crowd, belts around their schoolbooks, stood watching the Stones in awe. There were Brian Jones' clogs and brightly colored pegged pants. Bill stared at Jones' sublimely tapping clogs, gaped at Charlie Watt's impossible coolness behind his Ludwig drum kit, and covered his ears to the shrieks of the girls who in preorgasmic bliss were getting off riding the fat, low-end rhythms of the sexy, long-haired Stones.

But the cannabis-laden Summer of Love, a garlanded invitation to years of treacly virtuosity, was a few tossed daisies away from 1965. Fifteen years would pass before Bill would hustle himself at Peter, Keith, and Marek in a grimy diner in the East Village in New York City and start playing in the Fleshtones, a decade-and-a-half odyssey that took him all around the country, but never far from his beloved drum kit.

The Basement

"Down in the basement we
can make lots of noise."

3.
Blue Whales at The House

1) Pour one can of frozen lemonade into a pitcher.
2) Add one full can of Blue Curacao.
3) Add two cans of vodka.
4) Multiply above ingredients by 100.
5) Pour into garbage cans.
6) Invite lots of friends.

A sunny afternoon in the fall of 1975. Marek, Keith, Mike "Whale" Costello, and Bill Hattan are up in the attic, tripping their brains to dust. Seated around an opened door in the floor, peering through in a druggy bliss, they can see the house in diminishing perspective below them. They have a sense of an endless vanishing point. They're feeling suspended in the middle of some kind of infinite matrix.

Or something. They're babbling, really.

The simple three-story home at 20th Avenue and Murray Street in Whitestone, Queens, complete with attic and full basement, had stopped being merely an address, a point of conversion of two lines on a map, and had become—with hedonistic purity—The House. When the cramped basement apartment that Keith and Marek had been sharing became too tight, the two pals began looking along the retiring, tree-lined suburban streets for another place to live and detonate with mind-erasing parties. Hattan, a mutual friend, approached them and told them that his brother-in-law had a house that he was looking to rent. Did they want to go in on it? Keith and Marek went to look at the place. Structurally it seemed fine, though it was pretty dilapidated and run-down.

"Hey, c'mon. All it needs is paint," Hattan promised.

The selling point for Keith was the basement. He wanted a place where he could make a lot of noise banging away on the new Pearl drum kit that he'd bought and not have to worry too much about disturbing the neighbors. This place had a nice roomy basement, and an attic for Hattan to make over into his bachelor pad. Without much reflection Keith and Marek signed the lease, and they were moved in by October, joined by Keith's good friend Whale.

The first morning they arrived, Keith and Whale stepped out onto their front porch and noticed their neighbor to the west, Mr. Barclay.

"Oh, hi neighbor!" they hollered. "Good morning!"

"What's so good about it!?" Barclay grumbled, and disappeared gloomily back into his house. Thus began a tireless grudge between the elderly Barclay and The House, which would come to a reasonable close a year later after others in the neighborhood, supported by an influential local councilman, convinced Hattan's brother-in-law not to renew the lease.

Refurbishing of The House began, as much as four kids fresh out of their teens knew how to refurbish. Instead of selecting and ordering paint at a local store the expensive way, the guys bought a dozen or so cans of white paint at bulk and someone wandered in one afternoon with brown dye. What didn't get painted white that week got painted brown. So it was that The House interior was accomplished in white and shades of coffee, and because the exterior was already a rather sickly Indian corn/pumpkin color, the finished color scheme could only have been described as "Halloweenesque."

That would turn out to be appropriate. Throwing parties was the true reason that The House existed—the lease and zoning papers in Queens County municipal offices might as well have been filed under *Bashes, Too Many*—and the greatest parties were thrown on Halloween, that night of illusion and delusion. But every night was a party at The House. Whale came home from work one late night after his UPS job and found a group of people partying in his living room. Whale dove in gamely, smoking dope, drinking beer, sharing heavy-lidded grins. In the haze someone asked him if he knew who lived in the house. Whale didn't know who these folks were, and he never saw them again.

Blue Whales at The House

Marek had found his first job in New York, working in Long Island City in the Busila Building making rug-hooking supplies. He worked in their factory outlet store but the gig didn't last for more than a couple of weeks. The kid from Maine had a hard time figuring out the difference between a local and an express train, and he'd often end up all the way in the city, having taken the wrong train by mistake. He was late for work one too many times. He was told that the employee he replaced had been a retarded man. Who'd quit.

Meanwhile, Keith took some engineering and architectural drawing courses, gamely wrapped a tie around his neck, combed his bangs back, and began doing detailing for construction sites. Between Marek and Keith they made decent enough money, enough to buy them their weekends and the booze, acid, and nitrous oxide that made those weekends soar. Home by five, drink and play all night. Wake up on Saturday, pretend it's Friday. The games were adolescent, silly, and fun. Keith and Whale took to calling themselves the Young Police and jokingly rounding up local "hoods"—unsuspecting neighbor kids on skateboards and bikes in striped T-shirts. Like father, like son. One of Keith and Marek's favorite activities was to drive wasted around Whitestone at night. It was pretty easy for Marek to talk Keith into trying anything reckless, especially when Keith was drinking. One night they drove Keith's Volkswagen onto a sidewalk and down the entire length of Whitestone village, the car precariously squeezed between parking meters and storefronts with six inches of clearance. Laughing and shouting obscenities out the open windows, the boys made it the three blocks that constitute downtown Whitestone, and they got away with it.

The mayhem worked for the fellas, and for their widening circle of friends. The House became legendary, to local partygoers as well as to the 109th Precinct police, for the Blue Whale Parties that Marek and Keith threw. There were interim drinks, flavored milk concoctions called Chocolate Cows, and a nasty green-chartreuse libation dubbed Swamp Water, but there was nothing that these guys could mix with it that would make it at all palatable. The Blue Whale craze had taken off up in Wayne, which was where Keith was introduced to the drink. Marek's parents and their friends would throw infamous Blue Whale parties, and the mix was a little more potent in those days. A fetish grew up around the Blue Whale in Wayne, and friends began regularly sending Marek's mother tiny ceramic Blue Whales with which she decorated her home. Marek and Keith would eventually water the drink down because they had witnessed firsthand the aftermath of these rocket-fueled parties, including one legendary Wayne bacchanal where people's cars ended up going through camp windows in the early morning hours in a kind of joyful but careless mayhem.

A juvenile mad-scientist at heart, Keith continued to experiment with the mix, eventually arriving at the perfect combination that could sustain a party. Soon, he and Marek arrived at The House's signature: a garbage can full of the stuff. The consequences of these parties were often pretty lurid, but there were no fatalities or serious automobile problems, at least that anyone was aware of. Eventually people had to go home, and as the pitiless sun would come up over Whitestone, Blue Whale victims would be found littered about the neighborhood. One cracked morning Marek himself, having staggered around the neighborhood for hours, was finally found draped across a car. Much to the neighbors' chagrin, these bashes became an entertainment staple at The House. The only neighbors not too bothered seemed to be the family next door to the east, who liked the guys and found them genuinely friendly and relatively harmless, and the family across the street, a Rikers corrections officer (who'd probably seen it all anyway) and his wife and son. The problem was the officer's fourteen-year-old, who, when he wasn't working at the local hospital, would sneak across the street into The House during parties. The boy eventually started stealing cars in the neighborhood, and his parents figured that The House was a direct, and none too appreciated, influence. The teen wasn't the last neighborhood kid corrupted by The House's irresistible party vibe.

The soirees were fueled by more than Blue Whales and LSD. The music was always on, the music was always loud. Vintage blues, Motown and Stax, Stooges, some J. Geils, and a band that Keith had recently discovered, only they weren't all that new: the Sonics, purveyors of the grungiest, most intense garage rock & roll to ever come out of the Pacific Northwest. Keith and Marek loved their sound— rough, loud, distorted, and, above all, fun. Lenny Kaye's infamous *Nuggets* double album, a compilation of garage and one-off-bands, had come out a few years earlier, but the guys had been hip to much of that music already, its raw, indelible evidence strewn throughout The House in the form of the original 45s, thanks to Brian Spaeth and his younger brother Gordon. The records spun early into the morning hours, and the parties roamed from basement to attic and back down again.

And the basement held a surprise. Exploring the space on their first day settling in, ostensibly to set up the drum kit and soundproof the space as cheaply as possible, Keith and Marek discovered that the previous tenant had left behind a bass and a guitar. These were cheap, Japanese hollow-body guitars on their way out, the action two inches off the neck, but the boys looked at their surprise booty and then at each other: *What the fuck. What d'ya think?*

Keith had already started a band of sorts by this time called Twenty Flight Rock to take advantage of the basement space. The Blue Whale Bashes, as fun as they were, needed some live music to really open them up. Keith's first outfit, the Popsicles, led by College Point pal Bill Popp (who would later become a plumber-on-call for CBGB's and then an unsung power pop performer in his own right), didn't last long, and Keith had a musical itch that he was wild to scratch.

He was jamming in the basement with Brian Spaeth on bass and a local long-haired burnout named Freddy Osencoff on guitar. Osencoff was a shooting junkie who Spaeth worked with at Aul Instruments, an electronics company in College Point. The two would take their lunch hour and obliterate themselves on weed, then go back to work, goof on everybody, and get fired and then rehired in a dead-end tragicomic cycle. Keith and Spaeth began heading into Brooklyn, where Osencoff lived in a cramped apartment, for more structured rehearsals. Osencoff would often have shot up before they arrived, and further becloud practice by sipping from a bottle of Cutty Sark. Osencoff was pushing thirty but he looked forty-five, and the rehearsals lumbered along with awful Bad Company covers, Osencoff's own dubious songs, and periods where Osencoff simply nodded out in front of Keith and Spaeth.

"Look, why can't we do 'Little Girl' by Syndicate of Sound, or something?" Spaeth asked in desperation between tunes.

"No. That's crap," Osencoff intoned from his haze. "That shit's old." Sipping scotch whiskey from a smudgy glass, he looked up at Keith and Spaeth and lay down the first law of virtuosity: "We gotta do Mahogany Rush." Twenty Flight Rock was appalling, and didn't last much longer than the bottle of Cutty Sark.

With his amplifiers purchased for Twenty Flight Rock plugged in, Keith abandoned drums and he and Marek started fooling around with the guitars they'd found in their basement.

Problem: neither of them knew how to play a note.

Peter Zaremba was living in Manhattan now, the first of the Queens gang to move to the big city. New York in the mid-seventies was an exhilarating blend of cultural contrasts, teeming with the lowest-rung porn and the highest-rung arts and leisure, squalid poor and glittering wealth. And the city was teetering on financial disaster—within a year of Peter moving to Manhattan, President Ford would utter his infamous response to a proposed federal bailout: "NY: Drop dead!"

The honking, grimy stew was heady and flavorful to Peter. When he turned twenty he enrolled at the prestigious School of Visual Arts, on East Twenty-third Street, where he would study painting, drawing, and design. His draftsman aesthetic was made noisy by an intuitive love for B-movie trash and Mexican horror flicks. He enjoyed his classmates and teachers at the cutting-edge institution, and he positively thrived in the city, but his time at SVA was vexed. Peter knew that he should be there careerwise, but a combination of poor work habits, lack of focus, and distractedly attempting too many different activities would ultimately short-circuit his success.

Peter met and became pals with a fellow art student from Long Island, Jon Quinn, who was two years younger. One afternoon, Quinn was struggling with a class assignment. He was required to do a piece that was completely white, and as he was laboring in a studio Peter approached him, and over Quinn's shoulder, sniffed, "Oh, c'mon. You can paint better than that." Quinn spun on his heels and looked at Peter. "He had hair down to his shoulder, a ruddy complexion, a shirt that was way too big on him," Quinn recalls. "He was a long-haired kid who had long scraggly hair, this bird-ass posture. He was definitely geeked-out, but he was very, very committed. I knew at the time that he had aspirations of being a charismatic leader of his own cult."

Peter and Quinn quickly became friends. They were up late goofing around one night when they should have been working on assignments or critiquing projects, and their conversation meandered around to the subject of popular music. Fifteen miles across the East River, as Keith and Marek were just beginning to pick out notes on found guitars, Peter was dreaming up names for fictional bands. Quinn had also been conjuring up band names for kicks, a long list that included the Fleshtones. Independently, Peter was coming up with names such as the Pro-Styles and the Hi-Beats, and he'd also come up with the Fleshtones, as a pun on his daily painting and also as an echo of the kind of names that old doo-wop bands took. Grinning, wrapping their heads around the irony, Peter and Quinn got off on the fact that at the time there were so few groups named "-tones," a discredited moniker that was strictly fifties and mordantly unhip. That summer, Quinn was staying on Long Island at his parents' house when he got a phone call from Peter.

"I got two questions for ya, Quinn!" Peter said. "Do you mind if

I use the Fleshtones as the name of a band? And do you wanna move in with me?"

Quinn said no to the first, and yes to the second. He and Peter moved into a loft apartment in Manhattan near heady Union Square on Broadway and Seventeenth Street, a walk-up onto which the landlords had illegally tacked two rooms in the back over someone else's roof. The apartment featured floor-to-ceiling windows overlooking the bustle and romance of Broadway, and was simply enormous. "This place has got its own fucking weather system," Quinn said in disbelief the day he walked in. Peter got his own back room, with a hot plate, a sink, and a small refrigerator, reveling in an era when art students and other bohemian types could get a loft for so cheap.

The apartment was across the street from what was then Andy Warhol's Factory and around the corner from Max's Kansas City. It had been more than five years since Warhol drowned in a can of Campbell's soup on the cover of *Esquire*, and by the time Peter moved into the city, the Warhol crowd had moved on from Max's. With manager Mickey Ruskin, Warhol had taken the scene to One University Place, and then downtown to the Ocean Club on Chambers Street. Max's was now owned by Laura and Tommy Dean, with art director Peter Crowley in charge of booking. As Yvonne Sewall-Ruskin recalls in *High on Rebellion*, by 1974 Max's had become a chore for Ruskin, and the bar was drowning in debt. "The glitter-rock crowd had taken over the nightly scene, which drove the artists away. Many of them were now older and had gained some notoriety, were not hanging out as much. Mickey became bored with his own party. He had filled too many stomachs without filling his own pockets. This combination of factors—the fires, thefts, unpaid tabs, and drugs—contributed to Max's demise." The place still had its reputation as a cabaret and, as Peter, Keith, and Marek were to find out, that reputation would only grow when Crowley began booking some pretty interesting rock & roll bands.

Peter and Quinn often spent their evenings in the loft creating conceptual exercises that teased their notions of subversion and satire. One of the more memorable was Cool Europeans. The two roommates wanted to don black turtlenecks and, armed with Beat Generation–issue bongos, enter the SVA talent show to recite the lyrics to the Moody Blues' "Nights in White Satin" and other such pompous poetry. This was a subversive gesture on Peter and Quinn's part, and the talent show organizers refused to let them politicize the event and cut so deeply into the premise of Performing. The organizers accused Peter of making fun of talent. "I guess we were," Peter says. "I never forgave them for that. We realized they were helplessly square."

As an art student, Peter bounced between his loft in Manhattan and his parents' house in Flushing, and so he was never too far from the action in Whitestone. And as fun and wild and eye-opening as Manhattan was, the parties at The House nearly rivaled Union Square for kicks.

The Blue Whale Bashes, by this point renowned for blocks, drawing the most disaffected of North Queens youth, had entered a psychedelic phase, the aqua concoctions tempered equally with lysergic emanations. The local body count was rising. The neighbors were stirring.

What we need is some nitrous oxide, the boys thought logically.

So Keith and Marek made occasional afternoon rounds to local Queens hospitals in search of cans of nitrous to steal. When they weren't able to plunder the hospitals' supply under cover of darkness, they resorted to buying tanks from local bikers, or "hitters." On one happy afternoon the guys managed to score a five-foot tank with a quarter of laughing gas left, and they threw a huge nitrous party at The House where everyone got hammered and goofy. The tank sat around the house for the next couple of weeks. Eventually the nitrous ran dry so the guys put a wig and bra on the tank and kept their favorite lover in Marek's bed for a while.

There were a lot of costume parties at The House, and Marek threw himself into these affairs, infamously large soirees that drew kids, invited or not, from East Elmhurst to Little Neck, parties that live on today in the minds of those whose memories can still function. For the first costume party Marek, still with his Wayne long hair and cheap teenage beard, went as a poor-man's Jesus Christ. For the second party, yet to be jaded by the Lower East Side milieu, the country kid went as an artless "Bowery Bum." Marek borrowed his friend Ralph's thick black trench coat with the large "6" painted on the back that everyone had dubbed the "perv coat," rolled up his pant legs and, using peanut butter and catsup, made lesions up and down his leg and pasted toilet paper onto them. By all accounts the look was most authentic. Fooled partygoers gave Marek, passed out on the front porch by the end of the night, a wide berth.

Disenchanted with his job at the Busila Building in Long Island City and waiting for the pink slip to come, Marek began stealing merchandise from the factory. Among his ill-gotten cache were hobby kits and square Masonite clock faces, the kind onto which numbers could be attached but that had their battery-powered clock guts still intact. For one costume party the guys made a mask out of the clock face, onto which they painted some numbers and some heathen graffiti. One night, alerted to a costume party by yet another noise complaint, and eager to write summons, the 109th police knocked on the door. Out staggered Keith, as the son of a cop the one usually elected to deal with the regular visits from the men in blue. The cops stared strangely at Keith's costume: a bright orange lobster suit and a heavy-duty raincoat with a plastic jack-o-lantern over his head. Keith struggled to remain straightforward. Marek, wearing a full-length jointed cardboard Batman cutout—the kind usually hung on a child's bedroom wall and posed—came to the door to help out and try to explain things.

"Oh no, officers," the caped crusader slurred next to his shellfish sidekick, "we're completely in control. We know what we're doing."

Unimpressed, the cops walked into the front room, stepping over half a dozen drunk, half-clothed women sprawled on the floor. They issued everyone in the house tickets for disturbing the peace.

"If I caught my daughter here," one cop said to his partner, "I'd shoot her."

"You haven't read Baudelaire? *You die!*"

Late into a wild whiskey-sour party at The House, Rabbit and Gordon Russell Spaeth were arguing the merits of French Symbolist poetry, and somewhere in the murky passion of a drunken debate Rabbit crossed a line and got under Gordon's skin. Gordon's eyes bulged, his face simmered, and everyone present in the room knew that Gordon was on the edge. It was a razor's point at which Gordon, a ruggedly handsome local troublemaker, was often teetering. He was known around College Point, where he was born and raised, as the Rooster, a sobriquet that harkened partly to his shock of red hair, and partly to his fantastic, aggressive nature.

He was born on a blind street on September 21, 1951, three years after his brother Brian. He was an outsider who always felt cornered, suffering an isolation made especially painful by his difficult home life and by his reckless drug use that began when he was fourteen. Over generations, the Spaeth family had come to cultivate a good deal of bayside property in College Point, and Brian and Gordon lived their childhood years in a large home on the water by the Whitestone Bridge, with a vast yard and big gardens full of apple trees. Gordon's dad returned from a stint in the Philippines with encephalitis, and as the years ticked away the Spaeths suffered economic setbacks. One by one, the houses were sold off. By 1960, half of the property was gone. A large extended Spaeth family of aunts, uncles, and grandparents still lived within a two-block area, but the once-lush breezes off of Flushing Bay whispered trouble and dismay.

Along the idyllic waterfront Brian and Gordon as kids watched as ships and ferries glided by, picture-postcard moments illumined by sunsets draped over large lawns and dramatic lightning storms at night against the city line of Manhattan. "We had the prosperity of the 1950s," Brian reflects. "Twenty, thirty years later you begin to see things more clearly. There were a lot of contradictions: we were middle class but we had a beautiful house in which to live. It could have been fantastic, but there was this evil streak in my father's side of the family, cruelty and sadism, where the whole idea was to break a person's spirit, any kind of enthusiasm, crush it. And by the time you put all the pieces together, it's too late to punch father in the nose. Because he's gone."

By midcentury, a kind of hard-bitten hopelessness and ennui had settled in the Spaeth family marrow. After Gordon, another son, Wayne, was born with Downs Syndrome. Brian and Gordon would never be able to escape the long shadow of their family strife, the DNA of dysfunction tattooing them permanently.

During a couple of bruising summers, Gordon was forced to endure good-natured beatings at the hands of Brian and his cronies, and one humid day he was literally lynched by a couple of local kids in homespun borough fashion: they tied one end of a rope around his right leg, the other to a tree limb, and let go. Then they set the weeds on fire and left Gordon to hang there. Abused by his father, tormented by local hoods, Gordon nursed a grudge against violence in principle, even as his own behavior was often couched in aggravated fury, leading to his own emotional and legal troubles. Distancing himself from his more circumspect older brother, Gordon quickly grew into a rebel's posture, medicating his loneliness with booze, pharmaceuticals, and rhythm & blues and rock & roll.

Down the block from Gordon's house ran a dirt road parallel to an old railroad line. In 1959 Gordon, old enough to come home from school by himself, was walking down that road when he saw a shiny object embedded in the claylike dirt. He got down on his knees and dug out a big old Marine Band harmonica. He took it home and washed it out in the faucet with hot water. It's testament to how good they made the harmonicas in those days that it played. "I had an uncle who played the harmonica and the accordion and who wrote and played music, and on my father's side I had an alcoholic uncle who played the harmonica, too. There was a mailman who used to come by who played the harmonica, too. And my mother played the snare drum in a marching band at UCLA," says Gordon.

At age fifteen Gordon, flush with a surprise inheritance, picked out a Ludwig drum set. "This is 1966, music is exploding, and I'm really turned on. Then my father catches wind of it, and he says, 'No! Shut up and mow the lawn!' I was heartbroken. But in retrospect I'm glad there was a lawn to be mowed. As a result, my mother shut up, and I got depressed." Gordon got a job as a gardener at school, saved up his money, and bought another harmonica, a double-reed tremolo Echo harp that was designed for mournful Swiss melodies. "Meanwhile, I wanted to sound like Bob Dylan! I said, *Wait a second, something's wrong with me!*" A month or so later, Gordon returned to the music store and was told that he needed a Marine Band. His love affair with the instrument was born.

Gordon attended Flushing High School with Peter's older sister Sandra and with Andy Shernoff, a tall, gangly kid who would later transpose the "n" and the "d" in his given name, start churning out one of the early rock & roll fanzines, *Teenage Wasteland Gazzete*, and form the seminal punk band the Dictators. In 1969, Gordon and Shernoff got the same after-school gig through the Flushing High job placement program working in a factory packing twenty-three-shot revolvers for the police academy. "I have a distinct memory of Andy Shernoff holding a long rod with half-assembled police guns hanging on it," Gordon laughs. Neither punk lasted very long arming the local police force.

When he wasn't toiling in menial jobs, Gordon was becoming more and more passionate about R&B. He started earnestly tracking down old records, listening, memorizing liner notes, practicing for hours on end with his harmonica. At the age of fifteen he began sitting in with local rock bands at a Flushing club; directly across the street from the joint was a place called Paul's Stadium Bar, where some of the local African-Americans frequented. One night, after building up his nerve with numerous beers, Gordon walked across that street, strolled into Paul's, and ordered a drink. He was served reluctantly.

The house band soon took the stage: a tough, all-black R&B outfit called Clayton and the Mighty Cravens. Clayton sang and played a decent but minimal tenor sax. After the first set, Gordon approached Clayton and told him how much he enjoyed his band.

"You a white boy comin' into an all black bar just to hear me? You wasn't scared?"

"No," Gordon said. "I just like R&B."

"You a musician?" he asked.

"Well, I play the harp."

"You any good? 'Cause I like harp and this band could use harp on a few songs. You got a harp on you?"

"Yeah, I do," Gordon said. "As a matter of fact, I got three. I can play in E, A, and G."

"Stick around, Red. I'll call you up in the middle of the next set." Gordon nursed his single beer and waited. Though he was under-age and the only white boy in the whole club, he felt relaxed and juiced, dug the glamour and the danger, and he sensed little animosity. In the middle of the second set, Clayton called Gordon up and announced, "Right now we gonna have a harmonica player come on up here. I've never heard him before so I'm gonna take a chance on him. Come on up here, Red."

"Key of A, solo after the second chorus," he whispered to Gordon. The audience was surprised, to say the least, to see a white guy standing onstage. After the second chorus, Clayton gave Gordon a knowing glance. Gordon played a mean and jagged twenty-four-bar solo that complemented the song. After the solo, Clayton yelled into the mike, "Well, alright!" The crowd applauded enthusiastically, Gordon, his head buzzing, jumped offstage and headed to the bar to order a beer.

The bartender glared at him. "Your money's no good here," he said.

Gordon looked at the bartender knowingly. "Oh, uh-huh. OK. I gotta leave then?"

"Leave? Hell no," the bartender said. "You not only had the balls to walk in here but you played damn good harmonica for a white man." He extended a beefy hand to Gordon. "My name's Paul and I own this bar. You're always welcome here, Red."

Clayton asked Gordon to do regular guest shots and to be an auxiliary member of the Mighty Cravens, and for the next year and a half, every Friday night at 12 and 2, Gordon would play three or four songs with Clayton and the Mighty Cravens. His apprenticeship taught him both the thrills and the rigors of stage life at an early age, and Gordon felt good in Paul's place, away from the darkening vacuum of his home life, even as the racial lines he trespassed in the club further clarified Gordon's feelings as an outsider.

Gordon found increasing diversion and purpose playing at Paul's, and his daring drug use increased. "I was heavily involved in all of it," Gordon says matter-of-factly. "I was fascinated that substances could alter consciousness. I was a follower of Timothy Leary, Alan Watts. I dabbled in Zen Buddhism. I took LSD—a conservative estimate—two hundred times. My favorite hobby as a teenager was to watch Mexican horror movies with my brother on extremely high dosages of LSD. There was this one particular acid called Purple Football where if you took a whole one you'd come back a different person. I watched *At Sword's Point* and *The Brainiac* on half, almost three-quarters of a tab of Purple Football. I don't get flashbacks.

"But sometimes . . . "

Gordon had a very good buddy named Leroy, a bigger, stronger version of himself. Their favorite pastime, fueled in large part by booze and acid, was to enter local bars wearing girls' dresses to provoke people. *You don't like what I'm wearing?* they'd sneer. *Do something about it.* Inevitably a raging fist fight would ensue and Gordon's manic, wiry potency, dosed with the chutzpah of Leroy's psychotic bulk, would dilute the sorry competition. Gordon and Leroy often crashed out in a favorite abandoned house when they were searching College Point for a place to lie or a place to come down. In the middle of hazy circumstances that few remember now, they set the house ablaze, burning it right down to the ground. Around the College Point and Whitestone neighborhoods Gordon's fierce, bizarre reputation was becoming the stuff of legend.

He wasn't all wire and edge. In addition to his love of R&B and rock & roll, Gordon was not without his literary pretensions. He often would lapse into a cape-wearing, Romantic-poetry espousing alter ego he called "Lord Gordon." Lord Gordon would rise from the lightless, troubled waters of Gordon's psyche during drinking binges, showing up unannounced at neighborhood parties cutting a dashing, if suspect, figure of romance and pathos, roaming from room to room, or—across the length of a Whitestone evening—party to party, quoting Alister Crowley, indulging in all manner of flamboyant, Byronic excess, arguing aggressively with anyone who wasn't passionately enamored of Baudelaire, the nineteenth-century poet.

"Lord Gordon was one of many personalities that he'd have in his command, depending on what 'Gordon' he wanted to present to you," recalls Keith. "He was multipersonality for a long time."

Clinically?

"He was never diagnosed, but he definitely had many personalities he would fall back on with excessive drug and alcohol abuse."

Lord Gordon, or maybe another alcohol- or acid-drenched double, materialized one warm night in Hayden's lot in College Point, the site of the Hayden mansion, a beautiful century-old home one mile from Whitestone Park on the water. The pretty, sloping lot had once enveloped gentle marshlands, inviting visitors to lay on the grass and gaze down at the water. However, the mansion was abandoned by the early sixties, eventually destroyed by a fire, and was ultimately, in civic-minded thoughtfulness, filled in as a dump. A black hole, the lot began sucking into its maw the dregs of North Queens.

"In the late sixties and in the seventies Hayden's lot was one of the most depraved hangouts of anywhere I've ever seen," says Brian. The lot was infamous for ragged Toluol glue-sniffing parties, as there were a couple of factories in town and the kids were able to score big drums of the octane booster. "It happened pretty quickly, maybe by '67. People were still smoking joints, but there were a few hardcore junkies. Toluol was a scourge, an awful, awful thing. I saw people rip their underwear off because they needed a rag to soak the Toluol in."

By 1973, Hayden's lot's sordid reputation for fun and tragedy attracted local hoods and drifters, punks and junkies who would listlessly mill about scoring Quaaludes, LSD, and marijuana, and drink and drink until the drugs kicked in or their horror diffused. Gordon was a regular there, and death was always in the air. "I once had a duplicate who looked exactly like me who says he wanted to talk to me," Gordon says. "His name was Thomas Bannon, and on Halloween Eve he crashed right outside of Hayden's lot and was decapitated." The next day, as Gordon was heading to the dentist, a voice in his head buzzed, *Gordon, don't ever drive,* and lingered in him for weeks. "They say when young people die, their spirit lingers. And without a doubt I felt that I was in touch psychically and spiritually with this man. When I'd walk past his mother she would cry."

"I really wasn't hanging out with Gordon by this point," Brian says. "He was kind of off with his own crew of degenerates, an appalling crew, mindless, low-life, uneducated dirtbags. God knows what they did. I remember this guy Tommy Freudig huffing glue as he was driving his car, and the car would veer off and crash into the curb and he'd wake up, and Gordon would be in the backseat drinking beer with Leroy and they're all glued out. I think half the town died at one point. I saw one guy with a bicycle pump, sharpening it to use as a needle. They were unbelievable.

"I would always try to help Gordon out. I'd go to Hayden's and pull a glue bag off his head. I'd try to get him to stop drinking, I'd try to get him out of trouble, I tried to get him away from these clowns from the neighborhood, those jerks. But you really can't control or help someone if they don't want to be helped. Everybody begged him to stop drinking, to stop doing drugs and being crazy, and I always tried. I bought him a horn a couple times, always trying to bail him out of trouble. I tried to help him out."

These many years later so few remember the details, as they were sketchy to begin with. One humid night in the summer of 1974, Gordon was hunched over at a bar near Hayden's, drinking and minding his own. But very quickly the man sitting next to him started an argument. They bitched about a deal gone wrong, some ludes of shady quality, some stolen acid, a girl, the merits of Stax versus Motown horn playing—who knows now. Beneath the yellow street lamps, amidst the swirl of dirt and unsettled expectations, the altercation— enhanced by the fuel polluting both men—lit its own fire when the guy threw a beer can at Gordon, and before long the fight spilled outside and both were down on the ground, fists to faces and hands to necks, fighting wickedly. The brief, low-rent fight, tense though it was, was lost in the fumes of forgetfulness just as quickly as it arose.

The next day, Gordon greeted the early afternoon with a stroll down to Francis Lewis Park, a local hangout beneath the Whitestone-Bronx Bridge. Hungover, nodding off toward another vague, sunlit afternoon, he shut his eyes only to open them moments later and stare into the grim faces of three police officers. Gordon was always easy to find. The police arrested him on the spot for murder.

The dimly recalled fight hadn't ended in a blood-spitting, uneasy truce borne by exhaustion or momentary wits. In the maelstrom, Gordon had stuck his thumbs in the other guy's eyeballs—so went local lore, anyway—and threw him onto the ground, where his head unceremoniously, and with fatal results, thudded into the hard earth. Gordon Spaeth had accidentally killed a man, and he didn't remember doing it. "This guy was a drunk drug addict. Gordon was a drunk drug addict," says Keith. "I don't know what the fight was about. This guy also had a problem. He was on a medication for whatever his problem was and of course he shouldn't have mixed his medication with alcohol and the other things that were in his body, maybe Quaaludes."

Only twenty-two years old, Gordon Spaeth was charged with involuntary manslaughter and with leaving the scene of a crime. Subsequently he learned more about what happened after he'd stumbled home that night: a drunken homeless man had fleeced the warm corpse, and it wasn't until the itinerant squeezed a free drink out of the police that he confessed to that petty crime; until that point the cops had figured that Gordon had killed a guy and robbed him. Possessed of the little wits he had left after years of drugging and drinking, Gordon admitted the incident to the trial judge, who threw the book at him. "It was—it still is—a very murky, inconclusive thing," laments Brian now. "There were really no eyewitnesses to come forward." The dark unhappiness of Gordon's life took a tragic turn.

"I could've beaten the rap, but I told the truth," says Gordon. "To this day, I wish I had been the one who died."

Gordon's trial and subsequent conviction to a four-year prison sentence interrupted not only a young man's life, but the incarnation of Keith's first rock & roll dream. "Gordon's sentence for murder was pending," Keith remembers. "He was in and out of Rikers a million times for this manslaughter charge. Finally, the judge was going to sentence him. We all thought he was gonna get out on probation or on some type of lesser charge, do public service, have to report to his probation officer, and we'll have a lead singer for a band. We were rehearsing at the time Gordon went for sentencing. The judge sentenced him to Attica for four years! We were more pissed off about the fact that we didn't have a lead singer than we were upset about the fact that Gordon had to go to jail."

Gordon received a felony conviction and ultimately served three years of his four-year sentence in stays split among the Metropolitan Correctional Center, Attica State Prison, and Auburn Prison. "No one—and I mean, *no one*—ever does time in Attica and comes out the same man," Gordon says. "Attica is the most notorious correctional facility in the United States. You march down hallways by a giant guard, and more guards stand at every corner and click the counter as you pass. In the mess hall you ate your meals with teargas canisters hanging from the ceiling. I had to get a permit signed by the warden to play my harmonica. I swore that someday I wouldn't need any damn permit, and every day I practiced for hours. Eventually I was transferred to Auburn, and that's where I met Paul Bailey, a black man who'd been there for twelve years. He played tenor sax and had a degree in music from Berkeley—through the mail, I might add. That says a lot. He taught me music theory and I really learned a lot.

"In retrospect, I must say that state prison ruined me. Before I went up the river, I already felt like an outsider, an outcast with low self-esteem. Prison only reinforced those feelings. After two years being released from prison, Leroy died. It hurt me very, very badly. I became an intense loner. He was the toughest, nicest, and most loyal friend I ever had. His death changed me. Someone sold him poison drugs, and he died at age twenty-seven. No way was it suicide or an accidental overdose. He knew every damn pharmaceutical in the *PDR*, and he had a tolerance for drugs that was incredible. Lee died in '79, at which point I was attending college. I came back into society as far as I could.

"Then Peter Zaremba gave me a chance, when no one else would. For that reason alone, I'll always love that guy."

4.
Street Rock and Party Music

He's in the bathroom now, staring in the tiny mirror over the cruddy sink. Outside the door, a party rages on; he can hear the laughter and bottles, the loud music. He studies his face closely in the mirror, examines the terrain of acne scars. He runs a hand through his long bangs and screws up his mouth, willing a long-lost Sinatra visage, the same face he made when he was a little kid trying to get that rakish look down. *Francis Albert. There was a singer.*

Peter stares at the mirror a moment longer, then rejoins the party where the Dregs are revving it up. He and Brian Spaeth are the brains behind this outfit, before Gordon's murder conviction will put an end to the band's brief incarnation. Keith plays drums, a local kid Jim Peralta plays guitar, and Brian and Gordon play some bass and sing, respectively. Peter clings to the outside, grooving with the other partygoers, too timid and self-conscious to jump in the fray. He really wants to sing, wants to dive right in the middle of everything and take over and let his wild muse out and spread a good time for everyone. But something holds him back.

Peter met Tom Dale in 1968 when both were freshmen at Brooklyn Tech High School, where Peter was briefly a student. Peter discovered in Dale an extroverted figure through whom he could live out some of his more rabid and private fantasies.

"Dale was into some of the same things that Keith and the Spaeth brothers and I were into," Peter remembers. "He was really good-looking—somewhere between Tom Jones and Engelbert Humperdink—but he was ridiculously obnoxious. He was a *crimee*, and overbearing, and unpredictable, but he really did have what it took." Dale was especially overbearing with the local ladies. "He was always a man who overplayed his cards. No matter how good his hand was, he would overplay it." Using Dale, and with Brian assisting, Peter began as a kind of mentor and poor-man's manager to vicariously satisfy his urge to front a band, to grab a mike and see what the hell happened, to have fun and encourage everyone else around him to have fun. Brian and Peter made Dale the lead singer of the Dregs. Secretly, Peter wished that *he* was the one doing it, although Dale seemed to be so much more obvious. Peter so urged Dale that he leant him one of his prized 1956 Voice of Music ceramic microphones, which Dale subsequently destroyed.

Although Dale was a natural front man, when he got in front of people he often lost a lot of his natural braggadocio; allegedly, he resorted to bringing notes with him onstage. As he lacked the memory to remember the lyrics to the three songs the Dregs could manage, he was actually reading at a gig. "It was very embarrassing," Brian laughs. "The guitar player was so neurotic that, even though it was a summer night he was bundled up in a coat, and he wouldn't stand up and take his coat off. And he had a hat, on too. Not very exciting." Despite their dubious stage manner, the Dregs played free-form but lively jams, muscled along by the Spaeth brothers' love of rough-and-tumble obscure R&B and rock & roll, and especially Gordon's wild and impassioned harmonica playing.

The biggest Dregs show erupted when Peter's parents went to Florida late in 1974. "I threw a huge house party and a couple hundred kids came," Peter remembers. "Brian and I basically gave the Dregs their set. We supplied the music. One of the big things the Dregs did was Mose Allison's 'Parchmans Farm,' with Gordon singing. And I remember Gordon pulling out all stops in my living room in front of an amazed bunch of people. People were out of their minds. It was an out-of-their-minds house party."

"That party was a lot of fun, really good," remembers Brian. "It was the very, very first time that I had ever played in a band in front of people. I had to have quite a few beers because at that time it was as if kids had lost the knowledge that you could do it yourself and have a band, because everything at that point was, *Well, this is on the radio, these are professionals, you can't do that, you can't start a band.* Most of the people in the neighborhood were snobbish, spoiled kids who would ridicule us for even trying to have a band. But in '65 to '67 everybody had a band. It was incredible, a golden age. There's still tons of material we haven't heard out there, and it's all great."

Brian would ride his bike through College Point on pristine Sunday afternoons when he was a kid and, as families would congregate and barbecue in civic harmony, hear a young band of teenagers on nearly every block plugged in and playing, trying to get "Wild Thing" or "Louie, Louie" down, usually not very successfully. "It was incredible," he says, "like a revolution of the proletariat. That died out pretty quick because soon you had to have chops. Three chords were out. You had to learn exotic chords, you had to get really contemplative lyrics and all this pretentious crap." Gordon remembers the period similarly. "This was a bad time period for me because I'm trying to find someone somewhere in the no-man's land of Queens to play with," he says. "I wanted to put together an R&B outfit with clean-shaven guys with cool haircuts, and these guys had beards. One guitarist in College Point wanted to play 'Heart of Gold' by Neil Young. I thought, *This ain't gonna work.* This other guy wanted to play 'Cripple Creek' by the Band. And he had a mustache."

"Someone recorded that Dregs show at my parents' house, and I really wish someone would come across that tape because that would be the most amazing thing," Peter says. "They played 'On the Road Again' by Lovin' Spoonful, 'Twenty Flight Rock' and 'My Way' by Eddie Cochran, the Doors' 'Roadhouse Blues.' So obviously the set was great. Especially at that point in time, to hear a whole set of that type of music played live was unheard of, you know?" Gordon Lightfoot's "Sundown," a huge hit around this time, was defining the folk-rock sound of popular radio. The Dregs wanted to drown it all out.

As enamored as Peter was with Tom Dale and as fun as the Dregs' party shows always were, Peter remained restless, unsatisfied. His studies at SVA were interesting and compelling, his friends and colleagues there engaging and colorful, but he intuited that the rush he felt in sketching or drafting couldn't quite compare to the rush of seeing a particularly great band, or grooving to the live social vibe and the music on the great jukebox at Max's.

"I didn't really get what was going on in art at the time," Peter reflects. "Most of my ideas were throwbacks in one way or another. I was a pretty good draftsman, but I wanted to learn how to paint well. And that was way out. There was no one there who was going to teach me how to paint." Peter subsequently lost some respect for the institution. "If I was interested in making it in the art scene in New York, my teachers were the right people to be with. They would have set me up, and all I had to do was come up with a gimmick or a gig of some sort. However, I wanted to do this technical kind of painting. They didn't do that."

"Peter wasn't really prolific," Jon Quinn recalls. "One of the things we got drilled into us in SVA was that you had to produce a lot of work. He was committed to making four paintings, and that really was the kiss of death for him professionally." The big name to come out of SVA during this period was Keith Haring. "You couldn't stop Haring. If anything, Peter was the exact opposite of Haring. Peter was so good—small, precious Northern Renaissance–style paintings, very deliberate—but being a good painter was not in vogue. It was all about either conceptual or abstract art. If you were doing those kinds of paintings then you were in the illustration department, because that was not art. You were not politically informed. You were not a good Marxist if you painted pretty pictures. And Peter felt like, *Who are you calling a Marxist, you bourgeois rich bastards with your trust funds. You can afford to go to college forever!*"

"I really didn't know what to do with my ability or how to apply it to something valid at that point," explains Peter. "What I do with painting is so tedious, labor-intensive, and slow, that I figured the only way I could finish a painting was if the piece was only four by five inches. So I did *goaches* with huge frames around them. Pieces of gardens, no figures, some very controlled looking." One painting earned Peter some degree of notoriety among his classmates, a representational study of the rotting pipes in the corner of his studio. He worked for nearly a year and a half on the oil piece, his directed observation teasing from the ignored, workaday pipes an eeriness and a timeless peculiarity that many fellow students admired.

"This is me speculating here," Quinn says. "But I bet that Peter was doing his paintings and thinking that this was indeed art. It must've eaten him up, because he knew these were really good paintings." Disheartened, Peter found himself drifting more and more toward the SVA Film Department, where he found friends and where critical intellect was leavened by absurdist, good-time humor. Someone somewhere had gotten hold of 16-millimeter reels of the Three Stooges and was presenting them on student film nights. "I remember going into the amphitheater with a gallon of wine," says Brian Spaeth, whom Peter invited along to hang out at SVA and who eventually enrolled. "You could lay down on the floor, your knapsack under your head, you'd be chugging on the wine, watching the Stooges. Nobody'd bother you. It was really cool. You could smoke joints, do whatever you want." April Palmeri, an SVA student who ended up performing in Pulsallama and other artistic projects, dated Peter for a while. "We had access to projectors and screening rooms," she remembers. "You could just say, *I wanna do this*, and they'd let you. But sometimes the only people in the audience at the Stooges showings were me, Peter, Brian Spaeth, and one other person. We'd be the only people in the audience, and it happened a few times. It just didn't get people's attention."

Peter would cut classes and blow off afternoons viewing obscure Polish war films, delving into and exploring his cultural roots. Brian and Peter both enjoyed working on short animated films, but neither possessed the drive and ambition to actually finish much of what they started. One short film had great promise: a two-and-a-half-minute mock Mexican horror film. "We wanted to make it look authentic to a Mexican film," Peter remembers. "We had some pretty good ideas, like getting John Carradine's voice. We wanted to call him on the phone and try to talk to him and use that in the film. We had great ideas, but of course we were too lazy and we had the attitude that we couldn't really *do* things. It took a real strongly motivated person to actually get something done in those days. We should have just done it."

Peter was facing a growing tension. Because he was an accomplished draftsman he admired serious painters, but serious painters weren't the kind of artists whom he found lively and engaging, such as surreal Dadaists who moved closer toward Performance Art, locking art-opening spectators in the basement and wildly, capriciously subverting conventions. The disquiet between practiced skill and unpredictable nerve was beginning to pull Peter in opposite directions and would forever influence him as a man, a musician, and a performer. His favorite moments at school were often found not in studio but in the cafeteria, when he'd initiate loud discussions—with, among others, John Holmstrom, future founder of the epochal *Punk* magazine—about films and artifacts fading out of the American scene that he felt were important, obscure rock & roll and rhythm and blues 45s. More and more Peter found solace in rock & roll, and he'd stock the jukebox at SVA with 45s, "Heaven and Hell" by the Who, "The Ball Park Incident" by the Wizard.

"That was exactly what was needed at the time," he remembers. "Loud, obnoxious, very excessive, and brutal rock & roll."

In Whitestone, the first band to rise from the ashes of Twenty Flight Rock and the Dregs was a free-form ensemble called Concrete Block. After Keith and Marek discovered instruments in The House, they plugged in every day after work and started to jam. They had no ideas about chords or keys or tuning or the names of strings, but they turned the noise up very loud and put everything through Keith's fuzzbox with a lot of reverb. It didn't sound all that bad.

"Whale, who had no idea how to play drums, became the drummer," Keith laughs. "We would get together and just make this noise, and this was way before anything that would be considered Art Rock or avant-garde-sounding. We would make all these outrageous songs, but then we slowly but surely shaped them into arrangements and gave each one a title, and they sorta became songs."

What did the jams sound like?

"Horrifying and juvenile. But amusing."

Whale came up with the band name, an homage to the slabs of cinderblock that the boys would stack in front the drum kit upon which a concrete birdbath—"borrowed" from a neighbor's yard—sat adorned with a green plastic frog in the center. Whale pounded away gloriously on Keith's drum kit, happy to be making some suburban clamor. "The only other instrument that I had played up to that point in my life was an accordion," Costello recalls. "I took about six lessons before I dropped the whole thing. All I ever played on the drums in Concrete Block was the solo from Iron Butterfly's 'In-a-Gadda-Da-Vida.' One day while we were screwing around in the basement, Bill Hattan came down and started blaring away on some trumpet. We joked that it sounded like an elephant call so we convinced him to put a sock on his nose while he made noise with the horn. Concrete Block was a total fun goof."

The outfit veered closer to being a kind of musical theater of the absurd than any kind of rock & roll band with larger aspirations. What Keith and Marek saw most Queens bands aspire to was musical virtuosity, rock star pomposity, and local mainstream acceptance fostered by an ever-bulging, note-for-note catalog of cover songs of Top 100 hits. One such Queens outfit was the long-defunct Jon Montgomery Band, led by the eponymous "North Queens Glam God," as Zaremba remembers him. Peter and Keith would see the Jon Montgomery Band in 1976 at a forgotten bar under the elevated train in Woodside, Queens. "It was hilarious," Keith remembers. "The Jon Montgomery Band were horrible, like Bad Company. Even worse. I think they had a song called 'Hot Stove.' *She's a hot stove.*"

Sweat

(Years later, Keith and Peter Case of the Plimsouls would form an occasional pickup group when Case would visit New York City. Playing tongue-in-cheek covers of AC/DC and the like, they'd bill themselves as Hot Stove.)

Peter and Keith went backstage to meet Montgomery after a less-than-memorable show. Montgomery's local version of *Rolling Stone* magazine Rock Star Decadence was laughable. Sitting in a tiny backstage area, surrounded by local sycophants who had their star-worshipping telescopes turned the wrong way, Montgomery symbolized the fiercely provincial ceiling to which so many outerborough bands aspired. "Jon was holding court in the back room," Peter remembers of their meeting. "Under each arm he had a girl with long blonde curls just like his, and a bottle of some sort of sparkling wine cooling in an ice bucket on the table as befitted a man of his station. Jon dispensed some condescending advice on our material and haircuts and made a deprecating comment about the CBGB's and Max's scene. He did not offer us any 'champagne.'"

"Then he dismissed us," says Keith.

Marek had caught the tail end of the Queens scene that many of the Whitestone kids were into. "We'd go to Beggar's Banquet in Queens, which was where Twisted Sister played. But in those days they was a complete joke, a holdover from the glam and glitter period that didn't know to die. We were really told by all the musicians who Keith knew that there was the local Queens scene, the Jon Montgomery Band, the Jerry Laurie Band. These were local legends who were really excellent musicians, but they were still hooked into the belief that you have to play covers and have your own P.A. and light show to be a working band. They had no sense that there was a big gap between what they knew of being a musician and the musicians that were making the records they were trying to learn, the musicians who made original music. And there didn't seem to be any venue for these kids to make original music. You played covers. You were a tribute to some other established band."

What Keith wanted from Concrete Block was much simpler and less pretentious than rock-star virtuosity and local hero-worship: *Play some party music.* Which translated literally as: *Play some music at parties.* "We didn't know half the people who would come to our Blue Whale Bashes; the word would just get out on the street. 'Party at The House!' So people would come from all over," Keith remembers. "Then we started advertising that we had this new band that was gonna play. And of course everyone probably thought, *They're probably going to do cover songs*, Pink Floyd or whatever junk was happening. So we had this big Blue Whale party. We get set up, and it's packed with wall-to-wall people expecting to see this rock & roll band. I'll never forget the looks on their faces when Concrete Block started to play: their jaws are dropping, their faces are cringing. Girls are, like, crying. A lot of people were on LSD so maybe it was shocking, I don't know. It really was a gag we pulled on people. We really made it seem like we were this Serious Rock & roll Band with Our First Performance."

"I remember sitting and playing with the biggest grin on my face because it was all so goofy," says Costello. "Keith's dream was to be a rock star, and it really started there. He was prancing around doing the lead guitarist thing, and he stretched a cord too much, which toppled over an amp or two. People's faces were fun to watch. I don't know what they expected, but I feel confident that most people didn't hear anything that they expected to hear. I'd describe the sound as garage-acid-surf-heavy metal, with a touch of Captain Beefheart thrown in. It was unique. It was basically loud rock & roll."

"We had no aspirations," says Keith. "We just dug what we were doing. That was the aspiration." Concrete Block would provide the reckless party jams for many a basement soiree, scoring the aural deconstruction for the mayhem surrounding them. The basement became the grounding point for Keith and Marek's future musical explorations.

"I'm never gonna get a career as a painter," Peter said to Quinn apropos of nothing one afternoon as they walked together in lower Manhattan. It was the first day that the two had spent together in the city.

Quinn looked at Peter as though he'd snapped.

"No. No, there's no way I'm gonna do that," Peter continued, head down, his gait quickening. He looked at his friend sideways. "I'm gonna go be a rock & roll star."

Quinn looked up into the air. "Dude, you can barely play the recorder," he said. "There's no way in hell—if *I* can't be a musician, *you* can't be a musician!" Peter looked away and drummed his fingers excitedly on his hips.

"I don't want fame," he said quietly. "I want notoriety." They let a cab pass in front of them and walked on in silence.

"And that's what he got," says Quinn now.

Peter had bought a harmonica in 1971 while in high school and taught himself up in his bedroom to play along to some of his old Yardbirds and Kinks records. He learned the Beatles' "Love Me Do" and then the Yardbirds' "Got Love If You Want It," two wildly different personalities of the same reed-bending beast. In addition to John Lennon and Keith Relf, the Kinks' Ray Davies and the Rolling Stones' Brian Jones were early influences on Peter's playing (but not Magic Dick, whose virtuosic showiness in the charting J. Geils Band was a turnoff). Peter would soon delve into Southern and Chicago blues greats like Sonny Boy Williamson, Lazy Lester, and Billy Boy Arnold, loving the primitive transcendent sounds issuing from their breath and nerve, and the fact that their playing complemented a group rather than took center stage.

One night in the late winter of 1976, Concrete Block was jamming at The House while Peter was in visiting from the city. Keith and Marek asked him to sit in. "That was what I'd been waiting for for five years, simply someone to ask me," says Peter. "And from that day on, we've played together. I have no musical background. But I always had a lot of big ideas about rock & roll. And I just lucked out." Keith remembers how logical and intuitively right it felt to ask Peter to join Marek and him. "I knew he could play harmonica, but we never knew that Peter would write such great lyrics when we hooked up with him.

"And he came in with the name for the band."

"When we were rehearsing, or at parties if we were playing," Marek remembers, "people would jam in the basement and it would just become a fog in there, between cigarettes and/or pot and/or sweat. I don't think we ever had air conditioning down there. I remember in the light of a single bulb here or there just people all over the place while we're playing, jammed in there. And parties would generally be throughout the house and spilling out onto the lawns." The centrifugal force was always in the basement. When Keith, Marek, and Peter climbed out, blinked in the sunlight, and sniffed the air toward the west, what their senses tasted on the breeze was something enormously exciting coming from lower Manhattan.

Hilly Kristal opened CBGB's on the Bowery in 1973 as a venue for country and western acts, assuming that his neighbors wouldn't complain about country tunes and that that music would take off as a national phenomenon. It didn't quite turn out that way. Country music eventually took off, but it was shiny Texas and Nashville, not the grimy Lower East Side, that cultivated the genre. A year after opening his club, Kristal was struggling to make ends meet, driving a moving van on the weekends and literally living in the backroom of CBGB's, when he decided to let local bands play at the club, whether they could play Merle Haggard or not. Slowly but surely, bedraggled area musicians ventured into the ragged area and proceeded under-neath CBGB's awning to check out their prospects.

The underground art and music scene in New York had been spearheaded by Andy Warhol and his involvement with the Velvet Underground and with his own Exploding Plastic Inevitable in the late 1960s. When Warhol's days of holding court in the infamously decadent, celebrity-laden back room at Max's Kansas City petered out, the Velvet Underground too disappeared, to be replaced by underground's newest scene darlings, the New York Dolls. They played regular residencies at the Mercer Arts Center, but one day the Mercer crumbled, the back wall infamously crashing to the ground onto Broadway. Max's had a cabaret scene going and, after the Mercer collapse, was one of the only venues that would take chances on unusual artists and bands.

Kristal and CBGB's soon stepped in to fill that void. By 1975, his club had transformed itself from a derelict bar on an infamous strip of seedy, low-rent Manhattan into a club with a reputation as a place to hang out, drink cheap beer, and catch some exciting and very unusual rock bands. Kristal himself described the music and the growing scene in his club as "street music"—intense, nonmainstream music made by intense, culturally marginalized people who had close ties to urban ennui and social disaffection. Soon it would be dubbed Punk Rock. By early 1975, Patti Smith, Television, and the Ramones were regulars at the club, often playing on the same bill; Blondie, Talking Heads, Suicide, and the Dictators were soon to follow. None of these bands had record deals yet, and the crowds at their shows were filled—or, more accurately, semifilled—by friends and the other bands' members. But it would all change very quickly, as Patti Smith and then the Ramones and the Dictators got signed to major labels sniffing a certain marketability in Punk Rock. By the end of 1975, after CBGB's had produced in July the "Rock Festival Showcase Auditions," and rock critics like Robert Christgau of the *Village Voice* and Roy Trakin of the *Soho News* began writing frequently and enthusiastically about the scene, CBGB's rested on the cusp of national recognition.

Other venues would give rock & roll a shot around this time: Sea of Clouds Club on East Sixteenth Street (where the Heartbreakers and the Ramones would play on New Year's 1976), Club 82 at Fourth Street and Second Avenue (billing itself as a "New Concept in Rock & Cabaret"), Zeppz on West Twenty-third Street ("has Rock") where the Dictators played occasionally, Broadway Charly's at Broadway and Eleventh Street, the Great Gildersleeves Cabaret on the Bowery near CBGB's, and My Father's Place out in Long Island. Later, Heat ("Manhattan's largest rock dance floor") below Canal Street, the Rocker Room ("Rock Dancing") at East Forty-eighth Street, and Bottoms on East Eighty-fifth Street ("dance to live music uptown") would materialize. But for a couple of years in the mid-seventies, until Hurrah, Danceteria, Irving Plaza, Mudd Club, and Maxwell's (across the river in Hoboken, New Jersey) opened, the only two established venues committed to booking real street rock & roll were CBGB's and Max's.

Around this time, Peter was picking up the *Voice* in Union Square and seeing small ads for CBGB's. "We thought there might be something going on there," Peter says. "But it was a while before I got up the nerve to go. We were all so discouraged about music. The first time must have been around the end of 1975, because there was snow on the ground. I brought along a date for protection." He can't remember who played that night, but the image of Willy DeVille draped around the bar was certainly indelible. "The gummy floors reeked of a century's worth of piss and stale beer. There were lots of people wearing white shirts and black neckties *à la* Patti Smith, which was fine by me. I was beyond sick of hippies." There was a buzz on around town about the Ramones. "I said to Brian Spaeth, 'I see this ad in the *Voice*, they look right, they're not wearing makeup, no big hair, no Glam. Are we gonna go see these guys?' And one night April Palmeri said, 'Well let's go. Let's see the Ramones.' And that was the first time I saw them. I didn't like them."

Peter's experience with the New York Dolls was equally forgettable, though the Dolls' reputation as scene kings and their far-flung borough roots intrigued him. "Brian Spaeth got into the Dolls, and I remember him saying, 'I was at the Coventry hanging out with the Dolls, man, and they're really into all this music that we like. I was talking to them about Bo Diddley and Chuck Berry and the Yardbirds and stuff.' And I was poo-pooing it because they looked like Glam, and I hated Glam and all that Trans-Rock stuff." The pose turned Peter off, and with his infinite stubbornness, that was it: he was fed up with the Rock Star thing, and he was looking for a band that looked like his friends. He certainly found in the Ramones' torn jeans and thin T-shirts, leather jackets and tattered Keds a kindred dress code. Joey, Dee Dee, Johnny, and Tommy looked like scruffy versions of the kids who rode the Number 7 train in and out of Queens. "At the time, I didn't know that those guys were from Forrest Hills," Peter says. "I probably came across them, and probably even met them at some shows and stuff because I know they were at a lot of the shows that I was at."

There were certain rules and protocol that a band had to order to be taken seriously by the local cognoscenti. Tho intuitively rebelled against these rules, the attitude was ingrained in him that when he saw the Ramones onstage breaking all of those decrees, breaking them with intensity, speed, and volume, he was initially put off, wondering, *What the hell are they doing? Who do they think they are?* From his table at CBGB's that night Peter sipped his beer while the *Zeitgeist* in all of its heady and grimy glory swept around him. "I thought that all of their songs sound like a cross between 'California Sun' and 'Let's Dance.' If I was smart I would've felt differently."

The next day at school in the cafeteria, he bickered about the Ramones with a girl. "It's minimal rock!" she argued back.

"And then I started thinking about it," Peter says. *Yeah wait a minute,* he muttered. *The fact is I hate all those guitar solos anyway, and the fact is I do like "California Sun" so why shouldn't all of the songs sound like "California Sun"?* A lightbulb popped on.

"I remember having a great time that night, diving through the snow and slipping along the Bowery, just doing a toboggan right down the street. It was one of those nights.

"The second time, I brought Keith."

Keith would occasionally leave his architectural desk job blessedly behind him on the weekends and visit Peter in the city. Keith didn't come in as often as Marek did, but Peter had been enticing Keith by raving about the vibe in lower Manhattan. For Peter, the night was a vindication of the rethink he did about these guys playing street music in such a forceful if unorthodox way. For Keith, the night was nothing short of revolutionary. "Peter had told me that the Ramones do their own songs, which was unique. This is the year before the Ramones had a record out. The place was really packed! Milk and Cookies came on and they were pop sounding. I thought they were really pretty good. I thought, *These guys are playing all their own songs.* This kinda defied everything you were taught or believed about how rock & roll should be, that you have a God-like Band and you're in the audience and there's this invisible wall that separates you from the band. This was all brought down. That's what going to CBGB's did to me that night.

"Then the Ramones come on! And they were so fucking loud, but they were so fucking good. You could hardly hear the lead singer, but that didn't matter. They were just so brutal and raw, and we were trapped against the stage. It was the most direct thing—it was like having a gun aimed at you, seeing the Ramones. I noticed that Johnny Ramone was not playing all the lead licks that you 'had to play,' that Eric Clapton might play. It was just really simple and direct but really fun. And the audience just rocked and dug it.

"I walked out of there mesmerized. Everything changed."

Like Keith and Peter, Marek felt unsatisfied with the rock mainstream. "There was this rift developing between Keith and Whitestone guys who were into Genesis, jazz, and British art rock, and where British art rock was dovetailing with jazz was with Al DiMeola," he says. "The riffs were getting faster and faster and unplayable. No average kid could do it. You had to be a prodigy. And you were really losing touch with being able to identify with the musician. These guys would come over to The House and bring a DiMeola record with them, but then were turning up their noses at some of the other stuff *we* were listening to that was a little more lowbrow. We'd put on 'Strutter' by KISS, who were over the top. We loved that on their album covers it said, 'KISS uses Gibson guitars and Pearl drums because they want the best.' Which was so crass. The attitude was good. The Ramones were *completely* the other direction; it was like out of left field. I remember seeing the Ramones and just being floored. It wouldn't have dawned on me that that was going to happen. It wasn't coming out of *my* musical process, but I immediately identified with it. We were starting to rebel."

Hanging out at CBGB's and Max's, Marek began indulging his growing interest in Manhattan nightlife. He would often be accompanied on these late nights by Peter, who knew the Max's scene well since he lived around the corner, and by Peter's new pal Miriam Linna, a Cleveland, Ohio, transplant—"with a Pugsley kind of expression," recalls Peter fondly—who at the age of twenty arrived in New York City on the day of the Bicentennial and quickly became an enthusiastic and influential New York rock & roll booster. "Out of all of those guys I hung around with, I was Peter's pal," Linna remembers. "We were virtually inseparable for a long time. We weren't romantic, just best of friends. I felt like he was my brother. He was always wanting to have fun, so we'd go to these really weird places. He was a heavy-duty art student so he was hanging around with these totally off-the-wall but *incredible* human beings, super-talented. So we would have just a great time hanging out and having fun."

"It was mind-blowing," Marek remembers of the downtown scene. "You'd go down to CBGB's and see Blondie, Talking Heads, and the Ramones on the same bill for three or five bucks. They were starting to get a real buzz going at CB's so you couldn't get a seat at a table, but they let you sit on the floor in front of the stage. We would just grab a pitcher of beer at the foot of the stage." The scene at Max's was star-studded, also, downstairs in the wild backroom. "By that time it was all the local rock people, but all of those local bands were such self-made celebrities. And you can't *not* pick up on that. The energy of it was so infectious and powerful that I just got really caught up in it. I'm really shy, so I never actually ended up walking in there with the brass that they had saying, you know, '*Hey, Marek Fleshtone, nice to meet ya.*' I was starstruck by the whole thing."

The Ramones weren't the only band putting the lie to the merits of virtuosity. New York underground legends Suicide were another band whose influence on the guys would be incalculable. Marty Rev and Alan Vega played an intense and aggressive minimalist show, and with their sonic violence and conceptual attack mode they didn't fit into the soon-to-be-named New Wave movement. Peter heard about Suicide at the loft. His roommate would go to Max's almost every night and, wide-eyed, tell Peter what he saw there.

"Man, it's two guys, and this one guy playing this old beat-up Farfisa, and the other guy in black leather dances around and slaps himself on the face and falls down a lot!" he'd rave.

"I remember reading in the *Voice* that Christgau dismissed Suicide, calling them 'The Two Stooges,'" Peter says. "I thought, *If Christgau hates them so much I gotta check this out.* Keith and I went to see Suicide together and totally fell in love with them right away. Everyone hated them, you know? And we connected immediately to it. We became *real* devoted to Suicide. We'd go to all their shows and they became our idols." Suicide performed with an intensity that reached out, sometimes literally, to anyone who witnessed them live. "It's a little hard now to explain how totally revolutionary they were. Martin Rev played a beat-up old compact organ piled with a bunch of crummy echo units and a primitive rhythm box. He would just stand behind all this junk, flipping switches, immobile and bug-like in his oversized tripple-lensed shades. This would leave all the considerable stage, or offstage, action to Alan Vega. He performed with tortured intensity as if he was reaching out to an audience of fifty thousand in a place that would hold a few hundred, and usually much less as the 'show' went on, all the while shouting abuse at whoever was trying to control the situation at the sound board. Suicide is the only group I know that is actually louder between songs. They always galvanized what audience there was, usually against them."

Keith remembers Suicide's appeal similarly. "I used to sit up front because Alan Vega was so confrontational. You never knew if there was going to be a fistfight. You never knew what was gonna happen. He used to piss people off. This was part of the show. He used to go out in the audience and go up to people and say, '*Is that your girlfriend? Can I touch your girlfriend?!*' Just to get people going. And he would pick on the biggest, baddest looking guy. I don't know how he never got killed. It was chaos, insane. They'd make a lot of noise—with a beat—and to me it was pure rock & roll on some minimal level. I think when they first started doing shows at the Mercer Arts Center they would lock the backdoor so nobody could leave his show. If you came to a Suicide show you were locked in with Alan!"

Says Peter now, "Real emotion was something rock & roll was sorely in need of at the time. Everyone was so wrapped up in the size of Elton John's glasses or how many guitars Peter Frampton's roadies were dragging onstage that night. Martin and Alan brought themselves to the stage, stark and real." (Affection between the Fleshtones and Suicide wasn't one-way. "The Fleshtones had a fresh view of rock & roll," Martin Rev remarks. "Their live shows were driving and very upbeat, a new approach to traditional rock & roll with, of course, lots of new original songs which reflected their own unique approach to songwriting." The Fleshtones would record with Alan Vega twice in their career, in 1978 during sessions for their aborted first album and twenty years later while recording *More Than Skin Deep*.)

The Cramps from Cleveland also turned the guys on with their stripped-down rockabilly noise, savage fifties camp, and utter disregard for commercial trends. An added bonus was that Miriam Linna was the drummer, though her tenure would be short-lived. "I flipped when I saw the Cramps," says Keith. "It was probably the most amazing show I ever attended. I went to Max's on some Tuesday night to see Suicide, and the opening band was the Cramps, their first show in New York City. Within half a song my mind is blown. It was probably more shocking to see them than to see the Ramones, because when you saw the Ramones they already had a following. At Max's there were, like, twenty-eight people in the whole place on a Tuesday night and you're watching the Cramps do their thing for the first time in New York City. They had their gig way down, they were really professional, they knew what they wanted."

In the spring of 1976, Tom Scholz was busy in a vast Hollywood studio layering together the sonic mass of Boston's debut album. Across the country in a parallel universe, after a few jams at The House and a couple more months of confidence-building enhanced by Blue Whales and the buzz generated by CBGB's and Max's, the Fleshtones were officially conceived. What the band needed now was a drummer and a second guitarist to fill out their sound. Although Keith had been caught in the chain-link of Johnny Ramone's live buzz-saw attack and tattooed by the Cramps' onstage primitivism, he still hadn't quite avoided the local temptation toward virtuosity. He lacked confidence as a lead guitarist.

The goal? An audition at CBGB's. The future? Who knew.

CBGB'S sunday OCT. 3rd. 76

5.
The Curse of Al DiMeola

Gordon Spaeth was released from prison in the fall of 1976. "Mr. Dangerous" was back on the scene.

Tasting his newfound freedom sweetly, Gordon resumed his love-affair with music and mayhem. Though hardened by jail time, he fell right back into the swing of the party life in Queens and soon became a roaring regular at The House. The afternoon of the final costume party there, Gordon had excitedly scored a prize collection of old Motown 45s and LPs. Too covetous to play them on Keith's cheap turntable, he was roaming The House all afternoon clutching the records lovingly to his heart, a loopy grin on his face, muttering, *"Pre-disco Motown, Pre-disco Motown, Pre-disco Motown."* That evening, the party was raving, the costumes floating in and out of The House like so many rum-dum ghosts. As the alcohol ran low, the call went out for a volunteer to go grab reinforcements. Gordon dutifully answered.

About an hour later, the door flew open and Gordon, Leroy, and Jimmy Flanagan, a local pal, did a dramatic roll through the threshold and tumbled loudly into the foyer. "They looked like they had been blown from a cannon," remembers Peter.

Nonplused, and drink in hand, Keith peered out the front window onto Twentieth Avenue. "Hey Jimmy, where's your truck?"

"Oh, uh, I had to leave that behind."

"You had to leave it behind."

"Yeah, man. Man, I need some pot." He turned surreptitiously to Marek, and whispered, "*I gotta get fucked up, man! We just fucked up the truck!*"

In the confusion, Keith spotted Gordon sulking in the corner, carrying a 45 record in two pieces.

"Man, look at this, son of a bitch. It broke," Gordon cried to Keith. "You fucking believe it?"

"How'd it break??"

Gordon sat down on the couch, bleeding heavily, lost and inconsolable. He held in his hands the two pieces like they were epic tablets upon which was inscribed a language lost forever: *Pre-disco Motown, Pre-disco Motown*. He didn't really care about the damage to the truck, or his injuries, or how much trouble he—a newly released convict—was now in.

"Can I use your phone?" Flanagan asked Keith, *sotto voce*.

"Uh. . . . Yeah." Confusion swirled.

Keith overheard Flanagan talking to the police: "Yeah, I wanna report my truck stolen . . . I don't know what happened officer . . . I wanted to take it out, and it's gone . . ."

He gave the officer the license plate number, hung up, and wheeled around to Keith, grinning. "Where're the Blue Whales?"

Uh huh, right, okay. Gordon's bleeding. Flanagan's calling the police department. Keith was at a loss to piece together a bleeding face with a stolen van.

After a little prying from the guys, Flanagan finally broke down. He told Keith, "Well, Leroy and Gordon were behind me huffing Carbona. I didn't want any of it, believe me. I don't do that shit! But I couldn't help it. I kept inhaling the fumes and all of a sudden I lost control of the truck. I didn't know how fast I was going. And all of a sudden I started bouncing off cars and I guess I must've blacked out. The first car tipped us off that something was wrong, the second car slowed us down, and the third car stopped us! Next thing I know I'm standing on the street with Leroy and Gordon next to me!"

Like all tall tales, this story has been spun in different ways by different people over the years. Gordon sets the record straight: "Leroy and I had gotten into the death seat of Flanagan's car, and we started to head towards a bootlegger. We knew a bar that would sell us liquor at any hours, because we were infamous drinkers. We noticed that there was this car following us. Leroy knew that at that time any car with a license plate with a 'Z' in it was usually detectives, so we knew. Needless to say once we spotted them about fifty, seventy-five feet behind us, more vials, more pills, more illegal substances flew out of that van—it would've been Hubert Humphrey's dream."

In any event, Gordon and his pals didn't decide to pull over. They decided to gun it. They flew onto the Clear View Expressway dodging and weaving between cars like a scene out of *Bullitt*. They were zooming past the Creedmore Mental Institution when they ran into some vehicular resistance. "The first car that we hit was parked—it slowed us down and dented us. The second parked car we hit slowed us down even more. The third thing that stopped us was the gates of Creedmore!" The guys crashed through the gates in a hail of sparks. Panicking in the chaos, Flanagan slammed the car in reverse and tried to back up but the metal was against the wheels, and the more he stepped on the accelerator, the more smoke came out.

Meanwhile, Gordon and Leroy had been launched from the car and were now sprawled on the ground, dazed and bruised—their heads had hit the windshield at exactly the same time, and the windshield popped. "I was holding Johnny and the Hurricanes' 'Crossfire,' which was inside Junior Walker's double album," Gordon marvels. "That broke the crash. And here we were doing at least fifty miles an hour, but we were so loose because we were so drunk. Remember, I knew a kid who died decapitated."

The cops were hot on the guys' heels so Gordon and Leroy rolled in the bushes and then climbed up a telephone pole. The cops looked around wildly. *Where the hell'd they go? Godamnit they were ten feet away!!*

Confused and heroic, Gordon eventually climbed down from the tree and made it back to the party. "After that, Lee and I referred to ourselves as the Undisputed Kings of the Getaway," Gordon says. "Junior Walker saved my life."

"And they still came to the party!" Keith laughs. "The accident was just a thing that happened, an inconvenience. This is what you do in life."

Marek: "We sat there and got totally wasted as they recovered from their crash. And after a while it was if it never happened."

Keith and Peter were up against the Al DiMeola Curse. They needed a Master Plan.

Keith was now in a serious relationship with his high school girlfriend Judy Montiglione, and her hotshot younger brother Michael became the Fleshtones' first lead guitarist. "We were all like twenty-one, and Michael was sixteen. But he could play fairly well," Keith recalls. With Jimmy Bosko on drums, the band began rehearsing in earnest in the basement of The House, writing and playing only cheap and gullible originals because the guys didn't have the chops to learn cover songs. "We wrote our own stuff," says Marek, "the prototypical stuff that came out of Concrete Block. It was the earliest of Fleshtone songs, very simple, schoolyardy stuff like *Nya nya, Johnny's got a girlfriend!*"

Soon, Peter and Keith were knocking out nascent versions of originals: "Going on a Girl Hunt," "Rah Rah Rene," and "Critical List" (along with "Starfish in the Sea," "Love Cruise," "Code Three," and other amateurish ditties that didn't last long in the set lists). All of the songs were caught on Marek's cheap Hitachi tape recorder. Eventually they learned their first cover, a speedy, ragged version of Eddie Cochran's "Nervous Breakdown" that they would play for several years.

Marek remembers the diverse sources that the young band was drawing from during from this period—blues, Brothers Johnson, Sly and the Family Stone, garage—but he wanted a modern sound. "The Fleshtones weren't about trying to duplicate a period; we were always trying to be conscious about what was current and exciting, to keep the same mind-set of the older stuff but keep more modern elements in it." He adds, "We dabbled in reggae, and eventually it became so popular that we started to shy away from it. We were learning Desmond Dekker's 'Israelites' and Stevie Wonder's 'I Don't Know Why I Love You" off the *This Is Reggae Music III* compilations." The Fleshtones' reggae experiments were filtered, as all else, through the punkish verve of the time. "We sped the stuff up," Peter remembers. "Not quite ska, more rock & roll-ish." (Marek's memories are hazy here—"Israelites" never appeared on the *Reggae Music* comps, and Wonders' version of "I Don't Know Why I Love You" didn't, Desi Young's did—but the influences on the Fleshtones were certainly varied, common only to a bacchanalian vibe.)

For a spotlight, the guys had to settle for basement parties at The House; they formed the band to throw great big parties anyway, so it satisfied their growing, amphetamine itch. Word was out in Whitesetone that Fleshtone House Parties were bizarrely fun and chaotic. "After a while, other bands began to play with us, so you got a lot of value for your party," says Peter. "What I loved about those parties was that sometimes you'd be playing, and they'd turn out the lights and people would be dancing and making out and getting drunk. And dancing. It was cool. People were *dancing* to us! What a great feeling, that after all that time people are moving and participating. You really got a feel that, instead of *I'm up here and I'm doing this thing*, you got the feeling *We're all together, we're all one big organism.*

"There was no place for us to play in the city or Queens, and we didn't think we were good enough to play out anyway at this point," Peter says. "So we'd throw these parties, and we'd be blasting MC5 records and Stooges records, and some odder things like Wizard. And there was somebody who always wanted to put on Yes and stuff like that, and we'd take it off, put the MC5 back on, or Jonathan Richman." Richman, the baby-faced, heart-whole singer from Boston who specialized in remarkable, near-precious odes to the simple things in life, had recorded with his band the Modern Lovers one of the great rock & roll songs of the seventies, "Roadrunner." The song appeared in 1976, on his debut record on Beserkley, and had a big effect on the Fleshtones. "He was a huge influence for his very natural, vulnerable stage presence, and he's so honest," says Peter. "And all those things that are on that first album were things that we related to right away, that view of the world."

On May 19, 1976, the day Joey Ramone turned twenty-five, the Fleshtones loaded their gear into Keith's truck and with some trepidation drove into the heart of the Lower East Side and their first coveted Tuesday night audition at CBGB's. Peter used the office copier at Farrar, Straus, and Giroux, where he worked after school emptying trashcans, to run off hundreds of fliers. Before they played that evening, Peter was gracious enough to encourage the few Queens friends who did show up to drink around the corner—as the prices were a bit steep even at threadbare CB's. "We were very wound up and blasted out our handful of songs at a ridiculously fast tempo," Peter remembers. "Still, people liked us and some even danced along, an unusual event at super-cool CBGB's. We were invited back for another audition.

"Finally, we were a real band."

Jon Quinn was among the cheering handful. "Keith was fully formed as a musician," he recalls. "Marek came down off the stage and told me that he'd never played bass before, that he was just doing this to check things out. He was a really good bass player from out of the woods, and he was doing it immediately. But, Peter wasn't quite there yet. It was like he was still doing his paintings. The first time I met him at SVA he had his paintbrush and his rag and he'd be wiping, very preciously. He was doing the same thing with his harmonica at CBGB's."

The Fleshtones were already mixing into their set certain stage mannerisms in an attempt to appeal to the audience, gestures that would forever tarnish the band as silly to many critics. The guys wouldn't be averse to interrupting a tune so that a roadie could leap onstage to present Peter with a bogus humanitarian award, or ending a show by building a precarious human pyramid. Brian remembers that after each song "the guys would stand stock-still, smile a silly smile, and hold it for ten seconds. Somehow that was supposed to have an effect." Quinn recalls that during "Going on a Girl Hunt" the band would collectively shade their eyes and peer out, safari hunter-style, into the less-than-bemused crowd. The onstage goofiness was mainly inspired by Peter's love for the Bowery Boys' slapstick routines hatched to escape various jams and tight spots.

"We were horrible at CBGB's!" laughs Keith of the audition. "But we still passed. Hilly Kristal said to us, 'You guys aren't really that good. But there's something there.'"

All was not well. "Michael was so young that it was hard for him to play shows because he was underage and he had to go away with his family on vacations," laments Keith. The band was forced to cancel a summer audition showcase gig at CBGB's. "I think Montiglione was terrified to get up there, looking back on it," says Peter. "He made so many excuses of how he had to leave town that night, that he just couldn't stay and play that show. He totally screwed us up."

The band needed another guitarist, and quick, and found a technically proficient local guitar player named Danny Gilbert. "He had no idea what the Fleshtones were doing," Keith says. "He joined the group for, I don't know, eight months. This guy was all scales. He said, *You have to know these chops.* Peter and I didn't think in these terms at all. Eventually, we realized that working with Danny couldn't work because of where is mind was at. He liked jazz, rock-jazz, Al DiMeola was his hero. Meanwhile he's playing with the Fleshtones. Go figure that!"

Despite its unhappy chemistry, this early lineup of the Fleshtones—Peter, Keith, Marek, Gilbert, and Bosko—got noticed, in venerable *Variety* magazine of all places. Of an October 6, 1976, gig at CBGB's, the revered showbiz periodical noted that "The Fleshtones, a Flushing, L.I. combo who've been together but four months, are developing well with high-volume rock. Work appears needed in sound balance. But, when all can be heard, the Fleshtones rate attention." The brief writeup also noted Peter's "punk rock vocal style" and Keith's "effective via boyish" vocal quality, "a characteristic that could give the Fleshtones distinction." (Auspicious?)

A month later, Elliot Cohen, in the local *Aquarian*, wrote of a considerably more sloppy CBGB's gig. "Their short time of playing together really showed in their lack of professionalism. At one point, after some noises that really assaulted my sensibilities, lead vocalist Piotr Michael Zamben [*sic*] screamed out, 'Stop the music! We're out of tune.' A large segment of the sparse crowd left shortly afterwards." Cohen lukewarmly concluded by noting a barely recognizable version of Syndicate of Sound's "Hey, Little Girl." Two issues later, "a representative of the band" (undoubtedly Peter, assuming the nervy if naive mantle as frontman) sent in this rebuttal to Cohen's piece that ran in the "Wild Nights" column:

1) The Cohen review was reasonable. Time makes improvements.

Assuring that his prize influences were accurately noted before they were blithely dismissed, Peter added a second item:

2) The Syndicate of Sound classic is "Little Girl." "Hey, Little Girl" belongs to Dee Clark.

The band was searching for a unique, definable sound, and around this time some members of the Ramones showed up at a Fleshtones gig and afterward jokingly told Gilbert that the band ought to be renamed the Overtones, after Gilbert's moody instrumental that the band was tackling.

The guys could barely read the few exciting notices that they *did* earn for the noise around them: as soon as the Fleshtones cobbled together a rhythm section, it just as quickly fell apart. "Bosko didn't last that long," Keith remembers. "He was lost to the Jon Montgomery Band. He was enticed to leave us because, according to Jon Montgomery, the Fleshtones were laughable. He said, 'CBGB's is not where you go play. Those are punk bands for people who don't know how to play. That's nothing.' He convinced Jimmy that he was gonna be a star and they were gonna have a contract and a big major record deal. And Jimmy believed him and he went away, so that's when we had to get another drummer. So Danny Gilbert brought Lenny into the group."

He was born on December 3, 1956, eight years to the day after Ozzy Osbourne, a stellar coincidence that would forever mark him. He grew up in Flushing, in a musical home; his dad, a graduate of Julliard, was a professional musician and member of the NBC television orchestra. Thus young Lenny Calderon's apprenticeship began in his summers while his father carted him along on various jobs in the New York area: he watched as he taught drum lessons, conducted orchestras at City College of New York, copied sheet music by hand for, among other clients, Tito Puente, who would drop scores off at the Calderon house. One afternoon, his dad left him in the maternal care of Eartha Kitt, who rehearsed and babysat Lenny while his dad was otherwise occupied at a recording session.

Lenny's dad was always on call for studio sessions, and the high point for Lenny came when Mr. Calderon was hired to play on Napoleon XIV's "They're Coming to Take Me Away, Ha-Haah!" contributing to the novelty tune's odd, landmark percussive sound by banging on a tambourine and playing snare and bass drum. Hundreds of the infamous hit 45 were shipped to the Calderon household the summer that Lenny turned ten. Staring at the seven-inch slabs housed miraculously in the family stereo cabinet, Lenny felt both cool and lucky—and the family passed copies of the record out to whomever came by.

By the late sixties, his older sister had turned him on to Motown, the Stones, and R&B, which gave him a diverse taste at odds with his friends'. Soon, Lenny was enriched by the acid rock of Led Zeppelin, Blue Cheer (whose *Vincebus Eruptum* was the first album he bought, for two bucks down at Woolworth's), and, especially, Black Sabbath. "I was a big Sabbath freak," Lenny says. "I went to see them when I was thirteen or fourteen at the Academy of Music, and I just went nuts. I went to a big show on my birthday. It was the best seat I ever had in Madison Square Garden—I was in the orchestra—and Ozzy screams out, *It's my birthday!* and I jumped up, *It's my birthday!!* I have the treasured program from this show. A lot of people said I reminded them of Ozzy when I had my long hair." Soon, black-light rock posters were adorning Lenny's bedroom wall. Music was to become his lifelong passion.

He convinced Danny Gilbert, his childhood friend, to forget buying camera equipment with his Bar Mitzvah money and to instead buy a guitar so that Lenny could have someone to play around with. "We started playing at little community centers," Lenny recalls. "We played at the Quaker House and the Macedonia Church. We played anywhere where they would let us set up. And then I discovered that none of the drummers were ever any good at these jam sessions we used to have as kids. And one day I sat behind the drum kit, and my friends were behind me cheering me on! They couldn't believe I was playing the exact drum beat to 'All Right Now'! That's when I became the neighborhood drummer in Flushing."

For his first drum kit, Lenny's pleased and eager dad rummaged through his NBC take-home cache. "He pulled stuff out of the closet, professional stuff, but it wasn't a complete kit; I kept adding cymbals and things to it. I got my first real set in '69 or '70. A year later, the guitar was in the closet and I started playing drums. When my dad had all of his percussion in the house I used to set up everything, like timbales, bongos, these huge orchestral-type kits, in my room and I would just hang out there and play all the time." Lenny auditioned for and drummed in a few one-off bands in Flushing, mostly covers groups whose attention for composing original songs was as short as their hair was long. "I was in this phony progressive jam band, and we were imitating Yes riffs and Emerson, Lake, and Palmer riffs. Besides metal I'm really into progressive and jazz music also, because that's where all the hot drumming is. Regular pop drumming has nothing to offer. It's all just rhythm machines."

His friend Danny had been brought in to play in the Fleshtones, and one night he let Lenny know that the band were fruitlessly looking for a drummer. ("No one wanted to drum with us because they thought we were too silly," Peter says.) Lenny's audition with Peter, Keith, and Marek shortly thereafter was a far cry from his audience with the Dictators a few months earlier. The Queens band had released *Go Girl Crazy!* the previous year on Epic Records to a collective commercial yawn, and Stu Boy King was now out of the band. Adny Shernoff asked Lenny to play drums to "The Next Big Thing" and put him through a proper formal interview, including a grilling over his musical tastes and favorite bands. "I failed the interview with the author," Lenny says. "They'd ask me, 'Who's your favorite group?' and I'd say, 'Black Sabbath, Led Zeppelin'—I didn't even know there was a scene in New York going on." The gig eventually went to Richie Teeter. The laid-back Fleshtones weren't nearly as interrogative. "I went to audition in the basement at The House, and it didn't even feel like an audition," Lenny remembers. "It seemed like I was in the band already when I got there! That's the way the guys were treating me." Says Peter now, "We would've been smart to ask people their influences, but we assumed that nobody cared about what we cared about."

Lenny looked a bit like Joe English, the wooly drummer for the popular Wings. "We wanted him to cut his hair because we all had short hair," Keith acknowledges. "He never did, but we didn't really mind. Lenny loved all the music that we loved but he also had atrocious taste. We used to go to rehearsal and he was always smoking pot, one of the downfalls for Lenny. He was always turning me onto these records he was listening to, stuff like Judas Priest, KISS, Angel, UFO." One day at practice, no doubt epiphanous from weed, Lenny said excitedly to the band, "You guys, KISS is the bad side, the evil side of rock . . . of . . . of life! And Angel is the good side. Dudes, just look at their white jumpsuits!" Peter wrinkled his face and rolled his eyes—*Lenny, gimme a fuckin' break*—but he had genuine affection for his new drummer's enthusiasm. "He *was* super-amiable," Peter says.

Lenny joined the band as The House was imploding. The feud with Mr. Barclay had grown to epic proportions, fueled in large part by the din that roared weekly and by Barclay's elderly prerogative to crankiness. A group of weary neighbors had finally convinced a local councilman that the $300-a-month lease should not be renewed, witness the repeated incidents of obscenity, filthiness, and drug abuse. The end of Twentieth and Murray was in sight. "We had a final Halloween party, the Blue Whale party to end all parties there," Marek remembers. Someone came as an Abscam sheik with a big bag of play money, and the next day the cash was stuck to the walls, everything covered in Blue Whale. "We had to move out, so we were trying to do something with the tank of nitrous oxide, and we ended up throwing it out the back window and it lodged into the back lawn it was so heavy. And, as if ordained by the gods, Lizzie The House cat got hit by a car. So it was on this gray day, the last day that we were there, this overcast day, that we had a little burial in the backyard. We buried Lizzie. And then we moved. The end of the era."

Not long after the guys were forced from The House, Mr. Barclay died, the victim of one too many Curacao bashes and ride-cymbal crashes. To this day, Keith feels that it was the rock & roll that was truly sustaining him. Once the music and mayhem left, Barclay expired.

As the end of 1976 approached, the guys were on the prowl for places to live. Marek took the bridge over the East River and crashed with his sister in her small apartment on St. Mark's Place, the epicenter of East Village rawness and the start of an eye-opening tour of fun and annihilation for the kid from Maine. Keith moved himself and Judy into a nice, large three-bedroom apartment at the edge of Whitestone and there they settled for a couple of years, eventually marrying. Peter was still living in Manhattan, luring Marek along with him on long, long nights full of clubs and poppers and grins. With pals Miriam Linna and Gary Fakete, a talented, urbane photographer, he and Marek roamed the near and far edges of downtown Manhattan as only kids in their early twenties could: up all night, up all day, digging the dangerous, stomping, late-seventies New York decadence of crumbling urbanity and exploding nightlife fueled by an increasing intake of uppers and drink, sounds and nonsense, junkies and squares.

For Marek, the odyssey would end ten years later as he bottomed out in Tompkins Square Park addicted to heroin, as far from the parochial values of Wayne as he might have dared imagine. For Peter, the hip, coarse gleam of New York City in all of its cab-honking, early-morning clamor would forever tattoo him with potency and glee. He had the nerve, stamina, and fortitude to make it all last. Calling all Kicks, he was becoming a grinning Midnight-to-Six Man, mythically opposed to fatigue.

6.
I'm Just an Outcast

By November, the Fleshtones were gigging around town semiregularly, mind-blowing reality for the guys from Queens who had only picked up their instruments twelve months earlier. Danny Gilbert was soon out of the band, Peter having finally convinced Keith that the group needed only one guitarist with raw and jagged rhythm, not practiced and sustained *modus*. "I kept saying to Keith, *Do it on your own, do it on your own*. We could be a little rudimentary, a little primitive," Peter says. Keith was scared of the idea. "I could hardly play, I didn't know the name of my strings, I had no idea what the name of the chords were I was playing at the time. All of a sudden I'm the only guitar player! When I first started to play you didn't have guitar tuners and that was a nightmare for me. I dreaded it." Then Keith saw the Cramps. "And I thought, *Yeah, well, why not?*"

Lenny found himself in the unenviable position of having to fire Danny, who lived beneath him in the same apartment building. Little did Lenny know that he would later get similar passive-aggressive treatment from Peter and Keith. (Daniel Gilbert left New York for the Gold Coast shortly after he decamped from the Fleshtones, enrolling at the Musicians Institute in Hollywood. Years later he coauthored two textbooks on guitar solos. Since the late seventies he has taught regularly at the Institute, including courses in "Single String Improvisation," "Applied Technique," and "Fusion Workshop.") However awkwardly done, cutting Gilbert loose was the right decision. "When we started doing the four-piece gigs, we took off," Lenny remembers. "Sad to say, but as soon as we got rid of Danny we became a real incredible band. The Fleshtones didn't want to be a 'musical' band. They didn't want lengthy guitar solos. They just wanted to sound more like the Cramps or early Talking Heads. They wanted to sound less professional, more primitive."

The Fleshtones played two coveted, sparsely attended midweek shows at CBGB's on November 9 and 10. ("Still pretty rough" noted James Wynbrandt in *Good Times*.) Lenny remembers the sense of purpose, even of seriousness, that the band felt while playing and being seen at the already fabled club. "Usually in those days the CBGB's crowd was all of the other the bands, so you'd look out there and you'd see Joey Ramone, you'd see Adny Shernoff, you'd see all these guys from the other bands. So you always tried to play good. You never wanted to embarrass yourself. And there was always that air that there was somebody important out there. There was always people dropping names, *Oh, there's the guy from Chrysalis Records. There's the guy from Sire Records.* There was always some reason to get your shit together and play good."

The band was still happily plugging in and playing any house or loft party they could get in or out of Manhattan, and were slowly building a reputation as a fiercely energetic if not a niche-driven live band. A daydreamed record contract could wait: they now needed a new place to rehearse, the basement of The House having been relegated to the dustbin of (a semirecalled) history. A space out in Long Island City near Dutch Kills worked for a while, but they had a strong desire to be taken seriously, knowing full well that there was no place for them out in the provincial boroughs, that joints like CBGB's and Max's were truly where real rock & roll was played.

After a brief search, they ended up, appropriately enough, back down in a basement. Stephanie Chernikowski was a highly influential photographer who became a chronicler of the downtown rock & roll scene—her photos of the bands and scenesters who hung out at CBGB's and other New York City haunts would become the standard-bearers decades later—and she owned a basement on the Bowery near CBGB's that she rented out to the Cramps. The Fleshtones happily accepted the Cramps' offer to share the basement, but it was destined to be short-lived. "Some bad blood started between the Cramps and the Fleshtones," Lenny recalls. "They became very focused and very professional, and they kinda thought they were better than most bands. And, actually, they were."

I'm Just an Outcast

Peter remembers the more specific reason why the shared space went sour. "Stephanie kicked us out for making too much noise," he admits now. "Jon Quinn, Marek, and I stayed up one night making tapes with my father's old Voice of Music tape player, with the mysterious 'Add-a-Track' feature that we wanted to figure out. I made this horrible, weird voodoo loop of a dance thing. It existed with a second tape console and it was looping back into itself all night. We played it over and over until the sun came up. After that night Stephanie wanted us out. And as soon as we left and took our equipment out, the basement flooded and destroyed all of the Cramps' equipment."

Irony and comeuppance be damned: the Fleshtones were on the prowl for a rehearsal space.

He was a hazardous legend, an uncouth, semitalented musician who would hook up on occasion with local players, including Johnny Thunders and Jerry Nolan, late of the New York Dolls, at this time loose and succumbing to their addictions and playing in the Heartbreakers. Billy "Balls" Piano's reputation was borne of his other gig: he was an infamous heroin dealer, a major source of dope in the East Village. He owned a storefront across from Cooper Square on Third Avenue just around the corner from Eighth Street, and he rented the basement out to bands.

The confluence of flop houses and grimy streets above the Bowery was a no-man's land, a seedy haven for dealers and drunks, rarely visited by anyone without nerve or need. No one really remembers precisely what Piano might or might not have sold from his decrepit storefront: all there seemed to ever be in the window was a big white grand piano gathering dust. Anyway, Piano seemed more interested in his own cheeky, semi-adequate underground keyboard playing. "He played a raunchy old electric piano on top of an ironing board with fuzz boxes and wires hanging out of it," Lenny remembers. "The thing sounded like a wild, distorted guitar."

Piano's electric squall would score some pretty hairy times for Peter, Keith, Marek, and Lenny, who would rehearse in the basement on and off for the next two and a half years. The guys were equally frightened of and amazed by the small but dangerous Piano and his cool, risky vibe, and they began a literal immersion into the muck and humidity that was the perilous Bowery of the time. The Fleshtones were now at the epicenter of the East Village and were soon to be branded eternally—in a baptism by surreal fire—as a Manhattan band.

The intemporal atmosphere in the basement, with its earthen floors and damp walls, contributed to the primitive feel. "It was horrible," Peter recalls. "Underneath was a sub-basement, a cellar. In ancient times that area right around Cooper Union was a swamp and a pond. The sub-basement was always flooded with water, and even in the dead of winter hoards of mosquitoes bred in this basement. They would come flying out, so Billy had one of those old huge fans that he would turn on. They hooked that fan up in front of us while we rehearsed to blow the mosquitoes back."

Piano was often drug-laced and his behavior was, to say the least, erratic. The band would come back from a gig and roll into Piano's place at four thirty or so in the morning, start loading their gear in the basement; Piano would wake up, startled and disoriented, forgetting that the band was coming back, and fly out onto the sidewalk completely naked with a fencing foil in hand, ready to attack whoever it was who was breaking into his basement. "He was probably doing speedballs. You go completely off the wall at that point," says Marek.

In addition to Piano's capriciousness, the band had to deal with the remnants of the once-proud New York Dolls. Thunders, Nolan, and occasionally Arthur Kane were always down in the basement, jamming, and usually shooting up. ("The place was too much of a dump for David Johansen to hang there," Peter notes.) One night, Lenny sat behind his drum kit ready to rehearse when he noticed something peculiar. "I looked down and I thought there was paint on my drums, and then I realized that it was dried, caked-up blood! All over the skin, all over the side of the drums. Jerry Nolan had jabbed himself with a carpet tack because they didn't have any hypodermics in the house." (Lenny inadvertently took revenge. There was no bathroom in the basement, and he would regularly urinate in a glass bottle that, unbeknownst to him, Thunders and Nolan were also using to cook their dope in. The fluids would not mix kindly.)

"Everyone came to cop heroin at his house, and this was the period when I was getting disillusioned," says Lenny now. "I was seeing my childhood idols acting like junkies. I saw Glen Buxton from the Alice Cooper Band in Piano's basement one day and I couldn't believe it. I used to think of him like a God, and this guy was just hanging out waiting for his dope, you know." The guys became accustomed to Piano's reckless behavior and to his hangers-on, but the most bizarre element in his world wasn't the drug abuse or the dealing or the deconstructionist organ playing. It was *Igor*, a young man named Chris who Piano kept underground as his low-rent slave, a hopeless, drifter junkie whom he would literally lock in the basement overnight to guard equipment. "Billy controlled Chris by supplying him with dope," says Marek. "He lived in the basement like the watchdog. Chris would let us in, and his hands were like softball mitts because he'd been shooting up in them. Oh, it was horrifying. And as if I didn't have a clue then what heroin could do."

"Chris was like his slave, basically, and why not? The guy had nothing better to do," says Peter. "Billy would lock him in, but it was his deal, and he gave him a place to stay." A prurient and darker side of Billy and Chris's relationship would surface on occasion, when the master-slave dynamic appeared in ugly light. Billy would wrap a big motorcycle chain around the door to trap Chris downstairs and Chris would cry, *No, Billy, not yet!* "And this was not goofing around, this was the real thing," remembers Peter.

Piano was a psycho, shot dead years later by the police. No one knows whatever became of Chris. "Rehearsing with Billy 'Balls' Piano could have been a weekly situation comedy," says Peter now. "In the midst of all this constantly whirling around we sometimes could hardly get any rehearsing done. We would go there and would have to listen to Billy, a major speed freak, rant and rave for half and hour. He loved us, and he would say, *It's not you guys*, but then he would be ranting and raving at us too: *You can't do this. You can't come down here!!*" Peter adds, "I think they ripped the building down. It was one of the craziest places."

Secured with a regular if crackbrained rehearsal space, the Fleshtones concentrated on saving money, writing songs, and collaring gigs. "We were getting pretty spry on stage," says Peter. "Marek had dumped his Japanese bass for an old Mustang with a nifty racing stripe. Keith would spin across the stage, bashing his guitar into his odd rig of a Vox bottom and Traynor head to get more out of his $15 echo unit from Taiwan." Peter had discovered a pawnshop near SVA that sold Gretsch harmonicas, great rock & roll harps with a big warm sound, and the Fleshtones' sets were getting tighter, faster, the good times whirling into a frenzy. Could parties include an entire city?

The band was getting some surprising help with their set list, too. Near the end of 1976 Cathy Nemeth, a writer at the *Aquarian* and *New York Rocker* and friend of the band, handed them a cassette tape that she made after returning home from a trip to England. Among the songs scattered on the mix was a thundering, snarling ode that few in America had yet heard: "Anarchy in the U.K." by a band called the Sex Pistols. Digging the raw chaos and energy of the song, Peter quickly had the Fleshtones whip up a version down at

Billy Piano's, and they began practicing it well before it would make its American appearance on the Pistols' debut, *Never Mind the Bollocks*. The Fleshtones played the song at a midweek show at Max's on February 12, 1977, and duly received credit for the import: noted the *Aquarian*, "Exceptionally good rendition of 'Anarchy in the U.K.' was brought to the USA by the Fleshtones." The band would continue to play the song to raucous audiences up until *Bollocks* and its attendant hype and mania was unleashed several months later. ("Max's had 'Anarchy in the UK' in their jukebox," Nemeth remembers. "Maybe when people heard it there, they thought it was the Fleshtones!")

Choice of cover songs notwithstanding, the Fleshtones were starting to notice something unsettling: they weren't fitting into the rabid Punk scene of lower Manhattan. In terms of hype and local buzz, the Fleshtones followed the first level of the Ramones, Talking Heads, Blondie, the Dictators, the Dead Boys, Television, and the next level of Suicide, Tuff Darts, Shirts, and Mink DeVille. They failed to become "scenesters." Legs McNeil, coauthor of *Please Kill Me*, a comprehensive oral history of New York punk, doesn't even recall the Fleshtones on the scene during this period. "The first generation of CBGB's bands were the '74/'75 bands," says Hilly Kristal, owner of the venerable Bowery club. "The Fleshtones came shortly after that, unfortunately after we made the album *Live at CBGB's*. So they were part of the first generation, just two years later."

The Fleshtones' version of Punk Rock was bred in the fun and *joi de vivre* of the suburban basements and sixties turntables of their youth, not in the nihilist trends of politicized anarchy and safety pins. Their conscious breeding of black and white, dance and amplifiers was unique: when asked in 1978 what he liked, Peter replied, "Soul music. We're trying to get a little funky in a white sort of way." A touchstone for Peter had always been Archie Bell and the Drells, the Texas band of "Tighten Up" fame who sounded funky in a garage way. The Fleshtones were more interested in channeling the black intensity of Kid Thomas' obscure early-sixties recordings than they were in mining the ruffian street aesthetic of disaffected youth and dissonant, jagged rhythms. White kids happily misinterpreting black music, Peter would always say. Do That Jerk: the guys were more turned on by the last forty-five seconds of Wilson Pickett's "Land of 1000 Dances" than by No Future.

"Nobody had clear sixties influences like the Fleshtones," says Keith. "Everybody else was Ramones-and-Dictators 'Punk.' To me, punk music was the Standells or the Music Machine—American punk—which is more like what we were becoming. The idea was that we were gonna try and make ourselves like the early Yardbirds, but the fact that we were a band to dance to was considered uncool. Everyone else liked bands like Talking Heads and Television—bands that I liked—but we were getting condemned for being a party dance band. Some people called us a 'mindless twist band,' which we were! It didn't bother me that much because I knew that what we were doing was honest, real rock & roll. When we were competing with the punk scene and the art scene and then the art-rock scene that came in, we were considered unhip. *Twist band. Nothing there. What could be in a twist band?* It's insane when you think about that concept."

Andy Shernoff, who as the founder of the Dictators was at the start of the Bowery scene in the 'mid-seventies, feels that the Fleshtones were punk, but in an old-school way. "When the Dictators started we were obviously influenced by punk rock, but it was the sixties garage bands. Then it became that the Ramones really defined what punk rock was, and then every English band was imitating the Ramones. So in an historical sense the Fleshtones were punk, but they were also R&B, a little pop, a little art school." Richard "Handsome Dick" Manitoba, legendary frontman of the Dictators, feels that being called a mindless twist band "is a badge of honor! The Fleshtones were really Americana. They were watching B-movies and cartoons and comic books. That's what they were talking about. They had a real sense of humor, and they were good craftsmen with their music." But, the Handsome One adds, "It's hard to be taken seriously."

A lot of the hipster condemnation of the Fleshtones came right away, but the fact is that a lot of bands did like them. "Blondie were definitely fans of us early on," says Peter. "Suicide was a huge fan. The ex-members of the Dolls liked us. At that point, No Wave started to happen, which we *definitely* didn't fit into, but it turns out that Bradley Field of Teenage Jesus and the Jerks wound up being a big friend. Lydia Lunch actually liked us. Wayne County was a huge fan, and he helped us out a hell of a lot because he would let us open for the Electric Chairs at Max's. But they couldn't admit to it. That was their stance."

The Fleshtones were not part of the hard punk scene. "This was new music," Kristal reflected. "The Fleshtones were definitely alternative, if you want to skip to a few years later to when they called it Alternative Music. It was a very fresh, new sound. It had probably more dissonance than some of the older rock, but it was a new flavor, definitely new music. And it was not three-chord music. It was simple, but it *explored* music. The Fleshtones weren't really like Talking Heads, but their sound was closer to Talking Heads more than it would have been to the Ramones." Thirty years later, hundreds of wide-eyed bands from Good Rats to the Police have skulked beneath Kristal's famous tattered awning, plugged in, and played perhaps a memorable, perhaps a forgotten part of an epoch. Kristal has purchase on a wide and seasoned perspective, and he doesn't remember the Fleshtones as outcasts. "I think they were *themselves*, that's why they fit in," he says. "They were very good. They didn't copy anything. The Fleshtones just did it the way they felt, which to a lot of people is a drawback but I think it worked for them because they were good at it. Of course, it's always a drawback because record labels like to hear something they're familiar with. That always was a problem in that era." He adds, "I think one of the things about the seventies was there were a lot of new trends starting, and I tried to promote bands as being themselves, so all through the seventies a good many of the best of what came out of CBGB's were not like anything that had happened before. Maybe these bands were influenced, but they were themselves. And I think the Fleshtones were very *much* themselves."

Brian Spaeth, who with Gordon would soon be playing horn with the band on a semiregular basis, concurs. "The Fleshtones' music was definitely not following the cut. They weren't wearing leather, they didn't have any of the punk clichés. They were definitely one of a kind and unique. They were always trying to come up with that dance beat, and the emotions that they were trying to project were way different than, say, the Dead Boys. It was more complex, more subtle emotionally, not as far as the chords but subtle in the emotional feelings that they were trying to project. It wasn't that safety-pin-stomp-your-head kind of thing. It was more of a 1960s thing. There was tons of roaring energy, very heartfelt." The first six months the guys were feeling themselves out, not quite getting into their groove, "but after maybe the first eight months they got more confident and they started developing a following and a whole set of great songs."

Lenny felt that at this early juncture his band might have even been influential. "It seemed like people in other bands were trying to get the reverb sound, the early guitar sound that Keith was trying to get," he remembers. Patti Smith used to come see the Fleshtones at Max's and CBGB's and she'd stand in front of Keith and stare up at him, or keep her eyes glued to his skinny frame as he ran back and forth. A little while later she started playing a guitar, and it happened to be the same type of Mustang guitar that Keith was playing. That reassembled practice guitar was getting around.

Not recognizing his diagnostic accuracy, local critic Roy Trakin in the *Soho News* dubbed the Fleshtones sound "Amphetamine Rock." But a large and complicated dilemma was brewing for the amped-up, sped-up guys. A live dance band, a group dedicated to getting people up and moving and smiling and laughing to Kingsmen-like or I–IV–V stomping chord changes, the Fleshtones were encountering a big problem in lower Manhattan: few patrons were dancing.

"*Nobody* was dancing," remembers Miriam Linna, who wanted to lose herself at rock & roll shows in the goofy abandon of the Jerk and the Frug. "People have a hard time fathoming what that whole scene was like, but nobody danced! Oftentimes I really felt like I was the only person who was dancing at Max's, where they wanted you to sit down, or at CBGB's, where they had tables and people just stood around. The audiences were hugely, in proportion, guys. And it really seemed like the gals on the scene at that time were either photographers or writers. It doesn't seem to me like guys were going to shows with dates. There would just be, like, these lone guys. And they're not gonna dance!" Billy Miller, Linna's bandmate in the Zantees and later the A-Bones, and her future husband and partner at Norton Records, remembers, "People came into CBGB's and just walked around. None of those clubs were laid out for dancing. The tables went right up to the front."

As enamored as the Fleshtones were with playing Max's and CBGB's, they were increasingly frustrated. At some venues, the standing around got so bad that during sets Linna, always a stalwart Fleshtones fan, would grab tables and chairs in front of the stage and literally push them to the wall, scuffing the floor in her insistence to dance, dance, dance. Sometimes Peter himself would leave the mike—he was around it only half the time anyway—and hop off the stage to help Linna in her radical reclaiming of the rock & roll dance floor, the tables and chairs ending up in a pile against the wall while Marek's and Lenny's breakneck rhythms flew around them.

Unpleased by this rebellious display, management would frown and waitresses would get pissed off. "They'd yell at us while we were doing it," Peter recalls, "but while we're pushing away the chairs, kids would come up." At one point club management was going to try and throw Miriam out, but the band stopped them. "She would get shit for this, but she wanted to have room to dance with her friends," Keith remembers. "We had to find places where we could do this without having to worry about tables and chairs. At one point in time you did not dance to rock & roll. You were supposed to, I don't know, sit there and take notes. It was ridiculous. So the mindless twist band thought, *This is not a good situation!*"

The Fleshtones were making their point: rock & roll is about moving and grooving, and that's what the kids want. "That is what the music was about," Marek says, "that really simple stuff that was dance music in the sixties. And that's the stuff that we were playing, but at the places we were playing it just wasn't done. The fans wanted to do it.".

Peter: "So we took our case directly to the audience."

Fun + Movement = Purpose. The equation churned inside of him.

"Onstage I regurgitated a jumble of every dance I had seen growing up as a kid," Peter remembers, recognizing, naming, bumping into motion the heartlift that he and Keith felt and knew from their adolescent 45s. The fellas had plenty of artificial aid: they shook in the presence of go-fast uppers that helped them to physically approximate the spirit of rock & roll. "We were revved up most of the time on uppers and speed," says Lenny. "We were really into being awake! We used to take these pills that Billy Piano would send us called disoxins, really strong amphetamines. You used to take one and you'd get sores all over your mouth and you'd be gone for three days. We were taking lots of those! And if friends had cocaine, we would be snorting that up. It was fuel for the fire while we were out there staying up all night."

Peter's urge to dance, the ever-increasing alcohol and amphetamines coursing through his veins, the rock & roll in his heart, it all conspired with the rush of his twenty-two years and the glittering gauziness enveloping him. Uptown, a giant silver coke spoon was ascending into the star-filled black sky and a hundred and thirty-two beats pounded every minute. 1977 was the Year of Disco and Peter surrendered gleefully, although succumbing was a gradual process for the stubborn, skeptical guy from Flushing. John-Manuel Andriote observed in *Hot Stuff* that "disco's roots in black and Latin music, and its association with gay men, would give the music its uniquely exuberant emotional and sexual energy, but those roots and associations also caused mainstream Americans—the white middle class—to resist disco at first." Peter's initial disgust with disco, however, had little to do with the music's gay, racial edge, and more to do with the monumental intellectual preconceptions that he tends to throw in front of himself, inadvertent but adamant roadblocks toward his own enlightenment.

I'm Just an Outcast

"At first I was along with everybody else in saying *disco sucks*," Peter says. "To me, disco sounded artificial, and it stood for everything that we thought was inauthentic and glitzy. And as disco started becoming famous, there were really bad examples like 'Disco Duck,' which I put in the same box as what was happening to country music with the CB craze. It was a pretty bad time culturally in this country." But as had happened with the Ramones, and a few years earlier in Central Park when Sergio Mendes turned Peter on in ways for which he was unprepared, the passionate music of disco began to insist on its own urgency. "What I wasn't really thinking was that songs like 'Don't Leave Me This Way' by Thelma Houston and 'Rockin' Roll Baby' by the Stylistics are dynamic, unbelievable R&B. There were a lot of those songs I actually liked."

As he was warming to what German producer Giorgio Moroder was calling the "four-on-the-floor" thump and gaudy vigor of disco, Peter was being assaulted on two fronts by friends who intuitively knew that the energy of the scene would appeal to him. M. Henry Jones was a School of the Visual Arts filmmaker and down-to-earth guy whom Peter admired and regularly talked to about music and films. (*"How do they get those shots in those Mexican horror films? Can we do it without any fucking money??"*) Jones would soon occupy an eternal place in the Fleshtones' history, but at this point he was simply trying to convince Peter how great it was to go to Hurrah, a huge dance club up on West Sixty-second Street that provided an early epicenter for the scene.

"Pete, you don't get it," Jones said one evening in the loft. "You just don't understand what you're not getting. You don't understand what it's like to go to Hurrah. Everybody's there! You go there and, like, Warhol's there, and you can hang out with him. And Truman Capote."

"I don't care abut them," Peter said, suspicious.

"But you don't understand, like, the feeling you have," Jones retorted, wide-eyed. "It's like Max's in the sixties. You don't understand what it's like!"

Weeks later, Peter's good friend and fellow night owl Gary Fakete was urging him to check out the nightlife, the center of which had slipped down eight blocks to West Fifty-fourth Street, into a palace of high-energy hedonism known simply as Studio 54. "I don't care about that," Peter cried one night, reeling from the media-blitzed imagery on television and the papers. "I don't care what's going on there, the disco outfits and stuff!"

"You don't understand, people don't wear that. No one looks that way, and if you look that way you don't even get in." Fakete pointed his finger at Peter. "*You* are perfect, *you* will get in. For people like you, the music's great, man." Finally, one night Fakete grabbed Peter and Linna and hustled them into a cab and up to Studio 54.

"That was another night that changed my life," Peter says.

The discos pulsing in late-seventies Manhattan provided Peter with an irresistible outlet for his dynamism and curiosity about music, partying, and all-night energy—and for the memorable, untamed personalities lurking in the dark of what Albert Goldman dubbed "psychedelic country clubs." Soon joined by Marek's selfsame after-hours prowling, Peter was beginning to reimagine the Fleshtones as a conduit of danceable energy poised somewhere between downtown rock & roll and uptown disco, a fusion of two potent forces that would forever mark the sound and attitude of the band. It was a musical and social intersection explored by few groups bred in the East Village.

The nights were endless. The nights were endlessly fun. "I walked into Studio 54 and it was like dying and going to heaven," says Peter. "It was decadent, yes, but decadence is fun, especially good decadence, and this was decadence at its best. It wasn't burned-out decadence. It was decadence with energy and excitement. And sure enough, there was Warhol and there was Truman and there was Bianca Jagger and everyone, and you could hang out with them if you wanted." One heady night, Peter briefly sat talking with Warhol about music and the Fleshtones. The bleached Warhol approved of Peter's plans, and then urged him to chat further with Truman, and to dance with Bianca, which Peter did, his head spinning as the evening lengthened.

"You got into the hypnotic thing of the music. Every once in a while one or two of the tracks was just great R&B. That became a big influence on me. After a few times, it became so intense. 'Don't Leave Me This Way.' 'Disco Inferno' by the Trammps. 'You Make Me Feel Mighty Real' by Sylvester. It was R&B of the most passionate, and it was funny! It was rock & roll at its best! And at that point, the bands and musicians putting it down are the very people who should have been ashamed of themselves, because ninety-nine percent of white rock & roll had abdicated its real role as exciting music, as music with a beat, as music with passion, as music that meant something. Music was basically jerking itself off, pompous and boring as all hell. Soon I said, 'Marek, you got to come.' And he was the most open because he was living on St. Mark's.

"Marek and I became *addicted* to going to discos."

Father, father, lemme confess! The stoned Puerto Rican kid grabs a wary Peter around the shoulder and, laughing, snorting, looks back to his *compadres* for moral support. *Father, Father, lemme confess!* Peter was shaken, but relieved. He'd been mugged in Union Square park the year before, thugs jumping him in the dense, lightless shrubbery so hard to penetrate by the meek. They roughed him up pretty badly, taking his rent money, his crucifix, his shoes. But tonight, Peter was convinced that he had been delivered from the shit-kicking of his young life. He, Marek, and Miriam had been walking down a block somewhere on the West Side when Peter happened upon a complete priest's cassock and shirt in a trash can. His hair was shortish at the time (the exception rather than the rule), and to Marek and Miriam's giggles he donned the clerical garb, looking quite the earnest churchman. He wore the outfit all night at the discos, spinning and dancing up a storm to the delight of hooting partygoers.

Sometime around two in the morning, the trio turned a corner and walked right into the path of a gang of Puerto Rican kids, high and glinting. The trio had been expecting the usual: *Hey you white faggots, we're gonna kick your ass!* Peter's dressed up as a rock & roll priest to boot, a blasphemy that must be dealt with. But the lead hood walks up to Peter and surprises him: *Father, Father, lemme confess!* Their pure Catholic blood coursing but cut with booze, the street gang got Peter's joke, and everyone laughed, and the night went on and on and on . . .

. . . as Eddie Holman sang "This Will Be a Night to Remember" over thumping party grooves and Peter and Marek boogied through much of 1977 and 1978 in a glittering blur of dance floors at Studio 54, Hurrah, Paradise Garage, Le Mouche, Odyssey 2001. Indulging and nurturing their love for kicks and speed, they greeted dawns stumbling out of whatever Christopher Street dance club they happened to have closed. They became after-hours denizens, kicking their nights into gear at three or four in the morning. . . .

Hi-watt circuses, soaked in gin and dusted with coke, allowed Peter and Marek glimpses of the kickiness of the underground gay and transgendered world. Some nights they'd drop in at Cock Ring or the Toilet or the Manhole, infamous after-hours gay clubs where the music pounded along endlessly and the lights winked. The fellas were intrigued beyond reason. "It was out there, like the Velvet Underground unearthing the subterranean New York experience," remembers Marek. "It was really beyond the pale of a lot of the rock & roll people to do, but for us it was like an adventure into the nether regions of experience. We really were into it, all of that homosexual undercurrent that we used to love to flirt with." Marek and Peter soon became card-carrying members at Club 220, located at that number on West Houston Street, primarily a black transvestite joint with glitzy drag talent shows—a lip-synching Liza Minelli followed by a Diana Ross followed by another Liza and yet another Diana until Jackie La Frenchie would win it all—and sweat-soaked DJs spinning heavy-duty, high-energy R&B disco. Even though the patrons were patted down well on entry, nightly the club was raided by nightstick-swinging, skull-cracking cops responding to stabbings.

Cabs, cabs, over under sideways down in cabs: Peter had won a small arts grant, and Marek was spending whatever money he made, and whomever they ran with on any given night-into-morning was throwing long green all over the place. And Gary Fakete was well-known by the doormen. A favorite haunt for the group was the infamous Crisco Disco, located at West Fifteenth Street near the Hudson River in the heart of the dimly lit meatpacking district. Famed for its libidinal patrons and nonstop disco, the joint was grinningly celebrated for its stylistic *pièce de resistance*: a giant mock can of Crisco standing at one end of the cavernous room on top of which the DJ sat spinning disco mixes into starlight. The wink-and-nudge reference to the lard sometimes used as a lubricant in (mostly gay) sex was a cheeky reminder to Peter and Marek that they were in the raw nether world of boy-leather, cocktails, and poppers. (Years later the band would celebrate such homoerotic ambiance in their mock-heroic song "The Return of the Leather Kings.")

"You could buy drugs and speed at the coat check [at Crisco]," Marek says. "Their version of a drink was a dollar for a plastic cup full of vodka or gin and a splash. It was about pushing the envelope as far as you possibly could, fueled by lots of speed or coke or alcohol and going out and having as good a time as you possibly could, dancing all night." By nine or so in the morning, with the sun lifting above the wakening boroughs, Peter and Marek might end up at Cell Block, a lively gay/S&M joint where the music was still going, and where the boys could catch their breath and their tapped nerves could begin to settle. This was a whole other world that the boys were floating in and out of, with windowless black-painted doors, that if you knew the right people, opened onto cavernous warehouses where chains hung from ceilings and thongs of men and women shook.

"Marek and I talked a lot about trying to bring that energy into the Fleshtones," Peter says. "After a while, we probably found it *more* vital and intense than the downtown rock scene. The music was just so liberating, in the real sense of the word. Man, you'd just jump around and dance and work yourself free. And we're not talking about places where people went and did 'The Hustle.' We're not talking about *Saturday Night Fever*. This was a continuation of real nightlife that, for a while, went underground, the most direct continuation of the feeling and nightlife of the sixties. All of the people who were in on what made the sixties nightlife exciting were all there, the transvestites and the dancers and Andy Warhol hangers-on, so it was great.

"It was really exciting to be at a Television concert, but it was a *concert*. Even in the downtown resurgence it was more like, 'Well, let's look at this band play.' When we were at Crisco Disco, which was so different, everyone was just letting go. It was what rock & roll should've been doing, and wasn't doing."

At the Cock Ring, Marek and Peter used poppers for the first time. "At first I thought it was degenerate to do such a thing," Peter says. "At that point we were on who knows how many uppers, and we used to drink gin & tonics and, literally, I remember many nights losing count at twenty-five. We started huffing up 'locker room,' as it was called, dancing to some song, and Miriam and I were swinging each other by the arms and for a joke I'd swing her into Marek, and we're bashing into each other. I'm huffing up on the popper and someone slams into me and splashes it in my eye. It burned like hell." The inhalant would leave permanent brown stains on Peter's eye and hooded lids, the effervescent and dissolute disco evenings forever branded onto his face.

"When we were coming back later that night we ran into that gang of Puerto Ricans," says Peter. "It was such a beautiful ending. I figured these guys were just gonna kick our asses. But they asked to be absolved. They start confessing. Golden memories, golden memories."

7.
Soul City

The Fleshtones are hopping: house parties in Queens, loft parties in Manhattan, February 9 at Copperfields, an August buzz at the Terry Ork–sponsored "New Wave Festival" at Village Gate ("The Fleshtones were fun, not funny," wrote Alan Betrock admiringly), October 26 at CBGB's, and a happy handful of dates at Max's (February 16; May 3; July 27; August 12 opening for Wayne County; October 12). Apart from the festival and the exciting high-profile Friday night County gig, most of the shows were quiet, midweek affairs. At least the band was playing out.

Local press began peering through the steam left after Fleshtones shows. The upstart *New York Rocker* was an early, enthusiastic supporter of the band and would continue to back them for years. Two encouraging items ran in the February/March issue, one a "subjective guide to New York's Top 40 local bands, inclusion based upon originality, talent, and audience response." The Fleshtones earned four solid stars, beating out the Dead Boys and the Cramps but falling short of the Heartbreakers by half a star. Good company, indeed. "The Fleshtones manage to surpass nostalgia with good solid musicianship, vibrant originals and a captivating lead singer," *New York Rocker* reported.

A piece by Miriam Linna in the same issue was the first substantial look at the band, couched in a larger celebration of groups that Linna dug, like the Flamin' Groovies and Boston's DMZ and Real Kids, for whom "record contracts will be secondary as the fun element revives itself." In this important, generous piece, Linna energetically threw light on some bands that *Newsweek*, enamored with nihilist Richard Hell's Bowery blues, torn T-shirt, and track lines, wasn't talking about:

> As of late, a number of bands that for months had been submerged beneath the present punkers have been rising to the surface with a great new energy that will certainly change the trend of things to come, due mostly to the fact that their energies are positive, celebratory. Their main involvement is creating real rock & roll for modern kids, stuff to dance to, stuff to go crazy and fall in love and buy records to. The basic underlying factor? FUN. And the nifty thing about the whole deal is that they've subconsciously redefined the meaning of "cool" and the facetious rip-torn element is not there; it's like they're saying, look, we're cool and know it and we don't feel like proving it to you. Primo example: The Fleshtones.
>
> God bless the borough of Queens for producing such fine elements of true rock & roll fandom. God bless Queens. There's not much explaining or demonstrating left to be done about/for the Fleshtones: these guys have moved out of a quaking stage of doing what they were doing as an homage (come on, it HAD to be a tribute, what with that WE DON'T EVEN CARE IF EVERYBODY HATES IT attitude) to doing it because it really, truly is fun and 'cause the kids like it a lot.
>
> There's nothing left to say except that these guys are so detached from the present state of affairs that they might as well be the Blues Magoos—you watch them observe today's bands and enjoy them and then see them go home, forget about today, and slap on "We Want The Stones" like it were the anthem of the day. Their function: to make kids dance. This band is clean psychedelia, like even when they revert to a Real Oldie, it becomes a psychedelic revamp—maybe *controlled* is a better word—suffice it to say that these guys know the definition of cool and better yet, they KNOW how to dance.

In July, Linna dropped a reference to the Fleshtones ("the best new band in NY!") in the *Bomp Newsletter*, run by hip label-head Gary Shaw out of Burbank, California. It was the first mention of the band in the golden state, and within a few years, Los Angeles would be the band's temporary second home.

Emboldened by the good press, the Fleshtones got tighter live, Peter moving like mad, his harmonica wailing, Keith slashing chords and trebly leads, Marek and Lenny quickening the rhythms and coalescing into something remarkably intense and fun, delighting the guys themselves and surpassing any expectations they may had nursed during their blurry Whitestone bashes. "There was a certain nervous energy about Marek," says Lenny of playing in the rhythm section. "You were always waiting for a train wreck to happen, but it never really did. We always pulled it off." Peter and Keith were writing more songs, too: Keith usually supplied the riff or three-quarters of the tune, Peter the concept and words, a partnership that has lasted for decades. Early versions of "The Girl from Baltimore" and "The Theme from 'The Vindicators'" took shape and were detonated on stage next to hare-footed versions of "Sometimes Good Guys Don't Wear White," "Everybody Needs Somebody to Love," and "Wild Weekend."

Trusting more and more in himself, Peter was becoming wildly unpredictable offstage as well as onstage. The band might be rehearsing a certain set for weeks when on the day of the gig Peter would come barreling into Billy Piano's with a stack of new 45s, saying excitedly, *We're playing this song tonight! We're playing this!* "We were always on the edge," Lenny says, referring to Peter's infectious heedlessness. "That's why we always had that nervous energy about us." The band was positively blasting through their sets. One night after polishing off a typically revved-up show at Max's, the club's manager came up to the band in the dressing room, wringing his hands. "You know, you guys were really great. We're happy to have you here," he said to the sweaty foursome. "But I don't think it's fair of you guys to do a thirteen-minute set!"

The guys looked at each other and laughed: *Did we really do that?* Pills and thrills. They promised the next time that they'd play a little longer.

The Fleshtones were beginning to earn their local reputation for sonically demolishing the wall between themselves and the crowd, the whole thing a speedy dance party scored with smiles and rock & roll. *Everyone's invited! How long can this last?*

"It was hard to remember I was still in school," Peter acknowledges.

At SVA, Peter was growing friendlier with M. Henry Jones, the tall, wiry filmmaker with cool nerve and similar notions to his own.

Jones was born in Texas but moved to Buffalo, New York, when he was nine, and he started taking photographs after he received a camera at age fourteen (a reward from his mother for enduring dental work). His teacher had encouraged him to experiment with animation, and in high school he was turned on by Kirk Smallman's *Creative Film-making* text and got involved with the school arts festival, ultimately screening innovative student films from around the country. After high school, Jones interned on the staff at Artpark, an artists' colony south of Niagara Falls, shuffling artists and equipment to and from Buffalo. There was a great amount of experimental film happening in Buffalo in the early seventies, and Jones had planned on attending the university there, but several artists at Artpark, impressed by Jones' burgeoning talents—he had won the Kodak Teenage Movie Award for a claymation short—urged him to consider California or New York City. In 1975, he entered the School of Visual Arts on a full scholarship.

He met Peter in an animation course that fall. And for five or six hours each Monday they sat together, in desks apart from their classmates, learning with teacher Marty Abrams and conspiring together in their private appreciation of film and music. Very quickly, the boys discovered that they had as much in common as they were disparate. Peter enjoyed turning Jones on to rock & roll as much as Jones liked showing Peter how to turn a vision into something physically animated. They became good buddies.

"I had a lot of respect for Peter because he was a little bit older," Jones says. "Both of us were, for different reasons, wanting to make animated films, and a lot of it had to do with what we'd seen on TV growing up. He was talking about this Officer Blah Blah that had a TV show in New York, and I was talking about how when I was a kid I used to watch a show called *Kiddie's Carousel*, which he'd never heard of. We talked a lot about different types of collage animation. We were talking about it all."

Their late-night conversations leapt from one rapid-fire association and reference to the next, as they began electrically recognizing shared sympathies: two young art students thrilling in the moments of surprises and discovery in the art capital of the world. "Peter would spend a lot of time talking about the Mexican horror films that he liked so much," Jones recalls, "and then he talked about, say, the use of a shadow, and then I related that to *Beauty and the Beast*, and then we used to talk a lot about making films that would use certain props and lighting that would give the impression of having a much greater production value than it actually had. And we obsessed about this for a long time, looking at different movies and trying to figure out how they got different shots."

Kenneth Anger's infamous cult short *Kustom Kar Kommandos* from 1965 was a particular, and peculiar, favorite of Peter's: the four-minute film of a buff, young blond surfer boy polishing his hot rod with a pink powder puff has since become a touchstone document in gay and lesbian academic studies, and Peter dug the fetishistic gen-der-fuck that the film explored—not to mention the gorgeous souped-up vehicle itself and the golden West Coast ambiance in which it shimmered. In this obscure film, Peter watched one kid's mania couched in rock & roll parlance, and the vibe felt familiar.

"Peter would forever talk about polishing the hot rod in *Kustom Kar Kommandos*," Jones remembers. "That was what got us to music."

November, 1977. The Fleshtones are between gigs and rehearsals. "I Honestly Love You" by Olivia Newton-John, "I Love You Just the Way You Are" by Billy Joel, and "My Way" by the recently departed Elvis are among the Top 40 radio hits this month. Counteracting from the great punk beyond: both the Sex Pistols and the Clash have released their debut albums, and by the close of the year the music world would shift tectonically.

After a seminar one night, Peter and Henry Jones are lounging in Cosmo's Diner at Twenty-third Street and Second Avenue when Peter produces a scratchy 45 single from his bag. "I want to make a film that is *like* the 45," he pronounces to Jones and, apparently, to anyone who would listen. Jones stares at him. "The 45 is a single unit, man. I mean it's like a hit, or it's not a hit. It *may* be followed by an album, it may *not*. It's a thing of its own. It lasts two to four minutes. I want to make a two-minute film that's . . . just that, it's not part of anything else. It opens and closes. It's a complete unit."

Jones stares at him, fragments of historical videos flashing in his mind: the Beatles' "Paperback Writer" clip, grainy mid-sixties Italian Scopitones, Betty Boop animated with Cab Calloway.

"What the fuck?" he said.

"You have a hit 45. I want to have a hit video, a hit film. I want a single unit." Peter was getting excited now, shifting in his seat. Jones took the idea home with him and began to ponder it. "At that point, I had never heard of anyone doing what Peter wanted to do," he says. "Then I did some research and I found out there were these tone poems done in '62, '63—they were meant to be in a jukebox that would play the videos, they were sort of common knowledge—and that somebody had tried to do it in the fifties, somebody had tried to do it in the forties. But for a good twelve to fifteen years, no one had pursued that. They were very experimental, very arty. So I figured I'll do this film with Peter."

Peter already had a song in mind. He characteristically made a rockin' discovery in a used-record store where he fell in love with a tune on a budget album featuring a pre–Velvet Underground Lou Reed. "Soul City" was a grooving, upbeat, Motown-esque tune cowritten by Reed and performed by the appealingly amateurish Hi-Lifes. Recorded in "Authentiphonic Stereo Process," the song first appeared on the *Soundsville!* compilation in either 1962 or 1965 (sources vary) and was reissued in 1967 on *Out of Sight!* The gimmicky *Soundsville!* exploitation was likely the record unearthed by Peter, who dug the song's words—*People uptown, people downtown, listen closely to what I'm putting down*—which sounded a lot like his clarion call for a Bowery and Fifty-fourth Street merger. The Fleshtones would always love the suitably obscure "Soul City," and would record the song again two decades later.

Armed with a tune and a great idea, Jones and the band went to work. No one foresaw that the project would take a year and a half to complete and would eventually fry Jones' nerves. Jones threw himself into the making of *Soul City* with art-student devotion and focus. "It was a tremendous amount of work and it required phenomenal concentration," he admits. "But you're young and you have absolutely nothing to do except focus on a project. At the time, seventeen months was a whole lifetime just to make that film. But it was doable. At the time every single day was lived to the fullest, absolutely to the fullest."

Not blessed with digital manipulation that visual artists would grow accustomed to a couple of decades later, Jones was forced to manually and painstakingly assemble his psychedelic photo-animated film. He had an SVA-approved budget of $650, two hundred of which went to film purchase. He began by building plywood sets, one main stage for Lenny's drums and two different-size stages to compensate for the disparity between Marek and Keith's heights. "I wanted to make sure compositionally that it had all been laid out," Jones explains. He rented a bottom-rung 35mm camera, a few lenses, and a radio mike for Peter. The band assembled in a studio at SVA in November, Lenny's drumhead adorned with Peter's enthusiastic pen-and-ink copy of Dr. Smith from *Lost in Space*. Jones filmed one master shot, the guys feeling somewhat awkward tethered to the plywood stages but crunching through a noisy, garagey performance of the tune. The shoot went off without a hitch.

Sweat

What Jones wanted to accomplish with *Soul City* was twofold: film the band performing live in black and white and—taking his cue from the band name—color in their fleshtones with oil paint; and explore his interest in retina paths, in manipulating the viewer's eyes to follow a certain pattern on the screen and to remain pleasurably lost in that pattern, unwilling to move their gaze. "I laid the band out in such a way that visual cues would go from one to the next to the next to the next so it was in a circular pattern that was almost a spiral," Jones explains. "You'd go from Marek to Lenny to Keith to Peter, and then out of Peter you would go for the big picture again. It had to do with what later on was termed the 'Ham Sandwich Effect,' the concept of forcing people's eyes to be regulated to a degree where they would never reach the edge of the screen when then they might think about food or think about going to get a ham sandwich." More ambitiously, Jones hoped to "visually counterpoint the music of a subculture" with his film.

Jones spent the bulk of the spring and summer of 1978 working on the project, which burgeoned wildly, due mostly to his ambition and to the meticulous, labor-intensive nature of the photo-animation process itself. The work took its toll, and Jones quickly realized that the ambitious short was going to become his thesis project, the cumulative evidence of his talent and vision at SVA. Jones was certainly vibing on the fun and energy of the Fleshtones' ethos in the process: as a scholarship student, he had manufactured keys to the buildings at SVA and was familiar with the security guards, so he would work on the film all day, and then around six o'clock or so go get something to eat, meet up with the Fleshtones, go to the rehearsal space at Billy Piano's, check out the gear, pull it up to Max's, do a whole show with them, and then help them lock the equipment down, leave, go back to SVA, open the doors, check with the guard who was cool with it, and then work again until the morning. Oftentimes, Jones would work straight through the day, and then go and see the Fleshtones again that night. The band played Max's three times in August alone, so this became Jones' frolicking, feverish work routine.

Not that the routine wasn't without hair-pulling pitfalls. Jones would spend hours in front of projectors at SVA with his eyelids literally taped open, studying sophisticated, repeating filmed patterns as tests to gauge optical illusions and his fluctuating eye chemicals and retina paths. His typical diet during the *Soul City* project: cottage cheese, Entemann's chocolate-covered donuts, and No Doz pills crushed and dropped into strong coffee. A sympathetic teacher allowed Jones the use of his studio on East Thirty-fifth Street, where he would lug his equipment, chemicals, and poorly balanced meals on weekends and work from Friday night at 8:30 until Sunday morning morning at five. The *Soul City* project became an exactingly technical journey for Jones, an eye- and mind-opening immersion into visual design and execution possibilities. The end result was a widely influential short film, its international, well-earned reputation arguably more consequential now than at the film's debut.

With assistance from the studio of legendary documentary filmmaker D.A. Pennebaker, Jones was able to strike a 16mm print from the 35mm master. The final hurdle was the actual hand-painting of the individual cutouts from the film. "It was tricky," Jones says. "We'd look at the work print and choose the frames that we were gonna print, because each print was like eighty cents, which was an involvement back then. So I wanted to make sure that I was printing all the different photos I needed and *only* the ones I needed." This process was long and arduous, as Jones eventually made over seventeen hundred photo cutouts and assigned specific colors to correlating sounds produced by the band. A year and a half after filming the Fleshtones, *Soul City*—all two minutes and one hundred feet of it— was completed. The end result was a jagged and energetic strobe performance, with the rhythmic editing and cutouts creating a hallucinatory, double-vision effect that was both druggy and speedy.

Jones screened a rough cut of the film at a Fleshtones/Suicide weekend show at Max's on August 25, and premiered the finished film at the Museum of Holography on Mercer Street on February 22, 1979. Soon, the film was screening in New York art galleries, universities, media centers, and rock & roll nightclubs across the country. Writing at the time in *Film News Magazine*, Lisa Baumgardner, the innovative creator of the influential late-seventies *Bikini Girl* fanzine, wrote that *Soul City* "takes bold steps in the original portrayal of fleeting, intense psychedelic imagery through groundbreaking new animation techniques. . . . It is possible not only to *hear* music, but to *see* it as well, translated into rhythmically fluctuating hues that trick the eye into haunting hallucinations, in turn creating new colors and triggering an intense emotional response."

Within a year, Jones was screening *Soul City* at the Superfilmshow! series at the Metropolitan Museum of Art, and his career blossomed soon after. He was for many years a member of Depthography, a trio of artists in New York City creating four-dimensional imagery and animation, and in 1997 *Soul City* was acquired by the Eastman Museum of Imagery in Rochester, New York, for its permanent collection; the film is now featured on Jones' Snakemonkey Internet site. Jones never strayed far from his old friends from Queens. He was in touch with Peter on and off throughout the 1980s, and reunited with the Fleshtones in 1993 to film a video at Chichen Itza in the Yucatan Peninsula and on the roof of Keith's Brooklyn apartment building for the title track of *Beautiful Light*. In 2003 Jones photographed the cover and interior for *Do You Swing?*

Meanwhile, 1978 was pulsing. This felt like it might be an exciting— dare the Fleshtones say, a *breakthrough?*—year. Chris Stamey of the dB's produced a crude demo tape of the band down at Billy Piano's, the band received good press in New York, as well as notices in *Melody Maker* in London and the *Feelings* fanzine in Paris, and they gigged and gigged and gigged and worked up sweaty delirium at shows, visiting New Haven, Boston, Philadelphia, and Washington, D.C., for the first time.

And they would soon sign a coveted recording contract. Before long they would wonder if they had signed in invisible ink.

8.
Red Star on St. Mark's

Grinning if frustrated, the Fleshtones were wary of booking too heavily at CBGB's or Max's, and thus spreading themselves thin across an exploding local scene. But there were few other club options at the time. Loft parties were fun, and they played a couple of shows at My Father's Place in Roslyn Village out on Long Island, but the band's reputation was increasing in Manhattan and they had their sights set bigger. The band was playing fast and fun dance music, R&B-flavored rock & roll that depended to a large degree on audience feedback, on getting patrons up and moving and sweating and singing. "What we wanted to do was *connect*," Peter says. "We thought that if we didn't connect, then it didn't make a difference to us how well we played or didn't play, to us it's a bad show. We love that feeling that we're connected with the audience. If we're not, I go off the stage, and I know Keith does, just feeling horrible, like, *Man, I didn't do it. I didn't connect.*"

Late in 1977, Miriam Linna hauled Peter and his friend Gary Balaban down to Philadelphia to see the Flamin' Groovies on the heels of their *Shake Some Action* album, and though Peter didn't connect with the pop band ("Boy, did they like to tune up") he dug getting out of the city and spying on scenes in other towns. One event that inspired him to boost his own band's onstage power and to encourage crowds to translate that energy level was a weekend visit up to Boston early in 1978.

"Miriam Linna thought it would enlighten me," Peter remembers. "This was my first trip to the city that I have come to believe is simply the Hidden Rock & Roll Capital of the World." Neither Peter nor Miriam drove at this point, so they took a train out of Grand Central. The slow, gray trip took forever, but left ample time for refreshments and tapes of sixties garage music like the Sonics, whose grungy, absurdly intense "Pyscho" the Fleshtones were now playing onstage. "Eventually we were at Kenmore Square," Peter remembers, "descending into the basement club called the Rat where a full-scale battle of the bands between the Real Kids and their arch-rivals DMZ was under way. I had never seen anything like it. Not only were the bands battling, but kids were dancing all over the place in between waves of knockdown fistfights that erupted and subsided for no reason. The bands, aware that the battle was being broadcast over WBCN, were out for blood. This was the rock & roll Valhalla I dreamt of as a kid, and had been denied by the hippie-ing out of pop culture in the late sixties."

The trip marked the first meeting between Peter and Farfisa maniac Jeff "Monoman" Conolly (so nicknamed for his obsession with monaural recordings) whose likeminded band Lyres would, despite some infamous implosions, prove perennial, good-natured competition for the Fleshtones throughout the 1980s. At this point, Conolly was still helming DMZ, who debuted two months before the Fleshtones and were now on the cusp of signing to Sire Records (where they would suffer a career-careening production job at the concrete hands of Flo and Eddie). "DMZ blasted out a crazed mixture of sixties punk, psychedelia, and manic metal *à la* the MC5, the likes of which I had given up all hope of hearing," Peter recalls. "The Real Kids, led by the misnamed John Felice, were the exact opposite in all things except intensity."

The next day, Peter and Miriam visited Conolly on the edge of Beacon Hill. "His digs overlooked the old prison yard and Buzzy's Famous Roast Beef—I would often rue the fate of those luckless prisoners, so close they could smell that boneless rib sandwich I was devouring! With religious zeal, Jeff whipped out dozens of obscure discs from his collection of zillions of records. I was obviously in need of an education, but despite my overload I meekly managed to play him our basement demo. I was flattered when he commented favorably on the rather bizarre double-tracked drums on one of the songs." Peter came back to New York buzzing and renewed.

Meanwhile, the Fleshtones were surprised to be encountering their first bit of public-relations trouble. Georgia Christgau had written a lengthy piece on the financial realities of the lower Manhattan music scene that ran in the October 10, 1977, issue of the *Village Voice*. "Don't Be Denied: The Economics of a New York Rock Band" portrayed the rising scene and its attendant commercial lures and pitfalls, pitting successful bands like the Ramones and Talking Heads against comers like Sick Fu*ks, the Fast, and the Fleshtones. Though wide-ranging in scope, the article featured three prominent photographs of the Fleshtones playing in and standing outside of The House in Whitestone. They were the only band to be photographed for the piece, publicity that any group would crave; but the photo would come to harm the guys by its association with the high-visibility article.

The piece described the Fleshtones freshly booted from The House, dramatized as a typical struggling band balancing day jobs ("a taxi driver, a printer, a messenger, and a student living with his parents") with the paltry fiscal rewards of playing live rock & roll. Some innocent reporting in the fourth paragraph got the boys in a bit of hot water: "The Fleshtones' take at their only [*sic*] CBGB's gig was 40 per cent of the door, which is more than fair for an opening act. Except that most of the top-billed groups give starters a flat $100. Then a club can't get away with paying a band $10 apiece or telling them that $75 was deducted from the door to pay the soundman—both of which happened to the Fleshtones that night."

Although the article called into question the door politics of clubs in general and of Max's in particular, the CBGB's "deduction" reference—Joey Ramone laughingly referred to it as the "Hilly tax" later in the article—riled the club's management, especially the soundman, who duly connected the comments with the band in the photographs. Although he wasn't directly quoted in the piece, Marek was apparently the one who had talked to Christgau about Kristal's door management, and he remembers the fallout. "We got some really hostile vibes from Charlie, the engineer at CB's. He was the guy you called to do the bookings, but I remember being there one night and saying something like, 'Oh, why aren't we getting any bookings?' I got the impression that his feeling was, *Well, you guys shouldn't go shooting your mouths off*. We heard through the grapevine that Kristal got really pissed off about the mention of the 'Hilly tax.' Then it seemed like the gigs fell off."

"The 'Hilly tax' was a fee," Peter says. "They should've been more upfront about it. They could've just said, 'Well, we have a P.A. fee.' We had no qualm about money, but we mentioned it and we weren't supposed to, I guess. That went down really bad with Charlie, and I remember him throwing a reel-to-reel tape recorder down the stairs at us at the club. He must've really been enraged, because equipment costs money." The band played the club two weeks after the article ran, and then scored a major weekend there on February 2 through 4 in 1978, opening up for Suicide with the Contortions. But it took until May 5 for another booking at CBGB's, and after that they didn't get a booking until October 3, a long hibernation period for a hungry young band with a reputation playing in New York City.

Starting in June of that year the guys began playing more regularly at Max's, wide-eyed and sipping tall Blondie and Cherry Vanilla milkshake cocktails at the bar as the darlings of Wayne County, who had dug the band's version of "Anarchy in the U.K." "Peter Crowley and Wayne took us under their wing," says Keith. "I had never hung out with these guys, and they were kind of scaring me, here I was twenty-two years old. Wayne County's a drag queen and here I am a kid from Queens! They were *Flame on!* But they liked us, they thought we were great, and they were always really nice to us. I have to admit I was pretty young and this was *Woah, way out, man!*"

"It might have been the fact that we were playing Max's," Marek admits of the dry spell at CBGB's. "There was the factionalism there. I understand it—you hurt your draw if you're playing every week." Hilly Kristal remembers competition between his club and Max's being less fractious than current mythology suggests. "Peter Crowley was very astute at what he booked at Max's," Kristal says. "Bands needed more than one place to play, so maybe they, just by luck of the draw, played here more or there more. You eventually get a certain crowd that's used to going to one place more, and the bands feel more comfortable in one place than the next. It was good for me that Tommy Dean reopened Max's, and it was good for them that I was here, because you get a stronger scene when you have at least two places." And, Kristal adds, "We were sixteen blocks away, so you could actually walk or take a cab from one place to the other."

As far as the Fleshtones' indiscreet comments in the *Voice* piece, Kristal claims no memory of the controversy. "No. If they did object to the fact that I had very low deductions on the P.A., if they didn't like that, that was their problem. I didn't charge anybody anything. We had a man doing the P.A."

Peter formulated another theory many years later. "It might have been that Charlie was skimming this money, not Hilly. Maybe. Who knows? These are just alleged things, like Galileo, a theory, an alleged hypothesis. But after that, we couldn't get booked at CBGB's."

Unofficially banned from the Bowery, the guys began thinking from the ground up, looking around downtown for low-rent, upstart venues that they could co-opt and move into and make their own. They were careful not to overplay Max's, and even as special as that joint was it was starting to become a problematic place. "The audience at Max's is sort of boring," Peter said at the time. Keith added: "It sucks. They can't dance."

One legendary show during this entrepreneurial period took place at the Millennium Theater building at 66 East Fourth Street, ground zero of the early-twentieth-century Yiddish stage tradition. In 1978 the building was the sight of the experimental La Mama Annex Theater that had opened four years prior and that would soon inhabit neighboring buildings, establishing itself as the vanguard of Off-Broadway productions. The Millennium was up the block from the old Club 82, which had been a big drag/transvestite scene during the New York Dolls period. On April 15, between performances of Rimbaud and *Trojan Women*, the Fleshtones rented out the cavernous hall with two other local bands, Nervous Rex and the Mumps, posted fliers around town, bought small ads in the *Voice* and *Soho Weekly News*, and billed it a "New Wave Party." Three bands for three bucks, not a bad value. More than five hundred people showed up, and the show had to be stopped by authorities for fear that the pogoing dancers would wreak havoc.

"The Millennium was an old dance hall with a floating floor," Marek remembers. "This may be apocryphal, but they had laid a sub-flooring and then they had put rubber tires and stuff under the floor so that the floor would bounce. And you could dance all night and your legs wouldn't get tired. Now that was the myth. Whether it was true or not, I don't know. But I do remember the floor moving as much as six inches to a foot down the center with the people pogoing or dancing! We thought, *We're gonna tear the place apart!* It was a great, great show." Keith remembers the blistering Millennium show similarly. "That was a place we went to a few times, actually, and did some *great* shows. It was packed and people were dancing—way before Hurrah and Danceteria existed, which came in in the early eighties as the best New Wave clubs. The idea was that we could have this little space and bring our own P.A. and people could dance to the band! And that was not happening."

The Fleshtones were burning to keep playing, and through a bit of luck and native curiosity found themselves at the start of a wildly interesting and influential performing arts scene on St. Mark's Place, specifically at 57 St. Mark's, address of the narrow and nondescript

Holy Cross Polish National Church. "Club 57 was born back when there were fewer than a hundred pointy-toed hipsters skulking around the East Village streets, and a boy could get the shit kicked out of him for dyeing his hair blue," artist Ann Magnuson wrote in a reminiscence for *ArtForum*. "Girls fared a little better. We could parade about in our rockabilly petticoats, spandex pants, and thrift-store stiletto heels and get away with just a few taunts ('Hey, Sid Vicious' sister!') from a carload of Jersey assholes. That was in the late-70s, when the Bee Gees ruled the airwaves, Brooke Shields peered down from every billboard in town, and the nefarious isle of Manhattan still had a wild side to walk on."

Stanley Stryhaski, the straw-hat, old-style co-owner of Irving Plaza, was renting out the Polish church basement and was looking for some nightly alternative entertainment for the space when it wasn't being used for a Polish Students League. The low-ceilinged basement was dubbed "Club 57" by a few enthusiastic Irving Plaza artist-regulars and would soon become a nightly epicenter for a lively, provocative underground music and film performance arts scene, spawning Magnuson, Keith Haring, Wendy Wild, John Sex, Fab Five Freddy, Steve Buscemi, the all-girl percussion band Pulsallama, and many other offbeat actors, painters, filmmakers, and musicians who came to typify the late-seventies/early-eighties East Village art scene. Club 57 was soon waggishly dubbed "Little Studio 54" for its scene and scenesters.

Magnuson managed the space, and with her friends started the Monster Movie Club on Tuesday nights. Soon, Haring was curating erotic Day-Glo art shows, and theme nights such as Putt-Putt Reggae Night and Model Airplane Night allowed local hipsters to indulge in envelope-pushing conceptual art laced with irony. Word about the scene spread via dive-bar raves and posted handbills. Club 57 celebrated, and was duly celebrated for, its eclecticism. "The punk Do-It-Yourself aesthetic extended to every medium," Magnuson wrote. "Artists performed, performers made art, musicians made movies, fashion designers started bands, everyone picked up a movie camera."

The Fleshtones dug the basement because of its consecration of the underground pop-art aesthetic, its jukebox filled with sixties garage-band singles, and its proximity to their rehearsal space (and to Marek's apartment, so shabby and unsafe that he couldn't leave his bass behind). Plus, Stryhaski started renting the basement out for rock & roll shows, inviting covers bands at first but then original bands, a boon for groups looking for venues other than the Big Two, CBGB's and Max's. Some realities were dawning

on the guys. "We knew that we weren't going to get regular weekends at Max's, that they were really hard to get," says Peter. "And
we wanted our own atmosphere."

In keeping with the image of its patrons and performers, the
decor in Club 57 was ironic/tacky. Just past the front door sat an
overstuffed chair and a potted plant, oddly domestic *accoutrements*
for a nightclub, and yet the right touch for this homespun place. The
walls were painted hot pink and plastered with kitschy posters of
Donny and Marie (Donny's teeth soon blackened in with ink), teen
heartthrob John Travolta, a white plastic jumpsuited Elvis, and a
large map of the United States: a wry, sweat-curled gallery of the sort
of cultural icons deconstructed nightly in the club. An acoustic guitar hung on one wall, and red, blue, green, and yellow Japanese
lanterns glowed from the low ceiling.

Billy Miller, who by this point was playing in the Zantees, a band
that several times shared the bill with the Fleshtones at the basement
space, remembers the homey ambiance of Club 57 fondly. "On the
first night we played, Stanley ran out of beer, and he kept running to
the deli and buying six-packs and selling them for what he paid for
them," he recalls. "And then at the end of the night, he flicks the light
on, and he's like, 'Okay kids, here you go!' He's made little sandwiches for everybody. That was what was so great about the 57 when
it first started." April was a high-energy month for the Fleshtones.
They played Club 57 a week before the Millennium Theater show,
and then again two weeks after, and they really rocked the joint, the
pumping, sweaty mood harkening back to the reckless fun and abandon of Whitestone. The space held a maximum capacity of about a
hundred and fifty, and when the Fleshtones played the place was full.
"We created part of the atmosphere, instead of the club imposing its
own ambiance on the gig," says Peter, who loved the loose, amoeba-
like relationship at Club 57 between band and crowd.

Local critics started taking note as word spread. David Koepp
captured the essential spirit of a Fleshtones show at Club 57, cap-
sulizing the young band's sweaty animation and brio-over-virtuosity.
Reviewing an April 7 Fleshtones/Zantees gig for *New York Rocker*,
Koepp wrote, "Kids were boppin', jumpin', twistin' and shoutin' to
this wonderful rock & roll. It was a strange and beautiful night; you
could almost feel your sweat dropping to the beat. . . . Cousin, life
hangs out at the 57 Club. The bars stools are worn and comfy, and
the young man tending bar seems to have a smile and a good word
for all his customers. Every so often he'll even reach over and give
someone a big hug. When was the last time you were hugged by any-

one at Max's or CBGB's, let alone a bartender?" Koepp's small item was telling, in that it blended sincere raving with healthy skepticism, foreshadowing the band's career-long tendency to be pigeonholed by critics as fun but irrelevant. "Both the Zantees and the Fleshtones are gaining popularity here in the city," Koepp wrote. "But I wonder how they'd fare elsewhere? I get the nagging feeling that both groups are rock & roll antiques. . . . Both bands will have to use their initial base to reach another level of originality, but their hearts are in the right place. I love their spirit, their honesty and lack of pretense. The New York circuit is short on the former and overloaded with the latter."

Writing several years later, *New York Rocker* scribe (and future Rock & Roll Hall of Fame researcher/historian) Andy Schwartz remembered his own introduction to the Fleshtones at Club 57. "I found myself immersed in a tightly-packed crowd of dancing bodies and grinning faces," he wrote. "The front row of the throng stood only inches from the four piece band, which was set up right on the floor of the club and threatening to detonate the cheap p.a. with their sound. The tall, hyperactive lead singer shouted unintelligible lyrics and honked his harmonica into the microphone while executing a highly personalized combination of The Penguin, The Monkey, and The Camel Walk. The guitarist, his bangs falling into his blue eyes, hammered out power chords and twangy leads as he dashed back and forth across the 'stage' or charged into the audience. The bassist and drummer pumped away madly in a desperate effort to keep up with their companions pace.

"*WHO ARE THESE GUYS, ANYWAY?* I shouted in the ear of one sweaty celebrant. *MAN, DON'T YOU KNOW?* he shouted back. *THEY'RE THE FLESHTONES!*"

Amplified epiphanies aside, bands rocking the 57 floor didn't last all that long. By the end of the year, hipster poetry readings, art openings, and Magnuson's Tuesday night film screenings were starting to muscle out the bands. It was inevitable, as neighbors along the block had begun complaining about noise. "There *were* problems," Miller remembers. "Club 57 was right in the middle of the block, and if you could fill the place with people just watching movies, then you don't have problems with the people in the neighborhood." So, the Fleshtones were again on the prowl for a venue that could compete with Max's. Stryhaski would soon migrate Club 57 eight blocks north and, booking rock & roll bands, begin "Club 57 at Irving Plaza." The Fleshtones dragged their amps, guitars, and box of harmonicas and migrated along, becoming the first band to play in that historic rock & roll venue.

He had a "Detroit Haircut": half an inch on top straight up with butch wax, long sideburns, and "fenders" (long on the sides, squared in the back). He had the fifties *noir* look down pat—a juvie who'd stepped out of a Weegee photograph, and he spoke in the affectedly clipped, hardboiled street voice that was made infamous in the photo captions. As usual, Gordon Spaeth's reputation preceded him. Have sax, will travel.

Gordon began making walk-on appearances with the Fleshtones in the summer of 1978, a year and a half after being released from jail. "He was already a *dynamite* harmonica player," Keith says. "And he taught himself how to play saxophone in jail." Besides fighting off people who wanted to fuck him, this self-improvement regimen was one of the good things that Gordon did in Attica. He had saved up a bit of money after his release by moving into the guest room in his parents' house and working various menial, dispiriting jobs around Queens. "I was progressing pretty good on the saxophone when one day a strong gust of wind blew the door to my room shut with a loud bang," he remembers. "My father exploded, *Stop slamming doors, godamnit!* He handed me fifty dollars and threw me out onto the streets. I checked into the local YMCA and with great reluctance sold my tenor sax to survive. A short while later I scrapped together enough money to buy a cheap student model."

Gordon made his Fleshtones debut at Max's Kansas City. The guys, always bright about stage presence and keen, as the Beatles had learned in ruthless Hamburg, to *mach shau*, orchestrated his appearance with precision and mock-heroic grandeur. Gordon arrived dressed head to toe in black, with pointed suede shoes and the hairstyle that no one had seen in years. Gordon only knew a handful of songs, but Peter didn't care; he knew that "Mr. Excitement" was the missing ingredient. The Fleshtones started a drums-and-bass setup riff to "Crossfire" by Johnny and the Hurricanes. Resplendent in his suit and sharp shoes, Gordon sat patiently in the audience at a table, and at a prearranged moment stood up and came slowly through the audience with his saxophone in hand, looking like a psycho, staring straight ahead at the floor, inching his way up on stage, and then launched into "Crossfire" and started blowing hard sax. "Everyone was like, *Who is that guy?? Where did ya dig him up??*" Keith remembers. "No one in New York had really met him yet. So then Gordon started to play with us periodically. His stage presence was phenomenal."

Gordon and his older brother, Brian, would eventually tour and record with the Fleshtones as the Action Combo. In these early days, however, Gordon was strictly a part-timer, and he wouldn't really become an official Fleshtone for another four years. And even then, his alien stigma would haunt him. Reckless, wild, unpredictable Gordon was blowing his lungs out on "Crossfire" onstage every few weeks, channeling the old fire from the distant Paul's Stadium Bar, paying homage to the very song that saved his life that day in front of the Creedmore Mental Institution, a theme song and threnody to the kind of place he would visit all too frequently in coming years as his life unraveled.

Some days, Gordon would come home to his East Village apartment and taped to his door would be a message scrawled in Peter's handwriting: "Gordon, we're playing the 9:30 Club in Washington, D.C., tomorrow night. If you want to go, meet us at the rehearsal space at noon." For many years, this itinerant lifestyle would be the thin thread from which Gordon Spaeth dangled.

Peter and Keith couldn't believe their ears. Some record producer—his specific details have faded from memory over the years; he was probably an industry type with a bad polyester suit, a comb-over, *Variety* and *Billboard* in hand—had approached the band after a show at Max's and pitched them an idea. A surefire, can't-miss idea.

The Fleshtones could become the Punk Vegetables!

In 1978, Punk and New Wave were already on the cusp of commodification by the national media as a marketable niche, much as disco was being hustled to middle America via the roller discos and *Saturday Night Fever* dance contests that sprouted up seemingly overnight from Boise, Idaho, to Bangor, Maine. The punk aesthetic of torn shirts and safety pins, born in England but sanitized in America, was aided by the Ramones' cartoon pictures inside *Rocket to Russia*, and the neon pink triangles and skinny ties of New Wave metamorphosed from genuine disaffected anti-fashion gestures below Fourteenth Street. Co-opting a threat into something acceptable is an old, old tale, of course, as common to the human condition as any hunger. The Monkees were born of America's obsession with the commercial emporium that was Beatlemania, just as eventually the lovable "Disco Duck" waddled out squeaky-clean from the shady taboos of underground gay disco nightlife.

Ever since late 1975, when the guys started hearing "Little Johnny Jewel" by Television on the CBGB's jukebox, a 45 pressed into less than a thousand copies by Terry Ork, they craved a record of their own. The Fleshtones, hungry for commercial interest, stood in the dressing room at Max's, eyeing the industry man suspiciously as he offered to divert their sincerity into commodity.

"Uh . . . the Punk Vegetables . . . ?"

Yeah, yeah, you'll wear these costumes. Like Peter, you'll be "Peter Pepper"—I've got the rubber head and the costume all worked out—Uh, Keith, right? You'll be "Keith Corn," Lenny you can be "Lenny Linguini," and, uh, Marek, you'll be something like . . . "Marek the Asparagus Head," I dunno, you're tall.

"Uh huh . . ."

I wanna do a TV show, and I wanna start the show by opening up the act—the Punk Vegetables—you guys!—at CBGB's and Max's and it'll be—

"What are you, fuckin' nuts?" Keith asked.

—for like, kids . . .

Peter groaned and ran his hand through his bangs, thought despairingly of old *Monkees* episodes where the band goes on an audition and groups like the Jolly Green Giants are loitering. . . .

C'mon, whatdya think? Punk Vegetables! It'll kill! We can do a movie and then a record—I've got some song ideas, I know some writers—and then a tour and—well, I'll work up a contract. You guys've got the energy, the talent!

Peter laughed and shook his head. Nope. The Fleshtones had been pigeonholed for two years, but they were going to stick to what they were doing. They weren't about to run out and do "Punk Vegetables." Not that the idea of a record contract—any record contract—wasn't alluring to the guys. Miriam Linna remembers the half-hearted consideration the band gave to the Vegetables concept. "They were offered big bucks," she laughs. "They were really over a barrel: *vegetables and money, or Fleshtones and poverty?!*"

Fortunately for the band, a seasoned industry man with integrity, clout, and ambition was soon to check them out. And Marty Thau truly dug what he saw. He wasn't posing as a Record Business Guy. His legacy emboldening him, contract in hand, he could bring the Fleshtones to America.

He's an oversized man with a shrewd ear, and he lives comfortably. His office in his large home is lined with gold records, glittering testament to his four successful decades in the record business. Chairman Thau moves deliberately and acts decisively, and his brief tenure with the Fleshtones was a remarkable failure not because of any glitch in Thau's intuition or strategy, but because of desperately coveted funds that dried up as quickly as did the band's trust in him. His interest and encouragement of the Fleshtones at an early, formative moment in their career will never be forgotten by Peter and Keith. Indeed, they have recognized in the decades since the relationship flamed out just how loyal and heartening Thau's regard for them was. Thau was Thau, but they were young.

Before Thau discovered the New York Dolls in 1972, after catching their raw, exciting performance at the Mercer Arts Center, he had already carved a thoroughly impressive career in the record industry by trusting his hunches. His first job was a yearlong stint at *Billboard* magazine as an advertising trainee, where he quietly began taking note of the mercurial and lucrative trends in 1960s popular music. His counterpart at *Cashbox* magazine was Neil Bogart. Bogart eventually moved to MGM as a promotion man and was recruited by Al Rosenthal, head of the recently reactivated Cameo/Parkway label operating out of a small office in New York at 1650 Broadway, a prototypical music building housing publishers, writers, and record companies, along with 1619 Broadway a link in the West Fifties "Record Row." In 1966, Rosenthal recruited Thau and Cecil Holmes to do promotion for Cameo/Parkway. The trio shared a three-room office, and from that midtown perch placed a phenomenal twenty-eight records on the chart in their first year, including Terry Knight and the Pack, the Five Stair Steps, Bob Seger, the Rationals, and their super hit—and the feat that would forever endear Thau to Peter and Keith—"96 Tears" by ? and the Mysterians.

A year later, the owners of successful Kama Sutra Records, a label distributed by MGM, began to feel that they weren't getting the deal at MGM that they deserved, so they indulged a loophole which enabled them to start a new label that they called Buddah Records. There, Art Kass recruited Bogart and Thau from Cameo. At Buddah, where Thau was installed as Vice President of Promotion, the big hits came fast and would put their indelible mark on American popular consciousness: from 1967 until 1970, tunes like "Green Tambourine," "Oh, Happy Day," "Yummy, Yummy, Yummy," "Simon Says," "1, 2, 3 Red Light," "Indian Giver," and "Chewy, Chewy" invaded teen transistor radios and put Bubblegum on the map. Buddah grossed an astonishing thirty million dollars in one year alone. "Those records sold millions but the record industry hated them because they were teenybopper hits," Thau wrote in a reminiscence. "We didn't care because those teenybopper hits gave us houses, cars, bank accounts, and careers."

In early 1970, Thau left Buddah and moved on to Inherit Productions, where as a partner he was instrumental in selling Van Morison's *Astral Weeks* and *Moondance*, John Cale's *Vintage Violence*, and an assortment of other work from artists including Cass Eliot and Mike Bloomfield. But the climate of popular music was transforming. "With the emergence of the counterculture and the Woodstock Nation, the record biz changed," Thau reflected. "The Vietnam War, protest marches on Washington, the partisan politics of Richard Nixon, women's liberation, gay rights, racial strife, and civil unrest were just some of the issues of the day. A cultural revolution was underway and rock & roll was challenging the very essence of America's beliefs and principles. Youth-in-dissent, to the lies and deceitful ways of government, was the prevailing mood. The birth of FM radio and anti-establishment 'message music' was taking hold until Nixon diffused the revolution by threatening nonrenewal of their licenses. The record industry capitulated and followed suit. By the early seventies all you heard were singer/songwriters and soft, unthreatening sounds."

In 1972, Maurice Levy of Roulette Records offered to financially back Thau's new singles-only label, and among the first bands Thau envisioned for the label was the New York Dolls, whose over-the-top-attitude performances leapt outrageously from the softened musical climate. (Thau ultimately dropped the label idea.) Thau's vexed tenure with the Dolls has been well documented. Though the group never achieved the success that Thau envisioned, they became an infamous influence on and precursor to the New York Punk scene. Thau is blunt in describing his decampment from the crumbling band. "I chose to discontinue managing them at the end of 1974 because I didn't like their drug habits and drinking habits," Thau says. "That's the bottom line."

Thau's experience with the dissolute, disappointing Dolls didn't dampen his ambition to form a record label of his own, for which he could select, nurture, and market young bands that he felt possessed rock & roll spirit and commercial appeal. In 1977, he founded Red Star Records. The first bands he signed were Suicide and the Real Kids, who stood at opposite ends of the sonic spectrum but who in the Chairman's estimation shared something intangible.

The Fleshtones' fortunes changed dramatically in the warm, early summer of 1978, but there remains some speculation as to how exactly Thau connected with the band. "Alan Vega mentioned the Fleshtones to me," Thau remembers. "I always respected Alan's judgment on artistic entities and thought he had very good taste. He told me about the Fleshtones, and I went down to see them at Max's for the first time. And they reminded me of sort a New York version of the young Yardbirds. The Yardbirds and all those English acts of that English revolution was something that I really was into and respected and dug. I always thought the Fleshtones would be a great act to sign."

Keith remembers those heady first days associating with the legendary music man. "For me to make a record at that point in time was just incredible," he says. "To be in the studio and record this music I do? It was beyond my wildest dreams. So Vega comes to see the Fleshtones and sees that we are a true rock & roll band, and he flips. It was really because of Alan that our recording career started. Marty decides that he wants to rent a rehearsal space and audition the band. *You mean we're gonna play in a rehearsal studio in front of one guy and Alan Vega?* We do, and of course it's really uptight because we're a live band. But then Alan suggested to Marty that he check us out live."

Meanwhile, Miriam Linna was spending her days and nights drumming in the Zantees, working at the Strand Bookstore on Broadway buying up vintage smut paperbacks, writing pieces for *New York Rocker*, and generally supporting the rock & roll scene. Through her friends in the Real Kids she became Thau's secretary and press agent at Red Star, housed at the label's headquarters on West Fifty-seventh Street near Carnegie Hall. Linna claims now that Thau's memory of meeting the Fleshtones isn't entirely accurate. "I saw the Fleshtones before Alan Vega said *anything* to Marty. I had seen them, I clearly remember that. But—and I was actually pretty disappointed about this fact—Marty told me to write in a press release that Alan had discovered the Fleshtones, because I was a nobody, but Alan was a Red Star guy. So that's why I wrote that Vega had come to us, and I think that's how history has been written."

The faithful details may have vanished for good—Thau does not recall asking Linna to write that in the release—but what's certain is that when Thau saw the Fleshtones perform he was excited, and when the Fleshtones met Thau backstage they were impressed. (And they were relieved that he wasn't asking them to don vegetable costumes.) "The Fleshtones were a bunch of fun-loving, beer-guzzling working-class kids in the true tradition of working class kids going into rock & roll," Thau marvels. "I don't think they identified to whatever the politics of punk was in the American style or the English style, so as a result they were sort like outcasts. They didn't fit into any kind of niche except in the true classic rock & roll niche." He was certain that in the Fleshtones he had discovered magic: another find for his stable of legitimate, exhilarating rock & roll. "For some vague reason everyone warned us against involvement with Marty," says Peter. ("That sounds like the downtown rumor mill in overtime," comments Thau now. "It comes with the territory.") "But we had been knocking around the downtown scene for over a year and were dying to make a record. Thau certainly could introduce you to everybody, from Giorgio Gomelski to John Sinclair." Plus, Thau "had demoed Blondie, the Ramones, and other groups early on."

For the four kids from Queens, record contracts were mythical parchments that materialized in midtown skyscrapers, rock star biographies, or in their own speed-addled dreams. Feeling in over his head, Keith called a friend he knew from Day Old Bread, a band that had played with the Fleshtones at CBGB's several times, who knew a lawyer; he offered to look over the contract that Thau offered. Thau had extended the Fleshtones a $5,000 advance on the contract, an outrageous sum of money to the guys who instantly began dreaming of ditching their day jobs. "We go meet this guy who's got hair down to his ass, some kind of hippie who became our lawyer because we didn't know anybody else affordable," Keith remembers. "He proclaimed that the contract was no good, but we signed it anyway. At that point we had no idea about publishing, advances, terms of agreement, or royalty computation. We had no idea about anything. We wanted that advance, I can tell you. But we also signed away our publishing rights, which our lawyer advised us against. We wanted to make a record!" In actuality, as Thau points out, the Fleshtones signed away only fifty percent of their publishing rights, which Thau feels was not unusual or unfair.

Thau was focused and prepared, and things moved dizzyingly fast. The contracts were executed in June. Suicide was going to Europe to tour with Elvis Costello and the Attractions and then with the Clash on the Continent, and Thau was leaving with them. In Europe, he called back to New York to one of his partners and asked if the Fleshtones had signed and if all the fine points had gotten resolved, and to his relief they had been. Thau had produced Suicide's album in Ultima Studios in Blauvelt, New York, and he liked the facility and was on good terms with engineers Larry Alexander and Mitchell Ames. Thau set up an August recording session for the debut Fleshtones album.

Two years ago we found instruments in our basement. Now the country's gonna find us. The tops of the guys' heads were coming off at envisioning the chance to finally wax their sounds, to actually create a record that would come out with their own pale mugs on the front cover.

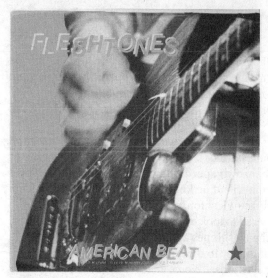

9.
Time and Tide Wait for No Man

Interviewer: Why do you suppose the Zantees and the Real Kids are lumped together with the Fleshtones?
Peter Zaremba: We're all hated equally.

Peter and Keith had to summon their collective suburban-*cum*-Manhattan worldview and write an album. Raised on obscure and forgotten one-off 45s and the odd groovy album track, the two friends felt the pinch of having to come up with material, even as they were beginning to write with some frequency. "We don't write songs as fast as we'd like to," Peter lamented. "It's always the words. What're gonna say? It's like a big deal."

For now, the Fleshtones could concentrate on igniting the stage. On June 10, they celebrated the Red Star contract by playing a fast and fun show at Max's with the Erasers. They opened the *Village Voice* that week and saw that they were billed as "Red Star Recording Artists," a career moment to truly savor. On July 1 they played a high-profile Saturday night slot at Max's, opening for Richard Hell and the Voidoids, whose *Blank Generation* had been earmarked by rock critics as Punk's Holy Writ and whose starlike presence guaranteed a packed show. Grinning, drinks in hand, the Fleshtones were in ascension on the local scene, with the press and a growing stable of friendly bands on their side. "At every gig one semi-influential person would hear us and say they liked it," Lenny remembers. "They usually made us feel good enough to go on." One night at Max's around this heady time, Clem Burke of Blondie sent drinks over to Lenny and Miriam, and the fraternal moment has stayed with Lenny to this day. "That was really cool, one drummer sending drinks to the other two drummers," he smiles.

In early August, the band loaded their gear and their nerves into Keith's truck and drove the forty-five minutes north up Highway 9A to Blauvelt. There they met Thau at Ultima, what Lenny would soon dub the "River of Fear Studio." ("His head was awash with lugubrious heavy metal imagery," bemoans Peter.) For a couple of weeks, the guys had to overcome any fears they might have and make a great rock & roll record. "They were reasonably prepared," Thau says. "They were where I thought they would be." High-ceilinged, Ultima had the shape and vibe of an enormous rehearsal space, and Lenny marveled at the soundproof tiles and the giant Hammond organs, in the warm presence of beautiful vintage equipment that he remembered from his childhood. Peter, Keith, and Marek plugged in and swallowed hard.

After two years of hesitant composing, Peter and Keith had a batch of songs, most of which had been stage-tested for several months, a year in some cases. They brought with them to Ultima one cover song, the Strangeloves' "Cara-Lin" from 1965, and three originals: "B.Y.O.B.," a shout-along ode to The House parties; the year-old "Judy," Peter's upbeat, childlike testimonial using Keith's girlfriend's *nom de plume*; and a new song Peter had just written, a propulsive four-in-the-bar anthem celebrating the radio sounds and homeland imagery that he grew up with and that he was calling "American Sound."

The band had to find a way to capture their sweaty, chancy onstage spirit onto magnetic tape, and the move from a cheering, beer-stained dance floor to the friendless, analog domain was a challenge. "We were turned loose to re-create all the great sounds from all our favorite records in our record collections, all on the same song," laughs Peter. He adds that "Marty was great about letting us add whatever junk we wanted to, no matter how superfluous. We added reverb from the amps, the ultimate seventies engineering sin, reverb from the board, and then reverb in the mix. But it still wasn't enough. After a while it was hard to tell what we were listening to."

From the control room Thau would ask, "How's this?" Then he'd turn a small knob. "How's this?"

The guys would shrug their shoulders. *Good? I guess?*

Thau had his own ideas, especially concerning Keith's novice guitar playing. "I tried to get out of Keith a certain guitar presence that was present in the Sex Pistols and the Ramones," Thau says, "sort of bridging them between that classic Yardbirds place and what the punk sound of New York was about." The basic tracks for "Cara-Lin," "B.Y.O.B.," "Judy," and the retitled "American Beat"—already earmarked by Thau as the band's first single—were laid down quickly. Thau and the band were interested in translating their essential energy, and so the pace of the songs was quick, the performances wound-up tight, too tight in some cases. A certain drunken, sing-along recklessness is apparent in these tracks but it's hard to tell whether it issued from nerve or nerves. Bum notes, microphone "pops," brittle energy, and amateur spirit abounds.

During a break in the sessions, Peter told Andy Schwartz in *New York Rocker* that "what we're trying to do in rock & roll now is bring it back to a level simple and infectious enough to dance to. Party music." Above all the guys wanted their studio tracks to be propulsive, to really *move*. "We always made sure that everything was danceable," says Lenny. "No matter how wild I got, I always kept things very danceable. I put this great disco beat on 'Cara-Lin' where I played two separate drum parts on top, one track of playing all over the drums and then one track of the hi-hat disco drumming." The Strangeloves' "Cara-Lin" embodied everything that the Fleshtones loved about rock & roll: an archetype of groove and rhythm. Put the song on anywhere in the world anytime and people will grin and move. The Fleshtones' version was one of the high points of these sessions, Lenny's darting drums dancing with Peter's cheap, ham-fisted organ and Keith's strident guitar creating an energetic rereading, replacing mid-sixties frathouse chants with late-seventies speed and punkish verve, finding as close to a punk/dance hybrid as the Fleshtones would in these early days

But what were they capturing on tape exactly? Peter and Keith brought tunes into the studio as the sessions resumed, including two, "Shadow Line" and "Watch Junior Go," composed literally on the way up to Ultima, "riding with Marty on Palisades Parkway," as Keith remembers. "Shadow Line," a moody, urgent number issuing from the wellspring of Peter's imagination and muscled along by Keith's psychedelic melody, was inspired by the Joseph Conrad story of the same name, a characteristic Conradian exploration of the thin line between adolescence and adulthood, innocence and responsibility. Peter, nearing his mid-twenties, was trespassing that line nightly.

"'Shadow Line' is about people who stayed up all night doing things," says Peter. "I was with a bunch of people and we'd finish playing at four in the morning and go off to the Crisco, and this place is packed with all sorts of people. Fine citizens. I mean, these people are not burning the candle at both ends. These people are on fire. So we'd leave there at nine in the morning and we'd go up to the Cell Block. You sit in there and you're wondering, *What the hell. I should have been asleep hours ago.* Here's this guy with chains wrapped around him, and that's definitely beyond the shadowline." Notable for the quickness with which it was put together, "Shadow Line" was an ambitious song, a plea from outsiders for understanding, and would do much to catapult the band's career in the coming year. The guys felt that the song was seminal and they would rerecord it three times within the next three years.

Also taking shape at Ultima were "Critical List," Keith's first song, to which he gave a weird, whiny, but effective lead vocal aided by Peter's wailing harmonica; "Atom Spies," a high-energy surf instrumental written by Keith and Marek; and "I'll Walk By," a middling Mersey Beat–styled tune from Peter that would see the light of day a quarter-century later. The band nailed two songs particularly well, veering close to the sweaty feel of a Max's or Club 57 gig. "The Way I Feel" was a hilariously fast statement of purpose from Peter, articulating his desires to connect in the best way he knew how: an audience-embracing, call-and-response chorus and nonsense singing. The song is in many respects the most sincere that Peter's ever written, a child-like, passionate sing-along set to a rocking beat, a hopelessly unhip marriage that he would spend the better part of his career defending— and the Fleshtones would be stubbornly, happily playing the song twenty-five years later. Keith's "Comin' in Dead Stick" was a companion tune to "The Way I Feel," equally reckless in nature, breakneck in pace, and frank in attitude.

In local fanzines at the time the band was adamant in stating that the ratio of originals to covers on their debut would be low. "We'll have maybe two covers at the most," declared Keith. They had planned on recording "Cara-Lin" and Kid Thomas' fabulous early-sixties burner "Rockin' This Joint Tonight," an obscure cut that Gordon turned the guys onto and that they raved up onstage, proudly aligning themselves with remote but impassioned black R&B when few New York bands beyond Blondie were embracing musical history across racial lines.

Indeed, Peter, Gordon, and Brian were relating to black R&B as intensely as they were to white sixties rock & roll, and Peter and Marek had begun to celebrate that in the discos. "Keith's background was more like my own; we knew the better-known rock of the time," Marek says. "But Peter, Gordon, and Brian were bringing in the Kid Thomas records, really zeroing in on a spirit that was there in the off-the-wall honkers and shouters that had influenced the white rock & roll that was coming out of Britain. The Shadows of Knight were imitating the Stones imitating Little Walter, but what Peter ended up doing was going *back* to the Little Walter." That wasn't that common in the New Wave scene, Marek notes, and "that was where the Fleshtones came out of." The Fleshtones tore through "Rockin' This Joint Tonight" at Ultima. The band flew and twenty-three-year-old Peter shouted and fiercely blew on his harmonica, an instrument that he was excelling at to a degree that surprised even him. His solos, respectful to Thomas' wailing, were blistering and real, creating a sound that only further distanced the band from what was happening in New York, allowing Peter to escape his geeky white suburban background and lifting into something universal, a clarion call for fun and rock & roll.

The band ended up recording two more cover songs for the album. They discovered "Soul Struttin'," a Bubblegum song by 1910 Fruitgum Co., on a shared album with the Lemon Pipers from 1968. The tune was as funky as the pop-conscious Buddah Records would get, but what was especially enticing was that Marty Thau had cowritten the track (with Tony Orlando, who would eventually marry Thau's cousin). Thau had always liked the song and was pleased when the guys decided to record their rendition in tribute; it took them three versions before they were happy. The band was dividing their time now between Ultima and Blank Tape studio in Manhattan, where Thau brought in Alan Vega, who took lead as the Fleshtones, wire-tight, played a memorable, atmospheric, psychedelic version of Suicide's "Rocket U.S.A." Vega growled and moaned his way through the taut song, and the utterly unique track could fit nowhere else on the album but in closing. "Recording with Vega was a great day, a cool memory," marveled Lenny. "Being that close to Alan was really cool." Peter cherished the experience, also: "Too bad we didn't do a few of his other things as well."

The Fleshtones spent the remainder of their brief time at Blank recording overdubs of vocals, handclaps, and various percussion. Thau had struck some rough mixes, volume presence, balance, and touches of EQ extras in the course of recording. All that was left was the final mixing, but the console knobs would soon be darkened by the long shadow of financial misery.

Meanwhile, gossip columnist Bea Flatte at the *Aquarian* was keeping close watch on one of her favorite bands. One bleary August dawn she ran into Zaremba on his way to Crisco Disco, and he was proud to tell Flatte that the Fleshtones had an album slated for September on Red

Star, with distribution by Bronze/EMI, to follow the release of their first single, "American Beat." "This is exciting news from a band whose sound ranges from young Yardbirds toward militant Roxy Music," Flatte gushed. "Keep a look out for the Fleshtones." The item ends by trumpeting the band's British Isles tour in the fall.

Peter gathered the guys together at Billy Piano's. The band was signed, the record finished. It was time to get no-nonsense about the future of the Fleshtones. Peter had fully assumed the mantle of leader now, painstakingly authoring a manifesto and handbook for the band, a guide on to how to succeed as New York City's greatest garage dance band.

He sat the guys down in the humid basement. *Here.*

Lenny looked down at his copy, nine pages, handwritten, stapled. *Shit, this is serious.* "Peter was worried about the image of the band," Lenny remembers. "It was something that I never worried about and I think that's what had them worried, that I didn't fit the image anymore. I *did* fit the image at the time. I did go with the short hair, and I was dressing as cool as I could! But I guess the Angel and the KISS records were really worrying them."

Lenny studied the handbook. The title read "How to make it big, sound great, interesting and artistic." Below that confident proclamation, Peter had drawn a scene straight out of the Old West: under a high sun a wooden sign read *Last Chance*, a vulture perched on one end. Littered on the sand beneath were struggling cacti and sun-bleached cattle bones. Peter wrote, in a curve around the tableau, REMEMBER, TIME AND TIDE WAIT FOR NO MAN!

Damn, this is *serious*, Lenny thought.

Lenny took Peter's earnest method-for-madness home with him. He read about Peter's obsessions with snappy percussion and an "adventerous attitude," his passionate calls on the band to rehearse and refine, to harness their energy toward the future, to avoid local examples of dull bands, and to dress the look. "We should never be reluctant to work on material until it is polished and at maximum rock potential," Peter wrote to his mates. "We can't afford to be *pat* and *lazy*." One of Peter's concerns was that many of the numbers the Fleshtones cover might be too identified with the "punk movement" and might be played out. ("This is a shame as we are just now beginning to really get them down," he lamentably scrawled.) His answer? Dip back a bit further. The Fleshtones, he wrote, can't be afraid to sound "unorthodox or 'old fashioned' or too *extreme*, it's got to get there, we've got to make it rock!" This, he reminded the fellas, requires practice. "Economy of Means is a *good* rule,"

as part of this, hand clapping, stamping of feet and shouting a real lot, will greatly enhance our allready exiciting stage appearence.

Speaking of Stage Appearence, we must have, well before the show, the clothes together that we will be wearing. Excuses such as; "It's too hot," etc. are the height of lameness and stupidity. Some members of the band have even worn suits or sweat shirts and preformed with utmost verve while others simply lolled about the stage dressed "comfortable". We are on a stage and people, sometimes a lot, are watching. Keep in mind bright colors and military gear and interesting casual clothing. If we are lucky

enough to ever get 2 nights at
C.B. 'G.B.s again we should try not
to wear the same thing twice. If.....
We should handle our selves a
little better than if we were
playing a off-night at Rumbottons
and Note that even bands from
places like _N.J._ are doing their
homework and getting pretty
hip.
We should really get going!

Lenny put the handbook down, and glanced out the window of his tiny apartment. He admired Peter's commitment to vision, his urge to merge the Troggs and the Rimshots, garage and funk. But he felt uneasy. He noticed that Peter and Keith were drifting more toward fashioning a specific 60s-influenced look and bearing for the band that involved thrift-store and vintage-clothes boutique runs. Lenny remembered that the *Aquarian* piece from August had raved about Peter's *Village Green Preservation Society* pink trousers, the sort of distinctive, sharp image that he was cultivating and was happy that the local press was noticing. That night, Lenny felt anxious.

"I kinda felt that Peter's handbook was directed towards me," he says. "Like, *Get on the boat or leave.*"

There were other problems with Lenny going unseen by the drummer. Marek was growing unhappy with Lenny's playing. "As much as I loved Len Calderon, there was a power struggle," Marek says. "He was smoking pot all the time, and he wasn't quite on the same wavelength as us. He was a great, great funny guy, but at gigs he just wasn't *driving* the band. I was trying to push it faster and faster and it was colliding with wuss rock. I think what I was trying to do in some ways was urge Lenny on, and so I would start pushing a little bit ahead of the beat." The problem was, for Marek, "he wouldn't pick up on it. And so I was really upset with it. I had this sense of the potential of the scene and the Fleshtones as a band to be really be big, but it was gonna require shedding our adolescence and really making some serious moves. We had to grow up in some ways."

Peter felt the same way, and he was beginning to apply his dominating energy toward getting the rest of the guys to tighten up, urging the band to *focus* and to not grow complacent about what was going on with the music. The New York/Boston bands that Peter admired—Suicide, Talking Heads, the Real Kids, DMZ—were intentional, purposeful, calculated conceptions, driven to be so. The Fleshtones might have originated out of basement jams in the boroughs, but Peter felt that they needed to start taking themselves more seriously—more, well, *professionally*—if they were to rise above. He would implore the band at rehearsals and during layoffs between gigs, *Look, if we're gonna make it, here are these bands that are, like, great examples of clear vision and intention, making a heartfelt, powerful statement. We can do that.*

Marek felt subtle resistance from Keith and Lenny. "Lenny was still living out in Flushing, settled into this cushy, domestic thing, smoking pot, holding down the copywriter's day job, doing the band, and he was happy as a pig in shit. Keith had some of the same thing going, but he was a little more driven. He was living with Judy out in Whitestone, and he had the swingin' apartment, the day job that could afford it. Based on his upbringing in Queens, the valuable things in life are to have a job, a car, and an apartment. You have your home really nailed down, your security, the source of strength." For Lenny and Keith, that was what was their foundation, their anchor, and "they needed that in a big way."

Marek, marveling at bands in Manhattan that were anchored by powerful drummers with killer personalities, implored the guys to get rid of Lenny. "You had the Voidoids with Bob Quine, Ivan Julian, Marc Bell, transitory drummers, but they were all stars. You had Marky Ramone, Clem Burke. God, Clem is still my hero! I was pushing them to get somebody else who was more hip and really a clock drummer, somebody who was gonna elevate the smeary, boozy quality of the band to something that any of the other bands on the New York scene would look at and go, 'You know, these guys may be simple, but that's intentional, and they can play that simple music as good as anyone.'" The Ramones were the prime example, and the Fleshtones weren't competitive.

Although the band was gigging often and looking forward to the release of the album (which they planned on titling *Blast Off!*), frustrations and band dissension were making themselves felt. They kept plugging in and playing: a Tuesday night gig at CBGB's on October 3, their first show there in five long months, a big Thursday through Saturday weekend there with Suicide in early November, and a Thursday-night show with Suicide and Walter Stedding at Max's on December 28. As the end of year approached, the band was dropping rumors in local fanzines that an early 1979 release of *Blast Off!* was pending. In truth, nothing was progressing on that front at all. The new year would see the Fleshtones play two high-profile shows—one out of state—but the release of only a sliver of the work done at Ultima. The band was forced to keep gigging without much product to support in order to stay visible and to make some pocket change, a fate that would dog them throughout much of their long, vexed career.

Mitchell Ames had liked what he heard at Ultima. As the assistant engineer, he was busy during the recording of the Fleshtones' album but not distracted enough to note the high-energy sounds coming through the board. Keith was still feeling some pressure as the lone guitarist, the spotlight at the studio contributing, and he sought (against Peter's protests) another player to complement him and the band. He'd struck up a friendship with Ames and asked him if he'd be interested in playing with the band. "This guy just seemed really right with his guitar approach," Keith remembers. "He played a lot like Keith Richards, and he kinda looked like him. I was going to be Brian Jones to his Keith Richards—that was the idea!" Ames began playing with the band at the close of the year: in January at Maxwell's in Hoboken, New Jersey, where they were among the first rock bands ever to play; a Valentine's Day show at Columbia University ("Rock Your Heart Away, All the Beer and Punch You Can Drink"); and a Wednesday night that February at Max's.

From the onset, there was some incompatibility between Ames and the guys. To Marek, Ames' musical gift was more Virtuosic than Human Riff. "There was always a schism between these guys who knew more about their instruments then we did!" he says. "We were certainly appreciating the Ramones as much as an Artistic Statement as it was a band, but our lead guitarists really weren't hip to that. They were much more old school, traditional. We kept picking people from that oeuvre because they were guys who probably could pick up some album and do the solo verbatim, and that always impressed us. But it always ended up being a problem when it came time to do the solo over Fleshtones material, which was inherently very simple stuff. And you couldn't 'unlearn' this stuff in these people. These were all really nice guys and musicians but they were coming from a whole completely different place, and we were looking in the wrong place."

In November of 1978, Marty Thau booked the just-opened Mudd Club for three midweek nights of Red Star talent that he dubbed "Red Star Express," harkening back to the Stax and Motown soul-revue shows of the sixties. The show was recorded with the hopes of releasing a live showcase album. "The Real Kids would have nothing to do with it," Peter remembers. "But all the other Red Star artists were there. As well as Suicide, there was Walter Stedding, who played brainwave-activated violin, and Von Lmo, a stream-of-consciousness performer who attacked his instruments and amps with a chainsaw." The Fleshtones played two solid if unremarkable sets on Tuesday and Wednesday nights, notable mostly for the debut of a new song, "F-f-fascination," that would serve as the band's swan song for Red Star, and for Peter's discovery offstage: "cocaine made me extremely uncomfortable." (For now at least, Peter would stick to beer and pills.)

A notice of the show appeared in *Punk* magazine, where the reviewer called Red Star "the world's strangest record label," but noted that when the Fleshtones played "everybody started dancing—unusual for a New York audience—but the normal reaction to a Fleshtones set." Alas, "Red Star Express," though well-attended, did not materialize into the promotional boon that Thau had envisioned. "Afterwards, the whole effort dissolved in obscure recriminations," Peter says ruefully. "The Express never left the station."

One show that did make a splash a month into the new year was the "Best of the New Wave Dance Bands/Battle of the Bands" at New York University on February 24—"a good idea that ought to produce some very hard-played rock & roll," wrote a hopeful Robert Christgau the week before in the *Voice*. Lou O'Neil, Jr. plugged the event in his *New York Post* column, fliers and advertisements blanketed lower Manhattan, and NYU promised a panel of "All Star Judges!" The Fleshtones competed with the Zantees and Nervous Rex for a $1,000 prize, due enticement for the guys whose advance from Thau had vanished quicker than they figured it would have. "We would be getting seventy dollars a gig," remembers Keith. "And here's a thousand dollars!"

The panel originally consisted of Chris Stein (guitarist for Blondie), Ira Robbins (editor of *Trouser Press*, a local rock & roll magazine that was growing quickly from Xeroxed-fanzine status), Meg Griffin and Dan Near (DJs from WNEW and WPIX, respectively), and Michael Shore (writer from the *Soho Weekly News*). In the confusion and push of the last minute, Robbins, Near, and Griffin bailed, and music critic Dan Oppenheimer and Georgia Christgau from the *Voice* filled in. Shore, for one, was impressed with all of the bands, but was positively blown away by the Fleshtones, who were keen on giving a high-energy show in front of a sold-out crowd at Loeb Student Center. "We played a very hot show," Keith remembers. "We wanted to prove something." The guys hit the stage "tossing packs of Camels to the mob," as Robert Christgau recalled, "then demolish[ed] Nervous Rex." After the band left the stage and the sweaty, panting crowd behind, Stein turned to Shore and said, "That's gonna be pretty tough to beat." Nervous Rex gamely tried, but the night clearly belonged to the Fleshtones.

Reviewing the contest in the next week's *Soho Weekly News*, Shore, though complimentary to the Zantees and Nervous Rex, could barely contain his enthusiasm for the Fleshtones. "The Fleshtones nearly blew the house down with a hard-charging set that seamlessly welded roots rock revivalism, streamlined R&B, and rousing 70s garage rock," he wrote. "Who cares if they owe more than a passing debt to the Ramones? So do the Clash. And besides, the Fleshtones have a boyishly winning amateurism and energy that is personified by lead singer Peter Zaremba's sloppy, good-natured charm. Theirs is an aggressively friendly minimalism." Shore's criteria was simple: how he liked the band, and how the crowd reacted, measured in large part by their moving and grooving. "What these criteria really boiled down to was *danceability*," he wrote, summarizing the band's musical, visionary ambition in a manner unique to the general New York press at the time. "With the advent of disco, people seem to have forgotten that rock 'n' roll can be great dance music too. . . . people danced in the aisles, in front of the stage, even in their seats in some instances." The Fleshtones were victorious. In addition to the thousand bucks, they earned some nice local press and even more notorious word of mouth: *This is a live band that has to be seen to be believed*. The band celebrated the victory with two consecutive weekends at Maxwell's, sandwiching the Wednesday night Max's gig in between. Their reputation was spreading wildly: the second Maxwell's show was stopped by the Hoboken police, who were obliged to give back money thrown at them by riotous patrons in an attempt to persuade the cops to allow the Fleshtones to play one more song (the crowd wanted to hear a reprise of "Atom Spies").

Two weeks later, a marveling Robert Christgau wrote a "Voice Choice" spotlighting the band to perfection. "Winning the first NYU Battle of the Bands," he wrote, "these guys were like Platonic ideal of high school rock & roll—out of tune, dropping the mike, doing stuff that was beyond them because they knew it would be wonderful in one way if they executed and wonderful in another if they didn't. I don't know if they can repeat—they were *up*—but I expect to find out." The Fleshtones were duly charged: re-create those great, sweaty, transcendent moments of rock & roll again and again and again, if they can. The gauntlet flung down, the boys had to prove over and over that they felt, knew, and trembled in the spirit. By mid-summer, the Fleshtones were being billed at Hurrah as "NYC's Best New Band." If only they had a record out with their damn faces on it.

Marty Thau's optimism was dimming quickly. His Midas touch couldn't make the long green materialize. "My partners felt that they didn't understand the punk game that I was in," he complains. More accurately, the folks at Bronze had listened to *Blast Off!* and had heard a poorly recorded album. Bronze Records didn't want to sink more money into a record that would likely flop. With a couple of key Red Star supporters having already jumped ship to CBS, Bronze, sensing market indifference to the Fleshtones, decided to shelve an album and single release.

Thau was defeated. Suicide had recently completed thirty-day tours with both Elvis Costello and the Clash on the European continent, amassing volumes of press, but Thau's backers wouldn't be swayed. Despite his platinum pop instincts and legacy of gold records, he was left without distribution for his own records. He could've scraped together enough money to press an album, but short of carting the boxes of vinyl around Manhattan and dropping them on the doorsteps of Bleecker Bob's and Rocks in Your Head, he had no way of moving them. Things stalled, and quick.

Thau was able to finance the release of one single. Dedicated to Miriam Linna, "American Beat" (backed with "Critical List") was released on Red Star in June, the picture sleeve sporting a close-up of Keith's Mustang-strumming hand, a frame from Jones' *Soul City*. Thau pressed up twenty-five hundred copies of the 45, but he had little realistic hopes of a million-seller. Though Blondie's "One Way or Another," Joe Jackson's "Is She Really Going Out with Him?" and the Knack's "My Sharona" were charting that month, the big sellers were the Charlie Daniels Band, Dionne Warwick, and Barbra Streisand. With little promotional support, Thau threw his first Red Star 45 over a pretty imposing cliff, and the lag time between Ultima and the single was unacceptable to a band whose dreams of the album had languished: "American Beat" came out one year to the day that the band signed with Thau.

"His part of the contract was fulfilled," Lenny recalls. "After that, we were still waiting and waiting and waiting for the album to come out. We were so disappointed because we all had our Suicide albums and our Real Kids albums on Red Star and we kept imagining out album coming out. It never did." (Thau would eventually sign a distribution deal with the ROIR cassette-only company in 1982 and release *Blast Off!* in that medium, using the raw mixes of the initial sessions. The infamous "first album" and various tracks from it would subsequently be released internationally by Thau over the next twenty years in cassette, vinyl, and CD formats via various licensing deals. Ironically, the Fleshtones' debut album, never officially released, has become their most-issued record. Call it a *Fleshtones Phenomenon*.)

Bitterness between the group and Thau would grow over the years, stoked in large part by naiveté, continental misunderstandings, and stubborn rumors. Keith recounts those meager days in the spring and summer of 1979, waiting, waiting, waiting for *Blast Off!* while his friends' records were coming out. He shakes his head at the Red Star mess. "Out of that whole record, maybe three or four things were considered finished," he claims. "The rest of it was supposed to be remixed, and there were supposed to be vocals done. Marty was smoking tons of pot. His publicist, Roy Trakan, was coming to the sessions and was always smoking tons of pot. You couldn't help but inhale these fumes in the studio.

"Most of the album truly was not finished," he continues. "All of these versions of *Blast Off!* aren't from master reels; they are from board-mix cassette tapes. Because Marty didn't have the money to pay his bills anymore, they wouldn't release the master tapes or the finished mixes to him. All he had was board mixes of what was being done at the end of the session to take home to refer to." He adds, "It gets even funnier. A year or two goes by, and Ultima Studio has a fire. The studio burns to the ground! There go the masters. Disaster. And to this day this record *Blast Off!* has been made into how many versions? How many record covers? Marty released it once and just called it *The Fleshtones*, because he thought *Blast Off!* was too juvenile. Come on! Finally, after twenty years, he got the right sequencing. Marty's a pretty funny guy. That's the saga of Red Star Records."

Thau is utterly bewildered that Keith would claim that a fire at Ultima destroyed the tapes. "That's legend," he says. "I don't where these stories come from. The Fleshtones circle was a very weird, uninformed circle. There was a perception that there was a fire, and that I turned my back on the whole thing. I've been in the record business all these years, so why would I turn my back on something? I went as far as I could with it. I just folded Red Star. I had the choice to keep it open or close it. I had no choice. I had no distribution, and I didn't have any money of my own to fund it the way it needed to be funded.

"I also read where Peter says that *Blast Off!* and even later versions of it on CD were, because of the so-called 'fire,' taken from a two-track tape. Well, yes, that is what you use when you manufacture records, two-track tapes. Sixteen tracks, twenty-four tracks, forty-eight tracks: they're all reduced down to two tracks because they've been placed together, the mixes and assemblies made where it's reduced down to two tracks, left and right stereo. That's what records are manufactured from. In Peter's simplicity, he didn't realize that. I got this inkling that I 'coldly folded Red Star,' the fire thing, and all of these elements, but I had no idea any of that was being bandied about.

"There was no fire, ever." In his office Thau points to a shelf loaded with reel-to-reel tapes. "I've got the Fleshtones two-track tape in there."

"American Beat" was shipped in June; copies ended up in Los Angeles and even trickled over the pond to London and Paris. "We were pretty proud," Peter recalls. "There was our 45 with its own pigeonhole at Bleecker Bob's. In our little world, anything seemed possible then."

The single received good notices, though enthusiastic writers were as apt to temper their comments with puzzlement over the missing album. "'American Beat''s booming wall of sound caught my ear," Richard Mortifoglio wrote in the *Village Voice*. "Though the mix muffles Zaremba's guttural Mitch Ryder vocal somewhat, lines like 'Heard it on the radio in my hometown' emerge often enough to make 'American Beat' a raving anthem for traditional-minded local bands who say no to the No Wave." Mortifoglio went on to consider the band beyond the vinyl: "Traditional doesn't have to be derivative, as Streng demonstrated at a recent headline show at Max's," he noted. "Streng is far more inventive, often breaking off from catchy retro riffs into interludes of echoing, subliminal minor chordwork. Zaremba forgot his harmonica the night I saw the band but played some Farfisa when he wasn't up front, which was most of the time.

Since his stage manner isn't as campy as, say, Lux Interior's of the Cramps, his enthusiasm, even his many fuck-ups, carry that much more conviction. Add to that Streng's shifting major-minor shake-downs and subtract the Fleshtones' sometimes distracting raveups, and you end up with just the right dose of high times and mystery."

Slash, the bourgeoning rock and punk magazine out of Los Angeles, published an effusive review that described "American Beat" as an "awesome recreation of a period in time (mid-sixties) when rock & roll was YOUTH music, not an Industry Business. This record captures it all-fuzzy reverb guitars, tambourines, harmonicas, gruff voices, oohhing backup—god, it's perfect, and yet still real and immediate enough to keep from being a museum piece. Like the Cramps, the Fleshtones have reshaped the past for the future, and I can't fault their faithfulness. The sincerity is overwhelming, you wanna blast this out of your car radio, even though they don't play this kind of music on the radio anymore. Ok, the tape deck then. It's a soundtrack for going a thousand down the freeway with no tomorrow, blast it in your den, do all the Shindig dances one the living room rug. This is the rock & roll we all nearly missed the first time out. Let's get it right this time. Hey, play that again!"

Perhaps most exciting for the guys were hearty European notices. *New Musical Express* in London wrote that the single was "a nugget from New York's best-kept secret weapon. The purest distillation of garageville gonzo genius this week (or maybe this year) comes from The Fleshtones, sublime practitioners of the rigorous punk four chord trick. Body crushing waves of sexy power surge and jangle to the front in a mad melee while the rhythm section bites on the beat with a zealous disregard for subtlety and the singer (a deranged specimen in the mould of Messrs. Saxon and Erickson) mouths off in full glorious spate: '*Can you hear the American sound / Don't wanna hear you put it down.*' This is an example of the beast at its most dangerous with American new wave's forgotten hero Marty Thau at the controls. History in the making."

Thau basked in the reviews also, and—despite the difficulties, the unreleased debut, and the small pressing of the single—hoped to continue working with the Fleshtones. What he needed from them was patience.

Marek had had it. He was feeling inklings of cultural and personal differences between himself and Peter and Keith, feelings that would quietly stoke and then grow over the next several years, and the frustrations with playing with Lenny and the interminable wait for *Blast Off!*

were chafing. Shortly after an August gig at Irving Plaza (notable for the other group on the bill, Boston's Lyres in one of their first visits to New York), Marek surprised the band by quitting.

"Keith, Peter and I had a meeting," Marek recalls. "They didn't want to fire Lenny. Peter was on the fence, but I think Keith was really loyal and probably a little scared of making such a bold move. It was a real radical thing to do, but I saw that as being necessary. So I said, 'The hell with you.' One of my big problems has always been blaming things on other people! I thought, *Okay, they're holding me back. My career would be great if it wasn't for these guys.*"

Marek didn't have to look very far for support and diversion. Some friends with whom he had hung out in Maine had moved down to New York, paralleling Marek's move of four years earlier, though they more involved with the art scene. Tim Rollins, a student at SVA and a rival of Peter's, Marek's cousin Julie (Rollins' roommate), and Marek started to hang out and kick around ideas. Liberated, Marek indulged his individuality away from the Fleshtones, as a musician and as a young man, and his escape from the counteractive Red Star debacle, and he wanted to start a band together with his cousin and Rollins, who had bought a jet-black Telecaster and was learning to play and raring to go. One red-letter night they ended up at a party in Little Italy thrown by Tom Carson from the *Village Voice*, who was hosting the B-52's after their New York debut. Marek met the band and was enamored of the quirky and spirited guys and girls from Athens, Georgia. He, his cousin, and Rollins decided to start a band called the RPM's (revolutions per minute), humoring their vaguely Leftist political bent.

Marek's departure also marked the end of Mitchell Ames' brief tenure with the band, and the Fleshtones were now officially, maddeningly, on hiatus. "American Beat" was out, and the band had been gigging fairly regularly and taking home increasingly larger wads of cash after each show (as much as $400 per member at a venue such as Hurrah) but Peter and Keith, miffed at Marek's decision, couldn't but help but wonder if the fates were conspiring against them. The guys rapidly replaced Marek with Walter Scezney, who they knew from other local bands, and who was a friend of friends. Scezney was familiar with the band's material and executed a relatively smooth transition, though Marek's distinctive playing and personality would soon be sorely missed.

There was a pressing reason why the Fleshtones needed another bass player so quickly. On the heels of "American Beat," the band had been invited to perform at a major festival in Minneapolis, Minnesota, by far their biggest and highest-profile show. Marathon '80, the New-

Time and Tide Wait for No Man

No-Now Wave Rock Festival, was held on September 22 and 23, 1979, at the University of Minnesota Field House. The idea belonged to twenty-four-year-old Tim Carr, a former rock critic turned assistant director of the Walker Arts Center, who wanted to showcase relevant, eclectic bands that he thought would dynamically preview the state of rock & roll for the 1980s. He assembled twenty-two groups in total, including the Records and Monochrome Set from England, Chris Stamey and the dB's, Richard Lloyd, DEVO, James White and the New Contortions, the Fleshtones, and many others. The festival was a major and ambitious endeavor, but would ultimately suffer from muddy acoustics, corporate disinterest, and the unhappy coincidence that the nuclear-protest MUSE concerts, headlined by Bruce Springsteen, were taking place the very same weekend at Madison Square Garden. The M-80 festival was exceptional enough that the *Voice* sent Tom Carson, who subsequently filed a major piece.

It didn't bother the Fleshtones to leave their prized hometown behind for that weekend. They brought along Brian and Gordon, and the lineup, though a bit shaky with Scezney still fitting in, worked its hardest on the cool, late-summer weekend. "That show is a big, fond memory," says Lenny. "That was probably the coolest gig we did because we actually flew and stayed at a Holiday Inn!" The flight gave the guys an opportunity to share close space with fellow musicians, a motley group that Carson called "an all-star football team of unrecorded New York bands, on their way to the big game." In the spirit Peter, for the humorous benefit of his fellow passengers, held up a *New York Post* with the headline BEATLES TO GET BACK. "A bad omen," Peter said to anyone who'd listen. "A very bad omen."

The omen proved feeble. The Fleshtones' performance was among the highlights of the festival. Commenting on the good vibes of M-80 despite lackluster local bands, rotten sound, and hesitant crowd support, Carson wrote that it was not surprising that the Fleshtones were the hit of the first day. "They were the closest thing to real punk yet," he wrote, "but with their r&b roots and Peter Zaremba's dance-party moves, they were also the closest thing to good old rock & roll—which was the one thing the crowd wanted. Even so, the band was tougher and tighter than I've ever seen them, and Zaremba's rangy stage presence and belting vocals had real assurance."

The reactions of the Minneapolis press, however, ranged from lukewarm to damning. "Neo-rockabilly shouters from New Yawk," the *Minnesota Daily* wrote dismissively. "The Tones displayed lots of energy, despite each band member playing in a slightly different time signature. And I don't mean intentionally. Nouveau garage." Wrote

Sweat

Christopher Farrell in *Sweet Potato*, "You can dance to the Fleshtones, although the truth about them is that you can dance to them but you can't listen to them. A New York new wave-punk band, they are a cross between Talking Heads and the Ramones. . . . Even with a single out, the Fleshtones show they are still looking for that material which will hold them in popular memory."

None of the tepid Rust Belt feedback bothered the guys much on the flight home—they felt that their duty was to connect not with critics but with the crowd, the guys and the girls grinning and jumping up and down and especially those tentative or suspicious ones lurking at the ends of the bleachers to whom Zaremba made frequent and literal gestures to come join the fun. They were nonetheless gratified to read loyal supporter Andy Schwartz's piece on M-80 in *New York Rocker*. He began by noting the band's uncertain start, poor monitor sound, and Scezney's inability to match "the popping, propulsive lines" of Marek's playing, "but they built up steam with 'American Beat,' 'Critical List,' and a funky, grinding 'Midnight Hour' (? and the Mysterians' song, not Wilson Pickett's). By 'Girl from Baltimore,' the 'Tones were roaring, and people were standing on their chairs, yelling for more. To see this band emerge victorious after a year of career disappointments and defeats nearly brought tears to my eyes. A tremendous performance."

Peter celebrated the show and his twenty-fifth birthday by throwing a gigantic party on the roof of his apartment building at East Eleventh Street. Hundreds of invited friends showed up and grooved until dawn to a DJ spinning disco glitter across the skyline.

Walter Scezney wasn't cutting it. He was clinging to his lucrative commodities day job that was too nice to throw away for fickle rock & roll. The guys, Keith especially, missed Marek; they'd been friends since adolescence and shared a simpatico that went beyond the stage. "I really thought that the band wasn't right without him," Keith says. "The Fleshtones almost broke up, the only time in our career. So I got back on the phone with Peter and Marek, and I'm trying to talk Marek into getting back with the band." Keith knew they need a new drummer. Peter agreed.

Marek hadn't missed the increasing discomfort of the rhythm section nor the delayed commercial payday with the Fleshtones, but he *had* missed playing rock & roll with his buddies. The RPM's never took off, and anyway an alternate musical direction would have had to wait: Marek severely injured his fingers while drunk one evening, nearly slicing his fingertips off after catching them in the hinge of a cellar door. He needed weeks to recuperate, and did so while Peter and Keith, with few options, jointly agreed to again place the Fleshtones on hiatus. It was understood between the three of them that when Marek was healed and ready to rejoin the band, Lenny would be gone.

The 1970s were finished. Disco was dealt a blow by backlash and saturation—the infamous "Disco Demolition Day" at Comiskey Park in Chicago had blazed in July—and New Wave was in ascension. The Fleshtones were at a crossroads. They had emerged from a basement in Queens courageously committed to playing unfashionable rock & roll, and after four solid years of sweaty gigs and nothing to show but a good reputation, an unfinished, unreleased album, and one single, the band was hungry, unsatisfied, and, most pressingly, without a drummer. They were becoming quietly desperate and wondered how steep the next damn hill was going to be.

In order to stay in pocket money, the guys had had to scramble for odd jobs again and ended up working together on a construction project. Marek and Peter got in on the job through Jon Quinn, and eventually Marek, who missed his buddy, brought Keith in as a glorified assistant. They were gutting an apartment building belonging to artist Frank Stella on Fourteenth Street between First and Second Avenues. The three rock & rollers slipped and slid in ill-fitting construction helmets, schlepping Stella's absurdly larger-than-life postmodern sculptures. "The queerest bunch of construction guys you ever saw!" laughs Marek. What had the makings of a scene out of a *Monkees* episode ended up smoothing over the rift between Marek, Peter, and Keith.

May 1980. Marek and Keith are sitting in the Stage Restaurant, better known as Bruno's, a narrow lunch counter on Second Avenue below Eighth Street. They're on their lunch break from the Stella building job, glumly eating their sandwiches, rehashing yet again the sullen desperation of the band.

. . . and Blondie's fuckin' huge, and the Ramones are fuckin' recording with Spector, the B-52's have a huge single out and their damn debut's probably gonna go gold. Even Nervous Rex are out in LA with Chapman. He'll probably make 'em bigger than the fuckin' Knack . . .

A tall, rangy man, who'd been sitting next to Marek and Keith at the counter, overhearing their despondent conversation, leans in.

"Well. I'm a drummer," he says to them quietly. "I heard you guys talking about. You're what. In a band and you need a drummer?"

"Yeah."

"Well, I'm a drummer. And I'm looking to play. I really want to get with a rock & roll band. What's the name of your band?"

"We're the Fleshtones," Keith says, wiping his hands. "I'm Keith. He's Marek."

"What's your name?" asks Marek.

"Bill. Bill Milhizer."

Damn, this guy's tall.

"Yeah, well, we're gonna do auditions," says Marek. "So give us your number."

Bill reached for a pen and a napkin. *This guy looks like Cary Grant . . .*

Ever-hustling Marty Thau had another project cooking. With the Red Star Express up on blocks, the producer turned his attention to a record compilation idea. "Howard Thompson, who was working in England when I made the deal for Red Star, was a friend of the owner of Criminal Records in England, and I was talking to him transatlantic," Thau explains. "I came up with the idea of doing a compilation, and Jimmy Destri of Blondie said he would produce it. I thought of it as potentially something I could do every couple of years, a series." Thau approached the Fleshtones, the Revelons, the Comateens, Student Teachers, and Bloodless Pharaohs (featuring a young Brian Setzer) to contribute two tracks each to the project.

"Thau didn't have much of a plan," Jimmy Destri remembers. "He had a feeling that it was time to round up the artists that remained after the initial industry rush on the first wave of bands— us, the Ramones, etc.—and bring them together in a collection that would be relatively easy to organize and pitch to a small label as a one-off collection of unsigned bands." The Fleshtones, as Destri remembers it, were the most notable band within the project. Happy to be thought of again by Marty despite the *Blast Off!* disappointment, the guys were charged to have a new recording gig on which to focus. And there was a bonus: as part of the deal, there would also be a U.K. 45 single of the two Fleshtone tracks released on Criminal Records.

The compilation, wittily titled *Marty Thau Presents 2X5* by Peter, came together quickly. Clem Burke of Blondie agreed to play drums on the Fleshtones' two tracks. (The guys were coy about Lenny's sacking. "I think they told me that their drummer was ill, or out of the area," Destri recalls with amusement. "Something less than 'Pete Best-ed' or exploded *à la* Spinal Tap.") Burke propelled the songs in his usual superb, muscular manner, and Destri added keyboards. Both songs were laid down at House of Music Studios in New Jersey: a taut re-recording of "Shadow Line," and the upbeat and loose "F-f-fascination," in which Peter extolls the virtues of looking at weeds along the East River and finding a Whitmanesque charm in daily suburban lore. The autobiographical song captured the joyful, heady excitement of youthful possibility.

"I think they had a good time," says Destri of the sessions. "I don't think they expected my kind of approach back then. I sorta giggled and twisted dials throughout the whole thing." Keith remembers the quickly taped sessions fondly. "Working with Jimmy was a delight," he says. "He was into other kinds of substances than marijuana. He was *really* into cocaine, so he was into working!" ("That was the blow era," Destri admits. "I was open about it. I shared it.") Although Keith had some domestic difficulties to overcome—Judy had shredded his guitar cords in the midst of a fight, and he had to dub some of the guitar parts later—both tracks came together nicely and proved that the band hadn't lost a drop of energy.

Destri recalls the Fleshtones circa 1979 as an original and honest band. "They made no bones about entertaining an audience and were never strained by the need to appear inventive," he reflects. They had a few problems for Destri, however. "I thought they were too locked in to a stylistic form to really get all of their intelligence across." Thau released *2X5* in the late spring of 1980, handing the cover art responsibilities over to Peter, who created a multicolor fireworks of the Red Star roster exploding over the Manhattan skyline. Acknowledged on the back cover was Marilla Palmer, Peter's new redhaired girlfriend, a lively Philadelphia College of Art graduate whom he met at CBGB's at a Revelons show. They would soon move into the East Village together and in 1985 would marry.

Limitedly distributed, the album received positive notices where it was discovered. Most reviews couched enthusiasm for the Fleshtones with bafflement and frustration over the band's missing full-length debut. Paul Rambali in *New Musical Express* wrote, "It's impossible not to talk in terms of promise, and I would gladly hear an album's worth of The Fleshtones right now, if not sooner." Toby Goldstein in *Trouser Press* remarked on the band's "blend of complex mystery," observing that "their updated garage-band intensity bodes well for their long-delayed first album; both 'Shadow Line' and 'F-f-fascination' are riddled with the tension that pervades the best of Television and the Thirteenth Floor Elevators. And that's a thrilling highway interchange."

Clem Burke agreed to play a couple of dates with the band to support 2X5. Recharged, the Fleshtones booked two gigs, at Hurrah on December 28 and at Irving Plaza on January 4 (though they ultimately canceled the latter). Peter and Keith, reckless and brass-bound under stage lights, were positively squeamish about confronting Lenny with the fact that his days in the band were over. "I saw the Fleshtones in a *Voice* ad one day" says Lenny. "This was after us not being together for a few months. I called up Keith and said, 'Hey, when are we gonna rehearse for the gig?' And that's when he finally realized that he had to tell me. And he goes, *I guess Peter didn't tell you, did he?* And I go, 'No, what . . . I'm not doing that gig, am I?' And he goes, *No, not really.* I got a weird vibe from him." He adds, "Those guys have never been able to face anybody and tell them that stuff. I'm the one who had to tell Danny Gilbert that he was out of the band. That was weird."

Just like that, Lenny was finished playing in one of the great rock & roll dance bands in the city. "I really wasn't disappointed," he says now. "I was a little hurt because they were friends, and there's always that part of it; you're hurt that your friends don't want you around anymore. But I wasn't insulted musically. Usually if you get thrown out of a band it's because you suck, and then you get depressed about that. Since I got thrown out because I was too *good*, I never really felt any animosity. But I always hated the way they did it. We never had meetings or anything like that to tell me it was coming, at least. I never did have any animosity toward the guys, because playing in the Fleshtones was a great springboard for me. I learned a lot about music."

After departing, Lenny briefly played with Mitchell Ames and then moved on to Thin Ice, a power-pop outfit that put out an independent single. In the mid-eighties he moved to the Bay area in California, playing in various death metal and heavy metal bands, and surprised the Fleshtones by showing up at a mid-nineties gig in San Francisco. Charmed, Peter invited him up onstage. Grinning and pleased, Lenny pounded along on a drum for a song or two, happy to be back onstage with his old friends from Queens. In 2002, he moved back to Flushing. He works in Manhattan in the computer/video industry, and in his spare time drums in the Dala Kings, playing just as fast and hard as he wants, and nobody tells him what to do.

At Bruno's, Marek and Keith ask Bill Milhizer if he can sing background vocals.

"Of course."

Bill asks Marek and Keith whether the Fleshtones have management. They . . . bluff.

"How confining are your day jobs?" Bill asks. He's free to go away on the road and wonders if they are, too. In fact, they are.

Unbeknownst to the guys, their paths had already crossed the past few years, beneath the dim lights of the Bowery and along the shadowy avenues of the East Village. Marek and Keith didn't know it that day, but they'd found their permanent drummer. The next hill would indeed be smaller, and what would follow would be a long, fun glide. But larger mountains are born of descents.

The Party

"I'm just spending all of my spare time
finding out how good it can get."

10.
Lucky Bill

Puppeteers Needed.
Apply now.
Travel Required Soon.

Bill Milhizer had never been west of the Mississippi. As pleasant as his childhood in upstate New York had been, he began to feel the restlessness common to all young men fresh out of high school. He bounced around local community colleges for a while—Hudson Valley, Adirondack—finally settling at Fredonia College, where he determinedly earned a bachelor's degree. The National Draft Board stopped pooling at around 190, and Bill had lucked out by choosing an implausibly high lottery number of 195. The Gods of Chance were looking down favorably. The East Coast imprinted in his marrow, Bill had wanted to enroll in graduate school at Rutgers University, but he was rejected. He ended up halfway across the country at Purdue University in sleepy West Lafayette, Indiana, charmed by their acceptance of his application and intrigued by their graduate program in social psychology.

Dismayed by the distance from New York, Bill was nonetheless happy to be just a couple of hours away from his older brother in Chicago. He arrived at Purdue in the fall of 1971. When he wasn't holed up with dense texts in the Psychological Sciences Library or doggedly canvassing the local community for his thesis research, Bill enjoyed the local bars, the local girls, and the extra green he earned giving drum lessons to various young sons of the Purdue faculty. His brother had shipped his kit out from Troy, and Bill bought his first drum case in West Lafayette. He set up, began practicing again in the basement of the house he rented, and started teaching at Miller's Music Store. He'd missed his drums dearly—more than he knew— and he enjoyed teaching, all of his chops and desire roaring back.

He finished his thesis—a sociological exploration of nonprofit volunteerism in groups ranging from Presidential supporters to the National Appreciation of Barbershop Quartet Singing in America— and he graduated from Purdue in the spring of 1973. Eager to experience sexy life in the big burg for the first time, he loaded up his drums in the oversized Buick that he'd recently bought and headed north on I-65 for Chicago. He knew a young woman from West Lafayette who was already in the city, and he moved in with her.

Bill was digging hanging out with his brother and soaking up the excitement and expanse of the big brown city, but he needed some money, fast. He knew that the Ludwig Drum factory was located in south Chicago, and he fancied working for the manufacturer of majestic kits played by Ringo Starr, Charlie Watts, and so many other drummers Bill loved and admired. He called up the factory one afternoon, and the foreman told him that they were going to need someone tall in shipping and receiving very soon. Bill was hired fairly quickly and soon was grunting and lifting raw materials off of the trucks on South Damen Avenue, shining drum hoops and loading up sets to deliver to some pretty celebrated drummers (among them Carl Palmer, percussionist *extraordinaire* for Emerson, Lake, and Palmer). He didn't last too long, however. The job was grueling, and Bill eventually heard the clarion call of upstate New York. On Thanksgiving of 1973, he drove back to Troy in his Buick warhorse, shrugged his shoulders the day his master's degree diploma arrived in the mail, and settled back into life along the Hudson River.

But quiet times with his high school friends and his parents soon made his hand-to-mouth existence in Chicago all the more romantic and appealing, and he resolutely moved back to the city in the fall of 1974. Bill was enjoying his latest job, working in a juice bar in the subway station downstairs from the Chicago Public Library, when on a break he noticed a small ad in the *Chicago Sun-Times* for a puppeteer company based in Skokie, Illinois. Bill had no experience with nor any particular interest in life-sized puppets and marionettes, but what appealed to him was that sorcerous phrase that leapt from the newspaper page in a Kerouac-like epiphany: *travel required soon.*

Bill: "I had been nowhere."

So twenty-six-year-old Bill could travel the country with a wandering puppet show and pick up three hundred balloons a week for the privilege. The organizers promised Bill that the troupe would traverse widely, starting in St. Louis and swinging through Chicago and the Midwest and then Hollywood and through the South. "The show required about ten puppeteers up on tiers, way up high on the scaffolding, and they literally needed a tall guy because the cross-unders—a short girl with her puppet, say—would be going under me," Bill says. "After a week of rehearsing they thought it would be pretty copacetic, so I went on the road with them."

Bill went as far north as Canada and as far south as Texas with the marionette troupe. He couldn't have predicted such a sprawling journey upon arriving for his second stay at Chicago. "We'd do two, three shows a day, package plans with schools, so we'd get all the kids coming. It was a beautiful show, with life-size marionettes, great prerecorded music and dialogue, over a hundred characters of all kinds. Trees came to life. It was all very magical. The parents just loved it. Then I became one of the drivers, for which I got paid even more money." (In later years on the road with the Fleshtones, Bill would get great kicks out of pointing out to his bandmates the various towns and venues in which his troupe performed.)

This theatrical tour lasted about a year. In August of 1975 Bill was again out of work, but had earned a hard-won and permanent glint in his eye. The seeds of his future infamous, roustabout lifestyle might well be traced to this country-traveling company of puppeteers, for which Bill could drift into the background yet contribute professionally and dig the scene all the while. Bill had seen the swollen country and he was glad. In giddy recklessness, he let go of his huge $140-a-month apartment in the Lincoln Park neighborhood of Chicago—one of the man's few regrets—and returned to Troy. One evening while strolling the neighborhood he ran into his old friend Gary Burke, who was now living in the East Village in New York City. Burke was involved with a loose theater group that leased the Wonderhorse Theater from playwright Edward Albee's producers, putting on shows and renting out the theater, all pretty low-maintenance; they happened to be looking for a jack-of-all-trades for the building, someone who could run the box office or paint or wear the janitor's uniform or do just about anything else that came up.

What do you think?" Gary asked Bill.

stily, Bill packed up his clothes, books, and drums and fol-
Burke down to the rake-hell wildness of New York City late in
st of 1975, arriving at about the same time that Keith and Marek
moved into The House over the river in Queens and found guitars in
their basement.

The Wonderhorse Theater stood near the Bowery across from the
LaMama experimental theater on East Fourth Street between Second and Third Avenues. The theater productions ran the gamut from
staged readings to full-blown performances, and Bill happily settled
in upstairs. He became the go-to-guy, the poor-man's everyman,
doing everything from replacing light bulbs to talking to the fire
department when they'd waltz in and pronounce, *Now this ain't
legal*, to going down to the Department of Buildings and searching
old blueprints. Burke's group rented out the theater to smaller, electric theatrical groups that didn't have a space of their own, or that
had so much going on that they needed a spillover space (such as Circle in the Square). In doing so the group managed to scrape together just enough money for the lease. Over the years actors and performers from Danny Aiello to struggling unknowns to Divine would
grace the theater's footlights. "Wonderhorse was a cheap alternative
to the expense of Broadway or Off-Broadway. It was spectacular living there," says Bill. But because there was only so much that Off-
Off-Broadway could charge patrons, eventually the Wonderhorse
would close because of the electric bill: so much power was being
used, from stage lights to the air conditioner, that the commercial
rate became murderous.

Bill would live at the Wonderhorse Theater—rent-free and wide-
eyed—for years. Indeed, Lucky Bill would live in New York City for
the next thirty years and accomplish something singularly amazing:
he would never sign a lease.

"One of the big casualties of the Vietnam War was that music had
become serious," Bill laments. "I don't mean that there weren't good
bands, but it was hard for them to get to the top with the serious, revolutionary music that was going on there. It had to pertain to the times.

"Fun music was a casualty."

Most of what was going on in popular music Bill happily ignored.
"I really hated the music," he remembers. "Some things *were* happening, spin-offs from the Yardbirds and everything, but I didn't
enjoy the tone of the radio and the DJ. It was very intellectual and
getting serious, and it wasn't the fun that I remembered. The only

thing that I could see about music was the way that it represented the political climate of the time, with the Jefferson Airplane, the Volunteers, the now-violent Rolling Stones. I liked music that supported whatever my beliefs were, but it certainly wasn't any *fun.* Sly and the Family Stone was a fun one, and the MC5 crossed the bridge of fun and radical; they were very fun to play at parties. That was quite an accomplishment." Bill recalls blasting "Kick Out the Jams" in the dorms simply to scare visiting parents on homecoming weekend: *Come see where your daughter's living!*

By the time Bill arrived in New York City, the street-rock revolution was stirring literally around the corner from the Wonderhorse, but Bill wasn't particularly interested in the Bowery scene. He'd sneak down to CBGB's, peer into the darkness, and say to himself, *Holy shit, I don't fit in here!* Bill joined the Musician's Union, and from late 1976 to the spring of 1977 scored a gig drumming for *Nightclub Cantata,* a musical at the Village Gate. Then things got lucrative pretty quickly. Bill kept super busy, able to earn a living as a professional drummer in a variety of jobs. He played in the production of *Agamemnon* (one of the Greek trilogies staged at the Delacorte Theater in Central Park) and, again through the help and connections of his friend Gary Burke, started playing in local cabaret bands. Burke had been playing drums with Andrea Morkovici at Reno Sweeney's at East Thirteenth Street between Sixth and Seventh Avenues, one of the more popular and hip cabaret clubs in the city. Reno's was an old-fashioned class joint where celebrities like Walter Cronkite, Lilly Tomlin, Shirley Maclaine, and Liza Minelli, redolent in dress suits or gowns, could saunter in to enjoy a show and make the society pages. One evening Donovan came up and danced onstage as Bill played feet behind him. Bill from Troy was starstruck.

Burke had gotten too busy with the theater and other engagements and asked Bill to audition with Morkovici and possibly sit in. Soon there were musicians dropping in at Reno Sweeney's who needed drummers. They'd see tall, handsome Bill playing and keeping impressive clock-rhythm and ask him if he would consider playing with them. "Soon I was playing there constantly," Bill remembers. "In fact, in the summer of 1977 I played there every night except Monday, from Memorial Day to Labor Day! The money was coming in like you can't believe: checks from Delacorte Theater, checks from the *Cantata,* and then playing every night at Reno Sweeney's. The first couple months I had to pay all of $150 a month for my room, but then I started staying rent-free. I really started socking it away and saving money."

Sweat

The Fleshtones and Bill were regionally close during this period. The evening that the Fleshtones were playing their second-ever gig at CBGB's, Bill was ten blocks away playing at Reno's. One night a couple of years later, Peter and some of his cheeky SVA buddies dropped in to check out Holly Woodlawn at Reno's and soak up some post-Warhol glitter. Bill was playing drums that night. He and Peter didn't meet, but many years later Bill remembers "a bunch of people who were sort of like wise-ass hipsters! They stood out, because everyone else at Reno got dressed up." (For his part, Peter remembers nothing of that evening spent drinking heavily. "I was carried out of the club," he says. "Actually, out of the bathroom. Then, out of the club.")

Seemingly overnight, things began to change for Bill. Near the end of 1979 the city, burdened by countless noise complaints, came down with new and strenuous rules about cabaret. "It could get loud with the crowds in there," Bill laments. "Shows ended at 2AM. The neighbors hated it. There were always problems." Around the same time that the Fleshtones and other bands were being muscled out of Club 57 for making too much noise, Bill too found himself the victim of volume. It was just as well. After three years, the theater and cabaret weren't so new and exciting to Bill anymore. He had wished that the money could have drifted in for longer, but he was really getting into something more important that would hopefully be a lot of fun at the same time.

Shortly after running into Bill at Bruno's, the Fleshtones decided to give him a shot. As Marek had been the most sensitive to Lenny's playing, he was duly dispatched to spy on Bill at a gig. Bill had recently been playing with the Harry Toledo Band, but at the time of his run-in with Marek and Keith at the Stage he had graduated to Derby, a synth New Wave band that bordered on Cars/Gary Numan territory. Marek showed up one night, sat at a table, and mentally played along as he watched Bill. "Derby was not memorable," Marek smiles. "Kinda quirky, kinda mean, pretty boring. But I watched Bill and I thought, *He's got that timing, that rhythm, the drive and the spark.*" Marek reported back to Peter and Keith, who told Marek to give Bill a call.

The band was auditioning drummers at their new rehearsal space. Moving on from the muck and mire of Billy Piano's, they'd relocated thirty blocks north into the infamous Hell's Kitchen neighborhood and the celebrated Music Building at 584 Eighth Avenue, a block below the Port Authority bus station. The landlords of this enormous, gray industrial building rented rooms at twenty-four-hour-availability to bands and musicians with enough dough. For the next couple of years, the Fleshtones would ride the freight elevator with, among other musicians and performers, a struggling and unknown Madonna. The band moved into Room 401 early in the year. Until the end of the decade, that room would become the site of not only high-spirited rehearsals, demo recordings, and songwriting sessions, but blowout parties, impromptu performances, and pre-production for albums, and it would serve as a desperate place to live for more than one band member.

Bill was more than a half a decade older than the other guys, and he impressed them immediately with his chops, his discipline, and his professional history. He channeled the exuberance of rock & roll drummers with the steady propulsive rhythms of Stax/Volt house drummers, filtered through the chops and old-school sensibility of Gene Krupa. All of Bill's influences nearly collapsed under the weight of Dave Clark. "I saw most of [the Dave Clark Five] shows as an underaged lad in upstate New York," Bill recalled. "I remember Dave Clark going on with his drums and starting the beat, and each guy in the band would come out and the place would go crazy." At rehearsal, Keith, a former drummer, studied Bill closely. "He was very good," Keith remembers. "Also it occurred to me that the guy's really tall and good looking—and a few months later my girlfriend at that time was looking at him and saying, *God, he's so handsome. He looks like a Hollywood star!* So that's how we got Bill into the band. If Marek and I had been talking about something else at that lunch counter, he might never had joined."

The Fleshtones debuted their new drummer at an unannounced gig at Maxwell's in early May. They played a dozen songs that night, including a new tune they threw together with Bill called "Feel the Heat," on which the former cabaret drummer could work up a sweat with super-fast Latin fills. Bill had had only the band's lively but purposeful rehearsals through which to gauge their onstage possibilities, and he was positively blown away by the energy that the band ratcheted up at Maxwell's. The group hadn't played out in nearly five months and they discharged their pent-up, powerful *joi de vivre* in front of a delirious crowd who had been waiting for the return of their favorite dance band. Behind his ageless 1964 Ludwig kit "Mr. Pro" blinked through the increasing sweat on his brow as Peter, Keith, and Marek threw themselves into each song with a tighter urgency than the last, yearning to channel rock & roll spirit and to again connect with a crowd. At the end of the brief set, Bill stood up with a final flourish and, beaming and dripping sweat in front of a roaring crowd, realized, *This is my new band and I love 'em!* Bill's first proper New York City show was May 9 at Danceteria, a venue at which the Fleshtones were the first band to play. The show, hailed in the *Soho News* as "the long-awaited return of prodigal garage-rockers the Fleshtones," was a rollicking success—the Fleshtones hit the stage at 4AM and tore the joint up—and marked the first time that Bill would play with the Spaeth brothers. The Fleshtones would be a big hit at Danceteria for the next couple of years.

For the boys it felt like the ship might be righted. Bill was officially in the band and he provided not only his eclectic and committed professional background but a dependable and effortless *man's-man* camaraderie, not to mention a love and capacity for drink that would prove legendary over the years. Bill was a good-time Charlie, his laid-back, smiling manner and dashing good looks providing the missing ingredient in the Fleshtones' simmering stew. The fellas would soon be clutching hands onstage and bowing before his drum set while Bill grinned in amusement.

The mythmaking, hit-making West Coast would soon come calling. Within months the band would begin a five-year journey with an influential major record label that would test the limits of their charm, their songwriting, their performing, and their career-damaging celebration of the traditional and the obscure. Would the Fleshtones fit in the American landscape?

11

Up-Front, Left Behind

The son of a C.I.A. agent, Miles Copeland viewed the world as a whirlwind blur of intelligence and opportunity. While his father was assigned as bureau chief to a Middle Eastern office in Lebanon, Miles and his younger brothers, Ian and Stewart, indulged their interest in music. By the mid-seventies, Miles and Stewart had each earned helpful experience in the music business, Miles as a producer and manager, Stewart as a drummer in Curved Air. After moving to London they began sensing the rumblings of a musical revolution, and Stewart formed a band that, after a name change or three, became the Police. Miles, always more interested in the marketing and production aspects of popular music, offered to manage the band. Unable to secure a U.K. label, Miles, then as now sublimely ambitious and confident, decided to launch his own label, which he called Illegal Records. The label's 1978 debut single of the Police sold in excess of seventy thousand copies, a fantastic number for an independent release. Emboldened, Miles branched out and inaugurated other U.K. labels, including Deptford Fun City and Total Noise.

In the late seventies the success of Stiff Records and the explosion of the Sex Pistols encouraged both American and English labels to take punk rock more seriously. Los Angeles–based A&M Records had become, along with Motown and Buddha, one of the most successful indie labels in popular music; encouraging and nurturing independent and unorthodox acts, A&M turned its attention to New Wave after being burned by the Pistols, who A&M had signed but then as quickly dropped due to the band's controversy (Johnny Rotten's band soon inked with Warner Brothers). In 1979, Miles struck up a deal with A&M to manufacture and distribute his records, asking for higher back-end royalties rather than higher up-front advances, and the partnership would thrive until the mid-eighties. Copeland called the new label I.R.S. and, as he still lived in England for much of the year, hired Jay Boberg, a bright young promotions man already employed at A&M, to run the American operations.

The original concept of I.R.S. was to plant an independent-label umbrella under which Copeland would distribute a wide range of indie and import records. Although some labels had already pioneered such a conglomeration—including JEM Records out of New Jersey, through which Marty Thau had hoped to distribute Fleshtones releases—the major label affiliation with A&M rocketed I.R.S. through the music industry ranks and helped the label to become a major player throughout the decade. By the end of 1979, Copeland had signed the Buzzcocks and was honing in on Oingo Boingo and a new, raw all-girl band out of Los Angeles called the Go-Go's. Copeland was looking for talent and scouring new indie releases in his office one afternoon when he happened to play *2X5*, which had kicked up buzz and good reviews in America and London. Copeland loved "Shadow Line" immediately, and he felt that the Fleshtones had an indefinable energy that Jimmy Destri had caught well. More important, he felt that the band might be commercial. He asked around and learned of the band's live reputation. Their kind of amped bravura, if backed by infectious and solid songwriting, might be marketable.

Meanwhile, armed with Bill Milhizer and flush with stability, the guys were searching for viable, dependable management. Jimmy Destri introduced the band to Bruce Patron, a self-described "hippie carpenter" from the Berkshires woods who moved to New York City in 1976. He had been a roadie for the Runaways and then a tour manager for INXS and Blondie, traveling the world with Debbie Harry and company as they rode the crest of *Heart of Glass.* "I was marketing to the Fleshtones that I was a big-time rock guy with major connections," Patron chuckles. More impressive than Patron's pedigree was his firm, passionate belief in, and love of, unpretentious rock & roll—Patron too was raised on the music of *Nuggets.* His distaste for the kind of British art rock exemplified by Yes and Emerson, Lake, and Palmer, or any band that earnestly attempted to turn rock & roll into a high art form, appealed to the guys.

"The Fleshtones were a cool band," Patron says. "There was no 'hipper than thou' thing with them. It was a great sound, a timeless sound which still sounds cool. And they were hardcore working-class kids. I thought that was a cool rock & roll thing." Patron felt that the Fleshtones were essentially complete: his goal was to try and sell as many records for this exciting young band as he could. (Patron did make some subtle suggestions: "My one vision was that Peter should work a little bit harder at singing on mike live. He was all over the place.") Intuiting that the band's fantastic live shows should complement a well-produced studio album, Paton began looking to increase the group's visibility and success on the road, to move them beyond the provincial New York-Boston-Philadelphia-Washington, D.C., axis, and quickly signed them to F.B.I., Ian Copeland's national booking agency. Patron ultimately had visions of breaking the Fleshtones in Los Angeles, as he felt that their music had much more of a trippy LA vibe than an ironic East Coast vibe.

Extended visits to the West Coast would wait for the time being. Patron wanted to get the band a recording contract as soon as possible, and through Ian Copeland he made contact with Miles, who made his interest in the band known. Before the fellas knew what was happening Patron was on the phone daily to Los Angeles negotiating a deal with I.R.S. By Memorial Day, most of the finer points were in place. The Fleshtones were initially suspicious of the upstart I.R.S. label, despite their new manager's confidence. Having been burned by the Red Star experience, and genuinely if naively feeling that, after four years of increasing popularity they were a big band deserving of a contract with a Sire or a Columbia Records, the guys— Peter especially—were hesitant to sign with Copeland's new independent music label, despite the Police's growing success. "Peter Zaremba is a very cautious person," Patron says.

However, Keith was impressed with Copeland's business acumen and commonsensical approach to exposing a new band. Keith began taking a responsible interest in the band's industry maneuverings and finances at this early stage, a regard that would by necessity blossom into managerial expertise by the end of the eighties. "The Copelands realized that how to break America was on the grass roots level," Keith says. "Getting out there and spending as little money as you can to get the band seen in as many different places as you can, and getting as many different journalists to come out and see the band as you can. It would mean not traveling in tour buses, maybe sharing the same bed. They realized this was a way to break a band and to get people's attention. The Police had already gone through America traveling in a van—just the three of them, a roadie, and their equipment—and this had started to work."

Particularly appealing to the Fleshtones was Copeland's offer to include them in a movie project then brewing at I.R.S.'s parent label. Michael White, a London producer of stage shows and films, including *Rocky Horror Picture Show* and *Rude Boy*, envisioned a filmed "music war" of New Wave bands battling across the spectrum of style and aesthetic but common to raw, frill-free energy. White was familiar with Ian and Miles in England and convinced them to come aboard the project as creative consultants; White then approached Gil Friesen, president of A&M Records, who suggested that the Copelands take more substantive roles. Ian, with the help of interested promoters, subsequently agreed to book nearly all of the bands for various U.S. performances while Miles would bring several other bands together with the Police for concerts in England and France. Director Derek Burbidge was hired to film each and every performance. To the Fleshtones, the project sounded similar to the M-80 Festival only with greater (literal) exposure, solid financing, and international distribution. Copeland was calling the film *Urgh!* and he pledged to slot the Fleshtones in with the dizzying array of fellow bands, from the Police, Wall of Voodoo, and the Go-Go's to Steel Pulse, XTC, and Echo and the Bunnymen.

Within weeks, the band started to feel the buzz generated by Copeland's interest and enthusiasm, and his major label alliance only intensified their reborn optimism. They surrendered happily to the Copelands' ambitious logistical know-how. "Recording for I.R.S. was gonna make the Fleshtones a national band," Keith says. "Everything was coordinated between Ian and Miles as far as where a record was released when, and Ian would then book the band into whatever territory Miles required to promote the record. I was already reading about the Copelands in the major music magazines. People were gonna hear about us. We were gonna play all over the United States, and we were gonna be in a movie."

Keith admired the Copeland brothers' fiscal frugality. "They really tightened the budget on a lot of things," he remembers. "Up to the time of the Ramones signing with Sire, the record industry was about big budgets, bloated spending, money being dumped into garbage cans. The Copelands spent more money on marketing and promotion. The whole idea was to get into a studio and get the job done quickly and efficiently, but to come out with quality tracks. And the publishing end of it was good for us too: we kept our publishing. That's what I.R.S. Records was all about. That's what this contract was about." The Fleshtones decided to sign.

Thau was surprised when Peter and Keith made it known to him, in the their vague and oblique manner, that they were severing their ties with Red Star. "I.R.S. was already on the scene, although they didn't tell me that," Thau remembers. "It happened too quickly for there not to have been something underway when we were separating." Thau was bothered by the hazy way that Peter and Keith abandoned him and his future plans for the band, the two Queens mates hemming and hawing, looking down at their pointy boots on Fifty-seventh Street one afternoon as Thau pressed them as to why they were leaving Red Star. "The Peter and Keith good cop/bad cop thing annoyed me," Thau says. "I thought that Keith was to blame, but Peter is actually the mastermind to the whole thing."

By the spring of 1980, the two-year experiment with Thau was finished. "They never trusted me. They had stars in their eyes," Thau says. "I was already at that point disgusted enough with the loss of my funding that I just felt, *Fuck it. I'm not gonna try to convince anyone of anything.* Their biggest problem was their lack of information, and a sense of independence that went a little bit too far for their own good. They're just victims of not being able to trust anyone."

Thau adds, "From time to time I would hear comments from people saying that *Blast Off!* was the best record, or one of the best records, that the Fleshtones ever did. And recently, I said to Keith that the record is perfect despite its imperfections, that its imperfections make it perfect."

Keith's response? "He said, *Yeah, we understand that now.*"

Though their dealings with Thau were strained, the Fleshtones, flush from signing with Copeland, agreed to play at a 2X5 showcase at Irving Plaza in June. Cofeatured on the bill were the four other bands from the compilation, the order of performance democratically determined by drawing lots. Tim Sommer covered the show for *Trouser Press* and was uniformly unimpressed by all of the bands except the Fleshtones, who played "one of the strongest and most exciting sets I've seen by an American band this year. Their pounding snarl-rock is in the tradition of the greatest American Primitives;

they are logical successors to the Stooges, Raiders and Dolls, bashing around the stage with a conviction and adrenaline level rare on this side of the Atlantic. What they were doing on the same stage with these other limp bands is beyond me."

Armed with that final kiss-off, the Fleshtones bid *adieu* to Marty Thau and Red Star Records. They were on their way to Sha-La-La La land.

The Fleshtones spent the summer of 1980 writing and rehearsing songs in the Music Building, getting the kinks out of "Theme from 'The Vindicators,'" "Feel the Heat," Titus Turner's "All Around the World," and new originals "Cold, Cold Shoes," "Hophead," and "The Girl from Baltimore." The latter was a Strangeloves-esque, energetic dance-of-the-month tune that Peter had high hopes for. At F.B.I., Ian Copeland booked three shows for the band in addition to the *Urgh!* gig in August: Hurrah on July 9, a triumphant return engagement at Danceteria on the 25th with new labelmates the Go-Go's (a show in front of a packed crowd that wouldn't begin until 4 AM), and the Ritz on August 13. Bruce Patron encouraged the band to shore up their energies for a September visit to Malibu, California, where they were booked at the Shangri-La Studio to record a five-song EP for I.R.S.

They needed a producer, someone who could capture on tape the energy, spontaneity, and spirit of the Fleshtones' sound. Patron's cousin had introduced him to twenty-six-year-old Paul Wexler, a budding LA producer who had done remixing for Allen Toussaint and production work for Van Morrison and Tin Huey. He'd also produced the Go-Go's successful debut single, "We Got the Beat," and had credibility on the indie rock scene. But there was more about Wexler that intrigued the Fleshtones: he is the son of Jerry Wexler, who, while at Atlantic Records in the 1940s, 50s, and 60s, helmed the sound board with Ahmet "Sultan of Rock" Ertegun for some of the greatest and most popular R&B and soul music ever recorded, from Lavern Baker, Ray Charles, and Clyde McPhatter to Joe Turner, Wilson Pickett, and Aretha Franklin. The Fleshtones were excited about their new producer, and only hoped that "Son of Jerry" might replicate his father's warm, fat, soulful sound and meld it with their garage and psychedelic leanings. This was an honest desire on the part of the band. It was hugely unfair to Wexler.

In addition to recording the EP, Patron's plan for the band was to book them in clubs in and around the LA area so that they could be seen onstage, not be judged merely by one 45 single and two tracks from a meekly distributed compilation LP. Patron hoped that they'd make a splash with local critics and fans, and in September booked the band into the infamous Tropicana Hotel on Santa Monica Boulevard, the first of the band's many visits to the "Rock & Roll Hotel" that since the late sixties had housed some of the most notorious musicians and artists in the business, from the Doors to Andy Warhol, and their telltale libidinous and crazed behavior. Over the next several years, the Trop would become the Fleshtones' home away from home when they visited Los Angeles, and the band's regional reputation was borne as much from the legendary parties they threw in their hotel rooms as from sweating up a storm onstage.

Some earlier commitments needed to be met first. On August 21, Derick Burbridge arrived in New York with film crews in tow to lens acts for the *Urgh!* movie at CBGB's and the Ritz. The Fleshtones were slotted to play their first show at the Bowery venue in well over a year. Ian Copeland pronounced hopefully (and accurately) that "the acts that we've got are not what's happening right now, but what's going to be happening over the next ten years." Burbridge filmed the Fleshtones following two support bands, Human Switchboard and Dirty Looks, before a surprisingly smallish crowd at CBGB's, given the hype and promotion drummed up by A&M and F.B.I. Although they were dismayed at having to play at CBGBs, where odd feelings between management and the band lingered, the Fleshtones tore through a typically frenetic if necessarily brief set, Peter doing nothing to indicate that he'd taken to heart Patron's advice to stay more on mike. In the *Soho News*, Ira Kaplan called the band's performance "superb," and John Buckley raved that it was "sublime," that "if this movie, F.B.I. or I.R.S. [does] something for The Fleshtones . . . then the Copelands deserve a certain degree of canonization." *Urgh!* was released in 1981 with an accompanying double-album soundtrack, for which the Fleshtones contributed "Shadow Line." (A version of Little Richard's "Dancing All Around the World," also recorded and mixed, didn't make the final cut.)

Ian Copeland himself lobbed an encouraging, if backhanded, compliment toward the Fleshtones as they prepared for Los Angeles: "Some of the bands on *Urgh!* are definitely a long shot, but who but us is convinced the Fleshtones are going to be huge?"

In September of 1980, the Fleshtones flew to LA for a ten-day stay. Though excited to be in the same town as the Whiskey-a-Go-Go, the Capitol Records tower, and Phil Spector's mansions, the guys felt like pasty-faced aliens visiting from the homey grime of New York, driving down anonymous, bleached highways, shielding their eyes from an enormous sun that never shut off. They certainly dug their glimpses of the nascent music scene: X, Los Lobos, the Blasters, the Plimsouls, the Unclaimed, the Leaving Trains, Wall of Voodoo, and other bands were forming, or would soon, circulating and playing area clubs, recording and releasing cheap independent records, and brewing a homespun culture of honest rock & roll.

But the guys couldn't rub the East Coast off of their skin; they'd been tattooed by New York's steel and smear. "I hated being in Los Angeles," Peter says. "It was appalling, an amorphous mess of suburban sprawl, like some endless Long Island with palm trees and taco stands instead of wholesome Carvel stores, hopelessly cut off from East Coast trends. The endless driving was like passing through the arteries of some kind of colossal, smog-filled jellyfish beached on the desert shores of California. Everything reminded me of *C.H.I.P.S.* or some other TV show that I despised." This wasn't Peter's first exposure to the gold coast. When he was seven, his father had driven the family out to Los Angeles, on and off the original Lincoln Highway, in a brief and fruitless search for work, and the family had resided in Los Angeles County for the entire summer. "It really socked it to me," Peter remembers of that stay. "Before that I thought everyone was the same, and that we were like everyone else. My idea of the world was from television. I thought I was Beaver in *Leave It to Beaver* and so was everyone else. Then out in LA I began to realize that we were immigrants, that my parents spoke with accents, that my father drove a truck, and that the rest of America wasn't like us." Peter carried this lingering, blue-collar, outsider status with him to Los Angeles nearly two decades later.

Though the Fleshtones had been together for four years, they'd had very little experience in recording studios beyond Thau and Destri's brief tenures turning knobs. "We were still not really sure how to make records," Keith says. "We knew what records we liked and we knew what we wanted to sound like, groups like the Strangeloves and the Honeycombs, things that are very wild-sounding, percussive-sounding. We loved tambourines, maracas, wild rock & roll, things like Richard Gottehrer would've done. At this point, we're a rave-up band with a Stax/Volt-feel horn section, and we brought Brian and Gordon, the Action Combo, out there with us to make this record. We think, *Well, this guy Wexler has had success with the Go-Go's. He's on the map. He wants to do us. He's Jerry Wexler's son. He must've learned something about the records his father made.*"

The band's instincts could not have been more wrongheaded. The taint of the disappointing recording experience with Wexler has stayed with the band to this day, a nagging reminder of shared culpability, woeful mistakes, miscommunication, rushed concessions, and continent-sized naiveté. "Wexler was an okay guy," admits Bill. "He was sort of new at it. We were probably a hard band to produce, being new at it and being conscious of being from New York with our own ideas. We were sort of ready to have a little punk attitude about it, almost like, 'Anything *you* say might be bullshit!'" Keith felt a bad vibe at the studio instantly. "Wexler had *nothing* to do with his father. If anything, what Wexler was trying to do was to make records *not* sound like his father. He's in the shadow of Jerry Wexler, so he rebels." The Fleshtones, Keith feels, "were basically his vehicle to rebel."

Nearly a quarter century down the line, Paul Wexler bristles at Keith's notion. "That's the stupidest thing I've ever heard in my life," Wexler says. "Anyone who knows anything about my life knows that my whole life has been spent trying to get *closer* to my father, not rebelling against him. Because you're not a clone of your parent and their taste, you're rebelling against him? That's a very odd idea to me. My father doesn't get reggae, he doesn't get rap music, he doesn't get Jimi Hendrix. Am I supposed to reject those things because they're not within his field of comprehension? If people want of clone of Jerry, my advice is to call Jerry! Which, of course, the Fleshtones couldn't afford."

Wexler feels deep regret now at helming the Shangri-La sessions and points to issues relative to the recording situation that were deeply problematic. "*Up-Front* was the only record I did as a producer where I didn't see the band live before I did the recording," he says. "I pleaded and begged with the manager. I said, 'I don't know what your band is like!' As soon as we got in the studio, I thought, *This was a mistake.* Zaremba was sulking from moment one. He was like, *I don't wanna do this.*" A big point of contention between the band and Wexler involved the Spaeth brothers. Brian and Gordon had been making walk-on appearances with the band for over a year now, and their raw, honking horns were meshing with the overall sound of the band, contributing a sorely needed R&B thrust. Peter had written "The Theme from 'The Vindicators'" precisely with the brothers' driving sax sound in mind, and the band wanted their ballsy, brassy riffs on the new record. But Wexler and engineer Jerry Napier unilaterally hired a session horn player for the recording. Bill remembers Wexler saying, "It's up to you guys. Do you want to get radio airplay or do you *not* want to get radio airplay?" *Of course we want to get radio airplay*, the band thought, *but this is the way we sound*. The uncredited horn player was hired and put clean and bright overdubbed parts onto some tracks, including "The Girl from Baltimore," Copeland's chosen single to compete on the charts with Steely Dan's "Hey Nineteen" and John Lennon's "(Just Like) Starting Over."

"We liked that Brian and Gordon sounded rough," Keith remembers. "We wanted to sound raw. We didn't want it to be jazzy. But Wexler and Napier bring in a studio LA 'cat' who does all the horn sections track by track. He's not listed on the sleeve. We didn't acknowledge his existence! I hated his guts, but it's not his fault. What did he know? Really, it was Paul and Napier. They were like a team. They were terrible. They're not fun, and they ruin rock & roll. They have no idea what it is, and they should've never have been involved in it. That's what I think of these people. What fools!" (Brian and Gordon play on "The Theme from 'The Vindicators,'" which interjected an amateurishness and ragged sound to that high-energy instrumental.)

Wexler rightly refuses to take full blame for the *Up-Front* sessions. "I listen to 'The Vindicators' and 'The Girl from Baltimore' and they sound great to me," says Wexler. "If those songs don't suck, then why did the sessions suck? Because the band fucking sulked!" Wexler, who somewhat condescendingly referred to Peter as "Boy Genius" throughout the sessions, recalls a moment at the studio when a distracted and pouting Peter began doodling on some Zig Zag rolling paper, relettering the Zs into "Zaremba," idly messing around, wasting time when he should have been focused and committed to recording. "Bruce Patron is looking at [Zaremba], and then Patron looks at me and shakes his head," Wexler recalls. "When we were away from the band, Patron told me, 'That's how he is.' I didn't want any of this, so I took Zaremba aside about halfway through the session and said, "Look, we're doing this now, so if you sulk through it, your performance and the record are really gonna suck. If you don't try, it's not gonna be any good.' And he started trying harder at that point. He gave the 'Girl from Baltimore' vocal after that and I think we came away with a couple of good performances." If Wexler had had his way, the Fleshtones would've been produced live in New York City in a big studio room facing bleachers full of handpicked audience members. "Every project should be run by the needs of the project, not the needs of the label, producer, or the band," Wexler says. "But I allowed myself to be pushed around. And the band has a right to be mad, because I did fall down on the job by letting myself be talked into that. Most of that EP should've been shit-canned and rerecorded—I'll be the first to admit it—but some of it shouldn't." The fault, Wexler feels, "didn't totally lie on our side of the board."

Peter and Keith regret that Wexler's goal seemed to be replicating the Knack's "My Sharona," the cleanly recorded power-pop classic that had been a *Billboard* number one smash the year before. "Think about New Wave records and the way they sounded," Keith offers. "They didn't sound like Motown records, they didn't sound like Phil Spector. They were very squashed, arid-sounding, dry-sounding, small-sounding. We're playing Wexler Rolling Stones records, we're playing him Strangeloves records. We went out there armed! We wanted to sound like these records we loved. We're talking about his father with him, and Stax/Volt, and we think that we're gonna make R&B-sounding records. And it was anything but that."

Wexler laughs: "If they wanted it to sound like an R&B record they should've gone to Muscle Shoals, not to Shangri-La."

The guys were suitably relieved when they moved into Phil Spector's famous Gold Star Studios—the site of many great Wall of Sound productions and where the Ramones had tracked the previous year—to briefly record in Spector's natural echo chamber (a process replaced industrywide, later in the decade, by digital manipulation). "Napier was a house engineer at Gold Star, and they were both inexpensive rooms where you could get a decent sound," Wexler explains. "There were budget considerations." The guys got off on playing at Gold Star, at least, even if they feel the band didn't take full advantage of the studio. Tracks were laid down relatively quickly, live in the studio with minimal overdubs, from roughly eleven in the morning to eleven at night. The band put to tape "The Girl from Baltimore," "Cold, Cold Shoes," "Feel the Heat," "The Theme from 'The Vindicators,'" and, in a curious exercise, the Rolling Stones' "Play with Fire." It had been Peter's brainstorm earlier in the year to record the B-side ballad as if the Stones had rocked the song up instead, as was often the case in the Stones' lengthy, organic songwriting process. But the end result was embarrassing. "We wanted to do 'All Around the World' but we felt that that was really the wrong song for Wexler," Keith admits. "If 'Play with Fire' had been produced well, it would've been a great idea. But working with Paul was very difficult."

"Listen to that fucking track ['Play with Fire']," Wexler exclaims. "It just doesn't sound like they mean it! If they're not into it, then why is it my fault? I was trying to accommodate them. It's like a car accident: both people want to get somewhere, and they end up not getting anywhere. I don't want to diss those guys, they're a good band. It does hurt me that *Up-Front* isn't what it could've been. It bothers the fuck out of me. I *am* angry. But I'm more mad at myself for making a beginner's mistake. I'm glad that they're still working. I'm not pissed off at them the way they have been at me."

The fact that the Fleshtones blame Wexler for how the record came out? Wexler says resignedly, "As a producer, you set yourself up for that."

The band soothed the arduous studio hours on their off days by soaking up the high sun poolside at the Tropicana, where they drank, relaxed, drank a lot more, and mingled with Nina Hagen and members of the Modettes and the Plasmatics. Not urgently required in the studio, Gordon was well-oiled for much of his stay, exhibiting the rough and unpredictable tendencies of his mercurial personality when booze-addled. "Gordon would go to the *nth* degree," Marek remembers of Gordon's road drinking. "We devised a profile that Gordon followed in how fucked up he was getting: there was *Gordon* and then there was *Gordon II*. Brian came into the room at the Trop and said, '*Gordon III* is with us this morning.'" The guys peered down at the pool and there was Gordon, beer in hand, cursing and muttering, wearing an incredible psychotic face. "He ended up sitting with Nina Hagen," Marek remembers. "She'd often be out there at daybreak in some monk's attire sitting by the pool or meditating, and Gordon would still be up from the night before and try to engage her in conversation. She was gracious, I'm sure."

Among the high points for the band was playing the Whiskey-a-Go-Go and the ON-Klub to packed, appreciative audiences, and a small tour up and down the coast with the Go-Go's. Afterward, backstage, the guys could only shake their heads at the obvious disparity between the vibe and energy with which they had just exploded and the anemic, generic rock & roll that they had recorded hours before in the studio. That aural gap would widen and narrow, widen and narrow throughout the band's checkered career.

Up-Front was recorded and mixed, the ten days were up, and the band returned to New York City at the end of the month. The cover of the EP was a memorable, purple-and-blue retro design of the four band members popping starlike from a burst, conceived by twenty-one-year-old Carlos Grasso, recently hired by I.R.S. and soon to become an enthusiastic supporter of the band and an important West Coast ally. On the back sleeve, the guys thanked Domingo

("Sam the Sham") Samudi and Larry Williams, two rock & rollers whom the band had hoped to channel in LA. The Fleshtones were unhappy with *Up-Front* and worried aloud about the commercial impact, but Patron urged them not to radio such dissatisfaction, to avoid blithely saying to people that they didn't like their own record.

Following a gig at Irving Plaza on October 10—at which the Fleshtones were billed as "I.R.S. Recording Artists" for the first time— Patron told the band that they'd been invited to record a radio show for a live satellite-beamed broadcast on the Radio France Network. Eager for more European exposure, the band happily agreed. On October 30 they assembled in Studio 12A at Manhattan's Acoustilog Studios in front of a handful of invited beer- and wine-drinking fans. The eleven-song, half-hour performance was a blast of smiles and shakes, as far aurally from Shangri-La Studio as possible. Indeed, the setup must have been what Paul Wexler had in mind in terms of the ideal way to record the Fleshtones. With one daredevil song crashing into another; with goofy Peter blowing harp and yelping and dancing and distilling the energy of the band and of rock & roll history into a fun and focussed frenzy; with Keith, Marek, and Bill as tight as humming wires, the Fleshtones firing on all cylinders were an untouchable rock & roll band, unafraid of looking or sounding nerdy or silly or uncool or mistake-prone, committed only to fun and connection. Tethered to headphones, they opened with an impossibly upbeat, skintight "American Beat" and closed with a sweaty "Little Latin Lupe Lu," in between offering a passionate "F-f-fascination," a sample of tunes from the *Blast Off!* and *Up-Front* sessions, a new, horn-driven original, "I'm Back," and a few blissful covers, including "All Around the World" and the Shadows of Knight's "Shake." As it turns out, this performance caused a stir among a certain rock & roll-loving segment of the Parisian audience who tuned in that night and laid the foundation down for rabid French enthusiasm that would culminate in a remarkable night at Le Palace in Paris two years later.

"We wish we did this one first!" said Peter moments before the band launched into "Little Latin Lupe Lu." Offering a sweaty, glad-handed thank you to the past, the Fleshtones were pouring it all out in the present. *Why couldn't our fuckin' record have sounded like this?*

Up-Front was released in November and reviews were generally positive. Those familiar with the band's live shows agreed that the Malibu studio had bleached out quite a bit of the band's raw energy. The band's first notice in venerable *Billboard* magazine was underwhelming: "basic rock 'n' roll with enthusiasm, feeling and enough competence to make it interesting. . . ." In the *New York Times*, Robert Palmer wrote that after *2X5* "it was a relief" to hear a Flesh-tones record full of "memorable" songs (despite the "rather ordinary version" of "Play with Fire"). "Apparently, the Fleshtones are aiming their music at the burgeoning dance-rock audience," Palmer wrote, "and if they can make a long-playing album that's as strong as most of *Up-Front*, they stand a good chance of capturing that audience."

In the *Village Voice*, Georgia Christgau complained that the record was "worse than nostalgia, it's retro," but in the *Daily News* an enthusiastic Bill Carlton wrote that "this is far and away the best record I've heard all day." (Two weeks later, Carlton urged his Christmas-shopping readers to spring the "delightful dance EP" on unsuspecting friends who might've have otherwise requested J. Geils Band's *Greatest Hits*.) The nationally distributed *Us Weekly* glossy also took note: in the "Don't Miss" column, next to items promoting the new Lou Reed and Dolly Parton releases, a review-er celebrated the Fleshtones' "fast-moving, strictly-for-fun EP." Accompanying the item was a prominent half-page shot from one of Bill's first photo shoots with the band. Bruce Patron and I.R.S. were spreading the word.

An anonymous reviewer in the *Blue Lunch* fanzine felt quite dif-ferent, the sheer bafflement of the notice reflecting the band's own disappointments. "Marty Thau and Jimmy Destri did much better jobs than the 'Corporate' Paul Wexler," the writer began testily, before trashing "a god-awful cover" of "Play with Fire," a "useless version with weak vocals." The writer continued, "Yep, I.R.S. have signed another group that they won't be able to market. This record will not sell nationally because The Fleshtones come across as a face-less, nondescript group. They don't deserve that." Unknowingly echoing Thau's wishes, the reviewer ended by imploring, "Go back to Red Star, guys, and be patient!" In England, the general response was similar. Remarked *Zig Zag*: "It's jaunty dancebang, indiscreet noise becoming ineffectual pop-blop, due to a lackluster perform-ance and a tired, effete production."

In Los Angeles, Miles Copeland had already voiced *his* opinion about *Up-Front*. He stared quietly at the acetate of the record as it played in his office, and then he stood up, strolled across the office, took the vinyl slab off the stereo, and threw it against the wall, smashing it into a half-dozen pieces.

This is not the Fleshtones!! he yelled. *What the fuck is this?!*

He called Paul Wexler and screamed at him. He called Bruce Patron and screamed at him, too. He told the two of them to go remix the goddamn record. *Do something!* he said. *This is not the band I signed!*

"I think they tried to remix it," says Keith. "But you can only do so much with how it was recorded. The record was done, the budget was blown, that was that. Miles was very disappointed. But he put it out. He believed."

12.
Roman Gods

We worked so hard on tours, Gordon remembers. *I was so tired when I came home that I stayed in bed for ten days. Sometimes there was no hotel, because there was none available or because mismanagement was rampant. But we developed such a sense of camaraderie. No matter what anyone says, when you go through things like what I went through with Bill, Peter, Keith, and Marek, you form a bond. It's almost like going through a war. I used to call it "campaigning." I consider myself very lucky, because it was like running with a bunch of outlaws. We were outside of society, we didn't have to take any crap from anybody, we could write any songs we wanted, we invented our own reality, we dressed the way we wanted, we didn't have to take orders from anybody, we didn't work regular jobs, and we were very good at what we did and at what we were supposed to do. What were we supposed to do? Show kids a good time, give a kid with some acne, a young teenage boy, the confidence to ask a girl next to him to dance. We brought a lot of happiness to peoples' lives.*

In December of 1980 I.R.S. and F.B.I. arranged for the Fleshtones' first national tour to commence to take advantage of the fresh EP and the positive word of mouth that the "The Girl from Baltimore" single might generate on radio. The Fleshtones played a few warm-up gigs opening for the Police, and on November 19 at Capitol Theatre in Passaic, New Jersey, were pelted by pennies and nickels from the large crowd impatient for the blond band riding high on the charts with "De Do Do Do, De Da Da Da." A week later, at Boston's Orpheum Theater, *Boston Globe* critic Jim Sullivan obviously felt different than the disdainful New Jersey patrons, describing the Fleshtones as "[b]rash and confident" and admiring how "[t]hey frequently threatened to careen out of control, but maintained touch." The Fleshtones wrapped up the year with an astonishing $10,000 payday at a New Year's Eve gig at Left Bank in Mount Vernon.

The *Up-Front* tour took them up and down the East Coast and back out to the Los Angeles area. Armed with the Action Combo for one of the final times, the Fleshtones piled in and out of vans, lugging gear, floating in beer, rocketing on cocaine, gagging down and sweating out hangovers, and learning to squeeze hours out of bleary mornings. Rehearsing the butt- and back-numbing chores of national touring that soon would become a decades-long blur of highways, hotel rooms, promoters, and interchangeable clubs, the band committed to testifying to the dash and brio of fun rock & roll for a country sometimes receptive, sometimes not. The Fleshtones were manifesting the relevance, or the irrelevance, of being a party band. During the next several years, management would send the tiring band out on many lengthy, grueling tours, hoping to promote and expose the band doing what they do best, sometimes without an album or a single to support. The guys were introduced to Americana embodied by long, lonely drives, highway rest areas, mom-and-pop restaurants, favorite girls in favorite cities, backstage coke and booze bacchanals, and the disorienting solitude of half-empty streets stumbled into after soundchecks. Hangover as Job Description.

"Forgotten Cities of a Failed Campaign," Gordon says ruefully now.

While Bill and I never really had steady girlfriends, between the two of us we pulled hundreds of women, some of them absolutely gorgeous, Gordon says. *Bill and I rarely returned to the band's hotel room. The women would pick us up and drive us home to their places. Mind you, this was before AIDS burst upon the scene. I remember waking up many early mornings next to some beautiful blond, and I'd always hear a distant train whistle. It was like a reminder that no woman could ever hold onto me, that I was chained to the highway and always bound for another town. It was too late for a normal life, too late for a steady girlfriend, because I*

*gambled with my life and I knew deep down inside that someday I'd
end up losing.*

Keith's memories of the first national tour are—at best—blurry.
"Beer. That's what comes to mind instantly. A lot of late nights, a lot
of lack of sleep, which at that time didn't seem to matter, a lot of very
over-the-top shows. Anything went from night to night, and the
show was totally changing, more free-form than ever; within each
song there was improvising." Response from the crowds, digging for
the first time the Fleshtones doing their thing, was wide-eyed and
panting and very encouraging.

Seven thousand feet above sea level, with Los Angeles and the
first small West Coast tour behind them, the Fleshtones approached
the infamous Donner Pass, where in the winter of 1846–47 migrat-
ing immigrant settlers suffered death at the brutal hands of Mother
Nature when snow closed the pass and the travellers were forced to
eat their dead companions to survive. The Fleshtones were blessed
with their first management-provided driver, who steadied the van
into increasing white-out blizzard conditions, but were nonetheless
wary of the elements and the sick history of those mountains. As
darkness fell, the guys started partying like mad, when out of
nowhere an enormous owl with a four-foot wingspan smashed into
the windshield. "It bounced off into the night and was gone," Marek
remembers. "We felt terrible, like we'd offended the Gods or something." Was it an omen?

The van continued to creep nervously through the wintry night of
the Sierra Nevada mountains. The guys were anxious now, but restless and increasingly drunk. "We've run out of jokes and we've run out
of alcohol," Gordon remembers. Somebody at some point, crazed with
boredom and fear, shouts, *Shut up, you motherfucker! Oh yeah, what
are you gonna do about it?!* And soon the guys are having a wrestling
match in the van, six guys on top of a thousand pounds of equipment.
The roughhousing quickly became excitable and contentious. Brian
Spaeth—who the guys had dubbed "Man Mountain Spaeth"—became,
despite his prized Valium score, the center of the scrum. "We're fighting, a donnybrook going on in the back of the van, a slugfest," Marek
laughs. "The roads were getting more and more filled with snow and
the traffic's slowing down, and we're finding that we're behind the
snowplows that have to open up the pass. At some point, a herd of
deer cuts off our travel. We're talking, like, seven to ten deer leaping
across the road in front of the van, and we have to hit the brakes. And
now the temperature is down to minus twenty."

At some point, Keith decided to turn and attack his childhood buddy. Marek wrestled with Keith and put him in a bear hug, and to try and break out of it Keith leapt to his feet and headbutted the window out of the van. "The whole window explodes and Keith's head goes through it," Marek remembers. "Everything comes to a screeching halt and we have to pull to the side of the road. We're up thousands of feet, it's twenty below zero, and we've got to drive the van. So we have our little tool kit, a black suitcase full of junk, and in there is bailing wire and gaffer's tape and all the things that you need. Out comes this spare bass drum head and we gaffer tape it over the widow. It doesn't really keep the van warm—we've got our coats on— but it keeps it from getting too bad. We weren't able to replace the window for the next week pretty much. We drove with the drum head over the side window for a week." The boys soothed their nerves the next day at Reno, hedging their bets against losses large and small.

Meanwhile, *Up-Front* wasn't selling, and the signs were ominous. On the day that the EP was released, the debut B-52's album went gold.

After a brief break from the tour, the band once again piled into a van, this time to head way down south. Lingering in the melancholy hangover of John Lennon's murder in New York, they indulged themselves down Highway 95 with beer, whiskey, and tape after tape of vintage James Brown.

Peter Buck, a young guitarist and vinyl collector in Athens, Georgia, worked in an indie record store, and there he found *Up-Front* and "A Girl from Baltimore" and dug them both. He was around fifteen when he discovered garage rock, the same time a lot of people did, when Lenny Kaye's *Nuggets* came out. "There were a couple songs on there that I'd heard of—I remember 'Gloria' and 'Psychotic Reaction'—but the rest of it was new to me," Buck says. "I thought it was the coolest stuff, so I immediately starting collecting those kinds of records. Then, when the punk thing happened I was totally into that, and then stuff started appearing that wasn't *quite* punk but it was on small labels. The Fleshtones were one of those. I read a review of their record and bought it. For me, it felt like they were a rock & roll band that got excited by punk rock and combined those two things. I never really felt like they were trying to be '1965.'" For one thing, Buck notes, "they had a whole lot more black influences than most bands." Buck corralled a bunch of his friends to go see the Fleshtones play at a popular Athens club, Tyrones O.C. Buck's own band, R.E.M., had been playing together for only a few months when the Fleshtones roared into town. "There weren't a whole lot of people there, but the show was *great*," Buck remembers. He hung out with the band for a while backstage and at an after-hours party. "We did the show to a smattering of people," Peter remembers. "All of the future R.E.M.er's were there."

R.E.M. would open for the Fleshtones a year later at the Peppermint Lounge in New York, at the dawn of the Athens band's ascension as alternative-rock legends, and play with them again in Los Angeles at the Music Machine in 1982. After that show, Keith and Buck sat out in an alley drinking beer and talking rock & roll, inaugurating a warm, boozy friendship that lasted for years. (A friendship in and out of *aqua vitae* memory: Buck recalls seeing a Fleshtones show from this period when afterward a very drunk Keith was under the assumption that the Fleshtones hadn't even played yet.) Buck would intersect with Keith and the band on personal and professional levels throughout the decade and into the nineties.

The Fleshtones were buoyed by the happy, sweaty responses at their shows. However, unease rankled the lineup. Patron suggested to Peter and Keith that they consider adding Gordon as a full-time member, jettisoning Brian and reducing the band to a more manageable (and profitable) quintet. Patron had initially thought of paying Gordon and Brian each a half-share—in essence making the Spaeth brothers the equivalent of one full-time member—but that situation proved unwieldy, so Brian had to go. Cutting him loose was a difficult decision for the guys, as he had been in the inner circle since the circle formed, was a great influence in terms of R&B and soul music and, perhaps most important, had been the only man who could keep Gordon in check when his drinking got out of hand.

The fallout for Brian would come early in 1981, shortly after the band played a highly publicized show in London as part of an American package of New York–area bands called "Taking Liberties." In between booking bands at Hurrah, promoter Ruth Polsky organized a U.K. show featuring the Fleshtones, Polyrock, the dB's, the Bongos, the Raybeats, and Bush Tetras, hoping to capitalize on the perceived English thirst for American rock & roll. "People in England are always looking for the 'Next Big Thing,'" Polsky explained to Robert Palmer in the *New York Times*. "And lately, on my last two trips over to England to hear bands, I noticed that people there seemed a bit bored, to be in a state of malaise." She adds, "I wanted to bring these bands over to England, so that British people would have a chance to see what's really happening here."

Polsky originally wanted to call the show "The Empire Strikes

Back." The event was well promoted by English trendspotters with cover stories and radio spots, and it was scheduled at the celebrated Rainbow Theater in London (where the Who had recently been in residence). The Fleshtones were excited to visit England for the first time, especially Peter, who was looking forward to spotting the street names and locales commemorated in the cherished Ray Davies lyrics with which he'd grown up. Before flying to London for the February 20, Friday night show, the band played a weekend in New York: Valentine's Day with Lyres at Irving Plaza on Saturday, and Sunday with the Rattlers at Left Bank.

They left the country with high hopes. Palmer had described the Fleshtones as a "wildly exciting rock & roll band," but their mettle and courage would be sorely tested by U.K. audiences. The Rainbow concert proved to be a great idea executed poorly. The partnering of several record labels and promoters resulted in preshow chaos, and at the last minute the production staff and lighting and sound crews were fired and rehired. Logistics became a nightmare. Despite the reasonable £3 admission and the hype and promotion for the *next* Next Big Thing, a mediocre crowd showed up at the Rainbow. Those who were in attendance suffered an indignant decision made by club management who, worried about overhead and poor ticket sales, refused to turn on the building's heat. Patrons stood around in a semifilled, cavernous hall cupping their hands together for warmth, their breath coming out in smoke plumes. Despite the conditions, the bands played well (Polyrock pulled out at the last minute), forging a unique camaraderie backstage based on their collective American background and the bunker mentality necessitated by the venue's chill, reflected in the crowd response as well as the air temperature.

The show was recorded on the China Shop Mobile, mixed quickly, and released later in the year on Stiff America as *Start Swimming* ("Sink or swim," Peter comments ruefully). The Fleshtones' two songs are fitting documents of the band at the tail end of the Action Combo era and further proof that Wexler hadn't quite placed his finger on the band's pulse. "Wail Baby Wail" is a raucous rip through the obscure Kid Thomas classic, a I-IV-V honking sweatfest featuring a false start, a rave-up ending, and a middle that threatens to fall apart. Peter isn't near the mike for half of the song, which serves as a showcase for each member: Keith slashes, Marek darts up and down his bass, Brian and Gordon stutter their saxes in the background until Gordon blows raunchy, patchwork solos, and Bill keeps the whole thing together with his effortless but intense backbeat. By the end of the tune the band had proven again how timeless a remote R&B tune can be made when updated with endless energy and good spirit. "Big Man (Calling Dr. Cranklin)," a midtempo sax-driven instrumental written by Peter, was an undistinguished number that apparently didn't make the cut during the *Up-Front* sessions. A bluesy version of "Wail," "Big Man" closes out *Start Swimming* in good spirit.

Zig Zag magazine was one of the few British publications eager to write well of the band's performance, though the reviewer dismissed the five other bands there as "garbage." "The best band of that particular night were definitely the Fleshtones," the reviewer noted. In a pointed review in *Melody Maker*, titled "Great American Disaster," Lynden Barber saved praise for "the wild and wacky" Fleshtones' performance, singling out Bill, "a drummer who stood half the time as he dented holes in his cymbals." The Fleshtones were, Barber notes, "the only band to get an encore. Oh, the thrill of it all."

The Fleshtones had work to do in Britain. Hopeful for valuable English support, Patron booked a three-day mini-tour of London to commence a week after the Rainbow show: February 27 at Dingwalls, the 28th at the Greyhound, and March 2 at the Venue. The band was wholly unprepared for the backlash that they would receive from critics and fans alike. There were pockets of the media and record-buyers that dug the band and made an effort to come out to the shows, but the general English response to the band was apathetic bordering on hostile, a disregard that would only increase a year later when the band launched a full-scale tour of England.

"I'm not joking when I say that touring in England scarred me for life," Peter says. "I was really keen to go to England before we went. But at that point it was too late. They had already gotten their anti-American backlash going. I felt that if we could be broken in England that that'd a good thing, because we intended to be a legitimizer to the United States. But people would've accepted things more if our record was doing well in Britain. It was the wrong time; it was way too late. They couldn't enjoy us." Peter believes that the English public has difficulty processing things that are a bit spontaneous, so they reject it and get angry. "They seem to respect more the idea of the Stage Artist who puts himself above the audience, whereas if you break that wall down they just figure that you're a blow-off band. We sort of dug the relaxed approach." It was an approach, Peter feels, that was "too American for them."

The guys felt like outsiders in London, especially when confronted with cultural differences. After the Dingwalls gig, the guys dropped into Hammersmith Palais, London's premier cool club. There they were faced with a peculiar rite: a bunch of British kids on the dance floor, the guys hanging out against the wall, not dancing, the girls out on the floor after having piled their pocketbooks in the middle of the floor, dancing by themselves around the small mountain of pocketbooks. "It was weird!" Marek recalls. "It was like they didn't know how to cut loose." When the DJ slipped on Grace Jones' "Roll Up to the Bumper, Baby" the guys said, *Fuck this. Let's go out there and show 'em how to do it!* tore their shirts off, and hit the dance floor jerking to every classic dance the could grin up, from the Frug to the Swim to the Monkey. "Their jaws dropped," says Marek. "They didn't know what to make of it." Gordon vividly recalls his introduction to the green and pleasant isle. "I stepped out in a brown shark-skin suit and this hideous English woman, and I use the term loosely, came up upon me and spat upon me and says, 'Go home, you Yankee Imperialistic rubbish!'" Such a warm greeting, and the fact that the bars closed at eleven, caused the hair to stand up on Gordon's and Bill's necks. Gordon: "And it was *warm* beer."

London did feature some solid gigs. "The show at Dingwalls built up good word of mouth," Peter says. "It was quite packed, and George Michael from Wham! was there. But because there was no room, he was actually sitting on the speakers. He was grooving on, and a lot of people liked that." Two contrasting views of the March 2 Venue show illustrate the band's initial critical reception in England. Writing in *London Trax*, Tom Hibbert praised the group's "beating heart" and their original, Bo Diddley/"Gloria"–inspired songs, "veteran concepts but The Fleshtones are in no way contrived; this is not coyly nostalgic revivalism—it's the real thing. Only when a shaky saxophone player appears to shift the style briefly to a cheesy woolly-bully jollity does the level fall below glorious." A different reviewer left the show with a cooler take: "The Fleshtones' first few numbers are exciting and stirring, with really mean harp playing and strange B-52's-ish falsetto choruses, but their brand of paraplegic R&B soon becomes innocuous, lulling you into the belief that they're just another wacky party band." The various barbs leveled from Fleet Street couldn't compare to the spit-laden curses lobbed the band's way by some of the more vociferous members of the audiences.

Brian Spaeth's memories of the Venue show have little to do with the band's performance or with the audience's reactions. That show marked the end of his tenure with the band. "A *coup d'etat*," he says dolefully.

He explains: "There was a very high stage at the Venue, a good six feet off the floor. I used to get really revved up for those shows and jump off the stage. As I was in midair, Zaremba—this is one of the weirdest things—grabs two maracas and hands them to me. I had to twist around to get them, and I landed off-balance and broke my heel. I remember thinking, *Oh boy, something is wrong here*." A French journalist had some hash, but Brian, a nonsmoker unaware that the French were rolling hash with tobacco, took a huge hit, and quickly got nauseous and green. "My foot was throbbing, and I ended up walking on a cane. It was horrible. That was the end for me. I was laid up for months. I was out of work and I had no money. And I found out, little by little, that I was out of the band and Gordie was in. What can you do? I was pretty hurt, pretty devastated. I wasn't expecting it, and it was pretty upsetting. I was really angry at my brother but I wasn't angry at Zaremba. I may be wrong—I don't really know the murky details at this point—but it seemed like he was the only one who didn't want to kick me out. But I don't care at this point." Ultimately, the choice came down to chops and money. Explains Peter matter-of-factly, "We took Gordon because he played alto sax, and he's a better player. He had more stage moves, and he could play a little organ." Keith felt the same. "Gordon had the presence, and he could play harmonica like dynamite. Brian just wasn't that great of a sax player. He was a great guy, a great friend, but he just wasn't cutting it. A lot of people were always talking about that."

Back home in New York, every painful step that Brian took echoed with the same refrain in his head: *Godfuckingdamn those guys!* He couldn't go out anywhere, couldn't work, had no money to live on, and all of a sudden his girlfriend didn't think that things were too cool between them. "That was how it ended," Brian laments, "in midair. Very strange." The Fleshtones, who had mastered the art of awkward and unprofessional goodbyes, were now launching them while leaping from stages.

In between the Rainbow package show and the three-day tour, the Fleshtones found their next producer. The resulting quick and productive recording sessions in an ancient studio in rainy East London would prove to be the sonic balm to sooth the pointed English hostility.

Richard Mazda had cut his teeth behind the sound board in 1979 as a twenty-year-old-member of Tours, a punk band whose independently released debut single, "Language School," sold out its initial small pressing in March of that year. Mazda fancied himself the coleader/cosinger of the band. ("It was kind of a Lennon and McCartney punk thing," he says.) Their Undertones-*cum*-Ramones sound kicked up some buzz, and after a six-label bidding war, Tours signed to Virgin Records in September of 1979. Mazda had arranged and produced the single on the fly and with a grounded, unschooled sensibility that would later appeal to the Fleshtones. "When I was producing the record I didn't really know that I was doing it," Mazda explains. "It's just that I had a bit more savvy and common sense than the other guys in the band. When we were in the studio in Cambridge, it was me saying, *That's horrible*, or *Let's not use that guitar*." Tours imploded professionally and personally, but Mazda stayed with Virgin Records throughout 1980 as a solo artist. By the end of the year, wary of bad blood between himself and the label, he asked to be released. He quickly formed the Cosmetics, a band that subsequently supported Tom Robinson on a tour of Japan in early 1981. Robinson passed Mazda's demos on to his friend Stewart Copeland of the Police, who played the tape for his brother Miles in the back of a limousine on the way to a concert in Birmingham.

Miles liked what he heard and contacted Mazda for a meeting in Miles' London house in Saint John's Wood. Mazda balked at Copeland's financial terms, which he found paltry. Though Copeland was offended, he was certainly intrigued by the Cosmetics and knew that as producer and arranger, Mazda was solely responsible for the sounds. "I told Miles how much I spent on the Cosmetics record, and I saw dollar signs in his eyes," says Mazda. "He asked me what I thought about being a record producer. I was so naive that I really didn't know what he meant. I was a boy from the sticks. I wasn't one of those people who read the backs of album covers looking for the names of producers; George Martin, Phil Spector, and Joe Meek were the only persons I knew. But I was cocky, and my attitude about producing was, *Hell yeah!*" Copeland gave some records to Mazda to listen to: the index masters to Wall of Voodoo's first record, *Dark Continent*, and the Fleshtones' *2X5* and *Up-Front*. "Miles was really keen on the Fleshtones," Mazda remembers. "He'd say, *These guys are great!*"

Mazda returned to Copeland's office three weeks later and flung the records down on his sofa. "These records sound like *shit*," he barked. "The groups are great, the songs are great, but they sound like shit." Brimming with youthful overconfidence and immoderate snottiness, Mazda convinced Copeland that he could do better. Mazda didn't expect much to come of the meeting, however, assuming that his attitude had overstayed its welcome. But three weeks later, Copeland called: *Richard, the Fleshtones are coming into town next week*, he said in his brash manner. *I've booked you a studio.* "There was no meeting, nothing," Mazda remembers. "But my over-confidence was so ridiculous that I said, *Sure, fine. Am I getting paid?* I was paid enough for me to think that it was okay. I was living in Bournemouth, on the south coast, and Miles put me up in the base-ment of his house in Saint John's Wood, on Marlborough Street."

The recording sessions were booked erratically. Copeland didn't know precisely what he wanted because the whole process had hap-pened so quickly. All parties hoped that the sessions would at least produce some workable demos. Mazda had been to the Rainbow show the week before, so he knew what the band was capable of live—"That show was great. There was one crazy moment where Bill was actually standing on his tom-tom beating out some weird beat. I can't believe the set didn't collapse under him."—but he duly noted the sonic disproportion between "Wail Baby Wail" onstage and "The Girl from Baltimore" as waxed. The week before the Fleshtones were due to play the Venue, Illegal Records manager, journalist, and gen-eral Fleshtones fan Nick Jones introduced Mazda to the band in that club's men's room. They were bemused by Mazda's energy and edgi-ness, his purple-dyed hair and painted fingernails, and they felt a simpatico with him immediately. "He was brash, really energetic, and enthusiastic," Peter recalls.

The following day the band arranged for two days of recording at RKO Studios, a tiny, ancient studio housed in, appropriately enough, a dingy basement. "I'll never forget those sessions," Peter says. "There was a typical Cockney coffee bar around the corner where we would go for our cups of tea and typical English sandwiches at that point, canned corned beef barely spread onto white bread. They would stack premade sandwiches up behind the glass counter where they'd get stale, or they would have hamburgers that they kept warm in hot water. That was England then. The guy behind the counter would actually say *Guv'ner*."

Flush with a meager stipend from I.R.S., the young men natural-ly gravitated toward beer to wash down the 15p sandwiches and to dispatch some good spirits. Their cultural shock toward warm beer notwithstanding, the boys made frequent visits to an off-licenses shop around the corner to fuel and inspire the sessions. "We discov-ered that the British had cans of beer the size of mini-kegs," Peter says, still marveling. "By the end of the session, Mazda couldn't open the door out of the control room because there were cans piled up knee-deep. I literally collapsed at one point in the sessions, laughing, buried under an avalanche of giant beer cans."

Watney's "Party Seven" cans—seven pints of *strong* ale—would become integral components of the band's gear. But the room's low ceilings, carpeted walls, and overall bygone feel weren't exactly inspiring, and before long Peter and Mazda were out on the damp London streets searching for speed. "I didn't have any contacts in London," Mazda says. "And we certainly weren't going to ring up Miles at the label and say, 'We need drugs!'" So the fellas went down the block to a local chemist and bought a half a dozen bottles of Benalyn cough syrup, with codeine-morphine sediment. "We let the sediment sink to the bottom, poured off the syrup from the top and got quite high on that," Mazda recalls with amusement. "That and the Party Sevens."

Mazda's production was reminiscent of Joe Meek. "Peter was always a fan of the Honeycombs and that wild sound," says Marek, "and that was what Richard was typical of: self-taught, eccentric, guided-by-voices kind of producing and engineering." Mazda blended antiprofessionalism with nerve and intuition, always on the lookout for inspiration and open to chance. "I hadn't been to the studio and I hadn't met the engineer," Mazda admits. "You couldn't describe the studio as state of the art. There was nothing plush about it. It was a very cheap affair." The antiquated tape machines at RKO, plus Mazda's lo-fi approach, suited the Fleshtones nicely, and they felt comfortable in a studio for the first time. RKO, however, wasn't too cooperative, breaking down every couple of hours. "We'd blow fuses and have to stop," Keith remembers. "That was a good excuse to go out and get some more beer. It was that kind of session. Those recordings were really good and a lot of fun."

Mazda found Peter a challenging singer to record. He was always moving and grooving in front of the mike, essentially launching a sweaty performance in the booth, and always drunk, so half of his vocals ended up recorded with him literally facing the wall. Mazda would flip the lights on and wail exasperatedly, *Peter! You're facing the wrong way!* Mazda eventually resorted to an old trick: he gave Peter a dummy mike which Peter threw around or semi-abandoned, and then Mazda recorded him properly on a second mike. "I used that trick on a lot of people," Mazda admits. "Peter was so used to making love to the mike, to swallowing the mike; he needs to abuse that mike. He would always go for the performance first." Mazda adds, "It was my job to let him."

A dead-in-your-tracks grind and growl was featured on "The World Has Changed," a new song from Peter and Keith and one of three tracks laid down swiftly at RKO, along with "All Around the World" and the civics lesson "R-I-G-H-T-S," with Keith singing. ("Keith was hard to record. He does not have a pop voice," Mazda admits charitably.) The sound and attitude in these recordings were as far from Shangri-La sonically as RKO was geographically. "The World Has Changed" bristles with barbarous energy, as if the early Yardbirds were dragged along the streets of the East Village, charged with low-rent amphetamines. Mazda encouraged the guys to layer on as much percussion as they could handle, and his literal hands-on production—he'd grab the reel, delay it, let go, the tape leaping and lurching forward recklessly—beat up the song to a rumbling, pulpy mass, the darkest, most muscular Fleshtones sound to date. The band would always consider the recording of "The World Has Changed" among their favorites. "I am *really* proud," says Mazda, who feels that the ideal way to hear the song is through the small speakers of a jukebox. "That record totally rocks."

Titus Turner's "All Around the World," filtered through Edwin Starr's funky, irresistibly danceable 1970 version, was a jolly, high-energy streak through sweaty R&B territory, the kind of song prized by the guys in that it was amusing, rocking, and suitably obscure. Marek wailed his first recorded solo vocals—the riotous *Grits ain't groceries, fried eggs ain't poultry, Mona Lisa was a man* chorus—and the whole bands churns, Bill's hiccupping drums and Marek's slap-bass echoing the song's strong black vernacular. Peter hollers the desperate words and blows harp ("We spent hours getting the filthiest harp sound possible," remembers Mazda) while the Action Combo, in what would be their last appearance on a Fleshtones record, honks happily behind him.

The raw immediacy of these two recordings came courtesy of the spontaneous luck that a lot of good rock & roll is born of: sessions cobbled together quickly, songs chosen on the fly, performances breakneck and loose. The band would try and recapture the energy of these brief hours in the studio for years to come. "Those were brilliant sessions," Peter admits. "We were in the right studio, and Mazda was still trying to prove that he could do it without stretching out too much. He had limited technology in front of him, which is a real plus, and he was very willing to experiment. It's a shame, actually, that we didn't have more material prepared right then, because *that* would have been the right time to record a whole album." Peter's memories may be burnished a bit by nostalgia, but a decade and a half would pass before the Fleshtones were this pleased with a recording session again. "We should have been locked down at RKO," Peter laments.

Roman Gods

"We should have been sentenced to record there."

Back home in March the boys laid low, recovered from their English hangovers, and gobbled up good, greasy New York burgers. They looked forward to the release of their "The World Has Changed" single in June. Sessions for the first full-length album were booked for that month at Skyline Studio on West Thirty-seventh Street. As the RKO sessions had gone so well, Copeland—still smarting from Wexler's botched job on *Up-Front*—agreed to fly Mazda over to helm the board. Peter and Keith duly wrote songs, and the band rehearsed arrangements in the Music Building.

On April 16, the Fleshtones headlined the enormous Bonds International Nightclub in Times Square (where two months later the Clash would famously play a two-week residency, selling out each show and paving the way for their American success). An historic link in the move toward rock dancing, Bond's was immense, the biggest disco that New York City ever saw, boasting a capacity of eighteen hundred. The Fleshtones played a "Spring Vacation Party" in front of an enthusiastic if thin crowd. "Three hundred fans showed up downtown to go up to see us and dance, and they essentially formed a row two-deep in front of the stage!" Marek remembers. "It was disheartening to be in such a huge place and not fill it, but the Fleshtones never could." A month later, the band played at the Peppermint Lounge on West Forty-fifth Street. The celebrated venue would become a high-profile, profitable home for the band for the next several years.

Songs for the new album were stage-tested and ready to be waxed. Richard Mazda flew from London to Los Angeles in March. He spent his time riding around in black-tinted cars, soaking up the California sun, and listening to the demo tracks cut at RKO. The pale Brit felt as if he'd won the lottery.

"I remember arriving at the A&M lot and walking into a conference room where eight or nine guys are sitting around, and they're all wearing those fucking pastel green, pastel pink, lemon yellow polo shirts," Mazda recalls. "There was a definite electricity in the air as soon as I opened the door. I was obviously for them the man of the moment. It was exciting." Mazda would be chosen by Miles in the next year to produce Wall of Voodoo's *Call of the West* (contributing his share to the making of "Mexican Radio" into an eighties alternative classic) but at this point his focus was on the Fleshtones. As was the label's. "To be fair to I.R.S., at that time they *loved* the Fleshtones," Mazda says. "They absolutely adored them, and definitely thought that they had some kind of chance." Jay Boberg acknowledges this: "The Fleshtones were a seminal band," he says, "and a lot of fun to work with."

Mazda, however, sensed that the Americana aspect of the Fleshtones might be difficult to market to some places. "The whole *Pebbles*/garage thing was never really big in the U.K., and the New York Dolls didn't do shit there," he says. "That whole New York flavor didn't really hit until Blondie, and the English didn't see the Ramones as coming from the Garage Rock tradition. So, one of the 'Tones' main problems was that the tribute that they would have paid to the Phil Spector sound and Garage Rock attitude would probably not have been very easily understood." He adds, "The Stray Cats were huge in England because Brian Setzer was considered a really good looking guy, a pinup. They had sex appeal. The Fleshtones had sex appeal for some people, but not in that way."

Mazda arrived in New York two weeks before sessions were to begin, and he checked in at the Iroquois Hotel in midtown—"because James Dean had been there"—where he stayed for the duration of his visit. His first time in New York City was of course intensely exciting, dwarfed as he was by the towering sky scrapers and the alluring bustle, noise, and rudeness of the city, and immersed in the energy and hustle of the Fleshtones' inner circle. "*Nothing* existed in England like the Music Building, then or since," Mazda marvels. "That was a new experience for me, that a band could rent a whole room with their equipment and go there anytime night or day. We virtually lived there while we were rehearsing." (By the end of the year, Bill would literally be living there.)

The rehearsals for the untitled album were lively and energetic. "Richard would listen to all of our songs and then he would have his input," Keith remembers. "We'd start rearranging, adding parts, and even before we got into the studio the song might've taken a new arrangement—maybe a new beat, a new groove—and then, as overdubs went down, he was always adding ideas that seemed to be making sense, that were adding to what was already there. He was totally in tune. In the mix we could focus more on what made everybody happy. Richard was very creative. He really was like a fifth member. That's why he was so great at that point." The guys respected Richard's musicianship and were pleased with his speed, focus, and "economy of means," one of Peter's favorite phrases. "Richard didn't waste time, and he was fairly direct." Marek recalls. "We'd talk about whether to double a chorus here, work on a transition there. We were pleased with how it all came about."

Sessions began in June and lasted roughly two weeks, the boys working from midnight to six for the cheap studio rate. The sixteen-track boards at Skyline were both impressive and suspect to the band, but Mazda made sure that, as best he could manage, the Flesh-tones' sound would not be diluted or squashed. The first day, Mazda and engineer Dave Liechtenstein spent six hours setting up Bill's drums and miking the shells to catch the perfect sound. The band was initially tentative, their suspicious eyebrows raised. "We were very much aware of mistakes, because everything was so miked," Bill recalls. "It was a little bit shocking at first. But everyone was exploring, feeling out and trying, still learning." The London sessions and the intense rehearsals in the Music Building were productive and helpful in that by the time the band arrived at Skyline, self-conscious problems such as mike awareness might be quickly resolved with humor and focus. Without many gigs to distract the band, they and Mazda concentrated intently on making as strong a rock & roll album as they could.

One of the first tracks cut was "The Dreg," the riff and the drumbeat for which Keith had written four years before, inspired after seeing the Cramps at Max's Kansas City opening for Suicide. Subtitled "Fleshtone-77" (stamping it from that seminal year in the band's young career) "The Dreg" was a churning groove featuring Keith's strident riff and Marek's "Electro Harmonics" fuzz bass. The song opens with Bill's incessant floor tom-and-snare beat, drizzled on top with wood blocks and snaked through with hypnotic feedback and Peter's personal vocal ("My heart says to my feet to follow . . . "). Marek staples the groove down with a fat, three-note riff at the end. The result was a psychedelic, propulsive drone unlike much else on Top 40 in the summer of 1981.

Tracks were cut quickly, purposefully: a new, frenetic version of "R-I-G-H-T-S" with Peter taking over on vocals; the upbeat, harmonica-laden "Let's See the Sun"; a lively if somewhat self-aware cover of Lee Dorsey's "Ride Your Pony"; the moody "Hope Come Back"; the emphatic *garage-cha-cha* of "Stop Fooling Around"; the driving "I've Gotta Change My Life"; an upbeat Gordon/Keith instrumental, "Chinese Kitchen" (through which Mazda laced a quirky beat that Gordon was never pleased with); and a final stab at "Shadow Line," slower now and trimmed a bit.

The band's natural energy, coupled with their new enthusiasm at working with Mazda and for a new label, translated into some rushed performances, and the producer ultimately suggested that they recut several tracks at a slower pace. "The sessions didn't sound right," Mazda remembers. "It wasn't that they were horrible, but they didn't have a purposeful feeling. The guys just got a bit excited." Keith wasn't sure that he agreed with Richard, but the guitarist was new at all of this. "I was still learning. We had that adrenaline going when you first get into a studio being a new band, so Richard made us record a lot of it over again, slower. Some of it is too slow when I listen back. Most of them should have been done quicker." Marek adds, "I know I always had a tendency to try and push the tempos, but I think in a lot of cases it was more out of an insecurity that it wasn't exciting enough, so it was like, *Play it fast. Give them a lot of energy!*"

Near the end of the sessions the band realized that they needed one more track to complete the album. They began fooling around up in 401 with a mean old harmonica riff that Gordon had recently brought in. Mazda was there. As the band started to jam on Gordon's riff, Keith took it over as a guitar lick and the guys knew at once: *Wait, wait, we've got something here.* Keith: "At that time, disco was still happening, and funk, and slap bass, which Marek was into, and as we're hanging out with Richard, we sort of put together this track without realizing that it was going to be the title track. That's what Richard was good at. Out of all of the songs on that record, that one he helped probably the most with, organizing it into a tune with an arrangement. All we had was a riff. Add a beat and a middle section, and slowly it turned into 'Roman Gods.'" The track was ultimately credited to the entire band. "We decided that there would be at least one big song on the album that we would share credit on," Marek explains. "The better songs, the ones that caught fire in our imaginations, were ones that we all contributed something to in some respects. That was where the group process had really jelled the most."

As "Roman Gods" evolved, an extended horn riff came into shape which would come to define the Fleshtones sound. The guys added a soul/frat call-and-response chorus, gleefully echoing the sixties garage spirit that they loved as well as mimicking the *Hey!*s shouted over the alley at poor Mr. Barclay all those years ago, a tribute to gospel spirit and juvenile behavior that the band celebrates to this day. By the time the song arrived at Skyline, Mazda had perfected the tempo and the changes, and he hired band friend Jon Weiss to join Gordon on saxes for the anthemic riffs over Marek's funky popping bass lines. The guys added a bit of live trickery: setting up a mike and amplifier in a hallway, they clapped their hands and banged a tabletop and a cymbal to the disappearing beat, the final sound on the record being the organic feel of skin and percussion. "Roman Gods" was born. The Fleshtones had their manifesto, their clarion call, their theme song.

Mazda's final touch on the album was to imaginatively link the tracks with some atmospheric noise. "It was some Indian chant, or some madness, we might have recorded it ourselves, or it may have been some noise that I found somewhere," he says. "You don't have total silence between songs at their shows, and so you don't want total silence between tracks. Never lose the vibe."

The album was finished by the end of June, and I.R.S. wanted a title. The guys submitted *Roman Gods*. The label wasn't especially interested and so the guys threatened them with *Gay Disco*. "That didn't fly with them either!" Keith laughs. Ultimately, Keith reflects, I.R.S. let the bands do what they wanted, "and that was cool. I run into more problems now with smaller labels. I.R.S. would let us do our own sequencing, album cover art, whatever. That was rare, at that time especially." The cover photo featured the guy's heads superimposed onto ruined Roman statues against a Day-Glo rainbow background—the groovy present meeting a long-ago past—and on the back were splashed photos of the band doing what it does best: playing live. "There was a lot about *Roman Gods* that we liked," says Marek. "But even at that point we were a little bit resigned to the fact that we might never get exactly what we wanted, because we didn't know how to get it ourselves."

On June 26, 1981, I.R.S. released "The World Has Changed" backed with "All Around the World." It did nothing commercially—riding the Top 40 charts that month were Phil Collins' "In the Air Tonight" and the Commodores' "Lady," among other balmy foils to rock & roll. For Ken Barnes, in the always loyal *New York Rocker*, the single "finally justified the shouting. 'World' is a brawling rocker." Writing in the *Soho News*, John Buckley hailed the song as "perfect Fleshtones. Featuring Zaremba's harmonica and his best singing to date, it's filled with Streng's dramatic chords, an insistently danceable beat, and one of the finest rock 'n' roll drum sounds heard in years." The trade publication *Record World* gave the band some industry buzz: "As the title suggests, time passes but this band is still rooted in some of rock's strongest traditions. The rave-up vocals . . . recall rockabilly greats and the explosive drumming demands shake, jerk, and sweat." London's *New Musical Express* proclaimed simply, "Manic and full of conviction. It will stand."

Word was getting out. The band celebrated the completion of the album and the release of "The World Has Changed" with a show at

Left Bank, but they wouldn't play the New York area again until December. Patron's master plan was to relocate the band to Los Angeles when *Roman Gods* was scheduled to be released in the late fall. The New Yorkers were heading back to the California Sun.

Much had changed in the greater Los Angeles area in the year since the guys last visited. Bands were sprouting, playing, and recording, many with a spirit and attitude similar to the Fleshtones'. Between 1980 and 1981, the Plimsouls, Green on Red, the Bangles, Los Lobos, the Last, the Unclaimed, Gun Club, Leaving Trains, Dream Syndicate, the Blasters, and the Long Ryders formed. Within a few years, many of these groups would be generally lumped under the "Paisley Underground" or "Roots Rock" labels, and their recording and club activity, and the rise of labels such as Slash, Enigma, and Frontier, created a tremendously exciting, fashion-conscious scene into which the Fleshtones landed in the autumn of 1981.

Patron intuited from the outset that clement Los Angeles would serve the Fleshtones well, despite their New York–centric attitude. "LA was much more receptive to the Fleshtones," he says. "That 'Dirty Water'/*Nuggets* sound was more of an LA vibe than a New York vibe, where I think the Fleshtones were seen as not dumb enough to be the Ramones, not sexy enough to be Blondie, and not kitsch enough to be the B-52's. They never really fit into the New York scene, whereas in LA they had a lot of credibility. There was more of that mind-set in LA for that kind of a retro act than there ever was in New York." The Fleshtones even found a personal tailor in LA who custom made tab-collar linen shirts for each delighted member. "I found the guy in East LA," Patron remembers. "He was the tailor for Nudie"—Nudie Cohn, the Russian-born tailor to such music luminaries as Hank Williams and Elvis Presley—"and he had his own Mexican East LA shop. Peter picked out the fabrics." The guys would wear these stylish, striped shirts with pride in several promotional photos (one of which would feature prominently in Gene Sculatti's book *Catalog of Cool* in 1982).

Phast Phreddie Patterson was a young journalist when the Fleshtones first visited Los Angeles, in 1980. Six years earlier, Patterson, born and raised in LA, had begun editing a small fanzine called *Backdoor Man Magazine*, which, though it would never receive the acclaim of *Slash* or *New York Rocker*, gave Patterson an outlet for his feverish, obsessive love for rock & roll music, culture, and history. In the fall of 1977, Patterson flew to New York City to interview the boogie band Foghat at some forgotten blues festival and stayed with his friend Miriam Linna, who was on the cusp of her tenure at Red Star Records and who had raved to Patterson about the Fleshtones. On Patterson's last day in New York, the two of them fortuitously ran into Zaremba on a side street in the East Village. "The next year, Miriam sent me a copy of the 'American Beat' 45," Patterson remembers. "At this point, I'm writing a column for *Slash*, a lot of which was devoted to old blues and reggae records and burger stands and what have you, but I happened to mention the Fleshtones record. I thought the record was so fabulous, and I wrote, *See 'em before they break up*. At that point, all the bands I liked seemed to put out a record, and then they break up, or never come to LA. I think it was the first ink that the band got outside of New York City."

Patterson saw the Fleshtones open for the Plimsouls at the Arena in Culver City, and he was blown away by their energy. "There were a lot of bands in LA that had energy. The Plimsouls had energy. X had energy. The Weirdos had energy. The Dils definitely had energy. But the Fleshtones had *otherworldly* energy. Nobody's like the Fleshtones. No one's ever been like them, and no one will ever be like them again." The Fleshtones were digesting their influences—Dave Clark Five, the Seeds, Motown—and the influences were mutating into something different, wildly exciting, and original.

In early October, Peter, Keith, Marek, Bill, and Gordon flew to LA and rented a house off of Melrose Avenue, in the heart of the scene. There, they would live and work for the next two months. During this period (and two years later amidst *Hexbreaker* touring) the band would often be mistaken by media and fans alike for an "LA group," so immersed were they in the party and club circuit, working furiously hard at area gigs and hanging out drinking with such scene players as Steve Wynn of Dream Syndicate, Peter Case of the Plimsouls, and Sid Griffin of the Long Ryders. The Fleshtones definitely made an impression in LA. "The level of what we were doing was scary," Peter claims. "You didn't really see it in California, which is very lightweight, with people pretending to act like the JD, the Tough Guy. We took the stage and it was a whole different thing. We were all very extreme characters back then, Gordon especially. We took to the stage at the Whiskey-a-Go-Go one night and we all had our own tall pitcher of cheap wine. We were drinking and running through the audience and harassing people."

The Fleshtones played widely while they resided in LA and on a subsequent visit early in 1982, with gigs at Club Lingerie, the ON-Klub, Cathe de Grande, Starwood, and the Whiskey. Additionally, they played two opening gigs for the Police at the Cow Palace in front of thirty thousand fans, where they were pelted with empty cans, quarters, and bags full of chili sauce. (They soothed their sores with their cut of the $300,000 gross.) They enjoyed opening gigs for the Go-Go's at the Greek Theater and at the Catalyst in Santa Cruz, and an opening slot for the Flamin' Groovies at San Francisco's Old Wardorf, an honor specifically requested by the legendary Groovies themselves. But not all shows were brimming: at some venues, such as the large Perkin's Palace in Pasadena, they would play to less than half capacity.

The neighborhood in which the guys lived was conservative: a light burning after midnight was a rare and undesirable event, and noise was a cultural aberration. Undeterred, the band did the best they could to re-create The House in all of its decadent splendor, dubbing the first abode they lived in "Zombie Hut," and after they were kicked out of there, the second "Cruise West." When the band wasn't gigging, they were partying, although at this point in the band's career that line was blurry at best, and often the parties would grow too large for their sublets. "We were already getting famous for our Blue Whale parties," Keith laughs. With both the neighborhood watchdogs and Miles Copeland awfully near, the guys sensibly opted out of destroying the house in which they were living and decided to rent a suite at the infamous Tropicana Hotel. "I sent Bill up to go rent it because we figured he was the most business-looking-like—I don't know how we came to that! The idea was that we would make this huge trash barrel of Blue Whale, and it became legendary. People in LA were not used to this. They thought that this was incredible. I invited everybody I knew: the Blasters, the Go-Go's, the Plimsouls, Los Lobos, the Unclaimed, Leaving Trains, Steve Wynn, Geoffrey Pierce, John Doe. I was never really close friends with Doe, but he used to love the Fleshtones and come see us when we'd play the Lingerie and the ON-Klub.

"We knew that the Trop was a great place, and that the hotel management didn't care. We'd invite sixty people or more who would show up and bring their friends, and you'd just get people to chip in money. I remember riding around with Gene Taylor, the big piano player from the Blasters, and we'd go out and get uppers because he knew where to get him. It was really fun. People from the record company would come and have fun.

"They would see no harm in this. Yet."

Steve Wynn was an LA rock & roll kid playing in local outfits who'd been a fan of *Up-Front* and *Start Swimming*, and he remembers the buzz that the Fleshtones brought with them to the sunny coast. One night at Cathe de Grande bar, where Wynn was DJing, he impressed Peter and Keith who'd had stopped in for a birthday party; aware of their presence, Wynn spent the evening spinning ultra-obscure sixties garage rock, scratchy tunes beyond *Nuggets* and *Pebbles*. Around the same time, Wynn was hanging out with Karl Precoda and Kendra Smith, the trio that would become the nucleus of Dream Syndicate.

"In fact, the Dream Syndicate formed at a Blue Whale party at the Tropicana," Wynn admits. "It was three in the morning, we were kinda drunk, everybody's having fun and it's really loud. And we said, 'We gotta do this!' The Fleshtones were the kind of band that make you want to do it yourself. Other bands you might love, like the Clash, but they seemed so distant, or you'd go see Television or Talking Heads and they seemed like brainy art students. You'd be inspired by them, but then you'd see the Fleshtones and say, 'This looks like so much fun, I've gotta do this, too!'" Wynn's fondest memory of the Fleshtones was their vibe of friendly inclusiveness. "The Fleshtones would adopt anybody in LA who was cool. I was still at the point of geeky fandom, so I was really excited to be hanging out, and you really weren't an outsider. You really were their friend and a part of their scene and the family. It felt like you were carrying on the legacy of Led Zeppelin at the Hyatt House." (A few months later, Peter enthusiastically talked up Dream Syndicate in *New York Rocker* after Wynn had given him a test pressing of the band's first EP. "Of all of the things that were happening at that time, that was the most exciting validation of what we were doing, that Peter Zaremba liked us!" Wynn exclaims.)

Keith met Wynn and many of his new rock & roll buddies through the Plimsouls' Peter Case. Keith and the like-minded Case, a street-toughened transplant from Buffalo, New York, and a budding songwriter, hit it off warmly and boozily. For much of the two months in LA. Keith was living in Case's rented house on Laurel Canyon, enjoying the ample floor space on which to crash, drinking with Case around the clock, listening to music, trying to write songs. Nights not spent gigging were free for everyone in the band— untethered to day jobs, wide-eyed in the blissful southern California sun—to live and play hard.

"Keith was an extremely enthusiastic cat," Peter Case says. "He was enthusiastic about what other people were doing, and he was always really excited to be playing guitar and to be in his band. He had a lot of energy. We shared a lot of common interests, too, like music and taking speed. He was really funny, and he had an appreciation of character and humor that I found very interesting. I always thought that the Fleshtones could've been a huge group, like the Beatles, if somebody would've just made a movie about them! They could've been like the Marx Brothers or the Bowery Boys, they were just such a great *group*. They had different looks that they would all get into at the same time, and the whole group was united behind the one direction. It was very powerful." The Fleshtones were the Plimsouls' brother band from New York. "Between the Fleshtones, the Flamin' Groovies, and the Plimsouls, we felt a kindred musical brotherhood," Case says. "It was always really fun to see them, because there weren't that many people who really cared about rock & roll. There were punk rock people, but not that many people knew rock & roll records or cared about Buddy Holly."

One of the more combustible results of the Streng/Case axis was the Action Dogs, a spontaneous joint teaming of the Fleshtones and the Plimsouls. "We wrote this song called 'I Can't Get Through to You' and recorded it at Pasha Studio, the same studio where the Plimsouls had cut 'A Million Miles Away,'" Case remembers. "We wrote the song on Friday morning, and recorded it that night. We were trying to do the whole thing super-fast." Case took a frayed lead vocal, Peter and Bill banged on tom-toms, Gordon threw in a trademark ragged sax solo, and the remainder of the two bands played up a storm on the call-and-response jam, the "super session" rounded out on piano by the legendary Uncle John Herron. On Halloween night, both bands took the stage at the Whiskey during a Plimsouls encore for raucous versions of the tune, plus Mountain's "Mississippi Queen," Elvis' "King Creole," and Gary "U.S." Bonds' "New Orleans." The show was recorded and broadcast on KROQ radio with the hope to feature "New Orleans" as the B-side of the single, but I.R.S. never released anything. ("I Can't Get Next to You" eventually saw the light of day in 1988 on *Time Bomb: Fleshtones Present the Big Bang Theory*, a compilation of various Fleshtone side projects. Case is currently assembling a Plimsouls live album that will feature a 1983 performance with Keith playing guitar on the Flamin' Groovies' "Jumpin' in the Night.")

Though short-lived—Keith stopped playing and hanging with Case more or less by 1984—the musical friendship was lively and memorable, a sunny snapshot of early-eighties LA rock & roll. "We were really buddies," Case says. "It was a whole moment of shared stuff. It was a really cool time."

In a *Creem* magazine article from this period, Peter was asked by

Roman Gods

Michael Goldberg why the Fleshtones stood their ground against the quarter- and chili-sauce-throwing kids at the Cow Palace show. "To show 'em who's boss, baby!" Peter bragged. Bill added: "The 'Roman Gods' idea is about a strong stance and pride."

The Fleshtones were always keen to stress the homegrown, patriotic sources of their sound. Sometimes this passion took obsessive dimensions, especially for jingoistic Peter: for the benefit of the *Creem* readers he traced the roots of Soft Cell's then-current hit "Tainted Love" back to the Standells, and in a sweeping gesture located much of the post-punk British music (Echo and the Bunnymen, Joy Division, P.I.L.) as coming out of American source material. "For us, since we're Americans, it's a lot more direct," Peter explained. "For me at least, it's the firmest foundation for the new rock 'n' roll." Asked by Goldberg what rock & roll should be concerned with, Peter answered quickly, "Emotion, release, beat, and rhythm. Virtuosity is not a main concern, although it is not necessarily a problem either. Though one should have much more mental command over what one is doing. Most people seem to let their hands do the talking as far as their instruments go, rather than their hearts or their heads. Rhythm, release, catharsis. These are the important things."

Then Keith leaned in. "Beer," he said. "Don't forget beer!"

The Fleshtones received some unhappy news near the end of the extended stay in Los Angeles. I.R.S. had decided to delay the release of *Roman Gods* until January. The Go-Go's first single, "We Got the Beat" (recut with producer Richard Gottehrer), reached number twenty on the *Billboard* singles chart in December; eager for their own release, the Fleshtones were disappointed by Miles' decision. Hoping to capitalize on the new fiscal year promotional budget and a relieved, post-Christmas market, I.R.S. dashed any fading hopes the band might have had that they would promote the album while they were still actually living in LA.

Back home in December after two months away, the Fleshtones played a triumphant Saturday night gig at the Peppermint Lounge, the large ads in the *Village Voice* warmly crowing, "The Boys Are Back in Town! Welcome Back to New York, Guys!" Bill, however, found a rude welcome: because the band was often on the road, the Wonderhorse Theater had to say *See ya later* to their lanky handyman, and Lucky Bill's rent-free days there were over. He needed new digs, and quick, and he made a desperate decision to move temporarily into the band's rehearsal space in the Music Building. An era of crashing on the floor and of washing up with industrial-size Handi Wipes would last longer than Bill, the Reluctant Bohemian, could have ever imagined.

As Christmas approached, the guys relaxed and disappeared to their friends and loved ones, their career optimism and expectations rising as quickly as their LA tans faded. The early press on *Roman Gods* was filling the guys with hope that their brand of American rock & roll might catch fire with the record-buying public. The band wouldn't be able to read many of the early reviews, however: in March, Bruce Patron sent them to Scotland, England, and France on an ill-conceived tour that quickly stopped any momentum that might've been building. The band thought that being battered with coins and condiments was bad, but through April they would face hostile U.K. crowds, dwindling European label support, and gray, gray, *gray*. Only when the clouds parted in Paris at the end of the tour did the Fleshtones see how much they could be appreciated by fans who truly understood the band's convictions.

13.
Et Tu Spiritus Dance

On January 7, 1982, the disco-*cum*-classical single "Hooked on Classics" went platinum in America, an auspicious market indicator on the day that also saw the release of *Roman Gods*. Reviews began appearing while the Fleshtones were enduring Britain. *Billboard* listed *Roman Gods* in its high-visibility "Recommended LPs" column, noting that "the results are not always successful but this freewheeling mix . . . is bound to strike a few chords with anyone who appreciates sheer sweaty fun"; a week later, *Billboard* featured the band in a brief "New on the Charts" article. In a three and-a-half-star *Rolling Stone* review, Tom Carson called *Roman Gods* "a terrific record" and raved that the Fleshtones are "passionately romantic and passionately angry, too. And passionately knowing about all of it. Every cut kicks in." The album's political message, Carson noted, "is under the surface: it's an insistence on treating the world as an adventure and persevering even when the adventure kicks you in the teeth. For my money, this simple, unaffected LP is the best rock & roll to come out of New York in the past year. And you can dance to every blessed minute of it."

In the *New York Times*, Robert Palmer, who was becoming something of a public defender of the Fleshtones, wrote that *Roman Gods* "is an exciting record, especially when the group's songs ('Stop

Fooling Around,' 'The World Has Changed,' 'Shadow-line') are as powerful as its infectious drive." He praises Gordon's "wailing" harmonica and Marek and Bill's "pummeling" rhythm section, and concludes, as most reviewers did, by musing on the band's potential for breakout success. In *Creem*, Richard Riegel noted how "absurdly up-to-date *Roman Gods* really sounds. Especially in harsh downtown 1982, a pop scene so dismal with fake 'progressives' like Christopher Cross. . . ."

In a glorifying review titled "The Great American Fleshtones" in *L.A. Weekly*, Robert Lloyd proclaimed that "The Fleshtones are America," that the album "may not be the stuff of Important Art, but it's the everlasting backbone of rock & roll." Joe Sasfy in the *Washington Post* called the Fleshtones "perhaps the trashiest and most irresistible dance band of the 80s," asserting that the band "escapes revivalism by delivering on the simple Dionysian promise that whatever we reveled in in the past can be made more pleasurable and intense in the present." Some pieces were borderline hysteric. In the *Village Voice* Marjorie Karp wrote a wide-eyed piece titled "Confessions of a Fleshtones Fan," in which she admitted to "symptoms" such as buying any record that bears their name, whether she's heard it or not, and if they've scheduled to play at such a place on such a night, "I will record it on my calendar and cross out whatever was there before."

Meanwhile, fellow Manhattanite Robert Christgau, self-described "Dean of American Rock Critics," was less impressed: though the record is "hooky and endearing, it's short on what one might call nuggets, which is why a whole side of unexceptionably jet-propelled tracks tends to lose momentum. In fact, whenever I try to concentrate for even an entire cut, my mind starts to wander, just like with Jackson Browne." *Roman Gods* received positive notices in Europe, especially in France, Germany, Holland, and Italy, where *Mucchio Selvaggio* placed it at number one on their charts page. In the U.K., Ian Pye praised the album in *Melody Maker*: "Far from retrogressive," he wrote, "this music represents a bold step forward for American roots rock."

What good were such reviews? *Roman Gods* debuted at number 174 on *Billboard*'s album chart, languished there for five undistinguished weeks, then disappeared for good. Even old nemesis Al DiMeola was charting ahead of the band. This would be the highest chart position that any Fleshtones album would attain.

Gordon was now on the cusp of becoming a full-time member. With Brian ousted, a move that would exacerbate tensions between the two siblings, Gordon found himself handling all of the horn and plenty of the harmonica work onstage.

Channeling the fun and mayhem he first felt onstage at Paul's Stadium Bar in Queens so many years ago, Gordon was enjoying playing rock & roll, living hard, traveling, meeting scenesters, and bedding women. Around this time he became friendly with English pop music impresario Giorgio Gomelsky, owner of the Crawdaddy Club and early promoter/manager of the Rolling Stones, the Animals, and the Yardbirds. "Giorgio introduced me to Lester Bangs and Robert Palmer," Gordon says. "I was familiar with Lester's reviews from way back, and Robert Palmer was impressed with my knowledge of R&B. Robert Palmer was to me more than just a critic: he could play sax, clarinet, and other instruments, and he was in Morocco before Brian Jones made it cool to hang out there. He also knew Paul Bowles. Some late nights I would spend at Giorgio's loft listening to exotic sounds coming from Lester and Robert. Quite heady stuff, indeed."

When *Roman Gods* was released and the band began to tour to increasingly complimentary reviews, Gordon, the loner, the outcast, Mr. Dangerous, soaked up the attention that deflected temporarily his unease and mental strain. "This was one of the defining summers of my life," he says. Keith was with Gordon in Whitestone Park in Queens when Keith asked him to become the Fleshtones' one-man horn section. "I didn't want to tell Gordon that we just kinda liked him because he's crazy!" Keith laughs. "The element of danger! That's what we wanted! No, he was a good musician. He was great to watch onstage. And it was this fifth wheel that we needed."

These many dim years later, Gordon remembers things differently. "Bruce Patron asked me to join the band as an official member," he insists. "It was right after *Roman Gods*, on which I played on considerable things, and I was getting along good with the fellows, but no one from the band approached me. Isn't it a bit strange? That gave me a complex that I really didn't fit in. And I suffer from severe depression and alienation, so I thought, *Gee, these guys don't really want me, Bruce does.* I don't know if I ever was an official Fleshtone."

At the request of I.R.S., the Fleshtones made a quick stop into Skyline before the British tour commenced to remix "Roman Gods" for a twelve-inch dance single. The seven-minute groove did well in clubs, peaking at number 29 on *Billboard*'s Club Singles Play chart. In February, the aborted sessions with Marty Thau were finally issued on the cassette-only label ROIR as *Blast Off!*, with liner notes by old *New York Rocker* pal Andy Schwartz, and in April I.R.S. released "Ride Your Pony" backed with "Roman Gods," the second single from *Roman Gods*. But the months immediately following *Roman Gods'* January release were tough. The band was inauspiciously launched on its U.K. tour with an unflattering review in the *Boston Globe*, wherein Steve Morse described a recent show at Streets as "full of strained, artificial fun . . . noisy and boisterous, but devoid of soul." The Fleshtones, Morse felt, came off as "an overwrought parody of garage music without really meaning to be."

Firmly entrenched in the U.K., the band forced themselves to remain upbeat. "We were offered to try and break the band in England, and a good amount of money was provided to bring us over," Keith remembers. "Bruce, of course, would get his fifteen percent of the gross, but he was new at being a manager. He was a road manager for Blondie; prestigious, sure, but he was not the guy who was cooking up the *idea* of Blondie or why they *became* Blondie. He was their accountant on the road who wanted to become a manager. I guess he figured that fifteen percent is a better deal for him. He wasn't looking ahead enough. It was a mistake, and I always look back at that." At the time the guys were questioning going to the U.K., but they went.

The guys found the climate in Britain more dismal in 1982 than they had the year earlier. The Fleshtones were the headlining band on this tour supported by Nine Below Zero, a lukewarm mod/R&B band, but outside of central London they were playing to increasingly dwindling crowds. In Europe I.R.S. released "Chinese Kitchen" and "Shadow Line" ("nothing very unusual," sniffed Barney Hoskyns of the latter in *New Musical Express*) but the label didn't commit adequate resources to promote the records. As a result, the band didn't feel it had the necessary support in the outlying English and Scottish burgs. The audiences that were there were small and unfriendly. The guys would hit the stage early in the evenings and were usually off in under thirty minutes. To polite jeers. "It was terrible," Keith says. "There was no interest." The handful of people who were at the shows spat at the guys, and the mood was tense and violent. Reviewing a Cardiff show at the Top Rank club in *Record Mirror*, Gary Hurr sums up much of Britain's evenhanded reaction to the Fleshtones: "Hailing from the rapidly-expanding Noo Yawk school of 'couldn't quite get the look right, but tried hard,' the Fleshtones make a scurrilous din but one that's not without its charms. . . . Their complete lack of sophistication made them strangely appealing."

By the end of the monthlong tour, the guys were exhausted and depressed. *Roman Gods* was charting back home, and here they were slogging through damp Britain without much label support, playing to largely indifferent crowds. To the guys, it was nonsensical. "I don't know why we went to England, to tell you the truth," Patron says now. "There must've been a reason. I'll take credit for it, blame for it, whatever. I was their manager." He adds, with frustration: "It was tough to package the Fleshtones onto other tours in America. With Peter being the big rock snob that he is, I couldn't have gone to Miles and Ian and asked for the Fleshtones to open for Squeeze. Peter's so condescending toward most rock bands that he'd say, *Squeeze? They're a pseudo-Beatles bad pop group. Why are we gonna open for them??* Peter would've knocked down any thoughts of trying to package the band. That was one of the problems with Peter. He's very condescending. I never felt like he was gonna gut it out."

Marek and Keith combatted the tour's low spirits one evening by "borrowing" Miles Copeland's sedan and driving recklessly through the slick London streets to visit Charlotte Caffey of the Go-Go's at her hotel. The trio spent the night lounging on beds, drinking Black Velvets, and listening to material for the next Go-Go's record. Labelmate Caffey had good reason to be imbibing that evening: while the Fleshtones were in Britain, the Go-Go's debut album, *Beauty and the Beat*, had reached number one on the *Billboard* charts. I.R.S. Records was prepared to ascend. Would the Fleshtones have what it would take to climb aboard?

The Fleshtones arrived in Paris for the tour's final show on April 15. Their mood improved as soon as they set foot on the great French capital. They checked into Hotel Caumartin and spent the morning giving press interviews with *Rock 'n' Folk*, *Rock en Stock*, and *Best*. In the early afternoon, they sat for radio interviews on Radio TSF 102 and *Boulevard du Rock*, and enjoyed a nice lunch at Le Ty Breixh along the Rue de Sèze. The treatment they received by the French press and C.B.S. Disques France (the European distributor for I.R.S.) was worlds different from what they had received in Britain. "After a month of torture in the faulty towers of every provincial English town by abusive knuckleheads, the worst treatment you could ever imagine, we were immediately treated wonderfully by the French," Peter says. "I had grown up, like most Americans, thinking that the French are silly people. *They're rude, they're too European, they goof off too much.* But we drove into Paris and the chestnut trees were just coming into bloom, the sun was beaming down, people were on the sidewalks having drinks, and we thought, *Oh yes. This is*

it. Especially after London, where the people were so beaten down, dreary, and shabby."

Even the warm and welcoming weather couldn't prepare the band for the show that evening at Le Palace. The buzz from the "Radio Party" show had only increased in Paris in the year and a half since its broadcast, *Roman Gods* was selling well, and Parisian fans and certain critics were very interested in seeing this wild New York City band. French promoter Alain Lahana explains: "The Fleshtones had all the talent, and were fantastic live, but were only appreciated by an elite in France. They could never reach the level they should have reached there, but they always stayed proud and convinced. We like *Beautiful Losers*." The Fleshtones, Lahana adds, "were amongst the best in that category!" The Palace show was promoted well and filmed for the weekly television show *Les Enfants du Rock* (the performance still shows up occasionally on French and Canadian television). Popular French band the Dogs opened the show to a rocking and primed audience, and just before nine the Fleshtones hit the stage—utterly shocked to find the venue sold-out, with over a thousand fans stomping and yelling for them. "We had just come from England where we had five people who'd rather piss on us than care if we were in front of their club, or dead in it," Keith says. "We walked in on something at Le Palace that we weren't expecting."

Duly launched by ringmaster Zaremba, Gordon was the first band member to hit the stage in the group's stylish entrance. At the time Gordon was opening each show with the theme from an old TV show called *The Defenders*. "It was a very pretty, moving piece," Gordon remembers. "I make it to the stage, play the opening theme, and within five seconds I know that this was not any normal crowd. By the third song we had them in the palm of our hands. By the fifth song, we weren't scared, but we realized that if we were to pursue it any further we could've caused a riot. We almost did." Keith remembers the chaos and thrill of the show's opening. "When we started the show we went through the audience, which kind of amazed them because this wasn't a small club, this was a sold-out theater. Entering through the crowd was something that struck us that night because of the situation. The audience, of course, never saw that before. I'll never forget that I got up close to the stage and the bouncers didn't know that we were the band! I'm trying to tell them in English, 'I'm in the band. I'm supposed to play!'"

The show fiercely culminated the tour. Exhausted but renewed, nearly in tears at the reception, the band let out all of the pent-up frustrations of the British tour in front of the rabid fans at Le Palace.

As in all Fleshtones shows, the alliance between the enthusiastic, eager crowd willing to let go and the band hyped to deliver increases the energy level on both sides exponentially. The equation became flammable at Le Palace. "It was totally packed, a great show, a big stage," Bill remembers. The Fleshtones tour through their set, opening with "American Beat" and charging through a handful of *Roman Gods* tracks, "Atom Spies" from *Blast Off!*, and a few covers, including a furious rip of the Sonics' "Have Love, Will Travel," and a streak through Del Shannon's "Move It on Over," Gordon supplying the R&B sax riff while Peter leapt from mike to packed crowd and back to mike again.

After several delirious encores the band was finished, or so they thought. Gordon remembers the near-messianic mood at the show's culmination: "When we left the stage, I stood upstage and saw Peter Zaremba—God's truth—being carried aloft, his feet never touching the ground from the stage to about three hundred feet back." Seized by the building's exalted vibe, the sweaty stamping and cheering, and the mood generated by the hourlong rock & roll party, the Fleshtones inaugurated a soon-to-be trademark gesture: they leapt from the stage as one and, singing and chanting down the long corridor that led to the front entrance, took their orgy out through the doors and into the streets. The five sweating guys from Queens had become pied pipers in paisley shirts.

"Hundreds of people followed us out onto the street, while we're still playing," Keith remembers. "We're just picking up whatever we could find, singing whatever R&B tunes we knew *a capella*, and the audience is joining in. They're all around us." The police were summoned and stopped traffic in front of the club. Bill: "The traffic couldn't do anything. The police came, mostly just observing and trying to get a handle on what it was, holding back traffic, making sure nobody got killed!" Peter recalls, "There were a bunch of *gendarmes* lining the street with submachine guns, holding the crowd back. As we approached them, we said, 'Peace, baby,' and marched through them and took over the whole intersection." The bacchanalian drift out into the streets was wholly spontaneous, as Marek remembers. "I don't think we were going out of the building a lot; later that became a signature thing to do, to get down in the audience. I don't know where it first started. That may have been it. I think Peter was definitely thinking, *This is some crowning moment, and how can we pay homage to that, what can we bring to it? This is such an amazing thing that the Fleshtones have come to France and the fans were rabid!*"

Sweat

"I felt like finally we reached out and were met with so much love," Peter says. "That was the thing that really killed me. We were like Edith Piaf. We were really respected as having thoughts, and we felt that." The crowd eventually followed the Fleshtones back inside the venue, and after the show dissolved, the band was treated by C.B.S. to a late dinner at Chez Gus on the rue Montmartre, escorted to the restaurant personally by the Hells Angels of France. The guys were buzzing, the toast of Paris. "You must see it to believe it," an epileptic reviewer wrote the next month in *Rock 'n' Folk*, a Paris fanzine. "I'm talking about the Fleshtones on stage. A rock 'n' roll cyclone . . . an American raid. . . . I can declare this, in a bombastic excess of advertising generosity: The Fleshtones live cannot be related! . . . It's not a stage anymore, it's a nuclear power station. . . . They came, we saw, they conquered." *Phew.*

Gordon and Bill usually roomed together on the road, as they shared a unspoken simpatico ("Bill taught me more with his silence than any lecture could," says Gordon. "He put up with a lot of my shenanigans.") and after the Palace show the two repaired to the hotel with some quality French wine. Gordon and Bill were as high on the show as on the Bordeaux, laughing and joking. Lounging on the hotel bed, Bill said, "Gordo, I'm not sure, but I think this is the greatest moment of my life."

Gordon turned to his pal. "Bill, it took you that long to realize this?"

A lunatic drunk somewhere in the hotel couldn't sleep because of Gordon and Bill's rejoicing, and he trowled the halls, banging on doors, the two pals guffawing, picturing a huge three-hundred-pound Frenchman with a curly mustache, a bull of a man. "He couldn't find us," Gordon says. "And the more he banged the more we laughed!"

The Fleshtones left Paris the next morning and flew back to New York, absently rubbing their shoulders and feeling the touches and slaps of a loving crowd. France would be a wildly hospitable country for the band for some time to come, and the site three years later of another memorable chapter in the band's turbulent career. "That Palace show was fantastic," Bruce Patron marvels. "That set their career up for the next fifteen years." However, the next Paris show at El Dorado was a debacle: the guys hit the stage late, there was equipment trouble, messy drugs. "Not all the same drugs," Peter remembers. "Some people were in forward, some were in reverse, that kind of thing. Bad move, a total disaster. We did a good deal to hurt our reputation with that show."

The band had little time to convalesce from the European tour. Through the lobbying of label publicist Betsy Alexander, I.R.S. had secured a coveted slot on *American Bandstand*, filming in Burbank, California, three short days after the Palace gig. The guys had an opportunity to meet the renowned and ageless Dick Clark. "It was mind-boggling!" laughs Keith. "You grow up seeing all of your favorite bands on his show, and you're meeting him. You're thinking, *How could this be?!*"

Sunny southern California beckoned again and the whirlwind year continued as the band flew directly to Los Angeles from London. The *American Bandstand* performance kicked off a cross-country tour in support of *Roman Gods*, even if the band had precious little time to rehearse and gear themselves up psychologically, not to mention pharmaceutically. They were scheduled to be in the television studio the next morning and were in the air for at least thirteen hours. "I remember looking out my airplane window at one point and I see polar ice caps and snow," Keith says. "Then I go back to sleep, look out later, and I'm over all these hot, hot sand dunes and the desert. It was really bizarre. The next thing I know I'm in LA, pulling into the Tropicana."

The guys caught a few fitful hours of sleep and dragged themselves into the studio at nine in the morning. Meeting Clark was a surreal and grin-worthy moment for the guys from New York, who were elbowing each other out of disbelief. Clark had come in from tennis that morning, so he had on white shorts and a white shirt, looking immaculate and tanned. Very LA. "He looked great," says Keith. "I was thinking, *Man, this is pretty cool. He's up early playing tennis.* We were already drinking. We didn't know what planet we were on! It didn't matter, we knew that we were lip-synching the songs so it was no big thing. We didn't have to really play!"

The affable Clark could tell that the band was more than a bit nervous as they hustled into makeup and then quickly positioned their gear over the world-famous AB logo on the studio floor. Keith was pleased to have scored a Coral Sitar from rentals, and they played "Roman Gods" and "Ride Your Pony," miming to a tape while around them the *American Bandstand* dancers were doing their thing to the American beat of the Fleshtones. "We were trying to get our own dancers in, but they rejected them," Keith laughs. "Eddie Munoz of the Plimsouls wanted to be a dancer, and some of our other friends. But they said they didn't look right. They were right!" Peter tried to talk Alexander into dancing on top of his Farfisa, but she begged off, fearing that she'd topple off of the organ and end up with her psychedelic miniskirt over her head on national television. Also taping that day was War, supporting one of their final pop hits, "You Got the Power," Richard "Dimples" Fields, Patrice Rushen, the Grass Roots, and, hilariously, a band named the Dregs (in truth the latest incarnation of Dixie Dregs, a southern rock/fusion outfit).

The Fleshtones commemorated the event that night with a wild Blue Whale party at The Tropicana, during which a black-clad Nina Hagen unnervingly disrupted proceedings by threatening to push a baby carriage—with a live baby tucked inside—into the filthy, rarely used pool. When they finally arrived back in New York, the band celebrated their first weekend back with two packed shows at the Ritz. For a June gig at the New Peppermint Lounge (the venue had dropped down to Fifth and Fifteenth Streets), the band was advertised in the *Village Voice* with an accompanying photo for the first time. The *American Bandstand* episode aired on Saturday May 15, during the show's twenty-fifth anniversary season. At that point, the Fleshtones were on the long American road to either success or oblivion.

The *Roman Gods* tour that criss-crossed the country in summer of '82 was the prototypical I.R.S./F.B.I. circuit. Sensing that he had potential star band on his hands Miles, in conjunction with many at the label, felt securely that the way to break the Fleshtones was on the long road, showcasing the band doing what they do best, creating wild, frantic, and fun shows at which the sweaty crowd loves the game and thrills in the wall between band and crowd coming tumbling down. Often the guys would begin the show in the dressing room, smiling and grooving with whatever friends and fans were hanging with them, pounding a drum and tambourine and gang-singing the opening tune as they'd make their way through the crowd and onto the stage, where both Fleshtones and the crowd seemed to say, *Hey! You're at this party too!* Peter's long curtain of bangs swung a hip metronome for the mayhem behind him as he hopped on bar tops and barely avoided decapitation from low-hanging ceiling fans. Usually the show ended in the same way, party-in-reverse back to the dressing room, the hotel, the tour bus. Peter, Keith, Marek, Bill, and Gordon were being their fun-loving selves, only amplified.

I.R.S. "Ambassador of Creative Services" Carlos Grasso, a big fan and supporter of the band at the label, remembers Fleshtones shows had "a kind of visceral nature that seemed to explode into abandon. It was one of those things that was inspiring as much as anything else, even on a personal level. I wish I could let go like that, particularly like Peter, who's so intelligent and knows about so many things. He'd just allow that part to be utterly devoid of any thinking whatsoever, just allow the elements to fall where they may. Being able to control the chaos in that manner was really amazing." Amazing, and draining. The band strove furiously to give more than one hundred percent at each and every gig (while rocketing on speed and coming down in Katmandu, *Well, it's a job*) and the endless touring was bound to catch up with them. As resilient as the guys were, they were one tired lot arriving home in New York City at tour's end.

Gigging, gigging, gigging would become the *modus operandi* for the Fleshtones for the rest of their long career. Poised at the end of the year with a critically acclaimed album, successful tours, and an appearance on *American Bandstand*, the Fleshtones couldn't help but wonder when their hard work was going to pay rewards. "If we don't make it, we'll just keep playing," said Peter prophetically. "They'll always be room for us, and there'll always be people who want to hear us. We wanna hear ourselves."

Gordon had more specific plans: "We're just waiting for that one big hit that'll turn us into drug addicts and junkies."

14.
Super Rock

Blondie, along with the Cramps, the Ramones, and the Dictators, had been one of the few mid-seventies downtown New York bands still active in the early eighties. In the autumn of 1982, Deborah Harry and company called it quits. The stalwart groups from the original punk and New Wave era were quietly vanishing.

The Fleshtones closed out the long tour schedule by teaming with R.E.M. at the Peppermint Lounge and the Del Fuegos at Maxwell's, dashing up to Boston in November to play at the Channel and appearing at Danceteria before Christmas at a benefit for the now-struggling *New York Rocker*. As Bruce Patron's band was playing out, he had stars in his eyes, only the Fleshtones weren't tethered to them. Patron was nearing the end of his tenure as the band's manager.

"I was fading away by the time of the Palace show," Patron admits. "When the Fleshtones and the Go-Go's toured the West Coast I really cemented my Go-Go's affiliation. Somehow I thought that I could be the tour manager for the Go-Go's and still manage the Fleshtones. I did try." Patron was with the girl group in Japan when it went down. "That's obviously a valid complaint from the Fleshtones, that their manager's in Japan. Nowadays you might be able to pull it off, with e-mail and stuff like that. But I was in love with the

Go-Go's and their whole vibe and that they were big." Rather than resign, Patron preferred to have the Fleshtones fire him. He'd been deferring his standard fifteen percent commissions on gigs for so long—allowing band members to keep a little extra green in their pockets after shows—that he felt he would have more leverage afterward if he didn't walk away. He was doing well enough as a tour manager for the Go-Go's that he could afford the risk. "The band made it right," Patron says. "Lawyers were involved, and I don't know that they paid me one hundred percent of what they owed me. But they made it right." Over the next couple of years the Fleshtones did indeed pay Patron's debt back, month by month, from performance earnings. The many days on the road earning the money would become the chief impediment to the band getting back into the studio in a timely manner. Patron's tenure was brief, but both sides have no regrets. "There are no hard feelings," Peter says now. "We should have felt that Bruce wasn't getting us, anyway. It would have required a real hotshot to get us anyplace."

The Fleshtones began searching for more stable management. The band was introduced to Robert Singerman by Ruth Polsky, organizer of the "Start Swimming" tour. Singermanagement handled the four other bands that were involved with that package tour, and Singerman was also friends with Jimmy Ford, a road manager who the band knew from New Orleans. Singerman signed on to manage the Fleshtones fairly soon after Patron left the fold, initially comanaging with Ford. At this point the band began living on a small weekly draw against current and future incomes, an arrangement that would become the economic base on which the band rested—for better and for worse—for the bulk of the decade. "I loved the Fleshtones' music, songs, lyrics, spirit, attitude, live performance, ingenuity, fun living, adventures," Singerman says. "I never focused on whether or not they were a good bet. I just wanted to have them perform in front of as many people as possible—live, radio, TV—for them, but also for the people/world. Fleshtone as a verb: *Fleshtone* Paris, *Fleshtone* D.C., etc."

Although *Roman Gods* had disappeared from the *Billboard* charts after five weeks, the band did much to promote the record and their own growing reputation as a phenomenal live band throughout the exhausting 1982 national and European tours. As the new year dawned, they laid low from performing, settling in for a couple months of songwriting and rehearsal sessions at the Music Building (where Bill was now firmly ensconced as a live-in resident). I.R.S. had renewed their contract with the band for another full-length album, and the time was ripe to build on the solid reviews and live support for *Roman Gods*, to break the band into the big time.

SUPER ROCK time.

Super Rock is all of the great elements that make rock & roll the great and vital thing that excites people, Peter explains. *All those things together and rolled into one without saying, "This is disco" and "This is garage rock" or anything—putting it together and rolling it up, as they say, into one big greasy ball. That's Super Rock.*

Bill: *Super Rock is taking the best, most exciting elements of rock & roll and exaggerating and amplifying them beyond proportion, with no apology whatsoever.*

The Fleshtones had a Concept. SUPER ROCK felt like the next natural step toward where their creative momentum was leading them, an amplified lifestyle where all of their influences—cultural, musical, and historical—were filtered and synthesized and revved up beyond belief. The band felt as if 1983 was the year that the previous seven had led to not only chronologically but *conceptually*, in a fated, organic, greasy ball of rock & roll culmination.

As the guys would sing years later, they were "armed with ideas," and they wanted Richard Mazda to again lead the sonic charge. But there was a problem: Mazda was exhausted. He hadn't recovered from the ingestion of speed and kicks while staying in New York during the previous year; such disport might have been standard for the ironclad Fleshtones, but it was a tad extreme for Mazda. "When I got back to England after recording *Roman Gods*, I felt so, so spent emotionally and was quite drained by the experience, rather like when a medium takes on someone else's pain," Mazda explains. "I went slightly crazy. My feelings about *Roman Gods*, and the whole experience, welled up in me, and I basically headbutted my bathroom window in a slightly psychotic episode. This is the stuff I don't lay on the band. It comes out somewhere." Mazda suffered some regretful business decisions during this period, as well. Much to his financial detriment he turned down recording R.E.M.'s album *Murmur* because he had committed to helming the Fleshtones' next record. Taxed by his emotional problems, he'd delayed the band by four months when he finally arrived in New York to begin sessions for the album.

Mazda hoped that the experience would be akin to *Roman Gods, Part Two*. "It wasn't," he says. "I couldn't work out at first what was going on, but Bill looked in very poor physical shape. He had lived in the Music Building without heat for the entire winter, showering at the YMCA every once in a while. He probably doesn't really know this—or, he didn't see it the way I saw it with my eyes—but his physical presence was smaller. He looked gray. He'd lost weight. I think it did him no favors at all. With Marek, there seemed to be no real spark going on in his eyes. That was to do with the heroin; he didn't really declare this stuff to me. It didn't seem as if the band was happy with themselves. There were tensions."

Despite their sublimely confident Super Rock ethos, there was indeed a lot weighing on the guys: road weariness, drug excess, increasingly dissolute lifestyles, pressure from I.R.S. to produce a hit record. When the band entered Skyline Studio in March, no one in the industry was prepared for the Year of Michael Jackson and the subsequent marketing shift wherein MTV music videos would become the pioneering and overwhelming barometer of public taste. The music video was set to replace the single as a record label's chosen means to deliver product to a national audience. Consequently, stylish and photogenic bands such as Duran Duran, Culture Club, Eurythmics, Wham!, INXS, Thompson Twins, Human League, Spandau Ballet, Flock of Seagulls, Naked Eyes—all of whom charted in 1983—had a leg up on artists whose image and fashion weren't their primary selling points. (The talented but ordinary-looking Christopher Cross, the Grammy-winning smash artist of 1980, famously declared that MTV ruined his career.) The rules had changed subtly but profoundly by 1983: an artist was as pressured to produce a video-worthy album track as he was a radio-friendly single, and the two products weren't necessarily one in the same. *Eye-candy* was quickly becoming as important a commodity in the music business as *ear-catchy*.

Miles Copeland and I.R.S. Records sensed this shift in the image-driven market, as well as the burgeoning popularity of twelve-inch dance mix records, and were committed to their brand of upstart and edgy rock & roll. By 1983, their stable was growing impressively: the Go-Go's had become million-sellers on the strength of *Beauty and the Beat*; R.E.M. had released a critically acclaimed EP and were on the cusp of issuing the widely influential *Murmur* and the single "Radio Free Europe"; the Alarm, Wall of Voodoo, and the English Beat were kicking up excitement and selling records. If there was any time in the Fleshtones' disorderly career when they were poised for breakout success, it was 1983. Radio was waiting. MTV was waiting. I.R.S. Records was waiting.

Waiting for what, precisely? Could the Fleshtones package and streamline their sound and image for mass acceptance? Could they retain their raw and lively spontaneity? Would they be relevant? The guys saw the Ramones as a cautionary example: by 1983, that seminal punk group had gone through producers Phil Spector and Graham Gouldman—and went so far as to remove their trademark leather jackets—in an attempt to create a marketable sound and image, but the results had been unhappy. The Fleshtones wanted to remain inexpert and energetic, but they believed honestly that the music they were producing was commercial music. Bill lamented at the time, "It's too bad that when MTV and the radio stations want to adopt a new format, they immediately think that new means a hi-tech sound. If it's not that, then it's not new, and there's lots of new music that doesn't involve a high-tech sound." The artificial sound common to records of the era was anomalous to everything that the Fleshtones stood for.

Initially, the band was lumped in with New Wave, one of the broadest—and most problematic—categories of eighties popular music. As John Dougan of Allmusic says, New Wave was essentially "all post-punk era music (starting circa 1979) that journalists, record-label A&R people, disc jockeys, and assorted music-biz folk didn't want to call punk rock." The Fleshtones certainly were not a punk rock band in the NY/U.K. tradition, and post-punk as a category was as broad and misleading as was New Wave, suggesting the difficulties and challenges posed by a band like Pere Ubu as much as the radio-friendly sound of DEVO. Ultimately, the Fleshtones would be subsumed in the catch-all categories of "Indie Rock" and "American Underground," but the labels that brought them the most trouble throughout their career would be "Garage Rock Revival" and "Neo Psychedelia." In terms of trendiness, niche marketability, and promotion, such branding might have been helpful, but the band chaffed at the narrow association, as they had since their inception. Bands such as the Three O'Clock, the Bangles, Green on Red, and Rain Parade in Los Angeles; the Fuzztones, the Vipers, and the Chesterfield Kings in New York; and Boston's venerable Lyres were soon to be generally lumped together by the media as "Sixties Revivalist" bands. In some cases, bands actively courted the look, sound, and attitude of sixties garage bands and strove to faithfully re-create a certain lost era via fashion, album design, gear, and equipment (the Bangles, the Dream Syndicate, and the Rain Parade, and to a lesser extent Lyres, exhibited obvious sixties influences but ultimately attempted to mix them with contemporary and more or less original sentiment). Some critics and listeners, seeing the Fleshtones in their vintage clothes playing their fuzz and Farfisa, failed to take note of the equally strong R&B, soul, and disco pulls on the band. The Fleshtones were playing Crazy Elephant's "Gimme Gimme Good Lovin'" and Sylvester's "Do You Wanna Funk?" at shows around this time. Not exactly Vox-&-Paisely territory.

What the Fleshtones wanted to do was revive the *spirit* of mid-sixties music. Joked Peter, "Scientific analysis of music never really came up with anything good except they found a lot of it was moldy. We want to revive not the music itself but some of the freshness." Marek added, "We're not a psychedelic revival band. We don't go in for the carbon-copy look and having all the Vox equipment and all that stuff. We're doing the same thing they were doing but we're starting from a different musically inspired base than they did." Peter always preferred to simply call the Fleshtones' brand of rock & roll "homemade." The band responded indignantly to the categorization issue in interviews, as well as in their bold new songs, a bumper crop of which Peter and Keith brought into Skyline.

Carlos Grasso feels that what Peter was trying to do with the Fleshtones was reflect both fun and abandon. "He wasn't going for a punk rock vision, although the very graphic, punchy elements were there, certainly. I think he was trying to fuse a couple of different things, but the Fleshtones were just as energetic as any punk rock band, had as much fire and fuel, lyrically, as well. If anything, Peter was probably infusing what amounted to the carnival elements, without it feeling like you were dealing with a circus. What I liked so much about the Fleshtones, and what very few bands were doing, was that they could be so much fun on the surface, but at the same time they were so aggressive. It was right on top of you, and then went through you."

I.R.S. wanted Mazda to record the new Fleshtones album in Los Angeles at El Dorado Studios, presumably to secure a flat rate and a highly recommended engineer. More likely, Miles and company wanted to keep an ear on the proceedings and add their input. Privately (and presciently, as it turns out) Jay Boberg and Grasso were concerned about recording the band again so close to their homes, wives, and girlfriends, worried that big-city distractions might manifest themselves easily and create chaos. But Mazda and the band won out and sessions commenced at Skyline, where some recent renovations provided the producer with a new Neve Board and Studio Deck. The rehearsal and recording *modus operandi* was the same: cobble together tunes in the Music Building, bang them into shape with Mazda's help, and ignite them in the studio. From the onset, Mazda was feeling the pressure. He had nearly scored a Top 40 single with Wall of Voodoo the previous year ("Mexican Radio" peaked at #41 on *Billboard*), and he knew that Copeland wanted a hit.

Unease percolated beneath the sessions, however. "There was one occasion where it just wasn't jelling," Mazda remembers. "Peter was all hyped, Keith seemed a bit muted, there didn't seem to be any lights on in Marek, and Bill seemed really fucked up, like he needed to go off to a health farm. I was sitting behind the control desk, thinking, *What is wrong with this picture?*"

Mazda halted the sessions abruptly, stepped briskly from the control room, corralled the band into a side room, and exploded. "You guys are *fucked up!!*" he screamed. He pointed to Peter: "You! You're on speed!"

He pointed to Keith: "You're on Valium!"

He wheeled around to Marek: "You're doin' heroin!"

To Bill: "You're just fucked!"

Lastly, to Gordon: "And you're drunk!

"You fucking idiots, You can't even do the same drugs! You're all pulling in different directions, can't you see it?!"

The guys were taken aback. "They were very sheepish," says Mazda of the incident. "Nobody said anything and it all went very, very quiet. I may have even called the sessions for the day. I said to them, 'If we don't get this together, it is not going to work.'"

The guys recall Mazda's impromptu lecture a bit differently down the years. Keith: "I remember Richard taking us up into a certain areas of the studio and sitting down, saying, 'We have to have a talk now.' And he'd talk to us for fuckin' half an hour about nothing. We started looking at each other, like, *He may be off his rocker, and he's our producer!* I remember him saying, 'If Miles Copeland finds out that we're on drugs, we're all dead men!' At the end of the sessions he was starting to lose his mind."

"Well, I was no Snow White," Mazda admits. Once during early rehearsals Marek and Keith turned to Mazda and, smiling slyly, told him that they were going to take a "stroll down Avenue D" that evening. In his naiveté, Mazda thought that they were referring to Alphabet City in the East Village. They were, of course, referring to dope, and asked Mazda if he wanted to go in on a dime bag of heroin and some beer that they'd pick up near Marek's place on St. Mark's. They were due to meet up with Carlos Grasso at his hotel that evening. "We went out as a little gang, the whole band," Mazda remembers. "There were some areas near where Marek lived where there were storefront drug dealers. We pick up the beer and the heroin and go back to Marek's apartment. This was definitely the first time I'd ever tried the stuff, and I thought it was stranger than any buzz I'd ever had. The evening became kind of farcical."

The drunk and smacked-out group piled into Keith's enormous gas-guzzler and drove warily up to Central Park West and the Mayfair Hotel to meet Grasso. As Keith blindly steered the car around the potholes that in those days dotted the Upper West Side, Mazda sweated the entire journey in increasing paranoia that Grasso was going to find out, go back to the label, and ruin Mazda's reputation. "I don't know *how* Keith drove uptown," Mazda says. "He was wasted, swerving all over the place. There was a rock & roll bust, if the cops had just pulled us over. Somehow, we made it up to the Upper West Side, and everybody suddenly got a little chicken about picking up Carl! 'Richard, you do it,' they said. 'You're the producer!' I don't know what kind of state I looked in. It was terrible."

Panicking in the swiftly rising elevator at the Mayfair, Mazda suffered the initiation rite for any first-time D user and vomitted in the elevator. He managed to clean up in a hall bathroom and, though he was high, his mind was racing. He couldn't very well tell Grasso that the Fleshtones were about to make an album with $80,000 of his money and they were stoned on heroin. "I had to lie to him, and I told him that we'd been drinking; I don't believe it, but he bought my story. To this day I've never told Carl. We later went up to the Peppermint Lounge, because we were all due to meet up Joey and Dee Dee from the Ramones. We went up there, hung out with those guys, had a great time, of course drank shitloads more beer, and dropped Carl off. He never knew what was happening."

Mazda had learned from that long, ragged evening to avoid dope, but Marek and Keith kept on during the sessions, and it began to put a distance between them and Mazda. The combination of increased drug use and the pressures on Mazda ratcheted up the level of urgency at the sessions, which soon went thousands of dollars over budget, much to the band's dismay. Bill tried tactfully to raise the issue of overspending with Mazda. "I sounded like a Philistine," Bill remembers. "When we hit the *obscene* $80,000 mark, I said that we're really going to piss off the label. But my one attempt at sober financial approach to recording was not to be heard." Bill adds ruefully, "It was the eighties."

"We were expected to make a hit record," Keith explains. "You go remix, and what you start doing is destroying a record. If that record had just been splashed down the way it was at first with the original mixes, which were much wilder and out there, it would have been a much better record." An early mix was played at an I.R.S. meeting that Keith and Peter attended with Miles Copeland present. "It's so retarded: everybody's in this boardroom with the Fleshtones listening to the mixes," Keith recalls. "Miles stands up and says something to the effect of, 'I can't understand what's going on!' so the album got remixed with a very mild and safe mix, the vocals very up-front and dry, which is really not the best way to mix a Fleshtones record. It wasn't only remixed once, it was remixed twice; it was almost like the company was mixing the record. They're on the phone giving Mazda a menu, a formula, and now this is costing thousands of dollars!" Mazda remembers that the original mixes were nearly dublike in their strangeness and force. "I would love to hear those," says Keith. "They probably were not as commercially viable, but they'd probably make more sense."

The label eventually flew Peter out to LA to help remix the sessions at Hit City West. "They wanted to keep an eye on us," Peter remarks. "I don't know how many weeks we spent mixing. They would listen and say, *Now bring up the voice.* So you'd bring up the voice, and then you'd have to bring up other things. It's totally finessed." Sessions were also marred by the increased hounding of Bruce Patron's lawsuit for back commissions. At one point, Peter was literally living at Skyline for days at a time, entering and leaving the studio disguised as a delivery boy to avoid being served papers by the process servers. "They never got me!" Peter crows. "But we went off the tracks really fast with that record. We had a lot of ideas, and there was just too much going on, what with being chased and harassed. There was too much speed involved, and that gave us even more ideas." Mazda was under the gun from the record company, and he started working harder and longer. "He started using speed for more energy," Keith remembers, "but also, I think, to enhance the effect of producing."

Despite the harried, fueled conditions, the album would ultimately be spared the mechanized sheen dating many albums from this era. The songs that the band were working on were strong, purposeful, brimming with confidence and attitude, if betraying a sore and frustrating admission that America was essentially ignoring the Fleshtones. "Deep in My Heart" was stirring and emotional (Peter's cheesy Farfisa solo notwithstanding); "BRAINSTORM" was a stern warning not to get unwittingly tangled in Peter's intellect; "What's So New (About You?)" was a self-evident smirk toward poseurs both on and off *Billboard*; "This House is Empty" was a midtempo ode to lost innocence (and perhaps a certain House in Whitestone, Queens);

"Legend of a Wheelman" was Gordon's rousing instrumental sprung from his preshow habit of shaving while listening to Spaghetti Western music, made monumental with Mazda's canyon echo; "Want!" was a throwaway nod to the Strangeloves with a rave-up chorus and bridge.

The band cut three covers at Skyline, more evidence of their comprehensive record collections: a barely recognizable "Burning Hell" by John Lee Hooker that the band whipped up into a pop-gospel hymn that was killing onstage; the obscure "Can't Get You Out of My Mind" by the Dantes from 1966; and "She's My Baby" by Johnny (Australia's King of Rock 'n' Roll) O'Keefe from 1956. Discovered by Peter buried in a mid-seventies Australian film comedy, "She's My Baby" featured a hand-waving gospelesque arrangement, with heavy percussion and trademark sax work from Gordon.

Four songs would come to define the sound and attitude for the album. The snarling "New Scene" was the album's strongest statement: *It's a mixed up, crazy time that we are living in today,* the guys chant against a powerful beat, *and I'm afraid it's only gonna get worse.* It was hard to tell whether the crazy times were personal or cultural, but the anxiety was palpable. According to Peter, "New Scene" was in part a dig against the sixties revival bands: "If they're so righteous about it, why weren't they doing it five years ago?" he asked at the time, championing the Fleshtones' own idiosyncratic history. "I was not happy [in] 1967. I was not a happy child, but I like all that music a hell of a lot. It's great." He adds, "Putting down people for not wearing the right turtlenecks is absolutely stupid."

If the Fleshtones' lifestyle had a theme song during this period, it was "Screamin' Skull," a shameless ode to taking speed and staying up all night. "We loved speed," Keith admits. "Was that song 'in praise of speed'? I don't know. Maybe it documented speed. That's different. We didn't really praise taking that stuff. The song doesn't say that at all." Despite the band's lukewarm defense, "Screamin' Skull" was indeed an unabashed celebration of wailing down Sunset Boulevard on rocket fuel, seeing triple with frayed nerves. *I can't sleep,* Peter moans, looking down at the pills in his sweaty palm: *these beans are all I've got.* The recording brought out the demons in Mazda: "We need devil laughter!" he yelled to the guys' delight and, with the studio lights shut off, stripped naked and screamed the bloodcurdling howl at the song's opening, impressing Ranking Roger, from the English Beat, who was visiting the sessions along with a reporter from *Cash Box.* A roaring, sax-driven number, "Screamin' Skull" would be a live favorite for years, often played at breakneck speed to increasingly slam-dancing crowds. The band wanted the song out as a single, but doubted that I.R.S., in the wake of First Lady Nancy Reagan's "Just Say No" national drug policy, would put much support behind a rockin' psalm to uppers, no matter how catchy.

"Hexbreaker" was another group-composed tune that took on an organic writing process. A rousing *frat hoodoo* against all things Anti-Super Rock, "Hexbreaker," with its horn-and-response hooks, would slot in next to "Roman Gods" as one of the Fleshtones' most recognizable and popular songs. "'Hexbreaker' was my idea," laughs Gordon, who brought in the riff on his beat-up harmonica. "The original lyrics for the chorus were supposed to go, 'They're raising the roof / They're high on vermouth / Becoming uncouth.' But they only took the riff." The band had high hopes for the wild "Hexbreaker" as a breakout dance song, and within the year would remix the track with engineer Dave Lichenstein for a dance club release. But "Super Hexbreaker" would only leak out on a European EP and never appear on *Billboard*'s Club Play Singles chart. ("At the time, I felt kind of offended that they'd gone and remixed material without talking to me about it," Mazda says. "It was a little bit rude, considering that they now say, *Oh, he was the fifth Beatle, the sixth 'Tone*. I don't think they meant any harm, but it wasn't very polite.")

The song that had the best if still slim chance to become a hit from *Hexbreaker!* was Peter's "Right Side of a Good Thing." Polished with Mazda's friendly, sympathetic touch, the song was a sonic crest of Super Rock: part garage, part funky pop, and a bit of New Orleans R&B tossed in. The tune was lyrically upbeat and catchy enough for radio, and Mazda sifted a grab-bag of Fleshtone Noise—Peter's gruff, lively vocal; background sing-alongs; Farfisa organ; wailing harmonica; wood blocks; a "Green Tambourine"–style Coral Sitar—and smoothed the edges, highlighting the tune's ample hooks. "We thought that that song would have been a good mainstream radio song," Keith says. "But I don't know why or what was going on. It always depends on who in the business was promoting that record for I.R.S. Records, who had the contacts, who was using what money to promote where."

Both "Screamin' Skull" and "Right Side of a Good Thing" were ultimately released as singles by I.R.S., but only in the European market. "America was not a singles market," explains John Guarnieri, director of A&R at I.R.S. "We were all hardcore vinyl junkies, but singles weren't really an entity in America. When Miles first wanted to start putting singles out with A&M he wanted to have them with the small holes, like in England. 'Single' was kind of a broad-based term; later it came to mean 'radio-emphasis track.' We released singles at I.R.S. because it was a collector's thing. It was fun." Perhaps Copeland took a marketing hunch based on Continental response to the band. Perhaps he was taking note of the American industry's general shunning of singles as commercial product. Or perhaps he was sensing that the Fleshtones would never be embraced by America.

The Fleshtones were bitterly disappointed by the label's decision not to release any domestic singles from *Hexbreaker!*, but they threw themselves into the making of the video for "Right Side of a Good Thing." I.R.S. flew the band out to Los Angeles, where they assembled at the Hollywood Hills home of director Francis Delia, whom Grasso had brought aboard. Essentially a filmed *bacchanal*, the lo-fi video documents the vibe of The House parties from so many years before at an exaggerated, So Cal, poolside level. I.R.S. catered the shoot, and the Fleshtones made trashcans full of Blue Whale and invited over nearly a hundred friends and fans to the house. "As soon as I saw the batches of Blue Whale, I thought, *This is gonna fly out of control!* and of course, it did," Grasso remembers. "It came to just under where the entire thing was going to fall apart and we weren't going to get a video at all, because everyone was so completely smashed. That one was great, great, great, great fun."

Peter hoped to re-create the *faux* strobe-light effects in Henry Jones' *Soul City*, and he played the two-minute film for Delia and his staff. What Delia delivered was a handheld mini-masterpiece of silliness. Interspersed with goofy soundbites from the guys ("You can't have a party without music!" Peter gushes), the Fleshtones positively swing, Peter's whipping head nearly flying from his neck, Gordon, mock-serious as always, banging two tambourines together while clutching his beloved harp between his teeth, Marek beaming throughout. Perhaps inspired by the Le Palace lunacy, the guys ended the song by marching outside to the pool (Bill dragging along his kick drum), where Peter led the crowd *a capella* through the song's chorus, happily filling everyone's drinks with the aqua-lit pool water.

The imbibing started early and lasted throughout the shoot, and the band had to run through the song several times for Delia to get proper coverage, so the scene at the end of the evening resembled a *Shindig* battlefield. "There were things that we ended up filming that never made it in there, people throwing up and passed out," Grasso remembers. "It was really out of control." But I.R.S. got their video, documenting the Fleshtones at their debauched best. The video received limited airplay on MTV (usually late at night) and was included on *The Beast of I.R.S., Vol. 1* video compilation in 1984.

Hexbreaker! was released on June 7, 1983. Michael Jackson's *Thriller* had firm hold of the number one spot on *Billboard*, followed closely by the soundtrack to *Flashdance*. R.E.M.'s *Murmur* was at number 71 and rising.

The memorable album cover, designed by Peter and Grasso, featured a "fey devil" photograph by George DuBose, who days earlier had shot a prescient promo picture of the band in front of flames, two flickers of which in a happy accident materialized over Keith's head as devil horns. For the album cover, DuBose rented a large studio and photographed the band against an enormous satanic silhouette as they bash away on their gear. Peter loved the setup but made one request: that DuBose droop one of the devil horns slightly. ("It was too perfect otherwise," remembers DuBose. "It didn't fit the character of the Fleshtones.") On the back, a trancelike Peter walks into fire as if possessed, and the colors and graphics were neon-bright. As the liner notes proclaimed, the whole enterprise looked and felt sunny and *new*. "The Fleshtones were always going to be what they were going to be," says Grasso, remembering marketing meetings where Copeland or Boberg would worry if the band looked "sexy" enough. "No matter how much you polished it or tried to put on the shine, there are always going to be a few dirt clods that are going to come through."

Reviews for *Hexbreaker!* were, again, positive. In the *New York Times*, faithful Robert Palmer called the record "a delightful surprise, a disk that captures the raw excitement of a Fleshtones live performance while suggesting that life can add up to more than a round of parties"; the album "offers constant variety" and gives "this enthusiastic but occasionally chaotic-sounding band a big, bright studio sound without dulling the edge of its intensity." In a three-and-a-half-star review in *Rolling Stone*, Parke Puterbaugh called the band "genius" and the album "[l]oose, sloppy and almost dublike," a "rearview-mirror study in fun." *Billboard* placed the record in the "Recommended LPs" column, noting hopefully that the "[t]ough-rock stance could have teen appeal, as group follows up 'Roman Gods' chart debut with a bigger, better effort sure to widen their audience." *Cash Box* described *Hexbreaker!* as "urgent, infectious, *essential* rock." And Ira Robbins in *Trouser Press* wrote that the Fleshtones "hit the nail squarely on the head" with the record;

because the band lives in the present time, "the sensibility that drives them into their musical domain didn't exist when these sounds were introduced. The self-conscious remove gives the band its modern edge." By the end of the year, *Hexbreaker!* had landed on the coveted Pazz & Jop Critics' Poll in *Village Voice* and graced several "Top Album" lists, including *Musician* magazine's "Pick Hits 83," where Brian Cullman called the Fleshtones the most underrated band in the country.

In Europe, the response to the album was characteristically positive, with glowing write-ups in French, Spanish, Swedish, Belgian, German, and Italian music magazines and newspapers, and high rankings on critics' year-end lists. The English reviews were mixed. In *Melody Maker*, Ian Pye wrote, pointedly, that "the party went stale. It's still mildly enjoyable stuff if you like this kind of thing, even while cursed with nostalgia and a vision that looks only backwards. . . . Familiar chanted choruses ring oppressively through the mind at the end of two sides, robbing the album of highs and lows. Ironically, it's all far too homogenous to be really authentic, desperately lacking in a few stand-out cuts to lift the whole affair beyond the average and despite the manic cover stares, 'Hexbreaker!' never goes really over the top."

I.R.S. put little promotional support behind *Hexbreaker!*, and the indifference from Hollywood irked the band and Mazda. "I think that the label was behind the Fleshtones initially," says Grasso. "But Miles wanted so much for these acts to go into the mainstream that he started making more hard-edged decisions on what an act should do. In the case of the Fleshtones, he was beginning to feel that, despite the initial energy, they needed to move up a notch and be more commercial—whatever that might have entailed in Miles' mind more than anybody else's." *Hexbreaker!* failed to chart on *Billboard*'s Top 200 and thus suffered an unfortunate contractual twist bedeviling any I.R.S. artist: an album that did not move a hundred thousand or more units would not receive the massive promotional and marketing push from the well-heeled parent company A&M, a drive that helped punch the Go-Go's and R.E.M. into national consciousness via advertising, radio, and tour support.

"I.R.S. liked the Fleshtones records creatively," insists John Guarnieri. "They felt that the best way to sell the records was to keep the band on the road. The Fleshtones always got college airplay, but I.R.S. was starting at that point to get into the 'radio trap.' Nobody cared early on, but with the success of the Go-Go's and things starting to click for the label. Miles thought that if you really want to sell records, you've got to get airplay." *Hexbreaker!* and *Roman Gods* came nowhere near selling in excess of a hundred thousand: industry estimates put domestic sales near twenty-five to thirty thousand for each, maximum, and, in fact, *Hexbreaker!* sold fewer copies than *Roman Gods*. From a business standpoint, by the end of 1983 the Fleshtones were effectively finished at I.R.S. Records. Their contract would be allowed to expire.

Fifteen years later, at the close of the century, when the average rock fan was asked about the Fleshtones he probably said, "Those guys? Yeah. Didn't they break up after *Hexbreaker!?*"

Miles Copeland had a resolute desire to squeeze what he could from his acts, and F.B.I. launched the Fleshtones on a cross-country tour starting in August. They flew to California and played the Plant in Studio City, Music Machine in LA, and Club Lingerie in Hollywood (opening for the "Original" Standells), then climbed into the van, leaned their heads back for some fitful sleep, and headed east: *San Diego; Phoenix; Dallas; Austin; New Orleans; Atlanta; Columbus; Cleveland; Chicago; New Hope; Buffalo; Boston; Philadelphia; Baltimore; Washington, D.C.; New York City. . . .* To a town, the band earned rave reviews among fans and journalists for their super-spirited, tireless shows, and the guys were discovering certain cities that were very hospitable to Super Rock, among them Minneapolis, Chicago, Atlanta, Baltimore, and especially Washington, D.C., where they began playing popular "Fleshtones Weekends"—two nights, four different sets—at the legendary black-painted 9:30 Club. The Fleshtones were the first band booked by promoter Seth Hurwitz to play at 9:30, a venue that modeled its seat-free, danceable floor on places like Danceteria in Manhattan. The Fleshtones would virtually become a resident band there throughout the 1980s.

Near the close of the tour, I.R.S. launched a somewhat feeble "Super-Rock Hexbreaker Dance Party" promotion in college markets nationwide, with tie-ins with local record stores: at the Fleshtones' Peppermint Lounge show on September 9, the final fifty couples in the competition danced in front of Peter and radio station and label reps. The promotion kept *Hexbreaker!* visible in the college-radio market, but didn't make much headway for the record anywhere else. As wild as the Fleshtones' live shows were, they simply weren't translating into record sales. Underrated and underselling, the band continued to gross well at shows, particularly in New York at venues such as Peppermint Lounge, the Ritz, and Irving Plaza. "As soon as someone would see the Fleshtones live, they'd be a fan," says Grasso.

"That was the most frustrating part with them, more than with many, many other bands at that time. If you just *see* the Fleshtones, it changes everything."

As go the Go-Go's, so goes I.R.S. Records, Miles Copeland infamously declared to his staff. The Fleshtones, unfortunately, would be left behind.

In October, the band made another brave attempt at conquering England, commencing with two support shows for label-mates the Alarm at the Savoy Ballroom in London where, it was rumored, Ray Davies and Mick Avory of the Kinks were in attendance. With Playn Jayne supporting, the Fleshtones played various dates around the U.K., culminating with a show at the legendary Marquee Club on October 31. In November, the guys flew up to Sweden for two shows and then down to Brussels for a gig particularly close to their heart, opening for longtime hero Alan Vega.

Staring down a particularly hostile crowd at an English club during one of these long evenings, the Fleshtones spontaneously threw themselves into a mock-heroic stance onstage: stopping playing, their sweaty arms folded, they glared back at the hooting unfriendlies in resolute, Mussolini-style. Thus was born the Powerstance. The humorous stage gesture would become synonymous with the band for the rest of their career. French photographer Richard Dumas snapped a number of photos during this tour that would pop up in the coming years, including one documenting the Powerstance that graced the band's live album, their swan song for I.R.S., in 1985.

On a day off, the band slipped into Fade Away Studios in London and cut a sprightly version of Lightnin' Slim's 1957 swamp blues "Mean Ole' Lonesome Train," featuring Keith's first lead vocal in five years. "It sounds great. We've really rocked it up," Keith enthused.

He added morosely, "I doubt anybody will ever play it."

15.
American Beat

The Fleshtones spent the early winter writing and rehearsing, lamenting the puzzling fate of *Hexbreaker!*, and playing gigs. In January, they visited the 688 Club down in Atlanta for the second time, securing a relationship with that venue that would prove helpful in a couple of years, and at the end of the month were back out in LA at the Music Machine. They tore home through the Midwest with a stop at First Avenue in Minneapolis, where if the guys were lucky an infamous, locally disbarred pharmacist named Pharmacy Mike might show up with any pill they wanted. They were then up and down the Mid-Atlantic region in February, and back rocking the Ritz in New York City. All with scant label support. The band was being hailed as "Our Local Heroes" in *Village Voice* ads and were even featured in the January issue of *Tiger Beat Star* magazine, wherein Bill urged his teenybopper fans to rub *Hexbreaker!* over any cuts or scratches they might suffer from in order to heal themselves. These were desperate times, indeed.

The band always tried to face the desperation with fervor. "During a good show—or even a really, really bad show—something just takes over," Peter explained of his onstage mettle. "In fundamentalist religious circles, it's called the spirit, and I'm most definitely possessed. Sometimes I have trouble explaining that to people, but it's not an act. Something happens, and I'm usually disappointed if it doesn't happen."

Primary focus for the band was working up demos of new material to send to Miles and company in the fading hopes that they'd be re-signed for a third studio album. Up in Room 401 at the Music Building, Marek set up his "port-a-studio"—essentially a glorified TEAC boombox with a four-track recorder—and the band spent several weeks laying down tracks. Jimmy Ford also managed to arrange a demo recording session in New Orleans to be produced by John Fred of "Judy in Disguise" fame. The guys had been building up collections of rollicking New Orleans "race" records for years, flipping out to the likes of Huey "Piano" Smith, Bobby Marchan, Irma Thomas, and Chris Kenner. They were becoming comfortable in the festive Crescent City and would become happy, drunken regulars at Mardi Gras for years. They approached the sessions with optimism, but upon arrival in New Orleans were greeted with a major thunderstorm of omenlike proportions that temporarily flooded their studio. "I don't recall seeing John Fred once amongst the floating recording gear and amps at the studio," said Peter of those sessions. "He might have passed his hand over the boxes of tapes at some point, unbeknownst to me."

Songs taking shape in New York and New Orleans were a motley lot. "Wind Out" was a gift from R.E.M. (they'd written and cut the track during *Reckoning* but felt that it'd be a better fit for the Flesh-tones); "Leather Kings" was Keith's stirring Gary Glitter–like instrumental; "I Need Something" was a rare number from Marek in which he was perhaps hinting at his growing dissatisfaction within the band; "In Need of Love" was an obscure R&B cover; "Fighting for a Lost Cause" was a self-evident barometer of the band's general attitude at the time. Of this batch, only a handful would see official release over the next few years, in one case as a cheeky in-joke. Most were destined for a bottom drawer in Room 401. I.R.S., looking for a radio- and video-friendly smash hit from the Fleshtones, was indifferent to the new material. Within months, the tape would be sent back to the guys with a polite but firm *Sorry, no.*

Although the band was being stiff-armed from Hollywood, Peter was becoming involved with a line of duty that would bring him out to that area on a regular basis. Miles Copeland had drummed up a deal with MTV for airtime to expose and promote independent bands and artists. "Miles threw this project on me," remembers Carlos Grasso.

"I knew nothing about television, but I got together with Jonathan Dayton and Valerie Faris, the directors of the program, and I essentially put the talent together and wrote the general scenarios. I thought that Peter was so special and that he'd make a really good host, because of his nature and his manner. And he's funny."

Cutting Edge debuted on MTV in 1983, airing once a month late on Sunday nights until roughly 1990 (dovetailing near the end of its run with the live Cutting Edge Happy Hour). The premise of the program, subtitled "Music, Interviews, Education," was to showcase indie music and artists, presenting the "cutting edge" of popular culture in terms of unorthodox, criminally ignored, or otherwise offbeat bands and visual artists via a lively format of performances and interviews. Featured on Cutting Edge in the first few years, in addition to run-downs of the CMJ Alternative Music Charts, were General Public, Echo and the Bunnymen, Jools Holland, Henry Rollins, the Psychedelic Furs, the Minutemen, the Blasters, Hoodoo Gurus, R.E.M., Moorisey, Flat Duo Jets, Red Hot Chili Peppers, Lords of the New Church, Jonathan Richman, and X. The Fleshtones were featured on an early episode with "Screamin' Skull" blaring in the background intercut with scenes of the guys goofing around flipping burgers in a diner.

The producers first experimented with a couple of regional hosts whom Miles had hoped would be more mainstream than Peter, but Peter ended up being the perfect fit, and he would host the show regularly from 1984 until 1987. His increasing comfort in the Southern California milieu, his loose if nervy presence in front of the camera, and the enthusiasm he showed for (the majority of) his guests, many of whom were quite obscure to the young MTV audience, were integral factors in the show's success and its eventual strong reputation. Cutting Edge paved the way for subsequent like-minded programs on the network, such as 120 Minutes, and Grasso feels that "Peter ended up becoming the kind of host that, as a blueprint, MTV ended using later."

Swinging his long bangs, Peter exhibited the right amount of cultural outsiderness to be considered hip, leavened with an almost hypersincerity and tongue-in-cheek earnestness. His hosting manner might be described as hipster au courant: here was a man slyly, if not entirely comfortably, aware of his own geeky coolness. Once a month, Peter would fly out to LA, settle into the Tropicana, and record band intros, "man-on-the-street" interviews, and the like, over a two-day period. By the end of his first year Peter was being paid $1,000 a show—not bad money, and the wad dovetailed nicely with the Fleshtones' decent paydays. On occasion, the television commitments interfered with the Fleshtones' itinerary. More than once Peter would fly into LA in the midst, or at the tail end, of a Fleshtones tour, arriving sleepless and exhausted; at times his voice would be noticeably hoarse on television. "He was always a trooper," Grasso insists. For years Peter would juggle his *Cutting Edge* responsibilities with his band and personal commitments. The marriage was not always happy.

While Peter was decked out in shades, propped up in convertibles, and driven around sunny LA, Keith and Marek were hanging out in the East Village at the Pyramid Club, a lively, memorable, and unique gay dive bar on Avenue A that opened in 1981 and quickly became a second home to all of the band members, who found the eclectic, cross-dressing, pure-fun vibe of the joint intoxicating. Peter's friend Gary Fakete had introduced them to the club, the happenings and clientele of which was in large part fueled by the same inspiration (and in some cases, by the same cast of characters) that drove the old Club 57. Ann Magnuson, Keith Haring, Wendy Wild, and others set the Pyramid's nights alive with gallery openings, drag shows, and DJ-spun glimmer; at one point, Nico lived in a loft upstairs. As *Time Out New York* noted, "The supremely grimy hole-in-the-wall" was much more than "a trannie tavern—it was the creative heart of a then-thriving East Village scene." The Fleshtones dug it and were the first rock & roll band to play there. "We were basically the house band at the Pyramid," says Peter.

The Pyramid Club did a good seven or eight years of being a unique club, "a mix of New York sensibility," Keith remembers. "Artists, musicians, drag queens, bikers, the whole thing would just groove. It was exciting every night, and there was always something happening entertainment-wise, Lower East Side entertainment, that made it just so much fun." The narrow club had a small stage and sound system, and in the mid-eighties Keith began booking shows on Thursday nights that he dubbed "Mod Teepee," and many side projects for the guys, Love Delegation, Wild Hyenas, Tall Lonesome Pines, and Mad Violets among them, would originate from the sleepless Pyramid scene.

The Fleshtones and the Pyramid made for a combustible, gender-fucking stew where on any given night film and theater happenings would simmer with John Sex stripping atop the bar to "The Theme from 'The Vindicators.'" The vibe at the club would usually accompany the band on the road. "The unofficial title for one Fleshtones tour was *Trapped in the Body of a Man*," Marek remembers, laugh-

ing. "I'm not really sure what that's supposed to mean!" ("We wanted to make people think," suggests Peter cryptically. "Who knows,
anyway?") Marek fondly remembers "the dear, late departed Ethel
Eichelberger on the bar playing the devil's own instrument, the
accordion, and there was a coterie of crazy drag queens who'd come
on the road with us, constant companions on some of the tours."
Pyramid co-owner Brian Butterick would at times stagger out onto
Avenue A at the end of the night with literally thousands of dollars of
cash in his pockets, and on impulse gather his friends, take a cab out
to Kennedy Airport, and fly to wherever in the country the Fleshtones were playing that night.

The Pyramid's bar-treading, drink-spilling crowds gleefully
ignored the cultural politics that were then blossoming. "It was a
very creative gay community that didn't have an ax to grind," Peter
explains. "They were all so gay that it didn't make any difference.
They might have been given a hard time, but everyone there accepted who they were to the point where they weren't self-conscious
about it anymore. They were basically making fun of drag queens."
The Fleshtones were utterly comfortable at the Pyramid. "For people
who felt that they missed out on some of the excitement of the sixties, the Warhol thing, the Pyramid was better. Every day and night
was great; it just kept going and going and going. The gay scene was
interesting and a lot of fun."

At the end of one long evening in the spring of 1984, Keith,
Marek, Butterick, and drinking buddies Michael "Kitty" Ullmann
and local legend drag queen Lady Bunny closed the bar and dragged
a bag of six-packs over to the band shell at Tompkins Square. The
drunken talk turned to the idle-headed idea of throwing a daylong
drag festival in the shell, an open-air invite to all of the most fantastic queens, fags, and straight-*cum*-inner-freakflag-wavers in the
neighborhood who wanted to groove to disco and sunshine. The
friends laughed into early morning hours, and at some point Marek
suggested that they call the event "Wigstock," as a parody of Woodstock and as a sly insistence on a required fashion accessory.

Wigstock debuted on a crisp Labor Day in 1984. Lady Bunny
kicked off the proceedings by belting "I Feel the Earth Move,"
sashaying across the stage to the delight of the small but enthusiastic crowd; the Fleshtones played, and in subsequent Wigstock's
would team up with Wendy Wild as a waggish "Jefferson Hairplane."
A cast of regulars would catapult the event into a major local scene;
both Ru Paul ("Supermodel: You Better Work") and Dee-Lite
("Groove Is in the Heart") launched their careers from the amped fri-

volity of the Wigstock band shell. By 1990, the crowds were numbering in the tens of thousands. In 1991, the event was moved to Union Square, and ultimately to the West Side piers, where the crowds swelled to fifty thousand, before Lady Bunny finally put an end to the series that had grown beyond anyone's wildest dreams on that beer-soaked, Uranian night back in Tompkins Square.

By the time Nirvana played their first New York area show at the Pyramid in the summer of 1989, the Fleshtones were dropping out of the scene. "The Pyramid became our home for much of the eighties," Peter acknowledges. "A lot of people assume that the band broke up in the mid-eighties. We didn't break up. We were at the Pyramid."

Meanwhile, Gordon was about to take an unfortunate plunge. In March he, Keith, and Bill went to see Jason and the Scorchers at Irving Plaza. The roots-rocking Scorchers were touring behind their expanded *Fervor* EP, and the place was packed and rocking. It had been snowing unseasonably heavily that evening. Gordon and Bill started drinking hard and early and by the end of the night the two buddies were trashed beyond repair. The clock on the wall had slipped into surreal overdrive, and before Gordon and Bill knew what had happened the show was over, and "Last call!" was bellowed out on both floors. Keith bid his mates *adieu* and headed home—Gordon and Bill had different ideas. After most of the crowd had left the venue, the two staggered about, dodging security, and managed to get themselves locked inside the building. "They thought that they could continue drinking for free!" laughs Keith.

Bill and Gordon were locked inside "accidentally on purpose," as Gordon acknowledges. "I can always out-drink or stay up later than all of the guys, because I'm a madman, but even I said to myself, *Holy shit, if the cops find me in here, they're gonna bust me for breaking and entering!*" Panicking, his head buzzing, Gordon remembered reading in a paper that ex-cons, when cornered, have a tendency to jump out of windows at amazing heights. "So I looked out the window, and thought, *Oh, man, that's only nine or ten feet. I can make that easily.* It's a blizzard outside and I thought, *Well, it's either this or going to jail.* So I said, 'Fuck this.'"

The Birdman of Irving Plaza jumped out the window but quickly realized when it was taking an awfully long time for him to hit the ground, twenty feet below, that he was in trouble. He hit the ground hard. "I shattered my heel, the slowest-healing bone in the body, and to this day I'm half an inch shorter on my left side, and it gives me back pains." When Gordon finally arrived home that night, drunk and cursing, his maimed heel gave out on his iced front steps and he fell and twisted his wrist, adding further agony. Gordon was laid up for a while, prone and ruing his latest sautéed adventure. "To the band's credit, they didn't fire me, they didn't lecture me," he says. "And Peter came to visit." Gordon continued to draw pay from the band's bank account while he was recuperating, a situation that didn't sit well with all of the members, and he rushed his rehab in typical recklessness, removing his cast prematurely and giving up his cane. "The band didn't know, but I was on narcotic painkillers for a few years. I was very slick. I knew a girl who's an optician and I would use stuff so they wouldn't catch me with dilated pupils. I was the only one in the band who never wore shades, but I pulled that routine a few times. The guys never knew.

"Couldn't the guys have said that I was in a car accident? Instead they said, 'Gordon jumped out a window!' It makes me sound like a suicidal maniac." He adds: "I'll confess to being a maniac, but I wasn't suicidal."

The month that Gordon began his convalescence, the Fleshtones received an unexpected offer from I.R.S. Records. Taking note of the popularity of the *Flashdance*, *Fast Times at Ridgemont High*, *Valley Girl*, and *Footloose* soundtrack albums, Miles Copeland had gotten his fingers into a middling Twentieth Century Fox production titled *Bachelor Party*, starring Tom Hanks and, among others, Adrian Zmed and Tawny Kitaen (whom Copeland was dating). I.R.S. would release the soundtrack, which featured exclusive label artists; lined up for the project were R.E.M., Oingo Boingo, Jools Holland, the Alarm, and others. Copeland wanted the Fleshtones involved, and so the band was re-signed to I.R.S. for the project.

Copeland had always loved the Red Star "American Beat" single, and the label felt that the band should rerecord that track as an ideal "Theme for a Bachelor Party." "If you get a song on a soundtrack, that can really be a vehicle to break a band," explains John Guarnieri. "Everybody knew that 'American Beat' was such a great song, but we knew we'd never be able to license it from Marty Thau because he probably would have wanted too much money. You could recut a song, depending upon what kind of contract you had, but there are certain statutes of limitations. I think that Miles thought, *Well fuck it, let's just recut it. If Thau doesn't like it, let him sue us.* Miles knew Marty Thau from back in the seventies. There was no fallout, as I recall." (In fact, Marty Thau learned of Copeland's tactics years later and was none too pleased. "That's the way Miles Copeland treats people and does business," says Thau. "The truth was, I had fifty percent of the publishing, and I never got paid my share, which would have been twenty-five percent of all the revenues that that song earned. The Fleshtones were actually $17,000 in the red in their Red Star account, which was nonrecoupable for me unless they earned royalties. I stewed over it for a while, and then just dropped it. That's the way Miles behaves, and that's the way he does business. I was pissed off. It was small-time shit. Typical of Miles. And also typical of the Fleshtones.")

I.R.S. decided to move on from Richard Mazda, and his days with the Fleshtones were over. "I have nothing but fond memories of being with the band," says Mazda. "But I think it's really rather sad that the last album I did for them came to be the last because of the bad blood over being overbudget. One thing about me, that I think is slightly different to other producers, is that I think that a way to develop a career is to *maintain* a relationship. We didn't get that far. It would have been interesting to do one more record." ·

The Fleshtones, however, were keen to move forward. Says Marek, "We kind of thought that Richard was kind of going off the deep end. He was doing his own recordings out in LA. We thought that he was hitting it a little too hard, that there was a little studio burn going on. We felt it was time for a change. Half the fun of being in the recording industry is that you've got all of these amazing producers out there who bring something to the records they work on, and you can switch producers. That was always part of the mystique: *Who are we gonna get??* You don't switch horses in midstream, but you can do so between albums."

Copeland decided to team the Fleshtones up with one of their long-time heroes, hopeful that the sonic simpatico would pay dividends commercially. Richard Gottehrer had been instrumental in forming Sire Records with Seymour Stein, and by 1984 he was also a leading rock & roll record producer, having helmed the boards for successful albums for Richard Hell, Blondie, and the Go-Go's, and having worked with other commercial-minded artists such as the Bongos and Marshall Crenshaw. Gottehrer's recognizable "Instant Record" sound, glommed onto artists as diverse as Joan Armatrading and Robert Gordon, was identifiable as smooth without being lightweight, accessible without lacking punch. As Marek remembers it, "There was no way the Fleshtones were *not* gonna bow before the master!"

Richard Gottehrer was a Brooklyn-born and -raised songwriter and producer who, with partners Bob Feldman and Jerry Goldstein, composed and manufactured pop songs in the heyday of the Brill Building, landing a number-one hit with the Angels' "My Boyfriend's Back" in 1963. Very soon, the British Invasion landed on American shores and work began to dry up for the talented trio. Hyperaware of the Liverpudlian blaze, Feldman, like any good industry man, wanted to jump in and feel the heat along with everyone else. He devised a ludicrous but hilarious scam: he, Goldstein, and Gottehrer would pretend to be three sibling imports from the Australian Outback, deck themselves out in matching black leather pants and zebra-skin vests, and pound tribal drums over simple, sing-along tunes. The ruse worked. America bought the Strangeloves (so named after the trio's down-under "last names," Strange), and propelled their single "I Want Candy" to the top of the pop and R&B charts in 1965. Successful cross-country tours followed, during which the straight-faced Strangeloves kept up their transatlantic farce, all the while riding the coattails of the English beat-group craze (they were nearly lynched in Alabama by a group unhappy with white foreigners singing black-sounding songs).

Gottehrer grew up loving R&B. "I learned all the Strangeloves stuff listening to Bo Diddley records and Howlin' Wolf," he explains. "I didn't learn it because I thought I could get rich, or exploit anybody, I learned it because I liked it. And I seemed to have an innate ability to communicate those ideas to my like-kind, middle-class white kids. It wasn't meant to be a life statement, but it turned out to be something that people remembered later on." The Strangeloves eventually hired a rock & roll band, the McCoys, to open for them on the road, and thanked the young group by writing and recording "Hang on, Sloopy" for them, which became a chart smash in 1965. Within a few years, the three hucksters tired of the game, but not before contributing some indelible rock and pop hits to the world, including "Night Time" and, of course, "Cara-Lin," which the Fleshtones had rocked up in their Red Star sessions and were continuing to play live.

To a man, the Fleshtones loved the Strangeloves' story: great rock & roll dance tunes with tongue-in-cheek humor and wild, palpable fun. Gottehrer was a pop legend to the guys, and his current success as a producer had only increased his value and coolness in their eyes. The Fleshtones visited Gottehrer in his New York apartment prior to sessions, and, as they would quickly discover, he was a blast to hang with. "It was like having this other kid hanging out with us," Keith remembers. "We'd be up in the rehearsal space, and we had a set of tom-toms just for him to play along with us. And he would go wild! It was blowing our minds." After Gottehrer was hired, he went to see the band play at the Palace in Hollywood and was impressed. He'd known a bit about them in New York, was aware of their reputation, and had kept track of I.R.S. releases.

April studio sessions were booked at the famous Record Plant in Manhattan, where tracks were recorded quickly and enjoyably. "It was pretty easy to work with the Fleshtones," Gottehrer recalls. "I was always good working with transitional artists, people that had the ability to be something and maybe you could bring a little more out of them. Remember, the Fleshtones are a live band, and translating that into the studio is not that easy. But it mixed together well. It wasn't very complicated or difficult. 'American Beat' is a great rock & roll song." Because Gordon was laid up with his heel and wrist injuries, he had to skip the sessions, a fact that he regretted for years. The band hired the Urban Blight Horns, a professional New York outfit and veteran session players, to play on the track, and Tony Orbach blew the tenor sax solo in place of Gordon.

The exciting "American Beat '84 (Theme for a Bachelor Party)" is vintage Gottehrer, opening with Bill's rousing four-on-the-floor drum call and Peter, Keith, Marek, and Bill stomping up and down on wooden planks. Gottehrer tightened the band's performance but delivered it loosely, shining the song's dynamic and hooks—the tambourines shimmer; the horns are bright and catchy—and packing a muscular wallop. "American Beat '84" is a spirited slab of rock & roll, capturing the Fleshtones' anthemic *animus* with style and aggression, and it was also their most commercial sound yet. The highlight of the song was Peter's pounding, raucous roll-call of American rock & rollers that closed the tune. He had sheets of paper in the studio on which he had scribbled various bands and musicians whom he wanted to honor, but the shout-out was essentially off the cuff:

> The Fantastic Johnny C., Freddy "Boom Boom" Cannon, the incredible James Brown, Floyd Brown, Chuck Brown, the Reverend Richard Penniman, Elvis Presley, and all the Kings of rock & roll, Lou Costello, the Intruders, the Illusions, Eddie Cochran, Buddy Holly, the Del-Vikings, Del Fuegos, Del Shannon, MC5, the Velvets, the Stooges, Louie Jordan, Roscoe Gordon, the Raiders, and the Wailers, and the Kingsmen, and the Sonics, Phast Phreddie and the Last, the Unclaimed, the Plimsouls, the Lyres, and the Real Kids, the Modern Lovers, Alan Vega, Los Lobos, the Gentrys, the Dantes, and the Headhunters, too, Mitch Ryder, Richie Valens, the Isleys, Parliament, and the Jackson Five, the Rivingtons, Donna Summer,

Martha Reeves, Richard Berry, Berry Gordy, Chuck Berry, and Louie, Louie, Louie, Louie, Louie, Louie, Louie . . . !

In giving thanks and respect to his heroes, Peter demonstrated the diversity of his and the Fleshtones' blues, R&B, and rock & roll tastes, with Del Shannon and the Jackson Five knocking heads with MC5 and Los Lobos, all spilling Blue Whales at a Super Rock cast party. (Peter ran through at least two versions of the catalog among the song's takes. In one, he hollered out "The Ramones!" but the official take omitted the legendary New York punk band. Allegedly, Joey Ramone was peeved when he heard the released version, offended that the Fleshtones would ignore his band. Years later, Peter cleared the issue up with Joey and, happily, Ramone dropped his grudge.) With Keith, Marek, and Bill chanting "The American beat!" behind Peter's litany, the last sixty-five seconds of the song are exhilarating, among the most exciting passages in the band's catalog.

The single was released on July 10, 1984, a week and a half after *Bachelor Party* premiered to decidedly cool reviews. Midsummer foes on the *Billboard* Top 100 were formidable: Huey Lewis & the News' "If This Is It," Eurythmics' "Right by Your Side," Bananarama's "Cruel Summer," and Night Ranger's "When You Close Your Eyes" were among the top hits of the month (as was Van Halen's great "Panama," the closest Top 40 would get to a marriage of the MC5 and Bubblegum). Copeland and I.R.S. loved the record and Gottehrer's production job, but the weakly promoted "American Beat '84" had little chance commercially, despite a cobbled-together video, and was not assisted by the movie's lackluster box office returns. The Fleshtones' reaction at the movie premiere didn't help the band's status at I.R.S.: sitting behind Hanks and studio execs, the guys openly and loudly goofed on the flick and then Keith, hungover, fell asleep.

"Hall of Fame," the B-side, was born in humid New Orleans as a funky, Lee Dorsey–type groove. "Marek had his port-a-studio set up in the hotel room," Keith remembers. "We were taking a whole bunch of crystal methedrine, so we were full of energy and ideas." Peter came in with the idea, wrote the lyrics, and put the groove together with the help of Keith and Gottehrer. White funk with tongue firmly in cheek, "Hall of Fame" is a five-minute dance tribute to figures whom the Fleshtones loved, from "The World's Greatest Scientists" and "The King of the Blues" to Carl Yaztremski and Earnest Borgnine. (Peter also gives shout-outs to Sylvester, Edwin Starr, and Liberace.) During the tune the guys unabashedly dub themselves "The Uncrowned Kings of Pop and Soul" and "The Five

Most Exciting Men in Rock & roll." (*Well*, they figured, *America isn't gonna.*) An appropriate sonic complement to the A-side, "Hall of Fame" generated some dance-club play, and was a live favorite for years. In France and Holland exclusively I.R.S. released an "American Beat '84" EP, appending to the two Gottehrer tunes the dance-mix of "Hexbreaker" and the "Mean 'Ole Lonesome Train" recording from the year before.

For Peter, working with Gottehrer was memorable more for the camaraderie than for the finished product. "Gotteherer's a wonderful guy, an original Brill Building *mensch*," Peter says with affection. "He's fun talking to about music and hanging out with. To a certain degree he was very open to all of our ideas, and he would know how to do all this stuff because he did it originally. But when all was said and done he still turned out the sound of the moment, the *à la mode* sound, which to me was lacking a bit in excitement. He always wanted to be on the cusp of what was happening, even in the sixties."

Gottehrer himself sensed a stumbling block on the Fleshtones' path to commercial success. "I loved both of those tracks because of the rockin' attitude," he exclaims. "But that was never what getting on radio was about. What came out of CBGB's was Blondie, the Ramones, Talking Heads, bands with songs and style that went in the direction of the bigger pop picture. The Fleshtones remained a little true to the looseness of the band roots, and it might have hurt them in terms of acceptability of contemporary radio. But it certainly didn't hurt them if they're still a band playing together. None of these other people probably even make music anymore."

The Hex was working. In August, the Fleshtones headlined a big-time "Local Heroes" show at the Bottom Line in Greenwich Village, with Suzanne Vega singing and Richard Hell reading poetry as support, but by fall the band's frustrations were mounting. For every sign of progress—the band was invited to accept sponsorship with Miller Beer in the national Miller Rock Network, a promotional boon that gave the band national exposure and tons of free equipment and gear—there was a reminder that the band simply wasn't selling records. The Fleshtones were again hanging by a thread at I.R.S.

Gordon was becoming increasingly despondent. "I had three saxophones, and I sold my baritone," Gordon says. "I was gonna go over to France, live with my girlfriend, try to form an R&B band. Then the phone rings, and it's Keith: *We're touring with Echo and the Bunnymen.* Being loyal that I am, I said, yes. But I have to think, sometimes, how different my life could've been if I would have gone on that plane and went there."

"Gordon would have been dead," says Peter flatly. "That's how it would've been different."

The joint tour with Echo and the Bunnymen, at the time garnering excellent press and interest for their stirring, moody, post-psychedelic music, was a bit odd, organized as it was not through F.B.I. but through various venue-specific promoters. The Fleshtones supported Echo and the Bunnymen, along with Billy Bragg, the English Socialist singer-songwriter. Beginning in August, the six-week tour brought the musicians across the country. At first blush, the pairing of the English and New York bands seemed curious, and the tour's early dates were marred by strife. The Fleshtones had to cancel their first two appearances, in Washington, D.C., and West Hartford, Connecticut, due to the mounting frustrations inside of Peter that Gordon and others had palpably felt. "I had been arguing with Marilla about the dates," Peter admits. "I had made a promise to her that I wouldn't tour, and yet at the same time I said to the band and promoters, 'Yes, I will do this tour.' It was great to be on, a big deal, and I really shouldn't have canceled those dates."

Peter was going to turn thirty in September, and he was no doubt taking stock of his personal and professional situations. "Peter was very depressed about the band and what we were doing at that point," Keith acknowledges of his friend, who was born of a darker disposition than the other band members. At this time Keith met with Peter at his apartment and tried to talk him into continuing the tour, suggesting that they may get a shot to do a studio album with Richard Gottehrer. But Peter balked. "He was very disillusioned with the whole thing. I said, 'Hey, there's still a lot here. We play in front of a lot of different people every night. This is a *good* thing.' And we decided to do the rest of the tour. I saw a lot there still." Yet, Keith adds, "It's easy to get disillusioned."

Ultimately, the guys got along well with the Bunnymen, particularly with Ian McCulloch, the pallid lead singer who displayed a winning diet of excessive drinking and who more than once after a gig roared off on his scooter with a cute girl on back, inciting the friendly envy of Peter. The bands indulged in Americana road and van antics, including an impromptu and self-financed (and wholly illegal) private fireworks show in the Arches in Utah. ("We hadn't passed a car in hours," Peter remembers. "It was beautiful.") The Fleshtones were grateful that Echo and the Bunnymen would lend their sound board and help with show lighting, and as the tour progressed, the Bunny-men would jam with the band onstage. "Every night, Mac and I'd go out and party, and just see what was going on in whatever town," Keith remembers. "It was a great tour." (The politically conservative Fleshtones decided against arguing with Bragg and his "bullshit, Pro-letarian nonsense," as Peter refers to the singer's liberal politics. "We figured that that was his *shtick*. The fact is, he identified with *us* any-way. Him saying 'the people': his 'people' are theoretical. We *are* the people, and 'the people' are all sorts, anyway.")

During the tour, most patrons would still be filing in as the Flesh-tones were playing, but by the end of the set they'd be responding enthusiastically. Characteristic was a Salt Lake City notice calling the Bunnymen performance impressive but "somewhat standoffish," and the Fleshtones' "a 180 degree contrast. They did the entire show in front of a closed curtain and were not afraid to interact with the paying customers in the front row. . . . Whatever you call it, I call it entertaining. The New York quintet plays with such exuberance they can win you over with a couple of tunes." Despite the good crowds, positive response, and sautéed simpatico with Echo and the Bunny-men, the dam burst for the Fleshtones on this tour. The guys—Gor-don, especially—were beginning to spin out of control in the eyes of I.R.S., and one particularly wild incident raised eyebrows. The Flesh-tones were scheduled to play at Irvine Meadow (since renamed Ver-izon Wireless Amphitheater), a large open-air theater in LA, and some I.R.S. Records executives were showing up to pass judgment. The night before, in San Francisco, the fellas had partied insanely on drink and methedrine, and in the morning, their heads cracked open, they realized they needed more drugs. Gordon had made a score the night before and his connection agreed to cop for the band, but unbeknownst to the guys, their road manager had scored some choice speed from the hotel desk clerk. Gordon never returned. The band boarded the plane without him, their road manager waiting behind for Gordon to come back to take the next flight down.

The Fleshtones flew into LA and were driven to soundcheck. Despite Gordon having gone missing, the guys were feeling pretty happy and worry-free with the speed coursing through them. Near-ing showtime, they began to receive frantic phone calls from Gordon and a mysterious stranger, promising that they were on their way and that they were only forty minutes from the venue. The problem was that the Fleshtones were playing in less than fifteen minutes. The guys brainstormed and decided to put "Legend of a Wheelman" fifth in the set. "We figure that Gordon will be there in time, and even if we hit the stage without him, we'll have him come on," says Keith. "So we're doing our show and sure enough, I saw the car pull up, the car door open, and Gordon coming running out of the car. He has the sax in his mouth, runs up on the stage, and I wave him up. We whip into 'Wheelman,' and he just goes in front of the mike set up for him. We thought it was fantastic!"

I.R.S. Records didn't think so.

This wouldn't be the last time that Gordon's recklessness affected the band's reputation as unprofessional wild men. In Chicago, Gordon, drunk and dosed with LSD, darted from the stage and vomitted all over Carlos Grasso's shoes. And this was *after* having had sex with the club owner's girlfriend. In Los Angeles a couple of years later, Gordon awoke one morning horribly hungover and wrapped up in an oversized rug: therein he had found some dicey solace after being chased from the backseat of a stranger's convertible where he was drunkenly crashing out, having forgotten his way back to the hotel. "I would say that my drinking, yes, was a factor at times," Gordon says.

After the Irvine show, the label said that because they had nothing that sounded like a hit and because the sound of the demoed songs wasn't satisfactory in the least, it might be time to part ways with the Fleshtones. Again.

The Fleshtones rounded out 1984 the way they began: assaulting late-night stages with abandon, including another "Fleshtones Weekend" at the 9:30 Club in Washington, D.C., in October (a show that acted as an apology of sorts for the canceled August date). During that same busy month the band rocked Irving Plaza again, and Keith made a guest appearance at an R.E.M. show in Passaic, New Jersey; it was over to Maxwell's in November, followed by a long, raucous gig with Barrence Whitfield and the Savages at the University of Maryland in early December, and, four days before Christmas, back down Route 95 to the 9:30 Club for another weekend. Four sweaty shows, four wildly disparate sets, another perspiring way to make $6,000. "Those sets at the 9:30 Club Weekends would all be different," remembers Peter. "We had no idea what was going to happen. It was like theater of some odd sort."

Playing, preaching, playing, converting. The road-weary, sleep-deprived, liver-taxing routine was becoming a grind for certain band members, some of whom would take an opportunity at the dawn of the next year to go not a little insane.

16.
The Fleshtones vs. Reality

The guys trailed a line of cocaine down from Manhattan, squinted in the light, and found themselves in the bright blue Caribbean. As Ronald Reagan raised his hand at his second inaugural and felt behind him the gust of a national rout, the Fleshtones were two thousand miles away, disconnected from American politics, culture, and air conditioning. Rick Shoor at F.B.I. attached the band to the Caribbean Festival Trianon, held on Martinique. The Fleshtones were slotted to play with popular French group Telephone and local artists Malavoir, Kali, and Poglo. The festival was programmed by Jose Hayot, a young, wealthy Martiniquean who with his equally well-heeled friends would soon become a friend in the Fleshtones' New York scene and an important, if short-lived, link in their career. "Jose's family was a major family on the island," says Robert Singerman, who organized the festival appearance with Shoor. "I'm fairly sure that some of his ancestors had been brought over by Louis the Sixteenth to colonialize the island in the seventeenth century. They owned rum, beer, bananas, gas, Kodak, and many other businesses on the island. Every person living on Martinique knew Jose."

Keen to enjoy some sun splash and to leave a bleak New York winter behind them, the Fleshtones were unaware of the *Night of the*

*Iguana-cum-*Super Rock anarchy awaiting them. The bands were assembled in New York, the mood ebullient, and as Marek recalls "everyone was already half in the bag by the time we got on the plane. Gordon, who's now sort of starting to move into another phase, has got a wig on—or maybe it was just his own hair and it was completely out of control—and he breaks out his saxophone. The plane is taking off and he's in the aisle playing saxophone, roaming up and down, and the whole plane is going nuts. He's playing his *Defenders* theme, something monumental! Finally, someone managed to get him in his seat. That was how it started. It didn't let up from there."

The promoter had scheduled a modest West Indies itinerary, including visits to Fort de France, the island capital. The band arrived a week before the scheduled show, *sans* Peter, who was otherwise committed and would come later. Upon arrival, the guys were astounded to learn that each group had a private island at their disposal, complete with a screened-in bungalow, a long dock, a cistern in the yard providing fresh water, a full cooking and housecleaning staff, and local fishermen hired to bring in the freshest catches for food. The guys duly named their retreat "Fleshtones Island," a little hummock coming out of the water. The maintenance man would materialize once a day on a boat and bring groceries, the cook would prepare lunch and supper, and then the guys would be stuck out there by themselves. The afternoons sizzled at ninety degrees, but by late night the trade winds would blow a gentle breeze. The house was stocked with rum, beer, and a huge vat of Planter's Punch, and with no TV or radio, the fellas turned to drink.

The tops of their heads coming off at the tropical *cornucopia* before them, Keith, Marek, Bill, and Gordon felt as if they'd been transported into a sultry Joseph Conrad tale. Shoor, who with Singerman was spending some time on the island, eventually found the sweltry goings-on too much to handle and headed back to Martinique's four-star, air-conditioned hotel. "The bathroom had no running water," Shoor recalls. "The toilet required dumping a bucket of water into it to flush it, and the shower was an enclosure outside the house with a hose running cold water." The Fleshtones weren't bothered by these low-rent accouterments and, bombed on Planter's Punch and reliving the Queens orgies of yore, roughed it in all of their hedonistic glory.

One afternoon, late in the day, the housekeeper's young son came in from the surf with a blowfish, and the creature was flopping on the dock, breathing its last. Gordon was so moved by this that he went running back to the bungalow to retrieve his saxophone. He began serenading the dying blowfish as the sun set, making a silhouette of compassion for the bemused guys. "This was so disconnected from anything else going on," says Marek. "We left civilization behind!" The long days grew more and more surreal as the effect of the alcohol built up in the guys' systems. One night it got to the point where they lost touch completely: Bill had gone out into the night, trapped and killed tiny lizards that he hung from his earlobes with paper clips, and returned wearing loincloth leaves. Gordon, at some point, had managed to make himself a loin cloth of bananas.

Around this point the guys began to get in touch with even more murky, libidinal urges. The appointed name for the island changed ominously from "Fleshtones Island" to "Balls Work Camp," so named after Keith's and his childhood friends' nickname for Keith's dad, who was the subject of the guys' jesting, inebriated fantasies that because of his Germanic heritage he was a closet Nazi. "He's *not*," Marek insists. "But he was portrayed as this strutting commandant of Balls Work Camp, like a Devil's Island kind of theme." Amidst the boozy, equatorial madness things became even more twisted, and the fun metamorphosed into "Balls Sex Camp." Gordon dashed to the kitchen and returned with a big bottle of cooking oil, urging everybody to grease him up. "It's time that we all fucked each other!" he bellowed. Laughs Marek, "There were no women on the island. Gordon's screaming at the top of his lungs, splashing oil on his ass, and we were saying, 'Yeah! Great!' making all of this noise!" Remarks a now rueful Bill: "It was *Lord of the Flies*, only with adults who shouldn't have been acting like kids."

Into this bizarre scene walked Peter, who'd arrived on the mainland earlier in the day humming the Kinks' "I'm on an Island," decked out like Lord Jim in his seersucker suit, straw hat, and carpet bags. He discovered to his shock that Fleshtones Island had rioted and thrown an insane *coup d'état*. "At one point Peter throws off the hat and takes off the jacket, and he's right in with us going nuts," Marek remembers. "But we were a little bit caught with our hand in the cookie jar—or somewhere! It had gone too far." Peter's arrival reeled the gang back in a little bit, and the next morning there was a sober pall cast upon the scene.

The guys nearly forget why they were in Martinique in the first place. After tearing around the islands with Hayot and his friends in tiny, souped-up Renaults, and partying at Telephone Island before the dawn and snuffed-out party torches greeted them wearily, the guys realized that there was a gig to play for over twenty thousand people. From a boat driver the band scored some local speed (named after the indigenous word for *calculator*, as the little pills were said to make one "sharp") and made it to mainland Martinique. The shows took place in a giant sugarcane field, and because tropical rains had poured for days the fields had turned into red, thick, clay-like mud. "Everyone was walking around with big wads of mud on their feet," Marek remembers. "It was two days of really fucked-up backstage slogging around, and then playing. I barely remember; I just remember being totally fucked up. When it was time to go, the blow would come out. We were playing like mad!" Singerman remembers that "the 'Tones put on one of their usual fantastic performances."

"Maybe the whole thing never happened," Marek muses now in disbelief.

Back in New York City, the chastened band cleared their heads and reoriented themselves toward reality.

Some domestic restructuring was in order. Peter was feeling rooted enough to marry his longtime girlfriend, artist Marilla Palmer, in May, at the National Arts Club in Manhattan. For fifteen years they'd live in a roomy apartment at Avenue A and Fifth Street, two blocks below Tompkins Square, throwing locally famed Christmas parties and indulging the rock & roll and art scenes perpetually grooving loudly beneath their second-floor windows. They would eventually be priced out of trendy Alphabet City and buy a house in Greenpoint, Brooklyn, in 2000.

Meanwhile, Keith's marriage to Judy had gone south, and they split up for good in 1984. Keith was liberated, ready to explode on the East Village scene, and in early 1985 moved into a small room on the first floor at the Hotel Rutledge on Lexington Avenue, in the Murray Hill neighborhood. The Rut, offering low weekly rates and welcoming transients and permanents alike, had become household of sorts for various itinerant New York rock & rollers. There, his cramped space augmented with a small hot plate, a fridge, and a burgeoning stack of records, Keith would live for nearly a decade, a cab ride away from the East Village. As a salaried musician, his nights would begin at eleven and end at dawn, his wallet gradually lessened of dollar tips, the only true expense in a downtown world of free drinks and after-hours clubs.

Soon after his marriage ended, Keith began dating Wendy Wild, a scene-making, shroom-eating, long-haired chanteuse from the Pulsalama and Club 57 scene. Until 1987, the two rockers would be *the* bead- and Day Glo wig–wearing couple of the Village, stopping in at as many shows as possible and playing together in Wild Hyenas, "always on the scene," Keith chimed, "where you should be seen."

One evening in 1943, Joseph Stalin listened to a radio performance of pianist Maria Yudina performing Mozart's *23rd Piano Concerto*. So moved was Stalin by Yudina's playing that he requested a copy. When informed that what he had heard was a live broadcast and not a recording, Stalin infamously ordered the entire orchestra and Yudina into a studio at three in the morning to re-create the performance. Two conductors panicked before a third relented. A 78 rpm recording of Mozart's concerto was duly made and pressed at dawn for Stalin's pleasure. An "Instant Record," Totalitarian-style. Henri Padovani, the French representative for I.R.S. at C.B.S. Records, had a similarly preposterous idea. Luckily for the Fleshtones, he was their friend and not their dictator.

Three years after the infamous Le Palace show, the Fleshtones remained hugely popular in France, and Padovani wanted to bring the band over for a two-week residency at the Gibus Club in Paris to record a live album. The angle? He wanted to press the album so quickly as to be on sale in the club while the band was still in residence; Padovani had grand visions of the Fleshtones signing copies of the record for fans days after they had played the show. The gimmick appealed to the band's sense of absurdist humor, and because at I.R.S. things were moving so slowly in terms of recording—and had possibly dried up entirely—the band leapt at the opportunity. Padovani sold the idea to C.B.S., and the plan was to release the album on I.R.S. exclusively in Europe. Richard Gottehrer had enjoyed his time producing the guys, and he agreed to fly to Paris to produce the record. "In France, and in Europe in general, the Fleshtones had a following," Gottehrer explains. "The European attitude toward rock & roll, or blues, or pure American music, is a lot deeper than American's attitude about it because this country is basically a mishmash of new people with no history or tradition. It's a great *country*. It's opportunity for everyone, but we don't hold anything sacred; we *pretend* that things are sacred. For the French, American rock & roll was not in their background."

Energized and focused on creating a memorable set, the Fleshtones worked up an amusingly presumptuous Super Rock Medley of "Theme from 'The Vindicators,'" "Hexbreaker," and "Roman Gods," as well as a "Kingsmen-like Medley" that featured the great sixties frat-band's "Trouble" and "Haunted House" merging with "Twelve Months Later," an obscure flipside by the Sheep, a name under which the Strangeloves had recorded a one-off single back in 1966. (The Fleshtones had made their love of all things Strangeloves clear to Gottehrer, who one day said, *You guys like this stuff?—I got a whole bunch of this junk lying around*, and to the guys' delight unearthed "Twelve Months Later." The Paris shows would amount to a tribute to Gottehrer, as the band would open each set with Bunker Hill's "Hide & Seek," the A-side to "Twelve Months Later.")

The Fleshtones were booked at the Gibus Club for nine shows over a two-week period, the gigs falling into two segments, March 5 to 9, and 13 to 16. Supporting were the Playboys. The first show was to be taped and mixed at a nearby studio the following day, the finished mixes mastered the third day in Amsterdam, and the record pressed the fourth and fifth day. (The album cover art by famed Belgian cartoonist Serge Clerc and the track listing were already waiting at the factory.) The album would then be assembled and shipped back to France, where in Paris *Speed Connection* would be for sale at the club on or before March 13, a week after the recording. For posterity, the second and third shows were recorded as well. The Fleshtones flew into Paris on March 4. The compressed mini-epic was destined for problems, and began inauspiciously: on the first afternoon, with a well-hyped buzz in the air, the band put on a show for French television and media, and sat for interviews. Unfortunately, the production lasted for six hours, and the band suffered multiple takes with poor monitors. Already nursing a mild case of laryngitis and a hoarse voice, Peter blew his throat out, leaving him a ragged mess for that evening's show.

Gottehrer brought along his trusted engineer Jim Ball to the City of Lights. "Richard called me a week before he was leaving," remembers Ball, who interrupted producing the Smithereens' debut, *Especially for You*, for the Fleshtones project. He had done some remote recording at the Record Plant and was used to working with capable crews, but prior to leaving, Ball had had no contact with the recording truck over in Paris. "When we got there all there was was two speakers, a mixing console, and a tape machine. They didn't have microphones. We were lucky they had a tape. It was really time to start scrambling. Somehow, we managed to put together the equipment we needed." Gottehrer was unflappable—at one point, he calmly turned to Peter in the midst of the cables/microphones scrum and urged him to try an exquisite wine that he'd discovered that day—but Ball was on edge. The night was revving up, the mikes were on, and a nervous Ball could hear the crowd chanting, *Fleshtones! Fleshtones!* He asked the sound guys if they had aligned the twenty-four-track machine. One of them who spoke a little bit of English, looked at Ball quizzically and said, "Oh maybe six months ago." Ball replied, "Well, just throw the tone reel on, and let's see what the machine looks like." To Ball's horror, every meter was pointing in a different direction. It was obvious that the machine hadn't had any kind of maintenance on it, probably since it was purchased.

Despite the production snafus, Gottehrer and Ball managed to get the first show on tape ("not too badly," remembers Ball). The band worked up a sweat the best they could in the sold-out club, but they were suffering from a bit of jet lag and Peter's voice was basically shot; he had been under doctor's order not to *speak*, let alone sing. They opened with a streamlined, supercharged version of "Hide and Seek," hauled out old chestnuts like "B.Y.O.B.," played a handful of the new songs, and invited Gottehrer to leave "Le Voyageur" remote truck to pound a Milhizer-assembled floor tom-tom onstage during the "Kingsmen-like Medley." But the show and the recording were marred. "The best thing we could have done was get a Nagra recorder, sit it in the back of the place, hang up two microphones, and record it," says Peter now. "They didn't do that."

Exhausted, Ball woke up at eight the next morning and began preparing for the four-hour window of mixing and overdubs booked at a rudimentary basement jingle-producing room at Le Grand Arnet in the bowels of the Champs Elysees. (Mixing had been scheduled at Palais de Congress, the best studio in town, but platinum-selling Duran Duran had unceremoniously bumped the Fleshtones' engineer.) Ball arrived, "still shaky from the night before," and Gottehrer showed up with tapes. "We tried to recut and overdub some backing vocals, because they had been so bad the night before," Ball remembers. After an hour or so, Gottehrer and Ball took a break and enjoyed a Vietnamese lunch where Gottehrer was in his cosmopolitan glory, urging his engineer to try this dish, that desert. They departed, but hours later than Ball wanted to. Walking back to the studio, Gottehrer passed a tack shop and decided that he needed to buy riding equipment for his daughter—this meant more delays for Ball. (Gottehrer had gleefully caught the shopping bug a day earlier when Peter took his producer out. "If you're gonna be on stage to sing 'Cara-Lin' with us," he'd commanded Gottehrer, "ya gotta look sharp!" They purchased suits, matching ties, and, for that Strangeloves look, leopard- and tiger-skin silk scarves.) Exasperated, Ball headed back to the studio alone. "We basically took that rough mix and put it on the tape," Ball laments. "We were out of time. I had my head in my hands. There was literally nothing we could do."

Padovani was putting pressure on Ball to finish the mix, as Padovani had a plane to catch to Amsterdam to master the album that evening.

"Here was my big chance to have a opportunity to make a great-sounding record in Paris," remarks Ball ruefully. "I was encouraged and supported all along the way that this was the way it was supposed to be." Keith and Gordon ducked into the studio to hear how the mixing was going, listened to about three minutes and, in horror at the poor sound, immediately ran out to the nearest bar and got bombed. When Ball and Gottehrer returned to the club later that night and overheard the Fleshtones onstage for their second gig, they were disheartened to hear how well the band was playing and how much better Peter's voice sounded, booming across the sold-out club. The second and third nights saw the band regain their stride, and by all accounts were tougher, leaner, and more boisterous performances than the vexed opening show. The Fleshtones had missed a great opportunity. Says Ball, "*Speed Connection* is what it is: a testament to how to do a record in a week."

The album went through the Instant Record process and was on sale at the club on March 13. ("Today it's not that big of a deal, with downloading and everything, but in 1985 this was an interesting scheme," Gottehrer reflects.) The band had been excited to score a custom-made cover by Clerc, whose work they loved, but were disappointed by the result, an inappropriate fifties-retro zoot-suited hipster leaping out of two oversized hands. "Clerc gave us some hand-me-down," Marek remembers. "He turned out not to be the nice guy we thought he would be." Graced on the back with a Richard Dumas photograph of a "Powerstance," *Speed Connection*, overly raw and warts and all, was released throughout France and Europe later in the month.

"When I.R.S. stateside hears the damn thing, they'll go nuts," Peter predicted, correctly.

The Gibus residency continued. The Fleshtones enjoyed the Parisian nightlife, soaking up the French adulation and the rock-star treatment. Marek began slipping quietly into heroin abuse, and the band would suffer an irking onstage debacle with the legendary, fading Johnny Thunders during the second leg of shows. But on the third night of the residency the band was graced by the presence of a friend.

Peter Buck was with R.E.M. recording *Fables of the Reconstruction* in London. As has been well documented, those murky and difficult sessions reflected in part the dreariness of the rainy English weather, and Buck was likely looking for a diversion. Somewhere along the line, Keith got on the phone with Buck, who lamented to Keith the fake uppers that he was taking and the general malaise of the R.E.M. recording sessions. Keith made a casual offer for Buck to hop over the Channel, and Buck joined the band onstage near the close of the third show—*Peter Buck, R.E.M., the Fleshtones COM-BINE!* Peter announced mock-triumphantly from the stage—and was immediately handed an out-of-tune guitar that Zaremba had just played and tossed down. "That's the high-powered road crew we were working with," Keith laughs. Buck's guitar precariously tuned, he joined the band on a stirring cover of the Eyes' 1965 mod tune "When the Night Falls," a rousing arrangement that builds in intensity from Bill's opening groove to a wailing vocal from Peter. After more necessary tuning during which a drunk fan memorably begs on-mike for more "Intoxication of the Fleshtones!" the band launched into R.E.M.'s "Wind Out," which ultimately bled into a spirited version of the Blendells' "La La La La La."

Buck was in the city for no more than twenty hours, and he and his buddies from Queens explored Paris kicks during their whirlwind time together. Shortly after Buck arrived, he'd been a guest of the band's at a dinner thrown at a local bar. "We'd bought a bunch of heroin from this woman who worked for the record company," remembers Marek. "There's record company people and all these hangers-on, and we're pouring the dope out on our hands under the table as we're sitting there, wiping our noses, doing this 'corporate' thing." At one point, Buck and Keith ducked into the bathroom to get high, but were mystified by an unexpected technical glitch: the bathrooms in France had slide-bar latches that activated the light, similar to an airline cabin. The guys couldn't figure it out—they closed the door behind them and started looking around for the light switch. So, giggling, they had the bright idea to build a fire out of a mound of toilet paper in the corner to illuminate their doping. Afterward, Keith and Buck made a nonchalant re-entrance from the bathroom as clouds of smoke poured out behind them. They came back to the table acting as if nothing had happened. "I don't think there was anyone there who cared or was taking note of it, because they were all partying in their own way," Marek recalls. The Fleshtones never endured much adult supervision, anyway.

Peter Buck downplays the situation now. "It wasn't a fire exactly," he says. "We lit some toilet paper to look around for the switch." Of the copious amounts of heroin in Paris, Buck insists dubiously that "It might've been around, but I didn't see it." He adds, "I had to fly back the next the day to finish [*Fables of the Reconstruction*], so

I got up at ten, hung over, and had to fly back through customs. They immediately spotted me as a probable heroin smuggler. If you go one day and come back the next, they think you're smuggling heroin. I had a little bag on me and I said, 'Look in the bag, I don't care. I just don't feel well. I'm kinda hung over. I was drinking cheap French wine until three in the morning.'"

"No wonder they searched him," Keith cracks. "He probably still smelled like smoke."

Johnny Thunders, who was living in Paris, made an unwelcome ingress into the Fleshtones' circle, showing up unannounced and playing with the band on March 13, kicking off the second leg of the residency. He wanted a return engagement. "The Gibus was Thunder's home away from home, after he had totally burned out the scene in New York," says Peter. "The French are very loyal about that stuff, and he was particularly popular among French rockers." The band, feeling as if Thunders was insinuating himself into their scene, tried to discourage him. "Thunders was self-styled rock royalty," says Marek, "and it was like we, as this second-generation band that we were, were supposed to bow and have him do this. And frankly, we didn't like that." *Speed Connection* was now on sale at the Gibus, and the band was abraded by Thunders' upstaging presence. Thunders had wanted to do a version of New York Dolls' "Pills" and Wilson Pickett's "Midnight Hour," and the band was especially keen on keeping Thunders off of the stage, as they hadn't rehearsed with him. "We'd had the set really worked out tight," Marek says, "a well-arranged set that we'd worked on and that we'd been tuning as the nights went on. We didn't want to fuck it up by throwing in something we were questionable on."

Marek had overheard amidst the backstage buzz that Thunders was currently clean and sober. "I had really good, heavy-duty brown dope that you didn't need to shoot," says Marek. "Keith let it slip to Johnny that I had some, or Johnny asked him. Keith kind of wavered for a minute." As Marek remembers, Keith subsequently suggested to Marek that he offer Thunders a line of dope. ("That I don't remember. That's possible," says Keith now.) "It occurred to me that maybe I could solve our problem," Marek admits. Somewhat devilishly, he laid out a thick line of heroin "that would've dropped a horse. I was doing a match head and that was enough to get me fucked up. Johnny just snorted the whole thing up and he said, 'Thanks man, that was great.' Well, within a couple of minutes he was reduced to a drooling pile of shit. He was sitting in the chair, and his chin was on his chest, and he can't talk because he had no tolerance, he'd been detoxed."

Relieved, the Fleshtones felt that their mission to detour Thunders had been accomplished. "We hit the stage and we're doing this kick-ass set," Marek continues. "In the middle there's this commotion in the audience. All of a sudden we see a corpse rising from the grave coming through the audience: Johnny Thunders is making his way to the stage. How many times have you heard of Johnny Thunders playing on stage so high that he can't even stand? We had underestimated him. We'd forgotten that if anyone could do it, Johnny could do it. So he crawls toward the stage, staggering and weaving back and forth, and makes it up. In effect the whole thing has backfired and turned into a nightmare because at least if he had gotten up there straight, he could've played the song." With Thunders precariously plugged in, the band managed to struggle through a horrendous version of "Midnight Hour," gamely following along with Thunders through changes that they barely knew. "I think it was the worst version of any song ever performed in the history of any type of music on this planet!" Keith laughs. "Actually, it almost would've been worth putting out on the record. You would've thought it was the Residents doing it. How can you twist this into something that's unrecognizable and horrid but funny at the same time? I wish I had a tape of it so I could prove it to people."

The bothersome dissolution that Thunders represented was made manifest on that sorry night. "He wanted to do his junkie act, but it wasn't an act," says Peter. "His whole projection of what it was to be a rock star and of what rock & roll was about, to me was not it. I was repelled by that." Thunders tumbled off the stage after the tune and that's the last the Fleshtones ever saw of him. Marek feels no remorse over having doped up a sober Johnny Thunders. "If it had happened today, of course, I wouldn't have been there to give him the dope," he says. "But they say, 'There are no victims, only volunteers.' So he could've said no. It's a big world out there and it's no surprise that he wasn't able to resist temptation. You're out there in the world and there's always going to be drugs and alcohol. It's up to you to not take it. So I don't regret having done that." Thunders died of an accidental drug overdose in New Orleans six years later.

Marek's link in the gaudy Thunders story illustrated his own deepening involvement with heroin while in Paris, an addiction that he now calls his "ticket to sobriety." The entanglement would only deepen and intensify in the years following Paris, and ultimately contribute to Marek's departure from the Fleshtones.

Marek met a young woman backstage at the Gibus early in the band's stay and fell in love with her and with the blissful, bittersweet lifestyle that she afforded him. "I hope she's still alive, dear girl," he says. She had first offered Marek coke but he was only interested in the oblivion of dope, and "it turned out that she was a junkie. I don't know whether she was strung out or not. She was a fairly well-to-do young woman, and her brother was an up-and-coming cartoonist. I thought, *Oh wow, this is so cool.* She was all hooked in with the cartoonist community. And they were big into the rock scene. In France, the cartoonists are on par with musicians. It's very interrelated."

Marek ended up spending the next two weeks living with the girl at her condo on the rue Saint Denis. Beneath their windows the local hookers strolled, and the building owner let her use a room in the cellar, which is where she had her private stash of heroin. "Her family made champagne and she had hundreds of bottles covered in dust and mud with no labels on them. So you'd wake up in the morning, she'd go get a bottle of champagne out from the cellar, fresh fruit from the vendors on the street, out would come the dope, and we'd just start the day off. And so I was in love." The affair ended more or less with the conclusion of the Fleshtones' stay at the Gibus, but the heroin lingered in Marek's life with the intensity of any complicated romance.

"I bought a pile of heroin that lasted me a week," Keith remembers. "It was really weird. But, I have to admit, fun."

Gordon wanted to name the record *Heroin Collapse.* The eventual title, *Speed Connection,* alluded to the dispatch with which the record was made and released, but the darker, drug-related reference—an in-joke kept from the brass at I.R.S. but winkingly dug by anyone inside the Fleshtones circle—was certainly faithful to the band's lifestyle, for better or for worse. "*Speed Connection* only aggravated relations with the bosses at I.R.S.," Singerman says. Indeed, I.R.S. had had it with the band, with their poor record sales, and with their increasingly adventurous ways of living. The band returned to New York in the middle of the month with few, if any, prospects for a label. They played to a packed house at Irving Plaza on April 19, and the ads in the *Village Voice* warmly welcomed them back to the states. Tired, drug-weary, career-precarious, the Fleshtones had a lot to prove. But who'd listen?

One of the many ideas tossed like a firecracker between Keith and Peter Buck was Keith's plan to keep recording, and on a sunny weekend in June he drove down to Athens, Georgia, to record an EP with Buck. The window of opportunity was small. Buck estimates that R.E.M. performed over three hundred shows in 1985, and during a brief break between the American and British legs of the *Reconstruction* tour, he invited Keith to record at John Keane's inexpensive studio. There, Keith quickly laid down drum tracks for three originals, "Way Down South," "One More Time," and a paean to driving blissfully down Sunset Boulevard called "I Got Wheels." Onto these Keith added bass, acoustic guitar, and vocals, Buck laid down his trademark twelve- and six-string guitar work as well as banjo, and Mike Mills of R.E.M. dropped by the studio to play some organ. The record cost a threadbare $320.29 to make and had an appealing, rootsy moodiness. "We were working really hard to finish a record in two and a half days," Buck remembers. "I was nominally producing, although we were both producing. We'd work until ten o'clock, and then run around until four in the morning." Keith said—"measuring by the trashcans full of beer cans"—that he was in Athens for three days. Coyote Records issued the three-song EP credited to Full Time Men in the fall of 1985. A year later Keith would corral Marek, Bill, and assorted friends and under Full Time Men cut "High on Drugs," a rollicking, autobiographical stomp celebrating the eponymous lifestyle. In early 1988, again mired in a contract-free morass, Keith would revive Full Time Men even more ambitiously.

Peter was also casting about for projects. Although his *Cutting Edge* responsibilities were keeping him busy—literally in the air—he was writing lots of songs and dying to record. The Love Delegation was more or less conceived at the Pyramid Club, where in the vapors of the long evenings Peter hatched a plan for a loose-knit enclave of musician friends that could cheekily testify to love, rock & roll, and all things groovy. Peter envisioned the group as a kind of sonic lifestyle garlanded with beads and grins (and benefits: Peter hoped that leading such an outfit would get him in free to the gay bars).

The band name came first. One night in Tampa, Florida, some Fleshtone fans roamed through the streets stealing flowers and presented the guys with garlands, proclaiming themselves the "Love Delegation." Duly christened, the group of Peter, Keith, Pyramid Club staffer and regular Michael "Kitty" Ullmann, Ricky Rothchild (late of Kristi Rose and the Midnight Walkers), and Jon Cormany expanded to include friends who dug and were around the scene, such as Wendy Wild and Barrence Whitfield. Peter initially saw the kitschy Love Delegation as an all-covers outfit, but accumulating a backlog of songs from the previous couple of years he soon expanded the idea as an outlet for his own material, much of which hadn't felt quite right at Fleshtones rehearsals. The Love Delegation based themselves at the Pyramid and, to a lesser degree, at King Tut's Wah-Wah Hut across the street, and those joints' lighthearted, boozy irony was laced throughout the trippy endeavor. One major source of inspiration was Vegas-era Elvis Presley, whose larger-than-life, archetypically American spectacle Peter found irresistible. He'd been in Sin City filming a *Cutting Edge* segment on celebrity imitators when a fake Elvis came out and did "C.C. Rider" Vegas-style. "Two things occurred to me: Elvis was so great [and] even someone who poorly imitates Elvis is great," Peter gushed. "When he got on his knees during the 'American Trilogy Medley,' and the laser cone descended upon him, smoke filled the stage, and Elvis froze in immortality. And John Wayne walked out and delivered a monologue about America. It was one of the greatest moments I ever had."

Armed with a stack of songs, Peter enlisted Jim Ball (recovered fully from Paris), and in August sporadic recording sessions began at the Record Plant. By November they'd completed an album's worth of tracks, ranging from the Fleshtones-esque "Let's Have a Good Time" and the Stax-influenced "I'm Gonna Knock You Out," to covers of Lee Hazlewood's "Some Velvet Morning" and J. J. Cale's "After Midnight." The whole affair had an enthusiastic, flower-power, East Village cabaret vibe, and Peter reveled in the opportunity to show-case his songs and groove with like-minded friends. Credited to Peter Zaremba's Love Delegation, *Spread the Word* was released on Moving Target in the spring of 1986; a dance-mix twelve-inch of "I'm Gonna Knock You Out" was released subsequently and charted well in parts of Europe.

The Love Delegation would play various one-off shows over the next year or so, often at all-night "Spread the Word" extravaganzas at the Pyramid. In January, Peter booked the famed Limelight night-club for a kicky "marriage and celebration" night celebrating the record's release; following a midnight "private prenuptial Cham-pagne toast in the Chapel" the Love Delegation played. In July, as part of the citywide New Music Seminar, the Love Delegation played an official record release party at the Saint on East Sixth Street, along with the Smithereens, who were celebrating the release of their acclaimed debut, *Especially for You*. Peter would revisit the Love Delegation a couple of years later, but the results of what he affec-tionately called his "secret weapon" would be unhappy and costly.

The Fleshtones vs. Reality

In September, Keith turned thirty. I.R.S. released *Speed Connection II: The Final Chapter*, taken from tapes of the third night at the Gibus residency. "[I.R.S.] were owed a record," explains Marek. "Or they had the rights to it and they thought to capitalize on it. Since it was in the can they weren't just going to give it to us. Maybe they could squeeze every last drop out of it." Ball had remixed the songs in July at a sane pace, the sound of the album much improved over the flatness of the first rush release. The track listing was slightly tweaked; added was a spirited run through "One More Time" as well as two songs featuring Buck. Their tenure officially up at I.R.S., the Fleshtones used the opportunity to sweeten the vocal tracks and mischievously drop in a demo recording of "Return to the Haunted House" *à la* the Kingsmen and *Got Live If You Want It*–era Rolling Stones. The canned applause came courtesy of *Rock Will Never Die*, a Michael Schenker Group live album recently engineered by Ball. "Take that, I.R.S.!" the guys snorted.

Peter created a humorous cover for the album, a pen-and-ink montage of half-true Fleshtones Paris shenanigans: a sports car, in flames, careens out of control in front of the Arc de Triomphe; a roulette wheel whips francs into the night; Lucky Bill struts with a comely Parisian showgirl under each arm. *Speed Connection II* stands as an excellent document of the band in Paris, the nine sweaty minutes of the "Extended Super Rock Medley" capping off the band's Super Rock era with aplomb. I.R.S. promoted *Speed Connection II* with less vigor than any previous Fleshtones release, and although the record picked up solid reviews in places ("The Kings of Super Rock are in rare form here," raved Chris Morris in *Musician*) clearly a period in the band's career was over and done.

1985 concluded and the Go-Go's, erstwhile buddies and labelmates, imploded into ego raving and drug use, their platinum career finished. The Fleshtones, though gigging more than ever to well-paying, packed crowds, were at a standstill born not of the perils of success but of the fickleness of creative inflexibility and an ever-splintering audience. A phase began of hustling for the ways and means to release their own records, a worrisome era for the group wherein they feared that they were being ignored, forgotten, or otherwise deemed an irrelevant party band. The guys couldn't have predicted that the exhausting and demoralizing process would last as long as it would.

John Mellencamp is riding high on the *Billboard* singles chart with "R.O.C.K. in the U.S.A." in 1986, and the paranoid, bemused Fleshtones can't help but wonder if the heartland singer hadn't learned a thing or two from their own "American Beat '84." Muttered Bill, "I can't imagine in my wildest dreams that [Mellencamp] didn't hear 'American Beat' and listened to it quite closely." A frustrated Peter echoed those sentiments: "It's easy for a band that's already made it to co-opt what others have been working on for years," he complained. "It just seems like a dynamic band like ourselves could have gotten a part of it. Somehow it's got to happen. It's got to. It's a matter of making records, and it's just got to happen. That may be the voice of desperation, but it's *got* to."

Living on a pooled income—Singerman estimates that the Fleshtones averaged approximately $1,200 per show during the time he managed them—the guys were keeping busy. Peter was fooling with the Love Delegation, Keith was downing Black Russians and aping early Jeff Beck playing drums and guitar in Wild Hyenas, Marek was creating Everly Brothers–style music with his pal George Gilmore in Tall Lonesome Pines, and Bill and Gordon were dreaming about reviving Action Combo with "Mustang" Mike, a security guard at the Music Building whom they'd befriended and for whom they had grand, if tongue-in-cheek, plans. (They'd gone so far as to grab a baseball bat and dark shades and shoot a "publicity photo" in front of the Tough Club, the former rough-and-tumble Tammany Hall speakeasy hangout on West Fourteenth Street.) But without much product to promote, the Fleshtones were forced to keep hitting the road, "peddling our rear ends all around trying to put bread on the table," as Marek complained.

At the end of January, the band played a weekend at the 688 Club in Atlanta and the next month made another visit down to New Orleans during Mardi Gras, where they partied around the clock but found time to open, with Let's Active, for the dB's at Jimmy's Music Club. While there, Peter also filmed segments for a *Cutting Edge* Mardi Gras special and scored a prize purchase. "The guys would come to Athens a lot and stay at my house," Peter Buck remembers. "Peter had just bought the 'Mardi Gras Mambo' 45, and the first time they came over they played it twenty times between two AM and six AM!" There were plenty of well-attended Mid-Atlantic-region gigs, including the always gainful Baltimore/Washington, D.C., axis; they earned over $7,000 for a March weekend at D.C.'s 9:30 Club. But fans and critics kept wondering aloud, *Where's the new record? Where's the new video?* In Manhattan, they began making regular weekend appearances at the Lone Star Cafe on Fifth Avenue at East Thirteenth Street, a venue that would replace Irving Plaza and Peppermint Loungue as the band's regular, lucrative Gotham haunt for the next half decade.

The Fleshtones vs. Reality

The Fleshtones had to make their living on the road, but trickling into Bob Singerman's office were still some one-off opportunities to record. The producers of a low-budget, campy horror movie, *I Was a Teenage Zombie*, approached the band and asked them if they would like to contribute a song to the soundtrack. Peter whipped up the title theme, and the band dropped into the Record Plant with Jim Ball to cut a speedy, humorous tear through Peter's beloved Herschell Gordon Lewis world of zombies and ghouls, a catchy song that nonetheless wouldn't do much to dissuade the general public that the Fleshtones weren't taking themselves very seriously. The soundtrack to *I Was a Teenage Zombie* was released in 1987, featuring songs from the Del Fuegos, the Smithereens, the dB's, the Waitresses, and others. The trashy, poorly received movie was destined for straight-to-video status.

In May, the Fleshtones headed down to Atlanta to record a few tracks at George Pappas' enormous Axis Sound Studio at the request of the 688 Club's owners, who wanted to release a compilation album of some of their favorite bands. Happy for the opportunity, the band cut four tracks: the horn-driven "Inner Groove," the lyrically downbeat "Too Late to Run," and, borrowed from the rejected I.R.S. demos, "I Forget How to Talk" and a substantial reworking of "Leather Kings." Onto a new arrangement of Keith's instrumental, Peter laid a personal lyric in which he documents being "down by the river where the big men go . . . out of the mist wearing black leather," a dimly lit world of "lots of flesh" with "all-night club hoppers, cocktails, and poppers" where he's forced to his knees at gunpoint. Twice in the middle of the after-hours rap the tune brightens into a tongue-in-cheek disco horn break, underscoring the song's origins from the Pyramid as well as the Meatpacking District/Crisco Disco/gender-blending days of Peter's youth. (And far youth: Peter fictitiously implicates his high school gym teacher in the song. Hints Peter: "You never knew who you're gonna find.") Retitled "The Return of the Leather Kings," the mock-heroic, homoerotic song was one of the odder if more compelling Fleshtones tunes to date. *688 Presents* was released in the spring; featuring "Inner Groove" and "Leather Kings," the compilation also included songs from Drivin' n Cryin', Dash Rip Rock, Arms Akimbo, and Vinyliners. The release kept the Fleshtones at least partly visible in a malevolent market.

Around this time, Peter admitted to a reporter that the Fleshtones had once visited a battlefield in York, Virginia, the site of a British defeat in the Revolutionary War. There the fellas knelt on the ground and vowed that they would never, ever play London again. Yet on July

Sweat

4, the Fleshtones flew to England for a one-off "American Independence Day Celebration" show at the Hammersmith Clarendon, with the Scientists and the Primevals in support. The show was well-attended, but the band's hostility toward England remained dogged. "We received our Independence Day show, especially the reaction in the press, as a bitter disappointment," Peter said.

Some journalists were on the Fleshtones' side. Nick Jones attended the show and recalls that near the end of the performance the Fleshtones led "a trail of happy smashed punters out of the dancehall down the rather elegant stairways into the foyer, out of the front doors, out into the smeared neon rush of Hammersmith Broadway traffic speeding past, and down the entrance stairs leading to the subterranean maze of tunnels." The paisley pied pipers literally enjoyed an English following on this sunny day. "I regained some semblance of consciousness in the band's hotel bar awhile later being interrogated by the Beastie Boys, who to my complete and utter amazement seemed to have heard of me," Jones continues. "I can remember looking around and seeing the smiling faces of Peter, Keith, and Bill, etc., and all their happy entourage chattering, laughing and grooving about the bar—and probably thinking to myself that this was indeed rock & roll paradise, and that absolutely nothing else ever needs to happen again." Indeed, Jones adds, "I don't think anything else ever did."

Lindsay Hutton, who since 1981 had run the Fleshtones fan club out of his Scotland home, was also at the gig, and in a subsequent issue of *The Next Big Thing* included a unique 45 single of two performances he'd recorded there, energetic covers of "Panic," a doo-wop tune by Otis Williams and His Charms, and the Fever Tree's psychedelic "San Francisco Girls." Credited to Thee Roman Gods, rendered collectible within hours, the small-press seven-inch was tossed onto the paltry pile of recent Fleshtones releases.

Paramount to the guys now was securing a record contract. Thus commenced the endless Era of the Indies.

Through friends and associates, Robert Singerman struck an album deal with a small independent label, Emergo Records, an imprint of Roadrunner Records & Music Publishing, a New York–based label later to be associated with popular heavy metal and speed-thrash acts such as King Diamond, Type O Negative, and Slipknot. The label would enjoy its considerable success in the future; in the mid-eighties Roadrunner was not yet a player. The Fleshtones wouldn't benefit from the distribution and promotional wealth of A&M (though the band rarely saw that, anyway) and they would have to record their album with a considerably lower budget than what was provided by Miles and company. These terms were generally fine to the guys: they felt that overspending on *Hexbreaker!* was chiefly that album's undoing, and they were looking forward to heading into a studio unburdened with options. With an office downtown on Lafayette Street, Emergo felt like a hometown label.

The Fleshtones and Jim Ball had long talked about doing a studio album together. Glad and relieved to be recording again, armed with a stack of tunes, the Fleshtones headed into the Record Plant committed to making their classic album. The New York Mets were in the playoffs when recording commenced, and the guys hoped that the steamrolling blue-and-orange would serve them nicely. (*Ya gotta believe!*) Certainly the old-timers at Smith's Bar and Grill, next to the Record Plant on Eighth Avenue, wished the Fleshtones well. Nightly, the band would repair to that legendary newsman's watering hole and raise their glasses to Mookie, Hernandez, Doc Gooden, and the rest of their beloved hometown Mets, waiting for Ball to come down and call the next band member in for an overdub. The band would come to refer to Smith's as "Studio D," a sly reference to Studios A, B, and C at the Record Plant. "I knew where to find people," Ball admits dryly.

Peter fully trusted Ball, and the band felt that they could get down and loose on their own funky home turf, throw a barbecue in the studio, and with kicks focus on their own vision and sound. "Peter and the guys were always up for things," remembers Ball. "They'd say, *Let's see how many people we can get in the studio shouting at the same time!* I invited some of my friends and family, and Peter's sister was there with some of her friends. We just threw a big party. Keith showed up with a couple of coolers of something strange-colored"—Blue Whale, no doubt. "That's how we made records."

The fun and lively sessions for the album would unspool, however, under a darkening cloud. Marek Pakulski was nearing the end of his tenure in the Fleshtones. He was particularly bothered with his stuck-in-place songwriting, his seeming inability to find his own voice as a writer and singer. "Marek and I would hang out at clubs late at night and bemoan the fact that we couldn't write songs," Gordon remembers. "But some people are songwriters, and some aren't." Bill recalls that Marek had reached the frustrating place wherein he was overworking to compensate for his deficiencies as a songwriter. "He had a great song that was so nice when he started it," Bill says. "Then he'd go up in this room up there alone and work and work and work, and when he finished it it wasn't the great thing that he came up with. Naturally, it never made it on the album." Marek's growing dissatisfactions were now keeping pace with his addictions. At the end of the summer, he quietly gave notice to the guys that he was leaving.

But then the Emergo deal happened, and the guys talked him into staying to record the album. Did he agree grudgingly? "I wanted to do the right thing, and not leave them in the lurch," Marek says. He had long been hoping to broaden the Fleshtones musically, mirroring his own personal if unspoken ambitions, and was feeling growing resistance from Peter. "I felt there was a very deepening gap between Peter and myself. There was certainly no one single fault but I think I was trying to put something in there that I thought the band needed, and that might have had slightly more sophisticated harmonic relationships between the instruments that had tended, in my opinion, to be a little monolithic. That was something that I wanted to hear. I think Peter had a clearer idea of what he wanted the band to be."

Many of Marek's frustrations simmered in the studio, where the songs that came to define Super Rock came into shape. "I might have been cutting off my nose to spite my face," he admits. "There would be something going on at rehearsal, the framework of a song, and I'd have a working bass line for it that I thought was appropriate. And if Keith was playing a C at any given point, in the past I often would have been playing a C or a C-based riff, but as time went on I might have decided to play something that was a harmony against that, and it was working in rehearsal." But, as often was Peter's tendency, when the band got to the studio, production became a last-minute-inspiration, under-the-gun thing. Peter's spontaneity would often clash with the band's arrangements, and when muse-blessed, Peter's infamous stubbornness could be formidable. "In preproduction," Marek continues, "you start scrutinizing what the working parts have been. Peter would say, 'Can you make it a little more this, that, and the other thing?' And I was unwilling to cooperate at that point. I was getting surly. I'd try some stuff, but after a while I'd say, 'You don't like this? Well, just tell me what to play!' There really is two to tango there, but I have to take responsibility. I had a bad attitude at that point." Marek ultimately decided to stay on for the balance of the recording, his deep friendship with Keith anchoring his best intentions and providing the flimsy rationale for denying his own addictions.

Marek struck a deal with the Fleshtones: he'd stay only if they paid his income tax. The guys had been self-supporting for roughly six years, and at the end of the tax year the salary covered the band's taxes.

"I figured that since I had finished the year under the band's umbrella that they would cover my taxes, because I certainly wasn't gonna have the money set aside," Marek remembers. "But they didn't do that, so I was pissed. I was mixing sound at a club called Siberia, and one of our power amps went down. I got in touch with Gordon and went and borrowed a QSC amp that had been given to the band as part of the Miller Rock Network, and I never gave it back. They owed me, and I figured it was an even trade. I ended up having to pay my own taxes for 1986, which I'd been promised I'd have paid. And so once that stuff was in my possession, I never gave it back."

The growing tension between Marek and the guys was a microcosm of Marek's larger personal issues. "I was so scared of people," he admits. "Since the early days of the Fleshtones, and before that, the drugs and the alcohol allowed me to interact with people. That's what allowed me to move to New York, to be part of the crowd, to do the band thing. And once I stopped and didn't have that, the recoil was awesome. It was very difficult for me to be around people. Heroin will do that. It obviates the need for people, whereas alcohol allows you to be present in social situations. Heroin says: *You don't need that anymore.* You and whatever your income is, the guy you buy your drugs from, and your house: this becomes your little triangle. And your friends leave you and it's like, *Who needs them?* In fact, the band was one of the controls that was keeping me going, because we were always on tour. I would use drugs when I was in New York and then use the tours to detox. But eventually I started bringing drugs with me on the tour. Peter was probably very unhappy about me because I was completely uncommunicative and unsupportive, drifting more and more into drug use."

Keen to Marek were the difficulties in maintaining the relationships among himself and Keith and Peter, a decade-old dynamic that tread upon mostly unexpressed personality issues, the roots of which dated back to Queens. "Keith and I had been friends originally and were really much closer than Peter and I ever were. In fact, there was a rivalry between Peter and myself. He may not have felt so, but I did. In terms of Keith's friendship, there was always a little tug-of-war going on there."

Despite the growing creative and personal strains, the Fleshtones concentrated mightily on the new album, which Peter decided to call *Fleshtones vs. Reality,* an ironic comment on just where the guys' moods were at this time. Hopeless but defiant, the determined spirit would come to define the rest of their vexed career.

As a kid in Flushing, Peter watched war movies on television and thought about the weird dichotomy between actors, sets, and special-effects and the actual historical story full of heroes, sacrifices, and blood. The tension between fantasy and reality, between imagination and fact, would always be present for him. In a real way, the Fleshtones existed as a kind of Platonic ideal to Peter. Even when waging victorious battles on small, sweaty stages against faceless, corporate Rock, the Fleshtones thrived and existed in Peter's own head where they ruled as groovy avatars of truth, tradition, and fun against historical obstacles. Around this time Peter began to steel himself for his ultimate, lifelong fight against the all-too-real forces of daily life that conspired against his utterly pure, frightfully naive, bravely honest belief: that the Fleshtones are one of the greatest rock & roll bands in the world. To Peter, ninety-nine percent of other current bands at the time—save for Hoodoo Gurus in Australia, and maybe the Bags and whatever scared-eyed young band Monoman Jeff Conolly was whipping into shape up in Boston—were pale imitations of those rare and pure ideas, one-off, obscure songs lost in the decades behind, sung by soulful black or Hispanic singers channeling dynamism and fun in forgotten studios in forgotten cities for forgotten labels, or (true to Peter's borough-bred heart) warbled pitifully by white geeks imitating those same sounds.

Peter was confident, secretly sad, and ripe for a good time. He modeled the songs on the new album in part on the Kinks' *Face to Face* album, a collection that had suggested the conceptual possibilities for rock albums and that had continued Ray Davies' musical rendering of people, class, and interior states. Peter would come to ruefully refer to *Fleshtones vs. Reality* as the band's "Magical Misery Tour of New York." As Pete Townshend once noted, rock & roll allows you to dance all over your problems, and the Fleshtones were amped to prove that correct. Although the $10,000 budget was relatively small, the Fleshtones felt liberated and confident coproducing themselves, and they were starting to learn how to make albums with a frugality borne of necessity. Ball feels that the band was embarking on their "classic album" in making *Fleshtones vs. Reality*: top-shelf songs, top-shelf studio, energy and attitude to burn. "Ball was trying to be modern in recording," Peter says, "but he gave us the latitude that we needed." Keith agrees: "*vs. Reality* was a great record, fun to make. There wasn't nit-picking like the way we were making our other records, but it was done very professionally at the same time, and it sounded great. Jim knew how to capture the Fleshtones without beating it to death and trying to get something that isn't there. A lot of producers will overproduce or reach for something, and by the time it's done, it sounds boring, dead. *vs. Reality* has the spirit, the sound, the songs. I think this was a great record." Unfortunately, he laments, "nobody ever heard it."

The band had nearly twenty songs from which to choose. "Another Direction," "Our Own Time," and "Nothing's Gonna Bring Me Down" (the titles indicative of the band's resolute optimism) dated from the two-year-old I.R.S. demos, and "The Return of the Leather Kings" and "Too Late to Run" from the Atlanta sessions were remixed and used. The Kinks-influenced "Way Up Here" was a growling riff of a song that featured a recorder solo borrowed from the Troggs (and Peter's memorable Queens-accented rhyme, "Way up here I can see right through ya / you're tryin' to make me feel like Lon Chaney, Jr."). The speedy "Mirror Mirror" was a reflective lyric set against Marek's marimba playing and a somewhat unoriginal guitar riff.

"The End of the Track," an inspired, funky, midpaced chant, was sleazily muscled along by Keith's porno movie wah-wah guitar and a bit of studio verité, a police car siren wailing a solo straight out of Peter's urban imagination. The Mid-Town North Police Precinct was located next to Ball's apartment on Fifty-fourth Street; bowing to the band's request, the producer gave the police station a shot. "I called up and said, *Well, officer, I've got kind of a strange request. . . .* I'm hemming and hawing," Ball remembers. The cop asked Ball who he was recording. Ball figured that that would be the kiss of death.

He admitted that he was recording the Fleshtones. "Oh," the cop said. "I know Gordon Spaeth!"

Ball groaned audibly on the phone. "We'd just gotten back from LA, and Gordon had been rolled up in a rug in a parking lot!" Ball laughs. He assumed that his request was futile. "But the next thing I know they sent a car right down, and it happened that one of the recording trucks was outside." Ball and Keith plugged in a two-track, standing in the middle of West Fifty-fourth Street with a gathering, gaping crowd on the block, checking levels while the cop went through the car's sirens, offering a long blast of each one. "That was one of my fondest memories of the whole business," Ball says.

The band recorded two covers for the album, a rocked-up version of Cornelius Brothers and Sister Rose's 1971 hit "Treat Her Like a Lady" sung from a ribald *royal we* perspective and revved up into a Yardbirds-esque hyperspeed at the fade, and "Jump Back," a yelping, guitar-heavy take on Rufus Thomas' 1964 Stax single for which the Fleshtones borrowed the Small Faces' BBC-radio arrangement that bore little resemblance to the funky, stop-start original. Gang-hollered with Keith out front, the ninety-one-second "Jump Back" is a great example of the deconstruction/reconstruction of black source music that the Fleshtones love, the bedrock of garage rock & roll that Peter affectionately calls "goofball, white misinterpretation of R&B." The bulk of the sessions for *Fleshtones vs. Reality* were completed within a month, and the album—on vinyl, cassette, and, for the first time, compact disc—was scheduled for release in March of 1987.

Among the ugly realities that the Fleshtones faced was Marek's sincere intention to quit. "He stuck it out a real long time," said Peter, who's generally quiet on the subject. "He definitely put in his time. Most people can commit a double homicide and get away with less time than that." Keith was especially upset about his friend leaving. Over the years, from long adolescent summer days in rural Maine to a smoky, sweaty basement in Queens, a fading mist of laughs and great times, Marek had become one of Keith's closest friends. "I loved Marek," Keith says. "I felt sad. He had a great voice, he was a great bass player, he was a great-looking guy. He was a Fleshtone. But he probably had had enough of butting heads with Peter. I'm sure his addictions would be getting in the way of the real world, but at that point I didn't realize how far he was into it. I didn't want to replace Marek. He was my buddy. But I realized that I had to."

Although Marek had promised to finish the recordings, he left before the album was complete. His last gig with the Fleshtones, lost in an ear-ringing avalanche of careening realities, was at the Lone Star Cafe on October 25, 1986, on the cusp of yet another wild Halloween with his wild friends, who were all now in their thirties.

Aware throughout the sessions that they would be the last with their friend, the guys began searching for a replacement. They were idly talking to Ernie Brooks, former bassist for the Modern Lovers, but were keeping their ears and eyes open. Keith was taking the pulse of the East Village nightly and happened to be in the Pyramid watching the Wigstock backing band (featuring Dmitri, who would in several years catapult to national fame and fortune in Dee Lite with "Groove Is in the Heart"). Keith zeroed in on the bass player, a tall, handsome young guy with bright eyes, dark Elvis hair, and a memorable jawline. He was smiling a lot, and was obviously a good player.

When the band finished, Keith walked up to Brian Butterick. "What do you think of this guy?" Keith asked.

Butterick glanced over at the stage. "Oh, he's the best. And one of the cutest," he gushed. "We love him!"

The Fleshtones vs. Reality

A Pyramid bartender and friend of the bass player learned of Keith's interest and arranged a meeting between the two musicians. At the end of a conversation fueled by Black Russians and rising enthusiasms, Keith asked the flabbergasted Robert Warren if he'd be interested in playing bass with the Fleshtones. Keith felt an energetic simpatico with the kind, soft-spoken Robert immediately, and the more he talked with him the more Keith felt that Robert was on the scene and in the know. Robert was considerably younger than Keith, Peter, and Bill—an unripe twenty-one when Keith met him—but he had already packed quite a bit of rock & roll living in his life.

Born and raised in Atlanta, Georgia, Robert Warren had first visited New York City in 1983 as the bass player in Ru Paul's backing band, Wee Wee Pole. He booked shows for that group at Danceteria and the Pyramid, and he fell in love with the noisy city. In 1984 he moved to Athens, Georgia, for a year, playing in Go Van Gogh and vibing that city's palpable tremors as the epicenter of alternative rock. In February of the next year he moved up to Manhattan for good, suffering the predictable first-year horrors of couch-surfing and menial jobs tending bars, washing dishes, and running off other band's flyers at a copy store. He finally found a small apartment on Avenue B and a steady job tending bar at King Tut's Wah-Wah Hut, and he settled in.

At some point, a friend had corralled Robert to see the Fleshtones at the Lone Star. "I was stunned," Robert says.

The guys invited Robert up to the Music Building to rehearse. He snatched up as many Fleshtones records as he could find downtown and learned all of the songs, digging the influences he hadn't noticed before, especially Marek's funky bass lines. "About a third of the songs I'd learned they didn't do anymore," he remembers with a laugh. "But it was great. I had done my homework and I wanted the gig so bad. When I joined, the Fleshtones were on a weekly salary of $250 that would go to $200 per week plus per diems while on tour. It was intense." Robert hung out at "Studio D," wide-eyed inside of dark Gotham haunts that he was now visiting nightly in the generous hands of legendary partiers.

Gordon, for one, was positively effusive about Robert. "Look at him! He's beautiful!" Gordon yelled to no one in particular, doing a jig down Eighth Avenue after a long, beery night at Smith's. "He's beautiful! We're gonna take him to Europe! It's gonna be great! *Our problems are solved!*" Keith remained cool, teasing Robert with the possibility of a tour of France, Italy, and Spain, including two opening gigs for James Brown in Paris. The guys played their hands close to their chests for a few days but, ultimately charmed by Robert's enthusiasm and his Southern lack of guile, invited him to play a gig upstate and to meet Singerman to discuss financial terms of life in the Fleshtones. Robert was a young bachelor with no expensive habits who lived simply. If he joined the band, he would make only a little less than what he made working around the clock at King Tut's and at the all-night copy store on East Twelfth Street. The gig was beyond his dreams.

On November 5, 1986, Robert played his first Fleshtones show, at Colgate University in upstate New York. Discounting rehearsals, it was only the second Fleshtones gig that he'd ever seen, and he was about to experience the joys and chaos of Super Rock baptism in the same way that Bill had six years earlier. Driving up to the show, Keith and Gordon told him, "We know that you know these songs, but you *have* to watch Peter and key off of him." Keith stressed to Robert that Peter's the boss, the ringleader, and he's good at it *but! everyone at some point misreads him and there's not a conversation onstage he can get furious when he's in a zone and it's not a good thing!* To Robert's relief, the gig went fine. The band was buoyant on the drive back to New York City, drinking copious amounts of alcohol, trusting the driver to steer them home through falling snow, another sweaty, exhilarated night of rock & roll behind them.

Robert could only look out the window at the receding hills draped in gray-white. It was raining when the guys let him off near his apartment in the East Village. As the van pulled over on a slicked street Peter began slurring to Robert, "Ayma drunken old fool, ayma drunken old fool, drunken old fool . . ."

Robert shyly pulled his gear from the van. Peter cleared his head and said to his new bassist, "I'll tell you how great you were. Later."

Peter never did. But in his own mumbling, side-glance way in the rain that early morning—tired, victorious, and stubbornly private—Peter already had.

Robert was intimidated by the prospect of filling Marek's shoes. "They were all Virgo's until I joined!" he says. "They called me the Hexbreaker. They were building this very imaginative and hilarious and compelling mythology about themselves. There were times, depending what chemicals had been ingested, when it would take on shades of reality. They conjured something and it had actually come into being, and they would riff for hours. I was quite entertained by all of their shenanigans." Robert's closest friends, aware of his aversion to hard drugs and excessive drinking ("I never did cocaine or speed, and never ingested that much alcohol"), warned him about joining a band whose saga of debauchery was storied, and growing still.

To his surprise, Robert found that some of that legend had been exaggerated on the streets, the bars, and in the mist of after-hours shows. "Truthfully, I did see a couple of things going up people's noses from time to time. But they are wise users of recreational drugs. They don't let it get in the way. Their tolerance and their stamina is deservedly legendary." Robert did once enjoy some head-lifting mushrooms with the guys while on tour in Durham, North Carolina. He hasn't touched the drug since, swearing that the single experience of shrooming with Peter, Keith, Bill, and Gordon, going to see NRBQ and then eating at a local Denny's restaurant could never really be topped.

The guys wanted Robert to play on the new record, languishing unfinished at the Record Plant. He went into the studio and quickly cut two tracks hitherto earmarked for Full Time Men and the Love Delegation. "Way Down South" was a full-band blast through Peter's tune on which Gordon blows one of his last recorded solos and Keith channels Tom Fogerty on lead Mustang, and "Whatever Makes You Happy" was a rock/gospel rave-up in 4/4, featuring Wendy Wild's wailing and Super Gang vocals from a handful of friends, including Barrence Whitfield. Onto this, Robert laid down a popping, disco-propelled bass line. Both songs rocked and capture Robert's dynamic playing with the band to perfection. Along with an original called "In My Eyes You're Dead," they would be the only songs that he would record with the Fleshtones.

Young Robert Warren had dipped his toe into a sonic whirlpool. He'd climb back out after eighteen months, breathless and a bit dazed, having learned the crucial necessity of sharp shoes, onstage education, and keeping his heart off of his sleeve.

17.
Time Bomb

1987 could have been the year that the confident *Fleshtones vs. Reality* broke the band. The guys felt great about the songs, sound, and homeland attitude of the new record, and like-minded groups the Georgia Satellites and Jason and the Scorchers were selling records. In retrospect, the fallout from the album was one of the most disappointing and bitter of the Fleshtones' career. Released in March (on Friday the 13th) *Fleshtones vs. Reality* featured the officially departed Marek on ten of twelve songs. In a friendly tribute to his decade testifying to Super Rock, Marek was included in the moody band photo on the front sleeve, the guys well-dressed and bathed in soft light, circling a ridiculously handsome Bill doing his best Cary Grant. Marek sports a rebellious Van Dyke mustache, an anomaly in a band politically against facial hair, and his eyes look tired and distant, gazing at the coming year of strife.

The back sleeve featured rambling notes from Peter that amounted to a Post-I.R.S. Statement of Purpose, the tongue-in-cheek diatribe doing much to explain the band's attitude in 1986 (and beyond):

> Somebody had to do it! And after waiting four years and studying
> the prophetic contents of "I'm Gonna Build Me a Cave" by John
> Lee Hooker, the FLESHTONES decided that they had to do it *Them-*

Time Bomb

selves! The FLESHTONES *are* the FIVE ELEMENTS—combining to provide their "special brand" of alchemy. . . . Passing the Philosopher's Stone over the discarded—Transforming the discredited—Rescuing *and* Revivifying the bones rummaged from the musical Glue-Factory. They reverse the rotting effects of reality, creating a world where a playboy (Horst Bucholtz) helps an FBI agent find a kidnapped Scientist. Our Kind of World!!! But, asks the mealy-mouthed, doesn't the FLESHTONES' collective pitching arm ever tire of lobbing curve-balls at boredom and pomposity? Can't anybody STOP them? WHO WOULD WANT TO!?!? Although Internationally known as "Nice Guys," the FLESHTONES henceforth operate on a SUPER-REVENGE MOTIF!, insuring "Great Music"—and lots of laughs as their plans invariably explode in their faces. Do Not Attempt to re-create these stunts at home, merely purchase this LP and let these "trained professionals" get your kicks for you. GO AHEAD, IT'S ALRIGHT. This is NOT just a brittle snag to momentarily break the head-long plunge into the chasm of obscurity—NO. This is a "rare opportunity," as well as a "standing invitation" from the FLESHTONES to step outside of time and claim the birth-right they hold in trust for You! The FLESHTONES VS. REALITY . . . *You* Be the Judge!!!

Few understood that Peter's tirade was only half in jest. He genuinely believed that the Fleshtones were a tonic for a country in need of fun, truth, and sincerity. Peter's overriding vision had been to begin and end *Fleshtones vs. Reality* on upbeat notes, despite—or because of—the more dispirited subject matter that the middle songs deal with: hopelessness, confused sexuality, and abject self-loathing that few Fleshtones songs had tackled before. "In the middle there's that nasty stuff, so it's sort of like a bad trip," Peter explained. "But then at the end you get that hopeful feeling. I don't understand why we're always accused of being so mindless. That's okay, because it's good to have fun, but some of the lyrics are pointed. The beat is so happy that people just don't realize it."

Fleshtones vs. Reality was accompanied with a generally unambitious marketing push by Emergo, which didn't have a lot of money to spend. Singermanagement did the best it could from its midtown office, blizzarding the release with a press kit packed with positive notices for the band, but Singerman and the guys soon discovered that Emergo's distribution scheme was paltry. Part of the problem was the label's many-tentacled approach borne of a diffuse, threadbare necessity common to an indie label. Recorded in Manhattan,

Fleshtones vs. Reality was manufactured in Germany, marketed from the Netherlands, and licensed and distributed in fourteen countries on fourteen different labels. Despite the global reach, the record was difficult to find months after its release due to various troubles along the distribution lines. "We had a problem in Europe," Keith laments. "It was on New Rose in France, and people there were still having problems, even though that was a top independent label."

The New York Mets won a thrilling victory against the Boston Red Sox in the World Series two months earlier, but local omens weren't strong enough. It appeared to the band that reality would again reign victorious and that *Fleshtones vs. Reality* was destined, as John Lee Hooker had put it in a different age, to go deep down in the ground. In its initial landing the record received excellent reviews. In *Rolling Stone*, J. D. Considine called the record "not simply the first Fleshtones album to realize the band's potential, it's the first time the band has been as much fun on vinyl as in the flesh." He went on to praise "The End of the Track" in particular, calling the song "exciting, entertaining, and entirely [the band's] own." *CMJ New Music Report* raved, delighting in the soul and funk sounds, noting that the guys mine their influences "with such spontaneous energy that the songs sound brand new and, more importantly, they're lots of fun. And that's the way it should be." *Billboard* called the record "top-notch," and *Cashbox* hailed it as the band's "best since '81's *Roman Gods* and perhaps its most accessible."

In the *New York Times*, loyal champion Robert Palmer wrote admiringly of the band's longevity and of the album's "straight-ahead, supercharged rock 'n' roll." He ended his brief notice, the last review that he would write of a Fleshtones record, with characteristic praise for a band that he so admired from their beginnings:

> On the evidence of "Fleshtones vs. Reality," they are playing better than ever. This is the first Fleshtones album that's as wildly and *consistently* energized as their celebrated live shows. The closest stylistic comparison would have to be the late 60s Rolling Stones, with tight, punching horns adding weight to their slashing guitar attack, as in "Exile on Main Street." But the Fleshtones are beyond comparison; this careening beauty of an album stands on its own from beginning to end, and that's the best kind of revenge.

Palmer noticed that the Fleshtones sounded relaxed and confident on this album, writing and recording from a place that felt, at last, like home.

Time Bomb

The Five Nice Guys had little chance. *Fleshtones vs. Reality* battled Michael Jackson's *Bad*, U2's *The Joshua Tree*, the *Dirty Dancing* soundtrack, and other commercial giants on the *Billboard* album charts. The Beastie Boys' *Licensed to Ill* was a good sign, an indication that raw, fun rock & roll still had its place in the hearts and wallets of kids buying records, but the marriage consummated there would see rap, R&B, and hip-hop come charging up the charts in the next several years. Even if the Fleshtones were able to release records steadily, they would suffer against the leading and splintering purveyors of popular taste and the increasing commingling of corporate labels.

When the Beastie Boys released their brilliant and brainy *Paul's Boutique* in the summer of 1989, the Bronx trio unleashed a thick sampling of disparate influences common to a vibe and feel. The sound, spiritually kindred to the Fleshtones' in borough-attitude and smirking fun, would mark the future of popular radio, and leave the Fleshtones in the dust. "When I first joined I thought, *I'm gonna help them write their hit!*" says Robert. "They still had a lot of desire to go beyond where they had been. I think, from what I can glean of what's happened afterwards, they became, *Alright, this is our niche. We're just gonna do what we do and do it better than anyone else.* Which is great. Maybe it was like that when I was in the band and I just didn't get it."

Now what? 1987 would see the band embarking on tours in attempts to bring *Reality* to the masses, long, grueling jaunts that were necessities born of diminishing band income. Despite debuting at number four on *CMJ*'s Radio Breakthroughs list and reaching number twelve on *Rockpool*'s College Radio Chart, *Fleshtones vs. Reality* wasn't selling well—Singerman estimates total worldwide sales topped out at a dismal fifteen thousand-plus copies—and the band had to hit the road again in order to earn pocket change.

Before embarking, they enjoyed a moment with one of their heroes, Andy Warhol, who was hosting *Andy Warhol's Fifteen Minutes* on MTV. Peter was still hosting *Cutting Edge* and providing national name-recognition for the band, so an offer was made to the Fleshtones to appear on Warhol's show. They filmed two segments for a special episode on "Romance," a lip-synch through "The Return of the Leather Kings" and a spontaneous, wholly inspired pairing with Ian McKellen, the renowned Shakespearean actor who happened to be visiting New York City. "The Return of the Leather Kings" showed the band at their campy best, Keith and Gordon pokerfaced throughout the mock-heroic tune, Peter whipping his bangs, Bill pounding out the beat on his overturned bass drum, Robert flashing beatific eyes throughout it all and looking plain tickled to be there.

The pairing with McKellen was fantastic: as the actor dramatically recited Shakespeare's "Twentieth Sonnet," the Fleshtones accompanied him in the background, creating ambient psychedelic music. The kind of marriage of high and low art prized by Warhol, the union provided all concerned with kicks. The guys invited McKellen down to the Pyramid with them after the taping, and he gladly came along for some alternative East Side *divertissement*. (When the performance was released the next year on the *Time Bomb* compilation, the Fleshtones were able to enjoy one of the more notable songwriting credits in recent pop history: "Zaremba / Milhizer / Spaeth / Warren / Streng / Shakespeare".)

The band spent the early months of the year indoctrinating Robert into life on the long road, playing the Eastern Seaboard/Midwest circuit (including a show at the Bayou Club in Washington, D.C., where Peter, pissed off at the promoters and indulging a rare nasty drunk, left the club in the middle of a song and never returned). In mid-April the band flew to Honolulu, Hawaii, and played their first ever gigs in the fiftieth state. On May 10 they departed for Paris and the start of a two-month tour of Europe, opening for James Brown at the Zenith Club, enjoying the Godfather of Soul more for what he represented than for his current state, a shadow of his former incendiary, groundbreaking self. In October, the Fleshtones would open for Chuck Berry in Barelona, Spain, in front of thousands. Neither opening slot did much to alter the guys' views of the two soul and rock & roll icons (although Keith got a kick out of Chuck Berry asking to borrow his guitar tuner). "All these people are our heroes," said Peter. "But it's important to remember we love them for their music. Confusing the music with the actual people, where one indeed exists, isn't really fair even to them and is kind of like judging a football player on his penmanship." Keeping things on the positive side, Peter said, "It was really cool meeting the guys in James Brown's band, and what's happened to him is really sad."

On this tour, a circuit fraught with an unusual amount of melodrama even for the Fleshtones, Paris rested at the midpoint between the ridiculous and the sublime. The band tore through France with their old pals Lyres in support, playing seventeen shows in nineteen days, displaying for young Robert a sonic, sleepless microcosm of craziness. For the new kid, popping his bass in the funkiest ways he knew, decked out in a pair of American flag stovepipe jeans, flattered that the band was playing one of his own songs ("I Can't Do Without You"), the tour was reckless vindication of the jaw-dropping admiration that he had felt for the band—*his band!*—as a live outfit. If anything, the energy level of the Fleshtones was ratcheted up even higher with Robert now in the lineup, as the young guy spun, high-kicked, and twirled his way out of Marek's receding shadow.

Robert lost track of the number of times kids would come up to him after shows and proclaim that the Fleshtones were the greatest band they'd ever seen. "We would breeze into these sleepy little towns," he marvels, "that were either totally Old World–looking or looked like they'd been rebuilt in the fifties after having been destroyed in the war—or a little of both—set up, do our show, kick ass, and leave in a cloud of dust, with smiles on everybody's face. That was one of the best things about playing in the band. The first twelve months was a golden period. I know they felt energized by my contributions, and I was just *so* into it. A lot of the times I learned stuff onstage or in the dressing room, but luckily a lot of the songs were easy to play, and *feel* was more important than actual accuracy. Atmosphere, attitude, and feel: all of which the Fleshtones have in spades." The highlight of the tour was a two-night stay at La Locomotive Club in Paris, broadcast over French radio. The wild second show ended with the guys leaving the club, gear in hand, chanting the refrain to an epic-length "End of the Track," and climbing into the trees that lined the street in front of the club, serenading a howling pocket of fans below who'd followed them outside.

The nadir came a week later in Decazeville, when the headaches endemic to touring took the frightful turn that all bands worry about and that the Fleshtones seemed to actively court this time around. "Essentially, Jamie Starr happened," Robert explains. Starr, the band's driver/soundman/tour manager from Minneapolis who had allegedly worked with Prince, had turned out to be a pathological liar. "A strong personality, he and Peter immediately clashed and did not get along. Jamie did some good stuff—got us road cases and wireless transmitters—but once we got to France, he started trying to divide and conquer the band. Very manipulative, playing band members off each other. Gordon—who I love—was always a bit of a loose cannon, and Jamie homed in on him and messed with his head."

Starr was jealous of Peter ("Starr wanted to be the star," Robert quips) and was bad-mouthing Peter to the press. It came to a head in Decazeville, where the audience was particularly rowdy and where Jamie got into altercations. "He was making decisions for the band and saying we wouldn't play, and he refused to let anything go." The band finally did play, and when the curtains parted the crowd was greeted with the alarming sight of a wasted, insane Gordon strangling Peter with his microphone stand. The show fell apart from there. "Peter slammed the stand into the mixing desk in front of Jamie, who was a big guy and claimed to be a Vietnam vet." Jamie gathered all of his equipment, threw Gordon into the back of the van, and abandoned the guys in the middle of France. "No Gordon! I don't know what happened to him. I can't recall if he headed back to NYC with Jamie or what," says Robert. The Fleshtones kept on going, a group of fans helping to drive them around in wasted circles.

Back from Europe, the Fleshtones watched in dismay as *Fleshtones vs. Reality* continued its disappearing act. The band was still hip enough to be name-checked in Bret Easton Ellis' novel *Less Than Zero*—in the middle of a coke deal, one character asks another for two backstage passes to a Fleshtones show—but modish Brat Pack literary references and good reviews notwithstanding, America's neglect of the Fleshtones continued gloriously.

In June, the band played at an *I Was a Teenage Zombie* promotional event at the Tunnel. (The flick was unkindly received: snickered a *New York Post* critic in a one-star review, "The only way to see this is in a zombie-like stupor. Bring a good book along anyway, just in case.") In the August issue of *Rolling Stone*, Emergo and Singer-management managed to wrangle a hilarious, if odd, two-page spread for the Fleshtones in the guise of a fashion layout with accompanying copy lauding the band for its survival. The guys posed in stylized garb straight out of *The Great Gatsby*, complete with stylish walking canes and wind-swept locks. Mexx-Men's Herringbone jackets, French Connection cable-knit sweaters, Sasson wool coats and shirts, Antique Boutique formal gloves: the guys looked as retro-contemporary as they'd ever dared. Decked out in a black-and-white cotton houndstooth suit, Bill earned his own full-page, striking his best 1940s Hollywood leading-man look while rakishly lifting his vintage hat with gray gloves. Lightheartedly or otherwise, the trend-sniffing editors at *Rolling Stone* wouldn't come calling on the band again for quite a while.

The cramped spaces of the van were beginning to confine Robert Warren. The age difference between himself and the guys, the drinking and carousing, the touring bugaboos, the political differences were all coming to a head. Robert was raised in the South by a single mom ("a hippy!" he crows proudly) and he found it difficult to stomach the guys' conservative and Libertarian leanings. The long, long stretches of lonely highways in the van, a septic tank of fierce hangovers and fiercer boredom, can cast unappealing personality traits into sharp relief.

In between gigs and bouts of soul-searching, Robert continued to indulge his love in playing with the guys. After Emergo folded due to mismanagement and dried-up funds the Fleshtones were again without a label, and Keith wanted to revive Full Time Men. He got in touch with Steve Fallon, who owned the Maxwell's club in Hoboken and the Coyote record label on which the first Full Time Men EP appeared. Coyote had recently signed a manufacturing and distribution deal with the Twin/Tone label out of Minneapolis, and Keith interested Fallon in bankrolling a full-length album. Keith turned to his trusted drummer and his new bass player for the rhythm section, recruited Gordon to play sax and harmonica, and asked local friend Rich Thomas (of Lower East Side Rockers) to handle lead guitar. Keith's Full Time Men *circa* 1988 was a grander master plan than the one-off duet with Peter Buck: this time Keith envisioned a dual-guitar rock & roll band that he could revive over the coming years with a revolving lineup equipped to handle his backlog of songs. Keith assembled the band in Jersey City and briskly cut an album's worth of tracks, all of which featured a heavy swagger and tongue-in-cheek *machismo* missing from most Fleshtones records. He handled the vocals and wrote or cowrote each of the seven originals, ranging from the boilerplate opener "Nothing's Gonna Stop Our Train" and eponymous fist-in-the-air band theme, to a "Way Down South" rewrite and a revival of the decade-old "Critical List." Three covers—Ida Cox's blues standard "Four Day Creep," the Creation's "Making Time," and Marvin Gaye's "Baby, Don't You Do It"—complemented the workmanlike but sturdy originals. ("I Got Wheels" and "High on Drugs" were added to round out the album.) Musicians and friends, including Peter, Jeff Connoly, Stiv Bators, Dave Faulkner, Pat DiNizio, and Michael Ulmann, dropped by the studio to sing or play. Full Time Men played a record release party at the Pyramid in June and *Your Face My Fist* was released semiwidely in November. An ill-fated mini-tour of Europe followed in the spring, plagued by poor distribution and planning, but Keith would continue to revisit his side band of buddies and like-minded rock & rollers for years to come.

Singing background on a couple of Full Time Men tracks was Anne Arbor, a young, dark-haired French girl whom Keith had met at the Gibus residency three years earlier. She'd moved to the United States in 1986 and, as Keith's relationship with Wendy Wild was ending, began to date her favorite guitar player. In the summer of 1987 Anne moved in with Keith in his small room at the Hotel Rutledge, enduring electrical shorts when the hot plate and stereo fired up, and handling the Fleshtones fan club for many years out of sheer fandom and love for rock & roll. "We did almost everything together, shared almost everything in those first years," says Anne. "Including the partying. More parties, more concerts, more tours, more clubbing, more travelling, more thrills, more cool people, more excitement than most people get in their lifetimes. And more love too. Enough of it to push through any difficult times." Keith and Anne would marry in 1991, and a couple of years later move out to (slightly) larger digs in Williamsburg, Brooklyn, years before that neighborhood became the epicenter of hip.

After the disappointing fade suffered by *Fleshtones vs. Reality*, Peter was also itching to record. Indulging disco and soul music, he revived Love Delegation for another full-length album. He arranged a deal with Skyclad Records, provided that he would assist in the financing, and dug into his own meager savings and borrowed money from friends and family to make the record happen. He ducked into Jersey City early in the year and cut ten Day-Glo tracks grooved with Keith playing guitar, Robert playing bass, Ricky Rothchild and Drew Vogelman drumming, and Wild and Ulmann singing; other friends contributed guitar, bass, and horns (and Bill was credited with a "Disco hi-hat"). If Lee Hazlewood and Nancy Sinatra had spent a weekend on acid, time-traveled to Studio 54, and recorded an album at dawn it might have sounded something like *Delegation Time*, a good-humored collection of workout R&B and smiley-face disco (including a cover of K.C. and the Sunshine Band's "Wrap Your Arms Around Me") smoothed by Peter's soft-touch production and Wendy Wild's impressive chanteuse vocals. It's a minor gem of a dance record, the songs amounting to a half-hour celebration of Peter's love of disco, funk, sixties music, and grins.

Peter felt great, but the album became nearly impossible to find upon its release, and it's more or less vanished. "A disgracefully obscure record," he laments. Skyclad's owner refused release and wanted his money back, but Peter was forced to admit in his lawyers' office that he was broke. The Fleshtones had just returned from a French tour where Peter had pocketed a couple grand and, under awkward circumstances, he was forced to turn the dough right over to Skyclad. "I thought that that record was gonna be my secret weapon," Peter says. "It was a miserable failure." Peter ultimately licensed the record through Singermanagement on Accord Musidisc in France, and it came out in early 1989. The embarrassing failure of *Delegation Time* cemented once and for all Peter's distrust of and disgust with the record industry.

The Love Delegation and Full Time Men recordings hinted at the pile of after-hours recordings compiled by various Fleshtones side bands since the mid-eighties. In the works for years, *Time Bomb! Fleshtones Present: The Big Bang Theory* finally appeared in April on Skyclad, documenting boozy nights at the Pyramid and various East Village haunts, apartments, and studios. The Fleshtones were represented by "I Was a Teenage Zombie," "In My Eyes You're Dead," "I Forgot How to Talk," "She Turned My Head Around" (one of Pakulski's final recordings with the band), and the Ian McKellen performance from the Warhol show. Full Time Men, Action Combo, Mad Violets, Action Dogs, Love Delegation, the Wild Hyenas, and Cryin' Out Loud (a Warren tune replacing a contribution from Marek's Tall Lonesome Pines) make appearances, the package a good-hearted hymn to the kind of Lower East Side after-hours silliness borne of men and women with colored drinks, kicky ideas, and too much time on their hands.

Late winter and early spring in 1988 saw the Fleshtones on and off the road, and Robert was beginning to butt heads with the guys consistently. Raised in an upper-middle-class home, he'd initially found the guys' working-class background alluring. "It felt so forbidden to me," Robert says. "They were way ahead of the curve in terms of the Political Correctness backlash." Not without their sardonic mean streaks, the guys would often tease Robert and his liberal politics. Simply to relieve the boredom of the road, the guys would try and get under Robert's skin. "Robert was very much into not being a racist," says Keith. "We all are not racist. But of course Gordon would start up on him to pull his strings. *Oh yeah? Can you name one black chess master that ever existed?* just to get Robert going. Of course, Gordon's not racist! And I think Robert didn't realize that."

One afternoon following the inaugural Martin Luther King, Jr. Day, Bill lobbed a loaded question to his buddies in the van: "Who thinks that Martin Luther King, Jr.'s birthday should be a national holiday?"

Robert raised his hand and looked around him in the cramped space. No one else had raised their hands. *Oh shit.*

After tense silence he turned to Peter. "Why do you think it shouldn't be a national holiday?"

Peter turned a heavy-lidded gaze at Robert. "Because it just focuses on one group of people."

"No it *doesn't*!" Robert demands.

"We base our beliefs on *reality*," Peter continued. "Not what we read in magazines." Robert rolled his eyes. The van rolled on quietly.

Keith laughs now about the incident. "We were all unified! Of course I think that King should have his holiday. That was just another joke we were playing on him. We're not like that."

"It was quaint up to a point," Robert says now with a smile. "Peter is the best debater. The other guys in the van rarely, maybe even never, went head-to-head with him. They would tell me, *Don't start with him because it's a waste of your time and you can't win*. But I'd do it anyway. For a while they read me and realized that they didn't want to ruffle my feathers too much. Then after a while they didn't care." Political disagreements were among the reasons that Robert began looking for a way out of the band. "I never would've thought that it would've bothered me as much as it did, but it did. It was Peter and Keith's band, their vision. They really got on my nerves and enraged me. But for the most part they were very gentlemanly, and they were great teachers in terms of being so passionate."

The final straw for Robert occurred when Peter failed to show for an Italian mini-tour with Elliot Murphy and the folksinger Phranc. The incident stretched to the limit the guys' tight-lipped acceptance of each other's personal quirks. "Something was going on at home to the point where Peter couldn't do the tour, or was pissed off at having to do it," Bill remembers. "We were at the airport, and Singerman was outside on the fire escape where Peter lived at Fifth Street and A, and he got up on the fire escape, anything to try and get him out." It is not in the nature of the Fleshtones to pry, to go in depth into private issues, especially domestic issues. "Peter's explanation was sort of like, *I had shit to do at home*," Bill sniffs.

Singerman convinced the guys to board the plane and fly to Italy in order to goad Peter to join his band; Bill protested from the outset, but his vote was the minority. "We went over there and it was horrible," remembers Robert, who sensed some friction between Peter and Keith regarding Keith's relative successes with Full Time Men. "These small-town guys have their reputations on the line. They booked the Fleshtones, they paid for advertising, they'd gotten their hopes up. We show up and stay in these hotels that they'd booked and eaten their food and gone to the restaurants, and then we wouldn't play! And then we'd move on and do the same thing in the next town, waiting for Peter to show up. He never did." Peter finally arrived in Greece, where the Fleshtones shared a two-night bill with Hoodoo Gurus and the Dream Syndicate at a giant amphitheater overlooking the sea. "We sucked," Robert says flatly. "There was only a handful of shows that I played with the band that I would say people didn't get their money's worth."

As far as personal issues, the Fleshtones are old-school; not much heart-on-sleeve stuff. "Quite refreshing in today's compulsively confessional age," Robert reflects. "At the time, though, I was really frustrated by the whole thing. None of the guys were interested in asking Peter what had happened, so everybody just let it go." Dave Faulkner of Hoodoo Gurus watched bemusedly as Peter gingerly balanced the home and the road. "Peter would be too chicken to tell his wife he was going on tour!" Faulkner laughs. "He had to basically sneak out and not come back for two weeks. If he had been more up-front about it, it might've been fine. It was just the way he did things. To avoid conflict, he created more."

The Fleshtones would later perform a makeup show in Italy at a beach near Rome. At the conclusion of the gig Peter and Bill jumped into the ocean and swam away as the rest of the band was finishing Jody Reynolds' "Endless Sleep," a tune about a guy who saves his girlfriend from drowning. "They had set the stage up on the beach," Peter remembers. "By the time we were playing, the tide had come up and there was water coming up under the stage. We were expecting to get electrocuted any second. It seemed like the only appropriate way to end a show like that was to swim away." Peter and Bill, tom drum in hand, ended up somewhere down the beach. "There was another party going on in an establishment on the beach," Bill laughs. "So we walked in there soaking wet because we didn't want to come back to the Fleshtones show area just yet. That would blow the exit!"

Robert was looking for his own exit. He'd met his future wife (Holly George, who had been playing in Das Furlines, Wendy Wild's *faux*-German punk-polka band, and who is now a writer) and was dumbstruck in love. "I had thought prior to joining the Fleshtones that all I needed was to play in a great rock & roll band and I'd be happy. I wasn't. That was a dismaying thought." Despite what some band members might have thought at the time, Robert insists that Holly did not try and talk him out of leaving the Fleshtones, although she didn't discourage him, either. "I was wanting to be a songwriter and be in my own band, and I didn't want to go on any of those long van rides with them anymore. Gordon went through a really rough ride, and that was hard for me to watch. It was diminishing returns for me after awhile. Truthfully, I thought that I was jumping off a sinking ship."

Further irritating Robert, Keith had promised to include a version of Robert's "I Can't Do Without You" on *Your Face My Fist*, and Keith reneged. "We recorded a blazing basic track of it," Robert remembers. "But when I changed the lyrics and the title, Keith objected—not outwardly—and left it off the album. He didn't tell me of his decision until tracking. My playing on all the other tunes, and the mixing, was done, letting me believe my song, which we'd added overdubs to, would be on the record until the last minute. That was actually the last straw."

Robert didn't think that the Fleshtones would cotton to his growing musical palette and artistic ideas, and he was right. At a rehearsal in May, Robert told the guys that he was quitting. "Peter saw it coming, but Keith was more hurt because he had really fought for me to be in the band." The Fleshtones had a repeat gig lined up at the Martinique Festival in June, and they begged Robert to do the show. Bitter, and a tad haughty, Robert forced the guys to implore him. "I was sloppy about leaving. It was immature stuff on my part. I was really young. Some of the stuff I did makes me cringe." Robert did finally agree to do the show, and on June 26, 1988, he played his last gig with the Fleshtones under an innocently clear Caribbean sky.

After leaving the Fleshtones, Robert Warren remained in New York City for several years, playing in a few groups and writing and performing his own material, leaning toward what he describes as a "folkadelic" sound. In the mid-nineties he moved to London for a year to play Buddy Holly in a West End stage production, and in 2000 released his debut solo album . . . *to this day* to critical acclaim, and in 2004 the follow-up, *Lazyeye*. He lives in the Catskills mountains of New York with his wife, Holly, and their son, Jack.

"I learned a lot from the guys," he says now. "When I joined, I was young and relatively ignorant of many things, and they imparted to me valuable knowledge that has enriched my life immeasurably." The guys introduced Robert to Sonny Boy Williamson, Frank Sinatra, Jr., the Stooges, Jack Lee, the Seeds, the Creation, early Yardbirds and Kinks, Lee Hazelwood, Humble Pie, the Faces, and countless other Super Rock Hall of Famers. "Many of these avatars of soul were brought to my attention through extremely lo-fi equipment, a handheld tape recorder in the back of a converted bread truck—our touring van on a couple of jaunts through France—or a shitty car stereo, or a Walkman." The music made its way to Robert's bones, "and there it has remained." He adds, "I can never repay that debt."

The guys taught Robert about more than simply music. "They shared their love of tab collars, three-button jackets, pegged trousers, Chelsea boots, silk scarves, Mardi Gras beads, a well-cut suit, and the value of a good haircut," he says. "I say all this with no archness. They taught me a great deal about the power of visual style. The irony is that at the time I sometimes rebelled against it. I was young and sometimes a little full of myself. As I've made my way in the world as a performer and a man, the lessons have come in handy." Robert is very glad that the guys are still at it, "delivering an endangered art form to a fervent audience and showing the kids how it's done. They are the Iron Men, the Masters. I feel lucky to have served on the frontline of a cause that still needs converts and folks to keep the flame alive." Robert Burke Warren doesn't worry that the fire will ever die, "not as long as the Fleshtones are still alive and active and spreading the word."

18.
Pocketful of Change

Frustrated at the turn of events, and not without a vague sense of dread, the Fleshtones began looking for their third bass player in as many years, watching enviously as their friends in R.E.M. signed a multimillion-dollar record contract with Warner Brothers Records and as pop-metal "hair bands" Motley Crüe, Poison, and Warrant swarm the Top 40, reaping millions of dollars and top-shelf tail. Their own audiences were rapidly dwindling, and no labels were expressing any interest in the band. Keith had indeed been irritated and distressed when Robert quit, and he took his departure personally. "It drove Keith nuts," Peter admits. "I think what bugged him most about it was that it had been his personal pick, and he was trusting his intuition with the kid. And I think it struck to his confidence. I mean, the disloyalty of it."

Gordon had been on a steep personal decline in 1988. His drinking binges were coming on furiously, resulting in missed appearances with the band. "My drinking was getting out of hand," he admits. "When a certain young lady of whom I was enamored committed suicide on St. Valentine's Day, I started to mentally unravel." The remainder of the year was a sad blur toward oblivion for Gordon. His sax was perpetually sitting at Gem Pawnshop on Eighth Avenue, and he was now practically living at the Music Building and hitting the risky Hell's Kitchen dive bars along Eighth and Ninth Avenues with increasing frequency. Those lonely tavern crawls—"my twelve-bar solos," Gordon wryly refers to them—would often end in dicey circumstances with dawn light glimmering off of the Hudson River. "There'd be many a morning when the band would find me near Port Authority and I'd have been mugged, my shirt would be ripped, my saxophone would be in the pawnshop. They'd give me an advance. I'd say, 'How many shows?' They'd say, 'Five.' I'd go across to the store, buy five sets of underwear, five sets of socks, five T-shirts, and throw them into a paper bag. They'd get my saxophone out of pawn, and we'd just go off."

Gordon was roughed up a lot, an easy target staggering out of after-hours clubs at four or five in the morning in a sports jacket and expensive shirt, carrying his saxophone. He often fought in self-defense, and almost got kicked to death at Port Authority one night by a group of kids. Gordon would occasionally threaten members of his own band with physical violence on the long overnight van rides, his increasingly splintering hangovers indistinguishable from his addled personality. "Venom and hate, just hate pouring out of him," remembers Peter of these episodes. "He was very vicious." Onstage, Gordon's playing was becoming predictable and rote, his choreographed moves with Peter strained and silly. More than once he'd have to turn to his band members in a panic, wondering aloud what the next chord is, let alone the next song. At the 9:30 Club he threw his sax down in the middle of the show and stalked off the stage, never returning. Later, he would miss several shows altogether.

Gordon's instability was already in evidence at the end of Marek's tenure with the band. "Gordon had been doing crack at the Music Building with the psychos who were living there, or whomever he was hanging out with, and we managed to bundle him up and get him in the van to go to this gig in Boston," Marek remembers. Gordon was convinced that he was setting fires in the area—psychically. "It was really scary. We all knew that it was really getting bad, yet at the same time—fear, denial, whatever it is—there was always this vicarious thrill of being with Gordon. No matter what kind of state he was in, it was nevertheless far more entertaining than most things that were going on!" All Hallows Eve in 1988—a calendar date that was at one time, far away, a time of fun and diversion—would become for Gordon Spaeth a dark and frightening psychosis, his portal into a decade of calamity.

Meanwhile, Keith was again on the lookout for a bass player to add foundation to the band's crumbling House of Rock. "It was very explosive being on Fleshtones tours," he remarks. "You had to be built a certain way to be doing this kind of insanity. I figured that now I want somebody opposite of Robert, somebody older who's been around the block, somebody who's not so pretty. Who do I conjure up? Fred Smith."

Fred Smith had been on the periphery of Peter and Keith's vision since the mid-seventies, playing in Television when that band was one of the vanguard groups at CBGB's. The group Jon Young once memorably described as "the ultimate garage band with pretensions," Television featured Tom Verlaine and Richard Lloyd famously swapping long, elegant guitar licks within experimental, psychedelic song arrangements. Their privately pressed 45 single "Little Johnny Jewel" became a legendary D.I.Y. document upon its limited release in 1975. Smith joined Television after having played in Blondie, and stayed with the band until their break up in the late seventies.

A decade later, Smith was playing with the roots-country outfit Kristi Rose and the Midnight Walkers, a band whose drummer, Ricky Rothchild, was a good friend of Keith and Peter's and who had played in Love Delegation. The Midnight Walkers weren't playing out much, and Keith proposed a deal to Smith: be a hired gun for the Fleshtones on a per-show fee basis. Smith agreed, with the caveat that once the Television reunion album that he was recording and producing was completed he would be contractually free to pursue Television full-time. The temporary arrangement worked for both sides. The Fleshtones were back in business. "Fred was great, from our school," says Peter. "He grew up in Queens the same way we did, the same sense of humor." Smith wasn't entering the fold as a wide-eyed fan eager to learn the entire Super Rock Cannon. "I'd never seen the Fleshtones," he admits. "I knew their name but I had no idea. We never crossed paths, as far as any of us know." Smith's memories of how he began playing in the Fleshtones are fuzzy at best. ("It was a bad time for me," he admits. "I was in the gutter.") But soon enough he was rehearsing in the Music Building, and he began to play area gigs with the band in late fall.

From the onset, Smith's stoic, unmoving presence onstage was in sharp contrast to the Fleshtones' legendary energy. "I was a total fish out of water," he laughs now. "They were very showy. They do wrestling moves onstage. They do the Powerstance. I remember the first time at the end of some show, Peter said, 'Follow me!' They all started marching into the audience, and I had never done anything like that with any band, especially with Television. There I went, marched around the room, got back onstage. It wasn't really my kind of thing but you had to do it! They're a lot of fun but I hated doing that. I hope that I never have to do it again." At the 8x10 Club in Baltimore, Peter and Keith called for an onstage pile-on and cornered a miserable Smith, laughingly throwing their bodies on top of his in a good-humored attempt to break Smith out of his shell. "He was such a straight guy that we tried to ruffle his feathers," Peter admits. "He didn't mind that." A telling photograph of the band was taken at a South by Southwest Festival show in Austin, Texas: the slow shutter speed captured Peter and Keith melting around a stock-still Fred Smith, as symbolic an image as any documenting Smith's brief time in the band as the dubious calm at the center of the storm.

By this point, gigs had become the sole means of support for the Fleshtones, and the guys had to look for part-time day jobs for the first time in years. "We were gigging a lot, maintaining the payroll, and paying people," remembers Keith. "You had to make a certain amount of money to pay the bills so you had to do so many gigs a month. It's what we had to do. We're in a big void now. We're in trouble. We all know that something's wrong." The band dropped into the Vipers' eight-track recording studio with Smith and, with Dave Mann engineering, quickly cut several demo tracks, including Spirit's "I Got a Line on You," Irma Thomas' "Ruler of My Heart," and one original, "Killing by Degrees." Pleased to be demoing again, the band headed down to Dessau Studios near City Hall and there Smith produced and mixed a more ambitious sixteen-track session over two days. The band recorded a handful of originals, including "Beautiful Light" and "I'm Still Thirsty," as well as a complete overhaul of *Hexbreaker!*'s "BRAINSTORM" in a new arrangement that the band liked. But the recordings failed to ignite. "The tracks were okay, a bit boring and stiff," Keith says. "We never got a record deal. We were rejected by most people."

The infamous Tompkins Square riots blazed blocks from Peter's apartment in the first week August, but the guys caught only wiffs of the fierce activism: they were on the road yet again, playing a handful of shows in Toronto and Montreal, a one-off gig in Portland, Maine, and a five-day swing through the Carolinas. Mostly, the guys were anchored in New York with few prospects. Tired, hemorrhaging money, and frustrated, the Fleshtones were dodging local rumors of drug problems and self-indulgent, messy shows, and were at obvious personal and professional crossroads. The problem was that both roads led into fog and uncertainty.

Sweat

The Fleshtones were scheduled to play at the Big Kahuna at Broadway and Houston Street on Halloween, and Bob Singerman was going to show up to check out Fred Smith. It felt like a big night all around. Iggy Pop, supporting his *Instinct* album, was playing at the Beacon Theatre on the other end of Broadway, and Keith and Anne were planning to catch the show after the Fleshtones' soundcheck.

Gordon never made it to the club that evening. He disappeared into a neighborhood bar late in the afternoon and when he emerged hours later he'd undergone a metamorphosis into the demon-laced man whom he had spent years ignoring, pleading with, and fighting off. Burdened with the guilt and terror of his girlfriend's suicide, years of excessive drinking and drugging wearing out his tired body, Gordon managed to make it back to the Kahuna but, finding it impossible to make his way through the door and into another night of oblivion, suffered a gruesome breakdown on the street outside. He snapped, repeatedly smashing his saxophone on the sidewalk outside the club until it was thoroughly mangled.

Then he vanished. Mr. Dangerous would become Mr. Invisible. No one would hear about him, or see him, for much of the next decade.

Lucky Bill's evening, meanwhile, had taken a wildly different turn. Always a wide-eyed fan of parades, he'd disappeared after soundcheck into the fun and madness of a nearby Halloween procession. He returned to the Kahuna tremendously drunk—even by Bill's standards—and the night fell apart frighteningly fast. "I remember being really revved up after seeing Iggy Pop," Keith says; dosed with ecstasy, he arrived at the club in great spirits. Bill, clearly in the worst state that anyone had seen him, staggered into the club as the band was in the dressing room. "And I proceeded to get drunker," Bill admits. "I was thinking that this is just gonna be the greatest show I ever played because I was in such a great mood, ready to go! And I really couldn't play. I couldn't play."

The Fleshtones hit the stage late and uncertain. Smith remembers the subsequent disaster. "Bill counted off the first song, missed the cymbal, and hit the floor! That was the first time I actually saw Peter scared. And things started decaying rapidly." Bill was on his ass grinning, and Peter and Keith, with paying customers glaring and Smith hoping to shrink away from the mess, made a split-second decision: at rehearsals Peter had jokingly suggested that the Fleshtones cover Thirteenth Floor Elevators' "Fire Engine" because Television used to open their shows with the song. The idea had never left the Music Building.

Pocketful of Change

The band struggled through a few numbers when Peter barked, "I'd like to introduce our latest member of the band, Fred Smith from Television! And we're gonna do one of their old classics, 'Fire Engine'!" Unprepared for Peter's spontaneity Smith froze, and then sheepishly started the bass riff, but Peter and Keith realized that the band was in big trouble. "'Fire Engine' sounded horrible. It was a disaster," Keith remembers. "The show ended with Bill trying to jump up in the air to come down for a big finale hitting his cymbals. He misses the cymbals, falls off the drum riser, and lands flat on his back."

Twenty minutes after hitting the stage, the Fleshtones were reduced to a prone and wasted Bill and an embarrassed and baffled Peter and Keith. Fans began to walk away in grumbling pockets, and the guys gamely packed it up, wrapping mike cords and tossing harmonicas into a sorry, beat-up box. They'd become silhouettes of dysfunction bearing the weight of checkered reputations and professional discourtesy.

Says Keith regretfully, "We still got paid, but we could've been arrested. There should be a law against people violating their contracts. You're supposed to perform a show, and instead you make a mockery of everything. That was probably the worst show that the Fleshtones ever did."

Among the disgruntled fans at the Big Kahuna that night was a twenty-seven-year-old sandy-haired musician from Toronto who'd paid his way in to judge for himself whether the local rumors of excess and tumult were true. He was a fan of the Fleshtones, but he'd been finding their shows more and more erratic.

Piece of shit band, Ken Fox groused to himself as he left the club and strolled down Broadway. *I'm never wasting my time on them again.*

The Hangover

"The only scientists we like are the mad
ones, the ones whose theories
will never work."
–Peter Zaremba

19.
Waiting for a Message

"'88 was great, but '89's mine," rapped Tone-Loc with the confidence of a young man poised for breakout success atop radio and record charts ripe for cultural change. The Fleshtones could hardly make such a cocky statement at the end of the 1980s, as an era of packed clubs and big paydays was coming to a close. Lean years were charging fast. This period was feeling suspiciously like the meager days from a decade earlier, when the Red Star Records sessions were languishing in the can, Marek had quit, and all looked desolate until Miles Copeland offered an invitation to a sunny poolside party that would last half a decade.

Would another helping hand appear? The Fleshtones bristled at their reputation, even if they'd been professionally reckless of late. They'd watched with envy and irony in 1985 as the Replacements, the latest avatars of alternative college-rock, graduated from Twin/Tone Records to major label Sire Records and a large contract. "Meanwhile, the reason we were getting thrown off of labels was the reason that a group like the Replacements were getting signed," Keith insists. "They had this mystique, this Johnny Thunders thing with Bob Stinson in the band. *Who knows what they're gonna do? It could be terrible!* And we were the ones who were getting ostracized. Funny, right?" With misfit Paul Westerberg's vulnerable, candid anthems and ballads buttressed by Stinson's guitar fury and drunken mayhem, the Replacements became in the mid-eighties the standard-bearers of alternative rock. The Fleshtones' version of desperate sincerity was far different from their post-punk peers', and many fans and critics would respond to the Replacements' songs and lifestyle more passionately.

The band had little time to take stock of their career, at any rate. They were scheduled for another Mid-Atlantic tour in November and early December (including a contrite makeup gig at the Big Kahuna) and a small tour of Spain that would culminate in a live recording released on Imposible Records by their promoter friends at Madrid-based Record Runner. The project was essentially an official bootleg: Imposible offered the band a thousand bucks for the right to release the recording throughout Europe, and they thought, *Why the fuck not?* At this point, any record out with their name on it was better than nothing. As no one had yet heard from Gordon, the guys swiftly replaced him with Paul Vorcesi and Nelson Keene Carse from the Urban Blight Horns. "You couldn't replace Gordon with one guy. You needed two!" Keith laughs. "Actually you needed a new angle. You don't replace Gordon."

Following their first appearance at the Lone Star in half a year and a jog down to D.C. and Virginia for some warm-up gigs, the Fleshtones flew to Spain in the middle of December. They hit Madrid on the twentieth—but Fred Smith barely made it. Recovering from what has been passed down in Fleshtones lore as one of the all-time shattering drunks ("Spanish-style drinking," Peter marvels) Smith, another in a long line of innocents caught in the happy web of Fleshtone Hospitality, played the show in splintered spirit only, his body wracked with the worst hangover that he'd ever suffer.

In the afternoon the Fleshtones corralled Smith to a local bar where they were known and popular, and there the friendly bartender asked Smith what he wanted to drink. Smith chose a Corvousier. "And without hesitation, the bartender handed me the whole bottle! Whatever anybody ordered, they were handed the whole bottle. Of course, I could only drink so much of that, and I'm not sure how much I drank. I *did* get a taxi, but the next thing I remember was this guy waking me up, and we're in the country with trees everywhere! He took me to the wrong hotel, outside of Madrid."

In awful irony it turned out that the band's hotel was only three blocks from where the cab had picked Smith up. Hours later he was taken back. He made it to the lobby, and as soon as he hit a hallway where he didn't think he could be seen, got down on his hands and knees and crawled to his room. At dawn, Smith managed to fall into fitful sleep. He awoke early afternoon in utter agony. He wouldn't be able to hold food down for three days, but did manage to gag down a cup of coffee and make it to soundcheck. "I knew I was in really big trouble. There was a wall I leaned up against during the show. I've never listened to that performance, because there were a couple of songs where I couldn't even move my fingers. I was just thumping away. I'm sure I held their performances down," Smith is grateful— and dumbfounded—that the guys were in decent enough shape to play. "I don't know how they did it."

The show at the Rock Club in Madrid is a solid document of the label-free Fleshtones drifting weeks after Gordon's sudden departure. The set list is typical of the period, mixing standards like "The Dreg," "Hexbreaker," and "Stop Fooling Around" with a few *Fleshtones vs. Reality* tracks and a handful of covers. Getting the Super Rock treatment in 1988 were the Music Explosion's slinky "I See the Light" in a snarling arrangement, the Gamblers' surf instrumental "Moon Dawg," Don and the Goodtimers' "Turn on Song," and the Customs Five's obscure and lascivious "Let's Go in '69." By this point, the guys had been regularly playing Bobby Marchan's finger-snappin' "Get Down with It" (filtered through a bit of K.C. and the Sunshine Band), during which the band would literally get down on the beer-soaked floor and Peter would often playfully halt things to single out an unlucky patron who wasn't "Doing it right!" The guys also introduced a cover of Stevie Wonder's "Fingertips" with which they would close many, many a sweaty show in years to come, eventually fine-tuning the arrangement by impudently dropping in the riff from "Roman Gods."

Despite Keith's amp exploding halfway through the show and Peter's mock-angry onstage warnings to Smith ("It's time we cut the lace off your panties, baby!"), the night went smoothly. The show was recorded with direct metal mastering and released on Imposible in December of 1989 under the title *Soul Madrid*. The Fleshtones' on- and offstage visual antics are always as fundamental to a show's success as the songs themselves, and with Fred Smith as Planted Pole, *Soul Madrid* reflected the band about as well as could be expected. The album featured an onstage photo in which the hungover Smith looks improbably radiant ("The miracle of photography and lighting," snorts Keith) and was, for anyone still bothering to look, proof that the Fleshtones hadn't broken up, or succumbed to drug addictions, or suffered the suicide of Peter Zaremba, or permanently relocated to Europe, or buckled under any of the current rumors dodging a band that was considerably less hip than it had been only a year before.

Somewhere during a long and terrifying drive in the winding, wind-swept hills of central Spain, high above centuries-old cities, Peter tuned in the radio to a local rock & roll show, half-listening as his own escalating blues competed with the sounds. "I was getting disaffected and depressed about our inability to do things, and the feeling that we're getting passed by," Peter remembers. One particular tune cut through his self-pity, and he listened in growing mournfulness, saying aloud to no one in particular, *Everyone sounds like us. Why can't we be on the radio?? Why can't we play like that??* At the end of the song, Peter realized that it had been the Fleshtones all along: the DJ had played "Watch This" from *Speed Connection II. Omigod,* Peter recognized with a start, *that was us!* Three years after the fact, and Peter couldn't even remember his own songs. He might as well be giving them away.

The end of the 1980s was difficult for Peter, professionally and personally. He was no longer hosting *Cutting Edge,* the second Love Delegation album had vanished, sinking him farther into debt, Flesh-tones tours were becoming increasingly leaden with headaches, and there was no interest in the band within the alternative rock industry. A surprising call did come from Hollywood. John Guarnieri, an A&R man at I.R.S. who had become a catalog exploiter and compilation producer, presented Peter with the welcome news that Miles was planning a Fleshtones best-of CD. With the guys' input, Guarnieri chose a selection of songs (ignoring various live tracks in the vaults), and Peter and Keith mixed two unreleased cover songs cut during *Hexbreaker!* Longtime Fleshtones supporter Chris Morris at *Bill-board* wrote the liner notes, which captured the essence of the band nicely (and included a recipe for the "Blue Whale").

Peter convinced Guarnieri to release the compilation under the tongue-in-cheek title *Living Legends,* as if the release were part of a chain of titles commemorating renowned bands. It was a joke borne as much from quiet desperation as from jokey confidence. "I wanted to give it that convoluted edge," Peter says. "It might have worked against it, actually." ("I thought it was brilliant," says Guarnieri. "Peter was always very, very clever, with a great sense of humor about this stuff.") The twenty-track *Living Legends* featured choice photos, including the cover shot from the *American Bandstand* performance, and remains to date the only digital source of the band's I.R.S. record-ings. The label printed approximately five thousand copies and, meekly distributed in late summer, the title was destined for out-of-print status before too long. In its brief in-stock existence, however, it gave hope to those fans who'd thought that the band had disappeared. "We were happy to have some kind of a release," admits Peter.

The guys were now nearly penniless. "We never saw a direct correlation between money and anything we were doing," Peter laments. "Like, *If you do this, you get this*. We were just doing stuff." They were experiencing diminishing returns on the endless roads, so Keith started driving a cab in Manhattan and Queens again, Bill managed to sublet rent-free apartments here and there, take on catering jobs, and sell pistol permits over the phone, and Peter, despondently searching the want ads, scrambled for any odd job that he could find, including a short, pathetically paying stint as a reservations agent for a subsidiary of Air France. "I was desperately broke," Peter says. "I was constantly having horrible, devastating arguments about money with my wife." He borrowed cash from Keith and sold his guitar to pay his rent; luckily Marilla was finding consistent, well-paying work in textiles as a designer, and was showing her paintings in Manhattan, selling the odd piece. But everywhere Peter turned he found creditors hounding him and/or his band. Onstage, he was taking to heart the words to the Kingsmen's "Long Green" whenever the Fleshtones would tear through that garage stomp: *the root of all evil.*

1989 was shaping up to be an *annus horribilus*. In February, Keith convened Full Time Men, along with Tall Lonesome Pines, the Vipers, and the B-52's' Fred Schenider, to play a benefit at the Pyramid for Wendy Wild, who was ill. For Peter, the spring brought the devastating personal loss of his mother, Madeline. "My parents had just moved to Florida," he remembers. "I was at the hospital when she was dying. The Berlin Wall fell right around that time. She missed it. It would have been a spectacular thing for her."

Despite the lean days, it never occurred to Peter, Keith, or Bill to break up the Fleshtones. The band's financial situation made it more difficult to tour the U.S. widely, though they were still reliable hits at Madri Gras and drew fairly well in major cities. They were finding more consistent and growing audiences in Europe, where loyal fans understood the Fleshtones' songs and attitude at a simple, gut level. At their core, the guys were held together by transient moments of exultation and fun on the rock & roll stage, and by their deep desire to make more records. By 1989, the *Fleshtones vs. Reality* sessions seemed like a lifetime ago. As spring turned to summer and the like-spirited B-52's scored a massive radio and video hit with "Love Shack"—the ephemeral pop ingredients of which the Fleshtones could never manage to locate in their own songs—the guys hunkered down for another summer festival tour of faraway Europe, unaware that a recording revival was just around the corner.

Fred Smith's interest had turned to playing with and producing Television as well as to Peregrines, a young, signed act with a promising future. His awkward marriage to the Fleshtones ended amicably. "When I joined, things were a little shaky, then things started finally getting solid, then they got shaky again," Smith admits. "Peter was getting unhappy." The beginning of the end for Smith came after forging through a freak ice storm to play Natchitoses, Louisiana, in front of a tiny crowd, where Peter started smashing up his favorite Farfisa organ, reducing it to a sparking heap. A telling publicity photo taken during this period shows four tired men lounging on a sofa in front of a *rococo* curtain, affecting cool but wearing drooping shoulders. Peter's eyes, hooded at their lowest, register little but fatigue and dismay.

With Smith out of the picture, Keith turned to the Dictators' Andy Shernoff, another stalwart from the mid-seventies Bowery scene and a personal hero to Keith, who nearly idolized the Queens-raised mastermind in a kid brother way, going back to the days when he and Peter would sneak into CBGB's. The Dictators had imploded in 1978 after their third album, *Bloodbrothers*, and in subsequent years Shernoff had kept busy writing songs, producing New York area bands such as Sic F*cs, Untamed Youth, and Adrenaline O.D., and managing the occasional Dictators reunion. By the end of the decade, he had his hands full with Manitoba's Wild Kingdom, a tongue-in-cheek heavy metal/hard rock outfit featuring three-fifths of the original Dictators. Wild Kingdom recorded their debut album in 1988, and Shernoff was waiting for the release on MCA and a subsequent national tour in 1990.

The Fleshtones were playing one of their last shows with Fred Smith in May, and Shernoff happened to be in attendance. "Andy hadn't seen the Fleshtones for a year and a half, and we did a real good show," Keith remembers. Keith asked Shernoff what he was up to and if he'd like to do a show or two with the Fleshtones. Shernoff said that he'd love to but, like Smith, couldn't commit to anything very serious for very long, as he was mixing the Wild Kingdom record that summer. The arrangement with Shernoff was temporary, but Keith was thrilled to be playing with him. "The Dictators are still my favorite rock & roll band," Keith enthuses. "They have everything that I think a band should have. I love 'em." Keith adds, "I love Andy. He's a great guy."

Shernoff swiftly learned the material in rehearsals and geared himself up for a June and July tour of Germany, France, Switzerland, and Italy. He relished banging around in a van with his old friends and felt liberated making music over which he had little control. "Just to play bass is fun," Shernoff says. "I was *just* being a bass player. I like writing songs and having a vision also, but I was perfectly happy not being The Guy." He rarely played in the States during his brief time in the Fleshtones, though there was a one-off gig at the Roxy on West Eighteenth Street with Sylvain Sylvain sharing the bill; the hyped evening, billed as a "New York Legends" show, with celebrities Liza Minelli and Jermaine Jackson in attendance, was duly noted in the *New York Post*'s Page Six gossip column the following week. But a major New York area show was rare. Mostly, the Fleshtones tread the Lone Star/Maxwell's circuit with Shernoff, who much preferred playing in Europe. "It wasn't that fun to play in the States," he admits. "It wasn't the same in the audience. I'll be honest about that. The Fleshtones weren't doing that many shows. They did a few New York shows, Boston, Washington, little things like that, East Coast fun. But when I was with them, we never went past the East Coast."

The European festival tour wasn't without its headaches. In Geneva, Shernoff had to abruptly leave the tour because of prior commitments, and the Fleshtones were stranded midtour without a bass player. "Shernoff left us flat," Peter remembers. "We had to beg Fred Smith to come back, and buy him tickets at the last minute. This turned the whole tour into a big disaster." For a couple of desperate days, as the tour dipped south into Italy, the band were without a bass player at all. "We had to get a friend of ours in Genoa, Stefano, to play bass, and we worked up a bunch of songs," Peter recalls. "It worked at one show, and absolutely, positively did not work at the big show in Genoa. That was the only time we were ever booed in Italy."

Shernoff was back in the fold for the duration of the tour, but the unease circuiting the band and their itinerary was difficult to stomach. The tour wound up in early August, and the Fleshtones returned to New York richer in the pocket but poorer in spirit.

Dave Faulkner was visiting New York City in the summer of 1979 on the final and greatest stop of a low-rent, whirlwind world tour. Born and raised in Perth, Australia, Faulkner had a fierce desire to escape the provincial isolation of western Australia and to experience the punk rock movement that had inspired his first band, the Victims. While in Manhattan, he picked up a copy of the Red Star "American Beat" 45 at Bleecker Bob's, loved it immediately, and discovered happily that the Fleshtones were playing Irving Plaza during his brief stay. The band was on the cusp of cutting Lenny Calderon loose, heading toward an ominous if brief career drift, but they never failed to enkindle the stage at Club 57 at Irving Plaza. Faulkner was blown away by the band's show, and he dug their sound, influences, humor, and energy. Their grinning, anthemic cover of Gary Glitter's "Rock & Roll, Part 2" was icing on the cake. Faulkner was baptized a sweaty Fleshtones fan that night. He returned to Australia with his ears ringing and his fingers clutching a stack of USA rock & roll records, with "American Beat" on top.

Two years later, in part as a response to that red-letter night in far-away NYC, Faulkner moved two thousand miles, from Perth to Sydney, and formed Hoodoo Gurus. By 1989, the Gurus were an enormous success in Australia, a regular presence on radio, charts, and award shows, but had failed to make much of a commercial dent in America, where the source ingredients for their brew of hook-filled, fifties- and sixties-style rock & roll and pop happily bubbled. Faulkner was a great songwriter, capable of composing heart-on-the-sleeve, lovelorn ballads, loud, ironic cock rock, and witty novelty tunes. Along the synapse rested a sonic array of popular culture touchstones that made Hoodoo Gurus a funny, smart, and tough outfit.

The Fleshtones—especially Keith and Peter, dazzled by Faulkner's like spirit, wit, and songwriting chops—had been fans ever since the Gurus hit New York City in 1984, supporting their debut, *Stoneage Romeos*. The Gurus were scheduled to play a weekend at CBGB's and Maxwell's on that visit, and Keith had been amped to check out the show in Hoboken. The Hoodoo Gurus' road manager unexpectedly called Keith and told him that the Gurus wanted to meet him. "So I ran over to Peter's house, because I knew that he had *Stoneage Romeos*," Keith recalls. "I quickly listened to it with the guitar in my hand, and figured out 'Leilani' and a few other tracks." Keith showed up at the gig and went backstage and met Faulkner, Brad Shepherd, and the other Gurus, who were positively psyched to be in Manhattan and meeting the guys behind "American Beat." Hours later, Keith, Marek, and Bill joined the Gurus onstage, and rocked out to a handful of songs during the encore. "We jammed and the audience loved it," Keith says. "It was packed, and it was a real exciting evening. Ever since then, I've thought Hoodoo Gurus were really a great rock & roll band." A relationship was born that night:

two bands with similar attitudes and sounds lost to mainstream America. Faulkner subsequently became friendly with Keith and the Fleshtones, a goodwill that lasts to this day.

In the summer of 1989 Hoodoo Gurus were fresh off of their successful *Magnum Cum Louder* album, and in between tours, Faulkner came to visit New York on a vacation. "Dave would come over to the States and hang out," says Keith. "He loved the Pyramid Club. He became friends with everybody." One evening, Keith and Faulkner were hanging out on Avenue A, staying up all night drinking and talking rock & roll, the New York Mets, and *Lost in Space*, when the conversation turned to the dreary state of the Fleshtones. Both men were enjoying the high and the company, and Faulkner was sympathetic to Keith's bitterness and frustration. At one point, Keith lamented the band's label-free plight, and frankly laid it out to his Australian buddy: *The Fleshtones need a record label!* "I wish you were an A&R guy," Keith joked to Faulkner.

"I am, mate!" Faulkner said. "I've got a label."

Keith looked at him sideways through his bangs. "Oh, big joke, Dave. *I've got a label!* What d'ya mean?"

"I've got a label," Faulkner insisted with a grin. "I'm part owner of Trafalgar Records. I'll sign you!"

This guy's out of his mind, Keith thought. *He's had one too many.* "We start talking more and more, and I realize that he's serious," Keith remembers. "I didn't know that because Dave had had very good success in Australia with Hoodoo Gurus—they had some number one singles—that he actually has a lot to say with what Trafalgar Records does." Within an hour, Keith and Faulkner began hammering out the rudimentary details of a long-fabled record deal.

The day after the Roxy show, the Fleshtones flew to Paris to launch their fall European tour. The monthlong swing went off without a hitch, save for a Halloween gig in Paris where flaming psychedelic pumpkins set Bill's kick drum on fire. Shernoff played behind his friends onstage for the last time, enjoying an up-close look at the band of hardening Queens mates who were playing rock & roll in somewhat dire circumstances and bringing smiles to their fans.

"People say that the Fleshtones don't get respect, but what's respect?" Shernoff asks. "I've been in the business a long time, and not that many people are still in the business from the time I was doing it. There were guys in the music business who were dismissive of the Fleshtones or the Dictators who are now selling shoes, or waiting tables, or who knows? And the Fleshtones are still doing it. You want respect of the fans. You don't want the respect of some guy at a record company who's trying to sign the New Hot Thing." As a seasoned New York rock & roller, Shernoff admires and utterly comprehends the Fleshtones. "You do it because you can," he says of the band's muscled, bruised longevity. "There are bands out there that have had hit, multiplatinum records that couldn't draw a hundred people in New York. But there are bands that have sold a lot less records that can do a lot more than that. The Fleshtones are out doing it, they're having fun, and it's in their blood. You don't ask, *Why did Muddy Waters play until he was eighty? Why did Leonard Bernstein make music until he died?* It's what they do. It's a part of your being. What else do you wanna do? One of the things I wanna do for the rest of my life is make music, and I know it's the same for the Fleshtones." Especially Keith, Shernoff adds. "He's a powerhouse. He loves making music."

With the help of lawyers recommended to them by Shernoff, Keith, Peter, and Faulkner began assembling the Trafalgar contract. Meanwhile, Bob Singerman was on the fringes, his purchase on the band's management increasingly tenuous. Bill recalls visiting Singerman's office during this period and watching hopelessly as faxes came pouring out of the machine, a waterfall, as Bill perceived it, of untended or otherwise ignored business correspondence. ("Any important business faxes were attended to," Singerman insists. "I wish there had been a waterfall of Fleshtone offers!") Singerman had his heart in the right place, but he had pulled one too many creative cost-cutting gestures for the guys' taste, such as when he required that the Fleshtones pose as a Scottish pop group in an airport in order to claim discounted plane tickets. "Bob Singerman in action," Marek snorts of that sorry episode. "You just had to grin and bear the ludicrousness; that kind of kept us going for a long time." Says Singerman: "It did pay the bills for the guys and got them to some probably great shows, otherwise impossible to make."

Keith was beginning to take stock of a sticky situation. "I'm the one getting the Trafalgar record deal for the band," he says. "I figure that this is a start, this is better than nothing, that as a matter of fact this might save us. I bring the deal to Bob Singerman to start handling, but then I start thinking, *I got this deal. He's gonna probably take a cut.*" The band's contract was up with their manager, and rather than renew, the guys took a step away and accessed the situation. "We owed Bob a lot of money on his credit card, I remember," Keith continues. "But he was making money from us at the same time, too. It was all fair, you could say." Keith got the guys together at the Music Building one afternoon and suggested that it was time that the Fleshtones part ways with Singerman. Personally, the decision was difficult to make, in that the guys had invested years with Singerman, but it was also professionally risky: in losing their manager the band was also losing their booking agent. The Fleshtones were really going to be starting at ground zero, and the result would be a decade of frustrations.

Singerman's feelings about his seven years with the band reflect sadness tempered by distance and perspective. "It was upsetting emotionally, as I'd been working passionately for and with them for years, but ultimately liberating professionally," Singerman says now. "They were angry that they never achieved the commercial success they wanted, figured I had something to do with that, which I can't deny, although of course I lived for it to work. It was a struggle, and they wanted to try other options, or do it themselves. They owed me significant—for us—money, too, and didn't want to continue living with a small weekly draw against current and future income. The investment of time, energy, and money that went into the Fleshtones' career from me could be nothing for a multinational company to invest, in man-hours and dollars, but it was a major part of my life and life's work, and something that I am actually and totally proud of having done, even given its lack of commercial success for them and for me. At least I know I contributed some intangible joy to many people's lives, though as always, would have loved to have done more."

Singerman and the guys used to joke, after the Rolling Stones tune, about being Under-Assistant East Coast Promo Men. They were renting and driving the vans, booking the gigs and travel, calling the radio stations, talking with the press, fans, bands, label executives, promoters, club owners, friends, agents, promo men, road managers, girlfriends/wives, technicians, soundmen, rehearsal spaces, studios, producers, engineers, video directors, accountants, lawyers. And, at times, doctors. "We were making the best decisions we knew how to make, given all the givens in all the moments," Singerman insists, "just for them to be onstage and allow people to go wild, dance or listen and be free in their own moments of frequent collective celebration, riding the wild pony, each in one's own hall of fame with everyone else, sharing love and wisdom of Fleshtoned sorts.

"One caveat to all this," he continues, "is that the Fleshtones, while a major—often *the* major—priority of my professional and personal life, were not my only focus. All during my management time with them I was involved with advancing and managing other artists,

Sweat

projects, 'loves,' and resolving career, financial, and partnership issues. While being at times conflicts of interest, there were always questions, just like now, of prioritizing one's time and making choices, sometimes complicated, even subconscious and difficult choices." With Singerman cut loose, the Fleshtones were about to embark on a half-decade spin through a half-dozen different managers, each with his—in one case, her—best hopes for the band running high. These baffled individuals would learn one certain thing: the Fleshtones are a hard outfit to manage.

As the 1980s closed, the Fleshtones were the most broke they'd been since cobbling together kicks and songs in The House so many years ago. Even as the material proof of their testifying—forgotten slabs of vinyl labored over in studios large and small—was rapidly disappearing, they were as committed to making and playing rock & roll as they'd ever been. Peter felt as if the end of the decade was conspiring against the band. The 1990s would find the guys battling on a different field than they were used to, fighting not only to be heard and seen, but to be remembered at all. Were the Fleshtones being erased from history?

20.
Better Days

The large, dark theater was a chapel of cool, but something was missing. The songs in one movie were too schmaltzy, and the suits and ties in the other movie too straight. But the overall effect was exciting to the young kid sitting wide-eyed next to his mother in a theater in downtown Toronto. The double bill of *West Side Story* and *A Hard Day's Night* was spectacle enough. There in the dark, Ken Fox began his indoctrination into the lyrical volume and gaudy thrill of popular music.

The real bang came a couple of years later in 1973, when the dewey, dark-eyed charms of Natalie Wood and the larger-than-life screams of Beatlemania were brought down to gut level. The New York Dolls were playing at Massey Hall in downtown Toronto; though only twelve years old, Ken felt the pull of the arena-sized power amps. "I was hanging out with friends who had the benefit of older brothers," he remembers. "We used to do whatever they did to try and be cool. If it was listening to the Dolls, then that's what we did. They bought a bunch of tickets and then overextended themselves and tried to sell us the tickets." *Of course we'll go!* Ken gushed in adolescent glee, but he had no idea how he and his buddies were going to pay, how they were going to get downtown, how they were going to get out of the house. Ken went to bed early, feigning sickness, then stuffed a dummy under his blankets and escaped out his bedroom window. He hooked up with his older pals who knew the downtown Toronto subway system, and little Ken dashed into the arena and sucked in the pot and the smoke and the sweat of the girls who were gathered to see the Dolls. "That was it, getting right up close to the stage," Ken marvels. He was taken under the wings of various audience members and protected that night. In between encores Ken leapt onto the stage and grabbed one of Jerry Nolan's drumsticks. He was so small, young, and quicksilver that if any Dolls security were there they would've been surprised that a munchkin could manage the feat.

"KISS opened up. After that, there was never anything else I wanted to do."

Ken Fox was born in Toronto, Ontario, on February 16, 1961, raised by Liz, a homemaker, and Terry, a hematologist, in an affluent suburb. A brother, Paul, and a sister, Alison, would come into the family over the next decade. Good-looking Ken was a soft-spoken, well-behaved boy who would indulge a growing intuition toward the sex appeal and excitement of rock & roll. His balance of charm and recklessness would come to serve him quite well as a traveling musician.

At age ten, Ken inherited from his grandmother a stack of pop records, including *A Hard Day's Night* and one of the numerous K-Tel compilations ubiquitous in North American households in the early seventies. "I distinctly remember owning the K-Tel record with 'Mony Mony' on it, maybe a Little Anthony and the Imperials song, and I think 'Hang on, Sloopy,'" Ken says. "I put on puppet shows to that record." He avidly listened to the radio that was broadcast mostly across Lake Ontario from Detroit or from Windsor in the south. "I got into white rock bands, and then I realized that the less and less commercial they were, the tougher they were. I found out that for every band like Grand Funk, there was a tougher, younger brother like MC5. So I was going in that direction. I was still into buying 45s, but the idea of longer songs, and then discovering the Stooges, came from living in proximity to Detroit." He would always find himself hanging with older kids, a fate born of his native enthusiasm and of a certain sophistication beyond his years; later he would play the role perfectly in the Fleshtones. "I was always, always, always the youngest," Ken says. "Later, when I became a musician, I turned it into a theory. I always try to be the worst musician in any group. That sounds cool to say and it's not really true always, but that way you struggle to catch up."

Better Days

Ken turned sixteen and moved to downtown Toronto with his family, his mother having become interested in jump-starting her career in television. "Only in retrospect do I realize what a big move that was," Ken says. "The opportunities in suburban Toronto were very small. I might have just turned into a beer-drinking lunkhead had I not moved down into a situation where all of a sudden it wasn't, *Can you drink twenty-four beers by yourself?* it was, *What do you do? Do you paint? Do you play music? Do you aspire to be an actor?* I would hang out in people's basements. Instead of getting comatose, they would have bands down there." In terms of sound and style, the avid music fan in Ken would often spot what these basement bands were doing right, and what they were doing wrong. Laid-back and easy to get along with, Ken might correct the words or the tempo of whatever popular song the local kids were trying to cover that evening, offering a helpful but unobtrusive hand.

Ken picked up a copy Japanese Fender bass when he turned seventeen, eager to play musical catch-up with an instrument that didn't demand much virtuosity. "The bass suited my personality," he explains. "I'm a team player. There is room for the foot soldiers, the guys who show up on time. I was never going to be a musical genius, or a guy who set things on fire, or the guy who wrote all the songs. What I needed to do was get in a band *yesterday*." Ken took lessons, learned to read music, and, deciding firmly that his higher education would come from a fret board and not from a college campus, left high school in the eleventh grade. He happily cashed in his dad's tuition trust fund and upgraded his gear. His friend, a keyboard player, was a big Emerson, Lake, and Palmer fan and he taught Ken the simple bass lines for "Theme from Peter Gunn" and "Fanfare for the Common Man." "And I was playing it!" Ken marvels. "We got a drummer in there and I was in a band within a day! It was absolutely great." But the guys needed a singer—that old problem—and they convened "all these nerds together." The band's first, halting gig took place at the Toronto French School (Ken still has a tape of the performance) but he soon left these guys behind and became a ladder-climber on the local scene.

Ken was finding media-darling punk and New Wave bands such as Blondie, the Clash, DEVO, and Joe Jackson poor substitutes for the first two Stooges albums, which to him were—and still are—the watermark for tough-sounding rock & roll. "Even the first Ramones album didn't blow my mind," he says. "It wasn't until I heard the token pop song on the second record that it made sense what they were trying to do: they were a little tongue-in-cheek, they were rocking, they were just trying to do the best they could. I did get it." A year of hanging out on the local music scene followed for Ken: he got his feet wet, trusted his intuitions with his expanding Detroit record collection, and played briefly in Suburban Crime and the Scenics.

In 1980 Ken formed the Raving Mojos, and everything came together; he could play bass, sing a little bit, and rock out in a band that emulated the Stooges and the MC5. The band thought themselves better in every way than Teenage Head, the competing Toronto punk/rock & roll band with a record deal for whom they opened some shows. "We had our whole creed down," Ken remembers. The Raving Mojos played briefly out of Toronto, but mostly in tone-deaf mining towns where the beer-swilling regulars couldn't give a fuck. "The frustrating thing was that there was just nowhere to go in that country," Ken laments. "A band from Toronto's got nowhere to go but the States. You've got this thin line of cities that goes along the U.S. border. You could go west to nowhere. Or you could play Ottawa, Montreal, and Quebec City. If you were really feeling adventurous you could go to Halifax or St. John's, way out on the East Coast. There was basically nowhere to play." Through the Mojos, Ken met Rob Sikora, who turned Ken on to this rock & roll band out of New York called the Fleshtones. He leant Ken a tape of the *Fleshtones Radio Party* broadcast from October of that year. "We would literally get so drunk playing air bass to that tape that we would be colliding into each other and giggling and yelling, *Marek! Marek!*" remembers Ken. "Ever since then I started learning Marek's stuff."

Ken would often go to see American bands play in Toronto at a venue unimaginatively named the New Yorker—there he dug, among other groups, the Cramps, Talking Heads as a three-piece band, and Pere Ubu, whose bass player was a big influence on him—and wonder why there couldn't be a similar reception for Toronto bands in the States. Meanwhile, Ken had become friends with a musician couple and members of the punk band the Androids who had moved from Toronto to New York City. ("They got out.") Early in 1982, they called Ken and invited him to play bass in their group. Semiseriously dating a girl named Carolyn who was on her way to school in New York, and who promised that he could be snuck into the country *sans* green card, Ken sensed that things were falling into place. He decided to make the move.

His friends' band soon metamorphosed into Smashed Gladys and landed a production deal with Gene Simmons of KISS through his Monster Management. Ken thought, *If Simmons is showing interest in this, I'll go down and check it out.* He got on the bus with Carolyn, his bass slung over his shoulder, and began sleeping on his friends' floor on East Tenth Street, in a building where he would eventually get his own apartment and stay for the next decade. One of his first cool New York moments came in early July when he gawked with dozens of others on St. Mark's Place, two blocks from his apartment, as Keith Richards and Mick Jagger made nice and slummed about while filming the "Waiting on a Friend" video. Ken followed Mick down from the Physical Graffiti building, and then he trailed the Glimmer Twins into the smoky and sweltering St. Marks Bar. And if Ken needed any more proof that he wanted to be a rock & roll star. . . .

With KISS in a holding pattern commercially and about to gamely enter their makeup-free era, Simmons was hedging his bets and hoping to jump on the lucrative glam metal craze with Smashed Gladys. Ken began playing with the group and, to his surprise, got along great with the "serpent-tongue" legend from Queens. "I'm probably the only guy in the world who has nothing bad to say about Gene Simmons," Ken smiles. "He was like a big kid with lots of money. We got along like a house on fire because of our love of horror movies." Simmons took Ken to see AC/DC at Madison Square Garden, and during Smashed Gladys recording sessions would often pass a yellow legal pad and a pen toward Ken under the recording console, and the two bass players would smile wryly at each other and play horror movie trivia.

Because of his industry reputation, Simmons was able to obtain rehearsal space and studio time on spec, and he sank lots of his own dollars into his pet project. Through Monster Management he booked an enormous soundstage from Studio Instrument Rentals, and there Smashed Gladys would tease up their hair and earnestly rehearse. Ken gamely played along, aware deep inside of himself that his fate could never be tied to this group. "It was awful, awful, awful," he admits. Simmons would show up at rehearsals and, seeing undersized Ken onstage, yell commandingly from the darkened seats, "You gotta hold your arms out!" extending his arms and triumphantly punching the air in the best KISS fashion. "There's gonna be fifty thousand people out there! You're just gonna be a little dot!!" Simmons would duly turn on his heels and disappear, having dispensed the most useful advice that he could think of. Hyperaware of commercial trends, Smashed Gladys' managers brought Def Leppard records into rehearsals and encouraged the band and their stable of songwriters to emulate whatever style would bring them onto the charts, originality be damned.

Ken's heart sank. "I felt like a whore," he says. "This wasn't the kind of thing I was into. I like good rock & roll as much as the next guy, but I was really only there because people were spending a lot of money and showing a lot of interest. It was my only reason for being in New York." Ken had trusted his friends and Simmons as if they were surrogate parents, but soon realized that they didn't have all of the answers simply because they were older. "I should have gone with my instincts. But had I, would I have done anything different? So many of my options were because I had no choice." As a Canadian without a green card, Ken couldn't obtain regular work and was thus somewhat beholden to Carolyn. After some hard thinking, and against their better wishes, they went down to City Hall and married in secret so that Ken could stay in the States and find legal employment. "It worked for a couple months, until she started saying things like, 'Why don't you ever introduce me to people as your wife?' Then she wanted to change her last name to Fox. She got into it."

Smashed Gladys ultimately lost Simmons as a backer when KISS' *Lick It Up* took off, and a frustrated but relieved Ken quit the group. Then followed the standard, well-worn period during which Ken became by necessity a hungry and determined bass-for-hire throughout Manhattan. "I had a little amp that I could pull around on wheels. I would show up at all of the little blues bars and wait to sit in. Next time I came back they'd say, *Oh yeah, that guy can play*, and I'd get a little further up the line." Soon Ken would supplement these provisional gigs by joining a quirky, XTC-like band for whom an unknown Joan Osborne was singing backup. After listening to Osborne pine after her own aspirations and dreams, Ken encouraged her to pursue a singing career, even lending her his guitar lesson texts (never reclaimed). Out of gratitude and a like-spirit, Osborne invited Ken into her new band, and he would play with her for the next year and a half. "Of course, I went on to fame and fortune and she went on to complete obscurity," laughs Ken.

After he left Osborne's band, Ken resumed his bass-for-hire, want-ad lifestyle with which he was becoming accustomed. In September of 1988 he spied an ad in the *Village Voice*: Jason and the Scorchers were looking for a bass player. Ken sent a tape and a photo. "Jason Ringenberg called me back and I talked to him for a couple of hours on the phone and we really hit it off." Ringenberg suggested that Ken hook up with the Scorchers' guitarist Warner Hodges, who was living in New York City. Hodges watched Ken play, dug his style, and urged him to fly to Nashville in January to audition. "By the time Christmas came and went, Warner and I had become such fast friends that, without me having even met any of the other guys in the band, he told Jason that I was the guy," Ken says.

"Ken adapted pretty well to our music, especially considering that it really wasn't his roots," Jason Ringenberg says. "The energy he brought to the stage fit right in with us. He rocked always." Ken was excited to join an established band with a good reputation and a major label, and he also thrived in his new big-fish-small-pond status in the South. "All of the sudden I was in Nashville and I was the new guy. They were still ruling the roost there. I was thrown in and I was the center of attention, but in a good way. Everybody was checking out the new guy." In his late twenties, Ken found himself in an ideal situation. His relationship with Carolyn was falling apart, so he took to extending his two-week rehearsals and tours into months-long stays in the music capital, hedonistic forays during which he struggled to define his role as a bass player and as a man. "I rarely came home. I was having too much fun. Drugs. Drinking at the Gold Rush. I was doing everything I could, having to keep up with the peer pressure of getting into this band late. I tried very hard to get a personality as far as where I fit in. All of a sudden the guys realized that I was getting laid a lot. Girls really liked me. They said, *Hey, that's what he does. He's not the musician of the band or the songwriter, that's what he does!* And of course, I played up to it. So I really went out after that, which led to the breakup of my marriage." Harassing fellow bandmates is habitual in any group, and Ken wasn't spared. Ringenberg laughs, "We always did get a kick out of the fact that Ken from Canada was playing in our country punk rock outfit, and we nicknamed him Country Ken Fox and teased him mercilessly about his Canadianness. He exacted his revenge by bedding with beautiful women all over the world while us old married geezers watched in wonder and jealousy."

Jason and the Scorchers were an odd band, bound more by mutual respect than deep friendships. Though their hard drug use had diminished, many days and nights in the band were still lost to blubbering, drunken, destructive escapades. And Ken fell right in step. "It's my strength and also my weakness that I'm a bit of a mimic," he reflects. "I tend to take on the personalities of those around me, and at times I tend to not have enough strength of my own convictions and personality to say, *No*, this *is who I am*. I tried to find my own sense of bad behavior that I could excel at. Like Levon Helm said in *The Last Waltz*, it was an 'adult portion.' I had a great time."

Despite the dissolute fun, everything collapsed at once for the Scorchers. The band didn't have the internal charity nor the strong-willed commitment to withstand too many financial setbacks. They were spending more than they were making, flying Ken, Hodges, and guitarist Andy York—all resident New Yorkers—into and out of Nashville on a whim, and the group ultimately suffered from aspirations of financial greatness that weren't being fulfilled. Ken played on Jason and the Scorchers' *Thunder & Fire*, released in 1989 on A&M, but the album wasn't enough to sustain the commercially and critically fading band, whose good intentions were usually sent careening in opposing directions. "The Scorchers were essentially falling apart then, but Ken was a shining light to us at the time," Ringenberg says. "He was quick with a smile or kind word and his complete dedication to what we were doing was invaluable." Without Ken, Ringenberg acknowledges, "the situation would have been much harder than it was."

The end came during a national tour opening for Bob Dylan, one of Ringenberg's heroes. The Scorchers had canceled the final dates of their own European tour to accommodate Dylan's people, who quickly laid down the law, including demands that no one approach Dylan—*Walk the other way if he comes near*—and that Ken and Hodges refrain from wearing the spurs on their cowboy boots for fear of damaging the carpets that Dylan coveted. (The road manager ultimately backed down on the last demand.) "We were always in perpetual fear of Bob," says Ken. Bad health and ill will detoured the end of the circuit, and when the Scorchers got back to Nashville they learned that their management team was dissolving, and that A&M had dropped them. Ken tried to rally the guys by suggesting that they stay in Nashville and drum up an independent record deal, but they looked at him as if they wanted to slap him. By the end of 1989, Jason and the Scorchers were finished.

Back in New York City for good, his marriage busted, Ken licked his wounds, prowled for fresh gigs, and commenced a post-Scorchers depression, the dim bottom of which looked to be his only option. Anne Arbor, Keith's girlfriend, had introduced Ken to Pomme Nicole, a French girl who'd road managed and booked the Fleshtones in Europe for years. Ken was walking down Avenue A with Pomme one afternoon when Anne flew out of the Pyramid. The group saddled up to the bar, and immediately Keith and Ken start talking. And drinking. Ken hadn't officially left the Scorchers, and he had respect enough for Keith that he wasn't going to tell him that he thought that the Fleshtones' best days were behind them. At the end of the conversation, Keith mentioned Full Time Men and suggested that whenever the Fleshtones and the Scorchers aren't touring that Ken come play bass with him. Ken said, *Sure, of course, call me if it happens,* and left it at that.

Nicole convinced Ken, who had sworn off the Fleshtones since the 1988 Halloween debacle at the Big Kahuna, to come see the band play again. He had really enjoyed meeting and hanging out with Keith at the Pyramid that he decided to give them another shot. He caught the band at the Lone Star Roadhouse, with Shernoff playing bass. And he loved them. "It was a great! I had a blast!" he says. "It was everything that they were supposed to be. It was funny, I laughed out loud at them, and it was really fun. I went to see them a couple more times and sort of met the other guys. Those dressing room scenes are always such a pile-on situation, with everybody yelling and spilling drinks and half of the Pyramid crowd sashaying through. It was a whole scene." That whole scene would soon come calling.

As the 1990s began, Marty Thau relicensed the *Blast Off!* recordings to ROIR for a CD release, the only "new" Fleshtones material on the market. The band celebrated the end of the decade with their first weekend at the Lone Star in three years, ads in the *Village Voice* crowing "Into the Nineties!" encouragingly. "Something more than an institution but less than sanctuary, Queens' own Fleshtones have been celebrating high-powered vacuity longer, and with more maracas, than any act in town," *New York Newsday* observed (accurately). The item concluded charitably that the band's stand at the Lone Star was "something of a reminder that they're still alive." In March, the Fleshtones made the first of several appearances at Woody's, the vanity nightclub project of Ron Wood's located at East Fourth Street, the site of the old Club 82 and across the street from the old Wonderhorse Theater, haunts from a foggy past. For two weeks in April and May, the Fleshtones swung through the deep South for a Jazz Festival Tour, collecting good-sized bonuses and playing to packed crowds.

When they returned to New York, Peter and Keith concentrated on writing songs and preparing material for a new album. Dave Faulkner offered to produce the record, and he flew to New York in June to work through Peter and Keith's new songs in the Music Building, cocking a novice producer's ear to the spirit and potential of the material. The new album would be released in Australia on Trafalgar—benefiting fully from BMG's considerable promotional, marketing, and distribution resources—and the band would be allowed to pursue and sign licensing deals throughout Europe and North America. Shernoff agreed to record the album with the guys as they began the search for yet another bass player, their fifth in as many years.

The Fleshtones played the Lone Star again in April, unaware that it would be their penultimate performance at that fabled club, and in May slipped down to Washington, D.C., to play at the tenth anniversary celebration of the 9:30 Club. The following month they headed up Route 87 to Dreamland Studios in upstate New York, south of the fabled Woodstock farm. Relieved to escape the heat and craze of New York (the city's murder toll would reach a record 2,245 in the summer of 1990) the guys were nonetheless put off by the "alternative lifestyles" dotting the small town of West Hurley. "We went to Woodstock proper once, and absolutely hated it," Peter says, citing some amusing resistance on the part of the locals. One afternoon the guys sat down at a local diner and were eyed suspiciously by "some hippy-dippy" waitress who took the guys' orders and then came back and told them, "You'll have to pay first." Peter cracks: "Think of all of the bars we've been drinking in all of our lives, with killers and whatnot. There the bartender poured the drink *first*." The guys soothed their irritations by settling in comfortably in a rented house a mile from the studio, where they lived for the ten days of recording. Providentially, a local television station was broadcasting *Lost in Space* episodes daily, and the guys and Faulkner indulged their mutual love for the show, adopting a merry theme for the recording sessions, taking to calling Dreamland the "drill site" after whatever expedition Dr. Robinson had been earnestly involved in in that morning's episode.

The B-52's had recorded "Love Shack" at Dreamland the prior year, and the single reached number three on the *Billboard* Hot 100. Could some commercial magic rub off in upstate New York? "If we had played well enough, maybe," speculates Peter. "But the B-52's took apart dance music and understood it better than we did. They distilled it better and did it better in a way that we just didn't put the effort into." The purposeful, dance-oriented songs that Peter and Keith brought with them up to Dreamland were marked by the heady vapors of years at the Pyramid, and by a certain anxiety born of frustrations and impatience. The bulk of the material reflected Peter's professional struggles and emotional declines of the last several years, but as always the guys were keen to balance the lyric blahs with fun rock & roll. "I'm Still Thirsty" was an up-tempo ode to the desires of living, playing, and drinking that still thrummed strongly in Peter; "Mod Teepee" was a funky celebration of the Pyramid and long nights lost to white lights and Black Russians; "3 Fevers" and "Armed and Dangerous," the latter Keith's garage rock homage to the Georgia Satellites, were breakneck and midpaced rips through the past that alluded to disquiet in the guys' personal history; "I Can Breathe" was an uplifting psychedelic-tinged paean to regret and loss with an exalted chorus; "Irresistible" was a somewhat labored dance floor workout; "Waiting for a Message" was an inconsequential tear through Strangeloves/Easybeats terrain that questioned the band's sad fate. "Let It Rip" and "House of Rock" were high-watt, rocking catharses for those same pent-up frustrations, both tunes amounting to sonic statements of purpose.

One song dated to one of Peter and Keith's earliest compositions ("Girlology") as well as a fabled session in front of Miles Copeland during which the guys played an original number called "Drug Addict"—unsurprisingly, Copeland felt that the song was jaw-droppingly inappropriate for I.R.S. The guys duly revived the main riff for "Living Legends," a pat-on-the-back dance-floor hymn to the Fleshtones' longevity, endurance, and battle against odds. At the time, Peter proclaimed, "In all modesty I think we can say that considering our achievements over the years, most of which have gone unnoticed by the world at large, yes, we have become Living Legends."

"Candy Ass," a mock-anthemic Gary Glitter–styled instrumental, referred to a favorite saying of Keith's father's, and not indelicately to what the guys saw as Robert Warren's frankly disloyal exit from the band. Ironically, Robert claims to have written the song's signature fuzz-bass riff in the Music Building. The Fleshtones don't give him writing credit. Years later, after he joined the BMI publishing group, Robert checked with the Performance Rights Organization and learned to his dismay that Keith had neglected to list him as co-writer on the several tracks that they had composed together. "It never came to a matter of money, but that really irritated me," Robert says. "They talk about being so principled. It just would have been a matter of writing my name down."

Before recording sessions commenced, Faulkner joined the Fleshtones on a weekend down to Baltimore and Washington, D.C., and he felt a strange and surprising attitude coming from Keith. "Keith had always been a very good friend, but now I was his boss," Faulkner explains. "And it wasn't easy." As the van sped down Interstate 95, Keith began downing Black Russians, leering at Faulkner, saying, *Look at me! Mr. Producer! Waddya gonna do about it?!* "It was funny, but at the same there was this undercurrent of attitude going on," says Faulkner. "I basically said to him, *Whatever you want to do, it's your life.* Keith was out of his mind. It was a nightmarish but hilarious weekend." For the next several years, Keith would have serious and taxing battles with his escalating drinking, remunerating long nights of fun and frolic with excruciatingly painful hangovers and animosity, both on the road and at home. He would redeem the nightmares with mirth until a calamitous weekend in Alabama during which he hit bottom.

Sessions went smoothly at Dreamland, a nineteenth-century converted church. It had been four years since the Fleshtones were last in the presence of knobs and boards for such a stretch, and they were acclimating themselves. Large stained-glass windows allowed the pretty upstate summer light to bathe the studio, but the sun couldn't altogether warm the chill imposed by Faulkner's *modus operandi*.

"As a producer, Dave knew what he wanted, but sometimes he was a bit too exact in what he was trying to do," Keith observes. "He wanted everything perfect. I can understand that, because when it comes time to mixing, everything is there proper, in perfect pitch and meter. But Dave was a bit too over the top for the Fleshtones." The guys deeply appreciated Faulkner's input: he was a great songwriter and musician, similar to Richard Mazda in contributing ideas for chord changes, guitar sounds, and arrangements. The guys trusted that his commercial-minded approach might pay dividends on Australian radio. But Faulkner was an audile soldier, and he wanted things done his way, the perfectionism straying into an area quite dear to the Fleshtones' hearts, and their livers: he unilaterally banned drinking from the sessions. Accustomed since the Whitestone daze of fueling rock & roll with booze, the guys were taken aback by Faulkner's edict and, juvenile delinquents to the core, they rebelled. "We were drinking our vodka and orange juice and our beer in coffee cups, so he would think we're drinking coffee! You can't change us *that* much," laughs Keith.

Peter is eternally obliged to Faulkner, but similarly mixed in his appraisal of the Dreamland sessions. "I love David," says Peter firmly. "David saved our asses. At this point we didn't know where to turn, and Dave came through. But he's a very compulsive and meticulous person, which made him extremely difficult to work with. We're a band that's always striving for a certain looseness, but Dave heard an album in his head. He needed us to make *that* record, and that was difficult, for me in particular. I don't sing a song the same way everytime—ever. But Dave would say, 'Let's do it again.' We got heavily into 'flying in' parts, taking parts of the master, bars that Dave thought were better, and moving them and reconstructing the actual master take." At one point Faulkner was importing individual *syllables* of Peter's vocals into and throughout the different takes, and even pitched the performances a tone sharper in Peter's headphones so as to accommodate the singer's natural, albeit flat, tone. Peter found that it did have its advantages: "It got me off the hook and I could go to the house for a while!"

Faulkner ultimately agrees with the assessment. "I was a bit persnickety about technical details and getting things just right," he admits. "I was a little bit uneducated, as well. I was overly obsessed, and I probably drove Peter crazy. I am proud, however, that I managed to get some of the best vocals that he's recorded. If I had my time over, I wouldn't have done that. I was driving my own band crazy at the same time with a similar approach. They rebelled, and for the next album they got a producer, and I wasn't allowed anything to do with it!" Faulkner regrets, more than anything, the indelible stamp of his own personality on the tracks. "I listen back to the record and I hear too much of me. I'm such a huge fan of the band, but I hear my voice on all of the harmony tracks. I think that I ran riot over the band, but by and large, there are some great things on there that I'm really proud of, and some great Fleshtones songs and recordings. *Some* stuff got through."

Leaning its lengthening shadow over the recording sessions was the Fleshtones' vexing bass player issue. While recording *Powerstance*, Shernoff had one ear cocked to Manitoba's Wild Kingdom, for which he and MCA Records had high hopes. As the sessions were nearing completion, the band began looking toward trotting through the usual European summer festival circuit—a financial boon for a band whose thrilling U.S. paydays were more or less finished—aware that Shernoff couldn't join them. Again, Keith was on the search for a bass player.

One track remained on the new, untitled album. The guys were looking for another bass player who could pop-and-slap in a funky manner like Marek used to; both Fred Smith and Andy Shernoff, though fine rock & roll players, were hardly channeling R&B through their practiced fingers. Keith vaguely remembered meeting Ken Fox at the Pyramid ("I was living there, basically"), recalling that Ken had told him that he learned to play bass while listening to the Fleshtones and that he was then playing in the Scorchers, one of Keith's favorite bands. Keith deeply regretted Ken's long-haired, Cowboy Punk/ Cheap Trick look—it might have been right for Alternative Nashville, but was wildly wrong for Super Rock—but he looked past it. "I told the guys that the way Ken looks will throw you, but not to worry," Keith laughs.

Sweat

"Keith's call saved me," Ken admits. "I had nowhere to go but down." Suddenly, things were moving quickly, and Ken was worried not only about the audition and recording, but about the precious little time he'd have to learn material for a European tour onto which he was also invited. Keith had the band run through a quick set with Shernoff playing, and taped it for Ken to learn as a template. Keith had given Ken a rough demo of "Living Legends," and Ken worked up a slap-bass part. "I always thought that Marek's style of playing was missing in the Fleshtones," Ken says frankly. "So, not only would I give a tip of the hat to Marek, but I'd put my own little stamp on it."

Ken agreed to meet the band at a rendezvous point in Manhattan to head over the river to the House of Music studio in West Orange, New Jersey, where the band was finishing the vocals, percussion, and guitar overdubs. "For some inexplicable reason, Peter is the first one to arrive," Ken recalls. "He's sitting on the sidewalk, probably nursing some terrible hangover, sweating profusely, his hands covering his face. He was looking homeless, actually, like he'd died on the sidewalk." Ken was tressed out with his long blond hair—"Guns 'N Roses would've kicked me out for looking ridiculous"—and he approached Peter and gamely introduced himself. Peter looked up with horror on his face, and slowly closed his eyes and put his head back in his hands.

"I really felt like I was off on a bad foot," Ken says.

Peter revived a bit in the darkness of the Lincoln Tunnel and the air-conditioned van. Ken tried making conversation, further eroding Peter's spirits by mentioning the Sly and the Family Stone–style twist that he'd brainstormed for "Living Legends." But as they drove on, Peter's native, headstrong vibe lessened, and he began out loud to reconsider Ken's choice. "And by the time we got to the studio, he was quite excited," Ken says. Faulkner, with his chordal expertise, helped Ken polish his part.

At rehearsal, Ken quickly faced a requirement of all Fleshtones. Keith planted a microphone in front of Ken as they were setting up their gear.

"I . . . I don't sing," Ken said to Keith.

"You do now," replied Keith. "You speak English? You got a throat? You sing in the Fleshtones." The swift recording went well, and the guys were pleased with Ken's energy and preparation.

Ken smiled as Keith approached him afterward. "Do you want some coffee?" he asked Ken.

No, I don't want some coffee. I want some fuckin' beer or something! Ken thought.

Keith winked and said, "No . . . do you want a *coffee*?" Ken peered into the coffee cup and saw the happy site of foamy beer. "This is a nondrinking session," Keith slyly intoned. "Dave Faulkner knows our reputation."

"I soon knew Keith's devilish look!" Ken laughs. Ken had a lot of coffee before that day was out.

Duly baptized, Ken settled willingly if awkwardly into the Fleshtones, feeling, for all intents and purposes, as the next hired gun. In July, the band flew to Europe for a month's work of festival gigs in France and Italy. They now had a finished record to crow about in interviews, though the album would typically languish unreleased for nearly a year. Ken lodged his boyish frame into the truck alongside Peter, Keith, Bill, and two new horn players, Steve Greenfield and Joe Loposky, and learned that barnstorming with the Fleshtones through small and large burgs was a thrilling, tiring, unpredictable whirlwind, an amplified lifestyle of grins, booze, and dawns. Nearly thirty and already battle-tested with the Scorchers, Ken had the mettle and good spirit to survive Peter's withering wit and inflexibility and Keith's brutal hangovers. The flaxen-haired bassist made his debut for the Fleshtones in July of 1990 in the north of France, nearly four years after Marek's departure. Neither Ken nor his new bandmates could've expected that such a midsize kid would become such a firm and right anchor.

Ken was chagrined early in the tour to learn that the placement of the bass monitors dated back to Smith and Shernoff's days, and had Ken playing far away from the front of the stage. Having convinced himself that he wanted to inject energy into this band, Ken convinced Keith and the roadies to move his monitors to the front; there he began to immerse himself in the nightly nuttiness of Fleshtone Fan Appreciation, happily learning goofy stage moves and onstage abandon, and learning to get out of Keith's and Peter's bullying ways, intuiting brutally quickly that the Fleshtones' *Never say no only say yes, the crowd will tell you if it works* ethic was different from any band he'd ever played in. And he very quickly had the facial scars to prove it. "Nothing prepares you for playing in the Fleshtones, because it's completely unrehearsed," Ken says. "You can only try and keep up. I was keeping an eye on Keith and Peter, and following them." After Smith and Shernoff's posturing, it took Peter and Keith a few shows to get used to the extra action onstage. Highlights were headline appearances at the Mediterranean Rock Circus Festival in Italy, where they played before a large crowd in a soccer stadium, spending most of the time in the large field in an attempt to get clos-er to the cordoned-off crowd, and for which they received enthusias-tic press. Exclaimed a typical headline: "Fleshtones. Un'esplosione."

But Ken came face to face with Peter's capricious onstage crazi-ness one night during this tour, in an episode known among the guys as the Infamous Trap Door Incident. Four songs or so into a set, Peter vanished into a false door at the floor of the stage, no doubt planning a resplendent reentrance into the club after wandering through the aged venue's vast catacombs. Ken and Keith, intuiting Peter's spon-taneity, each kneeled by the trap door, riffing on a note, *maching schau*, acting for all of the world as if this was planned. The band's roadie, however, grew concerned over Peter's absence and, fearing for his safety, leapt up on the stage and threw open the door. Ken warily glanced into the dark and saw Peter lying in a tiny hole, sweating and glaring up at him with murder in his eyes. Ken knew instantly that Peter felt that he had ruined his grand exit. Peter lurched up in a rage and grabbed Ken around his neck with both hands, threw him onto the floor, and began kicking him toward the front of the stage. Red-faced, Ken riffed and played along. Immediately after the show, he made clear to Peter in a furious confrontation that *You don't ever fucking do that to me again!* Marilla was along for the tour and hap-pened to have videotaped the incident; faced with the evidence of his folly and upbraided by his wife, Peter apologized to Ken the next day. But the new kid was branded. He knew from then on to deal with Peter onstage carefully and respectfully.

Much to the guys' relief, Ken cut his hair when the band returned home. "I realized that if the guys were gonna have me in the band—and at this point I *wanted* to be in the band—that I was definitely gonna get with the program, out of respect for them. They have a look, whether they like to think of it that way or not. It hasn't been contrived because they were high school buddies, but they do have a look. Plus, I was getting older and I knew the long hair had to go sooner or later." The new album, christened *Powerstance*, wouldn't appear for months, and Ken demanded that his photo appear on the cover. "I was always up to this point joining bands. The older you get, the chances of putting a band together at a grassroots level are less and less, and here I was joining yet *another* band." (When Ken played in the Scorchers, he hadn't appeared on most of the records that fans pushed under his nose for him to sign; he eventually start-ed scrawling the name of the musician he'd replaced. No one noticed.) Cobbled together from an on-the-fly promotional photo-graph, the cover of *Powerstance* featured four serious-looking men standing in front of a lava-imbued backdrop, Peter and Bill staring resolutely into the camera, Keith, wearing his trademark leopard-skin cap, looking askance. Ken affects his coolest *Hey I Belong!* look, appearing none too confident in what was for him a drastically shorn, if still shaggy, hairstyle.

In August, Ken was thrown onto the New York Super Rock blaze during his first sweaty weekend with the band, a Friday at Woody's followed by a gig at Maxwell's. Learning to balance preparation with abandon, Ken was slotting in as best he could, drawing upon his chops, his considerable knowledge of pop music history, and his love of the band's unrestraint. After a brief swing through the Mid-Atlantic region, a Halloween show in Boston, and an appearance at a Mick Rock photo exhibit at Woody's, the boys headed north up through Connecticut into Canada, where they played a half-dozen spirited shows from Ottawa to Oshawa, showing off their new "one-quarter Canadian content," as Peter had taken to referring to Ken. For Peter, things seemed to be jelling. "It was a new band. It felt great. It seemed like Ken was gonna work out really well, and he was really eager. And on top of that, he's a really, really good, really nice guy. Not too much weird attitude came from him. I didn't have any doubts about him, and he was much more stable than I was at that point. We all really appreciated that."

Noting that Ken left Joan Osborne to hitch his wagon to the Fleshtones' stars, Peter wryly remarked, "Placing his bets like that, I'm not gonna give him any money at the track."

In late November, Trafalgar Records flew Peter and Keith to Sydney, Australia, where they, Faulkner, and Alan Thorne sat at the recording/mixing console and gamely tried to breathe life into the Dreamland recordings. Faulkner feels in retrospect that these mixes damaged the tracks, the metronymic sheen buffed into a radio-friendly glimmer. The guys had one bright idea: Peter, self-proclaimed Acme Thunderer at these sessions, convinced Faulkner's sister Stephanie, an opera singer, to wail a high note during the crest of "Let It Rip."

Peter and Keith dug visiting Australia again and were excited and enthusiastic in the many promotional interviews and meeting various A&R and executives at BMG and Warner Brothers in Melbourne. They met and hooked up with many darlings of the Australian rock & roll scene at a label-thrown barbecue, including Rob Younger from Radio Birdman and members of the Saints and the Died Pretty, a grooving *mise-en-scène* of long hair, drinks, and paisley vests. "It was very exciting," Peter admits. Keith was in his element, so much so that he dragged out a trashcan and threw a giant Blue Whale Party in Faulkner's apartment before he and Peter departed the country. Every inch of the place was covered in blue the next morning. "You can have a Blue Whale Party in any part of the world at any time and it will work, I guarantee it," says Keith. "You could be in the middle of Africa, and this will make the natives happy!"

The mixes and album completed, Peter, Keith, and Faulkner turned to a harebrained idea that they'd batted around in New York: Hoodoo Gurus backing Peter and Keith for a one-off show. Dubbed the Gherkin Milkshakes (a slyly explicit reference to male ejaculate) they played a smashing set of Fleshtones songs at the Hopetoun Hotel in Sydney, a crowded venue packed with Gurus fans digging the two New Yawk frontmen doing their thing. One local journalist wryly observed, "That night will long be remembered for its frenzied scenes, reminiscent of an old Easybeats film clip, or at the very least, a balmy summer's evening on the Hill at the Cricket Ground."

The Fleshtones returned home shortly before Christmas. Hopeful that the cheer would last, they played a New Year's Eve show at Woody's, their last gig at that venue. Yet the accompanying ad featured a six-year-old photo of the band with the fading ghosts of Marek Pakulski and Gordon Spaeth. "The buzz for the band had been on in Australia, and it was working," Peter says. "But we couldn't get our visas extended and renewed for that year. It would've been a year and a half before we'd be allowed to come back. The 'Yankees' had used up their allotted 'Yankiness' in Australia on that level, and that was it. We couldn't go back."

The new year brought a thin shaft of promotional light, a "Random Note" entry in a February issue of *Rolling Stone* trumpeting the mixing sessions in Australia, including a photo of Peter and Keith affecting a Powerstance next to a bemused-looking Faulkner. By spring, *Powerstance* was out in Australia and generating good reviews, but 1991 would carry in its early months cool winds of anxiety for the guys.

During Robert Singerman's tenure managing the Fleshtones, he often faced a predictable query: "Is it *possible* to manage the Fleshtones?" After Singerman was cut loose, the Fleshtones endured a roulette wheel that would spin fruitlessly until the guys finally stopped the wheel and began handling affairs for themselves in the mid-nineties. Steve Fallon, owner of Coyote Records and Maxwell's, had expressed interest to Keith in managing the band, and he took over the reins in 1990. Saddled with his burgeoning retail interests and prioritizing his Hoboken club and record label, Fallon ended delegating much of his Fleshtones management to a young art school student and Maxwell's manager from the New Jersey suburbs, John Bruce. Bruce had tangentially met Keith years before while Bruce bartended at the Pyramid Club; at the many winking requests of Wendy Wild dancing atop the bar, he provided her boyfriend with an endless stream of Black Russians. (Bruce had also briefly met Ken years earlier, having gone to art school with Ken's first wife.)

"The Fleshtones were in Maxwell's one night," Bruce recalls, "talking about how they wanted to make a clean break from Bob Singerman. I didn't have any kind of experience or wherewithal to understand what it means to comanage a band, and I always assumed I would just be helping out Steve. But as time went by I ended up taking on and trying to do as much as I possibly could." Bruce had been a fan of the Fleshtones since his innocent days and long nights at the Pyramid, and felt that the guys, Peter especially, were part of a dying art of entertainers.

A gentle, wide-eyed kid with hair to down to his ass, boyish Bruce dove gamely into his first official task: to visit Singerman's office and clear out the Fleshtones' considerable accounting paperwork and royalty statements under the pretense of scanning the band's "books." Bruce was thrust into trying to appease Singerman, who, in Bruce's perspective, was making some noise about wanting in on the Trafalgar deal. "In fact," says Singerman, "I was due by contract debt repayment and cuts of this deal and previous deals, which I never actually even requested, even if it was discussed, as happens at every such management break-up." Bruce booked shows for the Fleshtones, drove the band to and from Woodstock for the *Powerstance* sessions, flew home from Paris with his pockets stuffed full of the band's twenty thousand francs payday, and helped to finalize the deal with Trafalgar.

Bruce couldn't help but notice how the Fleshtones were being ignored by a new generation of rock & roll fans. "MTV took over, and then there was a different aesthetic—bands like My Bloody Valentine, Sonic Youth, and Public Enemy, and 'clubby' things taking over from 'bar bands,' a term that you often heard associated with the Fleshtones but what was definitely something from the earlier eighties. It's a climate thing. Opportunity and timing is everything. Even at the time I could smell it and feel it. Being so close to the band and being able to smell and feel this thing was heartbreaking." Bruce sensed in the careers of the Feelies, Bob Mould, and other artists with whom he was also professionally associated that the industry was evolving in challenging ways. In the watershed year 1991, he and his pals would sit around their apartments playing My Bloody Valentine's *Loveless* album over and over and over, saying to each other: "Everything's changed." Bruce was torn between wanting the sky to open and good things to happen for the Fleshtones, and wanting to grab them by the shoulders and say, *Look around you. This is what's happening!*

The bottom line for Bruce arrived at the end of a busy, tumultuous year. Heavily taxed and dirt-poor, Bruce had to convince the guys that he wasn't quitting for personal reasons, but that he saw in the band a group of people who deserved something that they weren't getting, and he knew that he couldn't give it to them. He found it hard to stomach the difficulties and futilities associated with dealing with a record label and distributor halfway around the world, and having to lie to European promoters and say that the new album was forthcoming when it wasn't yet. After he quit, he did produce a low-budget but slick video for "Armed and Dangerous," but when Bruce left, Fallon was ultimately forced to admit that he, too, couldn't put in the time that the Fleshtones really needed.

The Fleshtones' brand of bad luck was sorry to witness. One afternoon at Maxwell's, a stranger from LA wandered through the door and reported that he had boxes of original masters from the Record Plant in the back of his truck, as the legendary studio was in the process of closing. Bruce opened a random box, and inside were the *Hexbreaker!* master recordings. When the guys heard of this, rather than get on the phone to complain or to track down lawyers, they snorted and turned the ill-fated discovery into yet another incident laughed about later over drinks: *Gotta rescue those boxes!*

"Everything for them became an episode of *Lost in Space*," Bruce sighs.

Fallon then phoned Leslie Aldredge, a promoter from Nashville whom he knew who'd supported the Hoodoo Gurus and other like bands, and who was friendly with the Gurus' manager. Fallon told Aldredge about the Fleshtones' predicament and current situation, although he shined up the prospects a bit in the pitch. "He told me that the band had a tour in France set up, a Warner Brothers deal in Europe, that it'll all be a piece of cake," Aldredge recalls ruefully. "Oh my God, it was anything but. Two weeks after I got involved, Warner Brothers pulled out. I was told to get on a plane and go get a deal for them in Europe, so I go to London and meet with labels." Ultimately, Aldredge licensed *Powerstance* to the Big Beat label in London, but she spent her time as manager picking up more pieces of crumbling deals than she ever bargained for.

As the band saw things, the Big Beat record deal was another link in a chain of bewildering events. Keith explains: "A big tour was being put together by a friend of ours in Paris that's gonna make a lot of money, eighteen or so shows at 2,000 bucks a show. We thought, *This is great—but we need a record out.* But Big Beat was not a French label that would do promotion with France that could connect you with radio, TV, press. We wanted to do the tour, but quite honestly we should've waited and gotten a proper deal for France and Europe, and put the tour on hold. Anybody in their right mind would've seen that." The Fleshtones ended up earning roughly half of what they were promised; during the months that lapsed between the planning and the actual gigs, the French economy suffered a surprising downturn. "The franc was worth shit against the United States dollar, and so as a rule the Fleshtones never play anywhere anymore unless we're guaranteed in U.S. dollars. But, of course, Leslie was managing the band and she had no fucking idea about these things." He adds, "But neither did I. You live and you learn." The guys quickly discovered that Aldredge was in over her head. "We realized that she was not too cool or swift, that she was always the kind of person moving a million miles an hour but not getting much done," says Keith carefully. "To put it nicely, we realized that she was not right for the Fleshtones."

Aldredge's brief tenure with the Fleshtones was vexed and unhappy. "We were not a good fit," she acknowledges. "It was a nightmare in terms of dealing with the Fleshtones, from my perspective. They had become accustomed to dealing with a certain level of success that they no longer enjoyed, but there was not necessarily the humility to go along with the new level. There were a lot of things going on that I found uncomfortable to deal with, a lot more demands from them than there were collaborative moments. Nobody likes demands being screamed at them." Though the band was willing to compromise, very often their high frustration level superseded arriving at any reasonable business or artistic middle ground. "We are not an easy band to work with," Keith admits. "We do great shows most of the time, but we were not that easy to work with, I know that."

"In retrospect, the Fleshtones were frustrated, and who else were they gonna take it out on but me?"Aldredge says. "I didn't really have a clue at the time as to their psychological makeup. Quite frankly, I think I did a really good job, and I didn't feel that I merited a lot of the treatment that came my way." Bill feels otherwise: "Leslie talked a better game. She sounded so good at the beginning, with contacts, names, everything like that. And nothing went anywhere."

Wading into choppy managerial waters next was Miles Barken, a clean-cut kid with the amiable look of a bank manager. Barken was friendly with the Vipers, and Singerman invited Barken to roadie in Europe for the Fleshtones. Barken had been a big fan of the *Cutting Edge* show and of the Fleshtones, especially Peter, and as a young kid he dug flying over and banging around Europe with guys whom he considered older brothers. Barken's metamorphosis as the band's manager was gradual, but by the time Aldredge was backing out ("She didn't give a shit about the Fleshtones," Barken claims) he found himself moving on from road managing and taking on more and more responsibilities.

To the guys, Barken didn't smell suspiciously of the CMJ/music biz scene as Aldredge did, and they appreciated his dedication, admiration, and business background. Bemused by his clean-cut look, they had high hopes that he wasn't in to merely chisel the band. But Barken hangs his two-year tenure managing the band onto the same sturdy peg that others have: frustration. "There was a lot of love for the Fleshtones in college radio and in the independent music scene, and they definitely had a strong fan base, but the record industry didn't want to throw money at a band that's not gonna go platinum." At nearly every turn Barken faced the commercial and marketing disadvantages of his band. He recalls chatting up a contact at Warner Brothers Records, trying to interest him in signing the Fleshtones, who by 1991 had been without an American label for four years. "The guy was a fan and loved them, but he just couldn't do it. He knew that his job was on the line, and how could he sell them?"

As Barken entered the fray, the Fleshtones were continuing to hop the oceans with frequency. 1991 saw the band, with Ken feeling more and more grooved each night, play Italy, France, Spain, Brussels, Belgium, Switzerland, and Germany in the spring, and England and Australia in the fall. *Powerstance*, its booklet laced with cheeky references to *Lost in Space* and monster movies, was out in Australia and England, and in October Trafalgar released a CD single of "Armed and Dangerous" backed with "Let It Rip" and "Electric Mouse" (an outtake from the Dreamland sessions). Big Beat swiftly licensed the release in seven- and twelve-inch versions, and at last the Fleshtones had a new single—their first in seven long years. Throughout Europe the band continued to energize large, appreciative, and enthusiastic audiences in both festival venues and small- to midsized clubs, warm support that lasts to this day and that morally and financially soothes a band who sweats and struggles to make $300 per show in front of thinning crowds in the United States. In Europe, advances and take-home pay were always considerably higher.

Keith took a glad break on July 14 to marry Anne Arbor in New York. Peter and Bill were dual best-men, Ken the ring bearer; the officiating priest hailed from Coney Island. The wedding and reception took place on the Mariner III, a vintage 1936 cruise ship that sailed majestically up and down the East River, the revelry eventually spilling inland to Brownies and the Pyramid and ending at dawn. Among the friends and guests was Peter Buck. R.E.M. was enjoying tremendous popularity with *Out of Time* and the surprising hit "Losing My Religion," and during a lively, drunken conversation, a giddy Keith convinced his old friend to produce some songs for the Fleshtones in the near future. The Fleshtones had to keep making records, and the hustling of an increasingly jury-rigged career continued.

In April and May, the Fleshtones were bumping around in their tour van in Switzerland and France and setting stages alight at night. Meanwhile, three pale young guys and a producer were holed up in a recording studio five thousand miles away in Seattle, Washington. Kurt Cobain's personal songs were jagged, difficult, anthemic, and inscrutable, and Butch Vig would smooth their inherent abrasiveness and present them as sonically hostile but thrilling tunes. Released in September, Nirvana's *Nevermind* would sell millions of copies, soar to the top of the *Billboard* charts, engender within Cobain a complex and mythical dissatisfaction, and change the record industry. Grunge was born and, like disco, punk, and New Wave before it, would soon be commodified, tailored, and packaged for the masses. As Stephen Thomas Erlewine remarked, "*Nevermind* was never meant to change the world, but you can never predict when the zeitgeist will hit, and Nirvana's second album turned out to be the place where alternative rock crashed into the mainstream."

The collision sent reverberations toward the wee Fleshtones, and in its wake the group was propelled farther than ever from mainstream relevance and commercial success. Where was the Hexbreaker now?

21.
The World's Most Unusual Blues Band

The end of an era heralded by a steep rent increase: such is daily life in Manhattan. The booming eighties were over but rents continued to skyrocket across the city, and the Fleshtones could no longer afford to rehearse at the Music Building. Bill's temporary crash pad wasn't in jeopardy—he'd been subletting an apartment on Fifteenth Street for years—but a certain long-standing age was bittersweetly banished. The guys managed to scrape together dough to rent room at Albert Caiati's Coyote Studios in Williamsburg, Brooklyn, and concurrently a funky space in Manhattan on Second Avenue, and it would be several years before they would glance into their collective fraying wallet, sigh, and hunker down, gathering their guitars and a drum pad and setting up in either Ken or Keith's cramped apartment, "doing our homework around the kitchen table," as Ken puts it.

The new era would be affectionately documented by Anne Streng, who in 1990 began distributing band updates through various "Hall of Fame" mailings, piecing together news, tour dates, national and international press clippings, gushing road diaries, and various photos and *tchotchkes* collected around the world. For roughly six years Anne ran the lo-fi Xeroxed fan club, first out of her and Keith's tiny room in the Hotel Rutledge and later from their Williamsburg apartment, keeping a core, ragtag group of Fleshtones fans united around the globe. In 1995, Steve Coleman started the band's official web site in London, for which he's still the administrator and international Super Rock Town Crier.

Peter Buck agreed to produce a handful of tracks that the guys hoped they could use to interest Trafalgar Records. As usual, Buck's window of availability was small: R.E.M. had begun recording *Automatic for the People* in New Orleans, and if the guys wanted to record an album's worth of material they would have to work around his and his band's schedule. The two sessions in Athens ended up book-ending 1992: one occurring swiftly in January, the other in December, sandwiching another long and grueling year of national and international touring and partying without a domestic album to promote.

Peter and Keith were happy to be working with Buck; they shared taste in music and humor, and the sessions, however apace and on-the-fly, felt right. "We'd been friends for years," Buck says. "I don't remember if I got paid, but that didn't matter. They trusted me, and they knew that we could do the studio inexpensively." In mid-January, the Fleshtones commenced three days of recording and mixing at John Keane's studio. Buck's marriage was unfortunately going south, so he holed up in a nearby hotel while the guys crashed at his large house, Buck happily providing them with all of the vodka and Kahlua they needed. The sessions produced "Mushroom Cloud," a midpaced psychedelic groove with a funky backbeat and a curious inhaling/exhaling rhythm, and "Worried Boy Blues," Keith's homesick love song to Anne with imagery of dying grasshoppers and a tear-stained river. ("I was in the right frame of mind," Keith admits. "I was very tortured and fucked up, too much booze, too much of everything all at once.") Two horn-driven songs were also recorded, a respectful cover of the Animals' "Outcast" from 1966, and the spirited "Powerhouse" (later retitled "Pickin' Pickin'"), an attempt at channeling Iggy Pop. "Treat Me Like a Man" was also cut, fated to be left off of the album.

At the beginning of the sessions, Buck, Peter, and Keith decided that the parties would consciously strive for a unique sound. "My feeling was that if you wanted the Garage Rock Fleshtones, they've done that," Buck says. "Let's do something a little different. And that's what they wanted. They do a whole lot more on the record: there's a little bit more psychedelia, there's a little funkier stuff in there. John Keane was helping push the ideas into a slightly different feel. I always wish that we'd had more time, and I might have remixed some things, but I think it's a really great record. It fits in with what they are as a band." Buck fretted about capturing the dare-devil spirit of the Fleshtones, but he was struck by their profession-alism in the studio. "A stage is real energetic, you just go where you're going," Buck reflects. "In the studio, you want to capture that, but you also want to get the songs. They were really professional about it. You wouldn't really think so; knowing them you'd think, *Oh god, it's gonna be a mess*, but they went in and said, 'We can do a record in a week, sure.' We didn't do any preproduction, so I would say, 'Two more songs tomorrow, guys.' It was up to them to come in with them. And they did."

The overall sound was indeed markedly different from anything the Fleshtones had taped to this point in their career, a fact that would ultimately doom the album to puzzled responses from fans. "I was listening to the Died Pretty and bands like that from Australia, bands that are much more hypnotic, psychedelic, and acoustic," explains Keith. "Musically, the Fleshtones drifted this way. Working with Peter Buck, I thought that it was a good combination." Peter, who adapted his lyrics to suit Keith's moody melodies, felt that work-ing with Buck and Keane was "really, really easy. These Southern rock dudes really accentuated the particular songs that we had." But, he laments, "there were certain sounds and effects that Keith and I wanted that Keane and Buck didn't know how to do. And so it didn't work out." The tremolo effect on "Mushroom Cloud" wasn't nearly as heavy and gimmicky as the guys wanted, ending up sounding less psychedelic and more Byrdsian. When R.E.M. recorded *Monster*—their sonically dense follow-up to *Automatic for the People*—they achieved the driving sounds that the Fleshtones had wanted. Cracks Peter, "It sounded like there was a voodoo ceremony and the bands' personalities were switched!" For his part Ken, still without his legs as the new bass player in the studio, didn't feel that his new band was cohesive yet. "We didn't work on that record very hard, nothing was really fleshed out, things were changing, we were going in without lyrics, putting arrangements together. I felt really unprepared while we were rehearsing. We didn't have a work ethic together." Peter's "Beautiful Light" was one of the earliest songs that he'd ever written, and many of his lyrics, as both Buck and Ken recall, were quickly brainstormed and scratched out at the sessions themselves.

The eleven months between sessions didn't help. In December, the guys returned to Keane Studios to wax the remainder of the record in a brisk week and a half. The bulk of the new tunes were brightly acoustic, finessed to the warm and breathable tones taped in January, and continued the sonic alteration of Super Rock with lyrics written by Peter and Keith, sensing their fortieth birthdays, that addressed large-minded themes from personal gratitude to bitter disappointments. "Big Heart" was a lofty and grinning midtempo *Thank you* to anyone who'd ever held the band together; "Not Everybody's Jesus" was a heartfelt, chugging grind layered with slide work from Keith; "Pocketful of Change" was an upbeat tune cowritten with Ken with lyrics that sat in opposition, Peter admitting that, after all these years of big nights and bitter dawns, he may have given his life away for a few good memories and a pocketful of change ("I got a little self-pitying thing going on there, but it's very truthful," Peter says, "driving back from shows and literally having no money and always being embarrassed. It's horrible."); "I Took a Walk" (later retitled "Take a Walk with the Fleshtones") was the closest here to bedrock Kinks-in-the-garage stomp, a joyous celebration of Peter's Alphabet City neighborhood made rousing by Ken's slap-bass and Keith's riff, which Peter had in his head since he was a kid; "One of Us" was a rare Keith and Anne collaboration, an atonal churn of a song bemoaning loss; "Beautiful Light" was another acoustic, large-hearted sing-along with gratitude for a warm and shining, but temporary vision.

"Whistling Past the Grave," perhaps the biggest departure of the lot, was a musically bright but lyrically abstract downbeat tune to which R.E.M.'s Michael Stipe contributed a stanza. At the 40 Watt Club late one night, Keith mentioned to Stipe that he needed more words for the song. When Stipe discovered that the song was sad he inscrutably vanished into the bathroom and returned with a few lines of lyrics; Keith felt they were perfect and they got used. "Push on Thru" was generic party R&B/Eddie Cochran ("B-material," Ken admits), but "D.T. Shadows" was a wholly original, autobiographical detour through the nightmare of detox: one crazy night years earlier Keith and Gordon had been holed up in a hotel room when Gordon began spouting a poem that he called "D.T. Shadows." Coked up and psyched, Keith ran after him and jotted down the lyrics. To Keith's amazement, two days later, after the coke had worn off, the words still had bite and depth.

By the second week of December the recordings and mixing were finished. The guys drove home into the teeth of the worst hurricane-grade storm to smash into New York in over a century, plunging the city into a state of emergency. Luckily, they steered the van through the streets during a slack period when the winds were temporarily mild. Was the blizzard a brash foretoken commemorating a successful new record? An auger of difficult storms to come?

In between sessions, the Fleshtones hit the road, buoyed by some heartening news in the summer. Miles Barken landed the band their first American record deal in half a decade. Ichiban Records was formed in Atlanta, Georgia, in 1985 (in a garage) by partners and married couple John Abbey and Nina Easton, essentially as an avenue for the transplanted Brit and Finn to indulge their love of blues and R&B. From the onset, Ichiban (a Japanese word that translates into the phrase "Number One") was identified as a black American music label, the roster of initial titles spanning blues to gospel, urban contemporary to jazz, and rhythm & blues to rap, and early artists including Curtis Mayfield, Clarence Carter, and William Bell. By the early nineties, gauging the gargantuan success of Nirvana and grunge, the label was interested in branching out to college/alternative rock. "I always thought that there was potential for the Fleshtones to get a good deal," Barken says. "I was very enthusiastic and idealistic about all of that, and for some time that was a shot in the arm for the guys." Barken opened shop in a tiny storefront on Thirteenth Street, between Avenues A and B, and set about to make the Fleshtones work. *How hard can this be?* he wondered.

Barken had initially struck a licensing deal with Ichiban to distribute *Powerstance* in America under the label's new Naked Language imprint, thanks in no small part to Kim Saade, an Atlanta college DJ who was then working at Ichiban in their marketing department. A big fan of the Fleshtones, Saade had gotten her hands on an import copy of *Powerstance*, loved it, and, weary of promoting the likes of Clarence Carter, drummed up support for its rerelease. After a bit of research, she cold-called Barken and interested him and the band in the label. "Nina Easton and others were into it, too," Saade says. "I think they thought that even if *Powerstance* didn't do anything in the U.S., they might make some money on it overseas. I was really excited. How many times do you get to put something together like this just because you really like the band? There was a lot of enthusiasm for the Fleshtones at Ichiban." The guys were grateful.

Ichiban issued *Powerstance* in November of 1992, well over two years after its completion. The band's first domestic studio release in five years received solid reviews (*Billboard*: "a glorious return"; *Pulse*: "a lean, mean distillation of everything there is to love about this hardworking New York institution") but middling sales. Barken was impressed with Ichiban's resources and promotion offices, and he was buoyed by the fact that the albums would be available in Tower Records. Barken began thinking ambitiously, and in addition to accompanying the band on the road and coordinating with promoters, he spent considerable time in his ramshackle office trying to convince I.R.S. to rerelease *Roman Gods* and *Hexbreaker!* as a double CD or, at the least, to allow Ichiban to rerelease the titles. "It seemed essential to me," Barken says. Unsurprisingly, I.R.S. balked at letting the masters go inexpensively, and Barken was stymied. "We were running into a brick wall. It's so strange to me that I.R.S. said, *We won't do it, but we won't let you do it, either.* They weren't taking advantage of their assets." Frustrated, he dropped the idea.

The Fleshtones—whom Peter had taken to semisorely calling "the world's most unusual blues band"—were back out on the road, their collective second home. The next five years would find the band away from New York for long stretches as an era of national and international, months-long, large- and small-club tours crested. By the end of the long decade the guys would be forced, under the weight of financial distress, domestic discord, and plain demoralized exhaustion, to reassess their touring career.

After the January session with Buck, the guys played a handful of gigs that tested Peter's voice, as he'd endured vocal chord surgery two months earlier. (During the downtime closing out the year, Keith reformed Full Time Men with Bill, Ken, and Andy York, ex-guitarist from the Scorchers and one of Keith's favorite players; they gigged around town at Brownies, the Continental, and the Lone Star Roadhouse). Peter's mended voice was strong. At a show at the 40 Watt Club in Athens, the guys blew away Richard Butler of the Psychedelic Furs who was in attendance, as well as R.E.M.'s Mike Mills. Afterward Mills found Keith backstage, and, sweating and wide-eyed, shouted, "I can't believe you fuckin' guys! You've been together, playing for so many years, you're still like a brand-new band." He slapped Keith on the back. "It seems like you've been rehearsing in somebody's garage for six months and finally got out and played for the first time!"

In February, the Fleshtones launched a seven-week U.S. and Canadian tour, ostensibly promoting *Powerstance* and road-testing the new batch of songs. Gigs were fun and riotous, the fellas ushered to and fro by longtime road manager and driver Jimmy Descant, a pal from New Orleans. The band hit eastern Canada, the Midwest, down to New Orleans for Mardi Gras, across Texas and the Southwest, up California through to Vancouver, with the usual looped and hungover shenanigans abounding, from regional food and illegal fireworks to a daylong visit to the fellas' favorite bar in the world (Findley's, in Baltimore's Lexington Market) and another run-in with

Sweat

R.E.M. members down at Mardi Gras. The guys suffered thousands of miles of cramped Americana van life, long drives begun too early in the morning or immediately after a sweaty show, and flopped onto and were too quickly dragged out of beds in their favorite hotel-chain *du jour*, the Knight's Inn. "The guys had turned me on to this purple palace long ago," Descant says. "Purple crushed-velvet bedspreads and drapes, gold relief scenes on the walls. The Fleshtones had great road rules to pass on. Always stay at the wildest, cheapest, closest place to the gig. Never eat at a place you've seen on TV. The best way to find a cool diner is to pull off for gas then ask someone where the place is that has good home cooking."

The fun spanned north and south: in Oshawa, Ontario, at the Star Club, the venue sold out of beer for only the second time in the club's history; the first time was when the Fleshtones had last played. Down in Corpus Christi, Texas, the guys played to a wildly appreciative handful who turned out to be the Spanish crew for the Columbus ship celebrating the anniversary trip across the Atlantic "They loved the Fleshtones and had a cassette that they played over and over on their trip," Descant remembers. "They invited us down to the docks and gave us a tour, complete with special unopened rum in the captain's quarters. The security guards finally showed up and the trumpet player, Joe Loposky, climbed up the crow's nest!" Afterward, the guys snuck into Mexico and enjoyed a local hideaway bar with taxidermy on the walls, a dusty unplugged jukebox, working men scattered and unimpressed, and six shots of Cuervo for $4.50. "Then in the early morning sun, watered-down streets and sidewalks, and a fresh bakery to get us back on the road," Descant remembers, shaking his head. The Fleshtones' cracked nutritional scheme worked well enough for them.

The guys arrived home sleepless and worn out at the end of March, but could rest for only one day. In April, they toured France with the Roadrunners on the Armed and Dangerous tour—eighteen shows in twenty-five days—and the wide-eyed speed continued unabated. Back home in May, the guys got a chance to catch old favorite Bobby Marchan in action at the New Orleans Jazz Festival, where they rendezvoused with Dave Faulkner and friends from Australia, drank beer, and wolfed down alligator po-boys, taking occasional rests for shade and redemption in the gospel tents. After a month of rest, the guys headed back down to New Orleans for a one-off show thrown for—and wholly financed by—a guy who simply wanted the Fleshtones at his thirtieth birthday party.

Fun under tall suns and shiny moons can drown out other realities for only so long. In early March, hours before a gig in Knoxville, Tennessee, Bill learned that his mother had died. He kept the news from his mates, played the show bravely, and then flew home to Troy afterward, requiring the cancellation of four shows.

The remainder of the year found the guys laying low in New York. Peter and Keith wrote songs, Keith and his Full Time Men played regular Tuesdays at Brownies, and the Fleshtones staged a couple of "Wild Girls Go-Go-Rama" shows in Brooklyn and at the Lone Star Roadhouse (plus a couple down in Athens, Georgia), sprawling gigs with over thirty go-go dancers onstage as the band tore through a typical set and Peter channeled Elvis circa *Viva Las Vegas*. The Ichiban deal was finalized in August, and at the end of September the guys flew down to Mexico for the first time professionally, playing a gig at Rock O' Titan in Mexico City and filming two separate episodes for *Picante*, a popular Mexican television show hosted by Maria Conchita Alonzo. She gamely lobbed questions at the guys, who were bemused to be center of attention in one of Peter's favorite countries. The taping occurred early in the morning but the Fleshtones loosened up and played two sets, rocking up a crowd who knew nothing about the band and persuading Maria herself to dance with Ken's bass guitar around her neck.

Back home, Bill was feeling the despondent pinch of the vicious and calculating bohemian lifestyle that he courted so well. As he cruised into his mid-forties, Bill was able to enjoy New York in the thrifty ways that he'd come to master over the years—free breezes and cheap beers at Ruby's Old Thyme Bar and Grill at Coney Island, dollar bets at the Saratoga and Aqueduct horse tracks, and gawking and hooting at the Gay and Lesbian Pride Parades along Fifth Avenue.

But grieving his mother, Bill was beginning to take a hard look at himself and his living conditions. "I was having to come up with six bills a month, and the band was not doing very much," he says. "I was almost getting my friend kicked out of his apartment for non-payment, and I thought, *What the fuck am I doing?* I was going a little crazy. Everything just sucked. I was thinking, *Should I even live in New York?*" Bill never considered quitting the Fleshtones, but he was at his lowest point professionally. "I remember at the time not wanting to leave the band, but being in the mood of trying to talk everyone into not doing it anymore. We were getting bounced around from manager to manager, with no interest, no visible means of support, no deals before Ichiban, nothing encouraging happening. Despite what the band had always meant to me, it just wasn't financial anymore. I thought, *This is getting rather sad.*"

Barken often approached them during soundchecks, worrying aloud that the guys looked so bummed out. "We were," says Bill flatly.

The Ichiban deal and subsequent flow of capital helped Bill's attitude immeasurably, as did a birthday party thrown at Brownies, where the guys surprised him by collecting enough dough from over forty friends to buy a new trap case, stool, drum pedal, snare drum stand, and cymbal. Bill's case had been rolling gamely on only three wheels by this point—a penetrating metaphor for the band's wounded years—and Bill accepted the gifts with great surprise, and even greater gratitude.

In December of 1992, Dr. Dre released *The Chronic.* Gangsta Rap's seismic impact in the record-buying public and industry would ultimately register as overwhelmingly as Nirvana's, and the Fleshtones were as far away from commercial relevance as they'd ever been in their career. Around this time, the band began playing with wireless guitars, allowing the chaos of a Fleshtones show new and nearly limitless possibilities of space and sound, Keith and Ken now regularly into the crowd and onto the bar tops, never without the ring-and-bottom of their beloved guitars. Audiences were slipping away. Sweaty and grinning as ever, the Fleshtones chased after them.

Peter had hoped to title the new record *Forever Fleshtones,* and he worked up a cheeky cover: he obtained a classic photo of the original 1960s Rat Pack posing in front of the Sands Hotel in Las Vegas and superimposed each of the four Fleshtones' heads onto Frank, Dino, Joey Bishop, and Peter Lawford. He festooned the image with a handmade, painted frame, but Ichiban, fearing lawsuits, would ultimately be too nervous to use the handiwork. (The image and original title were eventually used on the Greek release of the album later in the year.) Awaiting the album's release, the guys launched themselves on yet another cross-country tour in March and April through the Appalachians, past the Great Lakes, across the Rockies, down the Pacific coast, into the desert, through the Southern plains, and up the Atlantic coast, nearly ten thousand miles of travel—or, roughly, the diameters of the earth and moon combined—twenty-two shows in thirty-two days, a crazy geography of amplified fun, mayhem, and exhaustion.

Between New Mexico and Texas shows, the guys applied themselves to a diverting task assigned by old friend Billy Miller, who was assembling a tribute album to Sam the Sham and the Pharaohs for Norton Records. At a local record store they bought a copy of *Pharaohization*, the Rhino Records best-of for which Peter had written liner notes years before, and quickly banged out an arrangement of "Medicine Man." Ducking the high *Tejas* sun, they slipped into Michael Vasquez's Sweat Box Studios in Austin and made with the abracadabra, ham-fisting the tune along with local friends, cases of beer, Peter's cheesy organ, and the guys' fun-time background chants. "Peter had always been a bigger fan of Sam the Sham and the Pharaohs then anyone," Keith remarks. "He and Brian Spaeth were dedicated to studying this music and trying to figure out why it's so unique." (Ten years later, the guys would record a version of Jimi Hendrix's "Foxy Lady" and try to reinterpret it as the legendary Domingo Samudi might have, "the closest we ever came to what we say is 'pharaohizing' something," cracks Keith.)

The guys spent two weeks in June and July touring France, Belgium, and Italy, but Keith now had far more important matters on his mind: Anne had gotten pregnant in the spring, and she was due in the fall. In typical Fleshtone fashion, the birth of Keith's daughter would be wildly unconventional and unpredictable—another story to pass around and enter the lore. Anne went into labor three weeks early while she and Keith were vacationing in France, and Nascha was born on Thanksgiving Day in the heart of Paris (on the Ile de la Cité, considered the birthplace of the city), in the city's first and oldest hospital, next to the Cathedral of Notre Dame. A harried Keith assisted with the birth in halting French. Keith and Anne brought their daughter home to their new apartment in Williamsburg, Brooklyn, two buildings down from an apartment into which Ken would soon settle (after patching dinner-plate sized holes in the walls and floors). The two bandmates were now a dozen sloppy steps from the Greenpoint Tavern, a dive oft-visited and soon immortalized in song by the band, and both Keith and Ken settled comfortably in the neighborhood along the river, at this point still quiet, years before noisy Williamsburg would become the New East Village.

The new album, unimaginately titled *Beautiful Light* by Ichiban, was released in January of 1994. The band's new label promoted the record well, but typically netted tepid sales and little radio airplay. "I think that Ichiban wanted the Fleshtones on 'Ten,' a bombastic, crazy, big record," Barken remarks. "But *Beautiful Light* just wasn't in step with what music was at the time." Pop giants Mariah Carey,

Sweat

Pearl Jam, and Snoop Doggy Dogg were guarding the *Billboard* Top 200 with considerable might, and the Modern Rock Track Chart easily swatted away the Fleshtones with the likes of Gin Blossoms, Smashing Pumpkins, Soundgarden, and other post-grunge indie acts catching the eyes and wallets of twenty-something kids. Nonetheless, the album earned a four-star review in *Rolling Stone*, and *Billboard* was impressed, praising Peter's "evocative harmonica touches that tint the atmosphere" of the album's "good groove numbers." *Trouser Press* applauded "the less upward-looking" album for taking "a few slim chances and [coming] up a rootsy winner," while *Entertainment Weekly* felt that the guys had "crafted their most earnest release."

As always, the Fleshtones were a tough sell. Randy Sadd, a radio programmer at Ichiban, sums up the difficulties. "The Fleshtones had numerous fans throughout the industry, from the labels to radio programmers to writers at magazines," he says. "From the radio standpoint, we were able to translate some of that into air play, while others remained exactly that—hardcore fans. I think they had gotten used to the band being 'indie' band icons, that the idea of commercial success maybe was not in their mind-set for the band. The band had this hardcore, committed following that we tried to escalate into the mainstream audience. Even some radio stations would comment how the Fleshtones were their favorite band, but still wouldn't play them on radio." Perhaps, Sadd feels, popular-radio programmers thought the band "was to be experienced live but something not for the mainstream airwaves."

Sadd recalls a bittersweet moment in San Francisco at the Gavin Convention, a large music industry conference widely attended by record label employees, programmers, and directors. He'd brought the Fleshtones to the convention in February. The conference had been going on for a few days when Sadd arrived, and the band was scheduled to fly in and perform at a local club as a showcase for radio people. Sadd waited for the guys in the lobby, which around five o'clock started to get overcrowded and buzzy, packed predominantly with hip-hop artists, their entourage, and their label reps. Hip-hop was very hot in '94, especially so in San Francisco, and Ichiban had reaped some of that success with artists like MC Breed and 95 South. Sadd stood atop a wide lobby stair case and drew a look at the crowd. "It really was out of control with the amount of people jammed in there," he remembers. "Suddenly, I see in the midst of the vast hip-hop scene, there was a parting of the crowd in the middle of the lobby. It was the Fleshtones walking through with their own aura of sixties garage rock mod outfits and guitar cases in hand. The parting of the seas preceded them as they walked through the entire lobby until they got to where I was positioned. I distinctly remember cracking up to myself at the site, and thinking that they definitely carried a presence about them no matter where they were."

Alas, stylish entrances didn't have cachet in the current climate. MTV rejected "Beautiful Light," the band's first video in ten years, a choppy black-and-white tour of Chichen Itza, directed by Peter and old pal M. Henry Jones, who leant his cramped apartment for the performance segment of the video (which culminated in a snowy blizzard on Keith's rooftop). But it was hard to compete on MTV with the booty appeal of Salt-n-Pepa or the disaffected irony of Beck. (*Beautiful Light* would later receive a backhanded compliment on RockCritics.com under the category "Five Records You're Proud to Own but [Secretly] Never Listen To.") In 1994, Ichiban and Naked Language scored a Top 40 hit with Deadeye Dick's "New Age Girl," a novelty song on the mammoth *Dumb and Dumber* soundtrack. Ichiban had high hopes for "Beautiful Light," which became the Fleshtones' first domestic single in ten years, the lapse indicating how low hopes had been for any kind of commercial impact during the previous decade. Much had changed in the recording industry between 1984 and 1994, and the Fleshtones were being willfully ignored by Generation Xers more amped for the speed and pop nihilism of Green Day and the Offspring than for four aging party guys in paisley and boots. A release of "Take a Walk with the Fleshtones" disappeared commercially, too, Ichiban's waffling underscored by the fact that it was released only on slowly dying vinyl.

The chart disappointment of *Beautiful Light* was compounded by a big loss for Keith. In January, the band returned home to New York City after a brief tour of Spain. Upon arrival at Newark Airport they were told that their luggage had been temporarily misrouted and would arrive on the next flight. Two days later the equipment and baggage arrived—but for the bag carrying Keith's Mustang guitar. An anxious waiting period started that ultimately lasted for weeks, Continental Airlines staving off the inevitable for as long as it could with fruitless searches and disappointing phone calls. Keith realized that his chances of recovering his beloved Mustang were running out. The guitar was never located. Keith received an airline-drafted check for compensation, but no amount of money could have replaced the little practice guitar rescued in pieces from a box in an attic twenty years earlier. The Mustang was the perfect guitar for the band—it had rarely gone out of tune or required mended strings. More important, the guitar had become a symbol for the homemade, simple, intuitive ethos of the Fleshtones: *C'mon, glue it together and let's go!*

"If she'd just come back," lamented Keith, "I'd throw a huge party and invite everyone I know." He ultimately replaced the Mustang with a 1957 Silver Jet Gretsch, a very different glittering ax, but years would pass before the sting of the Mustang's disappearance would fade. The Fleshtones toured the East Coast, Midwest, South, Canada, and France again in the spring and summer, doing their best to promote the new album and to remind fans that they were still around and kicking. Peter turned forty in September. The world's most unusual blues band was driving around and plugging in, playing for those pockets of fans who wanted to hear them, but mostly for those stubborn remaining who Peter hoped were ripe for conversion.

22.
Pardon Us for Living,
but the Graveyard's Full

Miles Barken was beat. Like John Bruce before him, he'd become disgusted with a record industry growing more and more loathsome. "In order to be a good manager, you had to be a prick and a liar," he says unhappily. Flailing about pre-Internet—technology hospitable to the indie ethic—Barken was bedeviled by managing the Fleshtones and betrayed by the very idealism that had led him into music in the first place. By the end of the year, Barken was feeling the tension between business and friendships. "I was frustrated with the guys," he admits. "I was devoting my life to it and working my ass off for it. It was really dominating my life, and I felt unappreciated. When you love and are involved with something like that, you get burnt a little bit. I was starting to have to take the hits for them. I felt like I needed time away, a break from the guys." The Fleshtones' contract with Ichiban needed renegotiating by the end of the year and, after a sit-down, the guys "let Miles off the hook," as Keith puts it.

Keith himself was staggering on unsteady legs, his excessive drinking pushing a lot of people to their limits. "I was mad at Keith," Barken says. "I felt that he was letting us all down. For me to be committing so much time and life and energy to this and for Keith to be not only nasty but to not take it seriously? I wanted to say to him, *If you don't give a shit, if you wanna be fucked up or go out and do a shitty show, then I don't give a shit!* I don't think that they really understood why I jumped off, and they might have taken it personally. I don't know if they felt betrayed or abandoned, or if they felt that I was being selfish, but I was a little crushed under the weight of the responsibility of managing their lives."

Says Barken: "I wasn't managing a band. I was managing a group of men who needed help."

Despite the commercial oblivion into which *Beautiful Light* had fallen, Ichiban held hopes for the freshly inked Fleshtones and wanted to team them with a current, hot producer. Brett Green, a New York area attorney, and his booking-agent brother, Lee, had been recommended to the guys by Andy Shernoff. Brett Green examined and greenlighted the new Ichiban contract and subsequently recommended promoters, booked some shows, and licensed on the group's behalf, managing to land music from *Beautiful Light* onto MTV's *Real World*, and ultimately rereleasing *The Angry Years* and the first *Love Delegation* album.

But as did the managers before him, Brett Green sensed market and industry mutations, and he watched helplessly as even the Fleshtones' normally lucrative European circuits began taking hits. "The marketplace was changing, the following was dropping off, and we might've overplayed the market," Green explains. "It was getting to the point where if you're a casual fan and you've seen them once this year, do you need to go see the same band two more times? That's what happened in the U.S. as well. And clearly, when grunge became the vogue, the Fleshtones were well outside of that." The first name to surface as a potential producer for the next record was Butch Vig, who had helmed Nirvana's *Nevermind* and was subsequently in high demand. "Vig had told Peter that he was interested, but we got a run-around between his manager and his attorney," Green recalls. "He eventually got back to us and said that he'd love to do the project but that he was too busy. And I think that his budget would've been well out of control."

Vig recommended Steve Albini, who by the mid-nineties had been strongly associated with indie rock credibility, as well as with a certain prickly sensibility. Raised in Chicago, he cut his teeth in the eighties in the seminal punk bands Big Black and Rapeman, crafting noisily astringent, industrial post-punk/art-funk marked by a sonic and lyric hostility. He had also produced a smattering of small indie bands. A scene and industry gadfly from the onset of his career, Albini became notorious for avoiding major label negotiations, and after

Rapeman imploded—workers at pressing plants had refused to handle a product with that name—Albini continued his production work, quickly gaining, as John Bush in Allmusic Guide notes, "a reputation as a difficult man with whom to work, but one that could bring out the best from any alternative group." Albini has always preferred to be listed as a "recorder" rather than a "producer," and his trademark sound became identified with a razor-sharp middle range and discordant, often distorted and raging dynamics. By the middle of the decade Albini had worked with many bands, including the Pixies, the Breeders, the Wedding Present, Tad, Helmet, PJ Harvey, Guided by Voices, and myriad smaller bands, but it was his work on Nirvana's follow-up to Nevermind—1993's difficult, brilliant *In Utero*—that cemented his reputation as an inspired creator of storm and noise.

Albini insists that he doesn't let disparity between his tastes and the band that he's recording interfere with his job. "Do I like the music that I work on? A small portion of it," he remarked. "The majority of the music that I work on never registers with me on an aesthetic level. In the same way that if I was a gynecologist I wouldn't expect to be turned on all day, I don't think that if you work on something in a professional capacity that it has the same effect on you when you deal with it in your civilian life. I might hear a song two or three hundred times in an analytical sense, but it's not the same thing as my hearing the song to decide if I like it. It's not possible to have the same relationship to music that you work on to music you hear as a fan. If I tried to do that, either strictly work on music I enjoyed as a fan or even evaluated the music I worked on in that way, I would do a worse job. I would not be paying attention to the principle job, which is getting it on tape and not fucking it up." Ichiban and the Green brothers admired Albini's integrity and reputation, and the fact that he worked for a flat, relatively inexpensive $20,000 fee. They hoped that Albini's abrasive touch might work commercial magic for the Fleshtones. The band was scheduled to fly to Chicago in May of 1995 for a ten-day recording session in Albini's home studio, where they would also crash. Peter and Keith had a batch of songs worked up, and in rehearsals Ken introduced a couple of his own numbers. Ken didn't want to repeat the lax preparation that had marred *Beautiful Light*'s recording, so he implored the guys to really buckle down at rehearsals. "We worked hard on the material," Ken says. "We knew what we were doing. We were confident."

Inspiring the guys were recent weeks spent sifting through demo tapes dating from the mid-eighties: their friends at Imposible Records in Spain wanted to release an album collecting various discarded Fleshtones tracks, and Peter, Keith, and Marek sorted through boxes of dusty reel-to-reel's that recalled the heady but frustrating days at the end of the I.R.S. era. Tunes from the 1984 John Fred session in New Orleans were combined with demos cut on Marek's TEAC boombox up in the Music Building, one or two undated tracks, and a tune with Fred Smith from 1988. Imposible released the album, titled by Peter *Angry Years 1984–1986* and including his scathing, humorously honest liner notes, in 1994. The sound is predictably lo-fi, most of the songs bearing a nascent, unfinished feel. The collection documents the precarious state of the Fleshtones circa 1985 as they enjoyed their final moments under Miles Copeland's bottom-line benevolence.

The guys brought a batch of songs with them to the Windy City: Ken's "One Less Step" and "Let's Go!" were lively tunes slotting in well with the band's beery sound; Keith's "Hold You," his tribute to Nascha's birth, was given an oddly doleful tone by Peter's low-end vocal; the riffy "A Motor Needs Gas" name-checked fave East Village dives Holiday Cocktail Lounge and Brownies, as well as the Greenpoint Tavern; Peter's "Sands of Our Lives" continued the searching temper of the previous album, "Accelerated Emotion," and "Fading Away" were briskly paced tunes that belied themes of loss; "Nostradamus, Jr." was a riotous paean to the legendary prognosticator; "The Sweetest Thing" and "Psychedelic Swamp" were fairly generic. "We'll Never Forget" dated to the 1980s, a heartfelt, road-weary *Thanks* to fans around the world. The incisive bridge distills the Fleshtones' decades-old, morning-after attitude:

> *Now that you're gone, we try hard to understand*
> *but the silence doesn't hold the truth.*
> *Bitterness? There's just no use.*
> *Hold on, just the best we can.*

The tune ends with a bit of *audio verité*, a recording of some bartender hollering out *Last Call!* at some bar, the guys' late-night residence for so many years.

The Fleshtones cut four covers with Albini, Cher's "Train of Thought" in a R&B workout with dry-as-dirt harmonica, a primitive stomp through the Guess Who's "American Woman," an unbound reading of Jimi Hendrix's "I Don't Live Today" brimming with sloppy energy (Peter had wanted to record a version since the seventies), and the midpaced, blissy "High on Drugs" by the Titanics, a Boston band and one of very few contemporary groups that Peter loved.

("American Woman" would be left off of the album, as would be originals "Evil Mind," "This Is My Life," and "Stolen," a nimble tribute to
Keith's beloved Mustang guitar.)

The Fleshtones weren't terrible aware of Albini's history outside
of his work with Nirvana, and Albini had little familiarity with the
Fleshtones. "I had been exposed to their music passively in the eighties," Albini says. "I saw them play live a couple of times in Chicago."
Albini rarely concocts a plan for the bands he records, and his *modus
operandi* for the Fleshtones was predictably spare. "Their presenta-
tion is a pretty simple one, and their personalities are probably the
most important aspect of the band," he says, adding that any band
that plays live a lot "is easy for me to work with because they have
their shit together in terms of performance."

Albini had no reservations about recording a band coming out of
a different musical tradition than his own. "There are some bands
that come from such a different culture that it's hard to communicate, or even to give a shit about some stuff that comes in because
some people that are doing it have such different motivations. But I
certainly didn't have any reason not to pursue the Fleshtones
record." The sessions went smoothly and productively, and the guys'
preparation paid off in terms of tight performances. Bill, for one, felt
that he was being recorded the best since the 1980 *Up-Front* sessions. The overall sound taped by Albini was crisp, punchy, and energetic—Keith's new Gretsch sounded as sharp as a razor wire—and
captured well the propulsive thrust of the band onstage.

But the Fleshtones would remain deeply ambivalent about their
time with Albini. "It was a mixed bag," Keith says. "What was good
was that Steve basically liked to get everything as live as possible, but
the bad situation was that Peter's voice on that record sounds horrendous." Ken agrees, claiming that Peter had no support from Albini. "Peter's voice is thin, it has no reverb or echo. Up until the vocals,
the recording was sounding great—snappin' drum sound, guitar
sound, best bass sound on record that I'd ever done—and all of a sudden it was like driving into a wall. *Smash!* In a studio, Peter's either
inspired or he needs a lot of coaxing and direction, and there was no
support from Albini. He didn't care."

Ken was particularly incensed over what he felt was Albini's
botched job on "One Less Step"—so angry with Albini and with
Peter's vocal that he had to walk around the West Side neighborhood
in Chicago, calming himself down. "The song was getting no help.
Peter was doing the best he could—I'd tried to prepare him with the
demo, and I felt a little chagrined that he probably hadn't worked on

it that much—but Albini's attitude was that the guy can't sing, and the song's as good as it's gonna get. And we had a lot of other songs to do." To this day Ken won't listen to the record. "I knew when I walked out of the sessions that I didn't like it," Keith admits. He would get a lukewarm response from many of the band's European fans, especially to Peter's bewilderingly at-sea vocals. "It was the wrong choice to work with Albini. He's a brilliant person—and he would always let you know about things, he's a megalomaniac, he truly is!—and generally a cool guy and a funny guy to be around. The project went smoothly and we got a lot of work done, but I just wasn't happy with the record." Like Ken, Keith finds it difficult to listen to the album now.

For Albini, the Fleshtones clearly didn't knock it out of the park. "It was a reasonable crack at what the band sounded like, but I remember being a little disappointed that at that stage, after they'd made so many records, it would've been nice for them to have made a record that was somehow a notch above what they'd been working on," he says. There was no tangible reason why the sessions never jelled, although Albini suggests that Peter and Keith might not have brought top-shelf material with them. "The best song on it was a cover of another band's song, 'High on Drugs.' So I think that gives you an indication." He adds, "It didn't feel like anyone was fully committing to the project. There wasn't anybody in the Fleshtones really excited about any of the music. It was almost as though the band felt, *Well it's time to make a record. We better do it.* It would've been nice for them to have really hit a home run."

Brett Green's biggest problem with *Laboratory of Sound* was that the album doesn't capture the band as they are live, despite Albini's recording technique. "I've been to countless Fleshtones shows," Green says. "Sometimes the crowd's in the club staring at the stage and the guys are coming in off the street playing with their wireless instruments, and Bill's banging on whatever he can bang with the drumstick. They would do sets where Peter's singing on the top of the bar in the club for the whole show. That was always the fun, that they were never a conventional live band. *Speed Connection* couldn't even capture what the guys were."

Despite the disagreeable outcome, working with Steve Albini became a turning point for the Fleshtones, an epiphany that subsequently redirected the band toward a do-it-yourself, homespun aesthetic that would feel both intuitively right and long overdue. "We went into the studio with more of our old, lackadaisical way of thinking about working in a studio," Peter admits. "We thought, *Okay, let's whittle us a record.* And Albini doesn't do that at all. He's quick. And I dug that about him. That inspired me a lot."

At one point Albini turned to Peter and said, "What the fuck are you doing? Just make a record. Why do you guys even need a producer?"

The question opened the clouds over Peter's head.

Laboratory of Sound was released in September, one week before Keith turned forty. Ichiban was at this point distributed by Capitol/EMI but struggling economically and internally (the label's fortunes would deteriorate after founders John Abbey and Nina Easton split up and Easton departed to start her own label). The label put decent support behind the album, but sales were flat, topping out above twenty thousand units, anemic totals similar to *Beautiful Light*. The Fleshtones gamely played a show in New Jersey at a Capitol Records boardroom in front of label executives and some old fans, but whatever decent, out-of-the-box album sales there were weren't sustained.

Among the artists ensconced on *Billboard* were Hootie & the Blowfish, Goo Goo Dolls, and Alanis Morissette, who was all of a crawling two-year-old when the Fleshtones formed in 1976. "Let's Go!," "One Less Step," and "High on Drugs" were each released as CD singles (the latter in France only) but none penetrated the charts, despite *Billboard* applauding "Let's Go!" as a "goofy good-time rocker" with "[r]apid rock riffs and carefree vocals [that] should keep album and modern rock programmers singing for more." Peter was stymied by Ichiban's publicists, who again overruled his choice for the album art, an in-joke photomontage of the guys devolving from Bill in a lab coat to Keith as a long-haired hippie rock guitarist. Ichiban chose a somewhat dull, green-and-black color palette and a generic cover image of a scientist at work. "To avoid sales and people noticing the record, Ichiban actually came up with a camouflaged record placed next to other brightly colored records, so that no one would even notice it," says Peter, drolly. "And many people didn't."

Reviews for the album were mixed, some critics noting the spotty song quality and the curious sonic mismatch between the band and Albini. Jamie Roberts in Consumable Online noted that the album "contains a lot of the straight-ahead grungy rock that one might expect," and that Peter's vocals "just manage to pull off even the more questionable numbers," adding that "[t]he punchy, short numbers don't give you enough time to think about what you actually liked about the tracks; you just remember that they rocked." Also weighing in were upstart indie music magazines *Magnet* ("If there were any justice in this world, a band like the Fleshtones, with more than 15 years of chaos and fun under its belt, wouldn't be scuffling for a living") and *Alternative Press* ("Another retro-with-a-purpose release").

Writing in *Trouser Press*, Ira Robbins lacerated *Laboratory of Sound*, describing the album as "one experiment the Fleshtones probably shouldn't have tried." Writes Robbins,

> It's tempting to blame the letdown on "engineer" Steve Albini, but other than razorblading Streng's guitar tone with his patented anti-lapidary trebling action and organizing inappropriately harsh and thin sound, he doesn't appear to be at fault. Nor does the hedonistic ethos expressed in "High on Drugs" seem responsible. No, it's Zaremba's generally ineffectual songwriting and distressingly sharp singing that keep the album from matching the easy appeal of its immediate predecessor. . . . [T]he monochromatic rock performances of constricted melodies leave *Laboratory*—the casualty of inadequate preparation and overly casual execution—a disappointing write-off.

A few weeks after *Laboratory of Sound* began appearing in record stores, the editors at *SPIN* magazine published *The SPIN Alternative Record Guide*. The Fleshtones weren't among the bands selected for inclusion, as if the guys needed more proof that their relevance was diminishing. Former *SPIN* editor Eric Weisbard explains that the Fleshtones were caught between two moments. The garage rock that fueled early punk wasn't as powerful an influence on indie kids like Weisbard after R.E.M., and by the mid-eighties, when Weisbard came of age as a critic and began covering music, bands like the Fleshtones, Lyres, and the Slickee Boys seemed outdated. "The new energy was in reviving the Velvet Underground, or anchoring a scene somewhere, or taking arty hardcore to the next level, or finding weird characters like Alex Chilton and Robyn Hitchcock to embrace," says Weisbard. "We listened to *Pebbles* and the like, but not as obsessively as folks had just a few years before. And by the time I was choosing bands to include, it just didn't seem like the Fleshtones had amounted to a significantly novel band to include in the pantheon."

The guys embarked on a modest tour in November and December to promote an album that they hated. They'd taken to covering Johnny Thunder's anthemic "I'm Alive" as a sonic tonic to a numbing decade. In order to defray costs and logistical headaches, they cut their horn section (to the dismay of some fans), opting for a leaner, four-man sound in which Peter's up-front harmonica supplanted brassy ballsiness. Following a Halloween show in Annapolis, Maryland, they dipped into the South for a few days, flew to France for a week and half of gigs, and then to Spain for a handful of dates.

Meanwhile, Brett and Lee Green were nearing the end of their brief tenure. "Peter was very pissed off because of the last European tour," Green admits. "They didn't make much money, and we got the blame for that. But honestly, I can't put people in the seats." The Green brothers had taken ahold of the Fleshtones at a tough point: Ichiban was collapsing, and a dicey relationship went downhill from there. "I don't think that the band could complain, at least during the first two years," Green continues. "They were touring U.S. and Europe a lot, considering that they didn't have a hit and that Ichiban wasn't selling a tremendous amount of records for them."

Green has put any bad feelings behind him. With fresher perspective he can understand his frustrations, especially with what he calls Keith's "fear of success." "We could never get a record out that really captured the band," he laments. "More people didn't get a chance to experience what they were live in their prime. And getting these guys a publishing deal wasn't an easy thing, because there wasn't a lot of money out there, and they weren't doing the type of music that easily lends itself to licensing for film and television." Green adds, "At some point, there was a decent amount of understanding that they simply weren't where they were five years before." But, he is quick to say, "The Fleshtones played the same if there were two or two thousand people in the audience. They never shortchanged whoever was there to see them. They never acted embittered." With the Green brothers cut loose, Keith would permanently take over the reins as the band's manager, cobbling together label and distribution deals and booking his band around the world from a tiny overflowing desk in his cramped Williamsburg apartment.

In December, the Fleshtones travailed the bleak Midwest, ending the month with a New Year's Eve show at the 9:30 Club in Washington, D.C. In the first few weeks of the new year they were driving through the snow and gloom of Canada, whatever hopes they might've had of being renewed by the gusts of New Alternative trends fading quickly and quietly. Twenty years after banging fun and recklessness together in a basement in Queens, the Fleshtones were driving out the end of a long tunnel. Blinking into light long regarded as myth and rumor, the guys approached a fork in the snowy roads: one direction led toward role-playing on a stage long overplayed; the other down a less fashionable but cozier sidestreet that brought the band—at long last—home.

The Remedy

"I must hold in balance the sense of the futility of effort and the sense of the necessity to struggle; the conviction of the inevitability of failure and still the determination to 'succeed'—and, more than these, the contradiction between the dead hand of the past and the high intentions of the future."
—F. Scott Fitzgerald

"The Fleshtones have stared in the face of success and laughed."
—Peter Zaremba

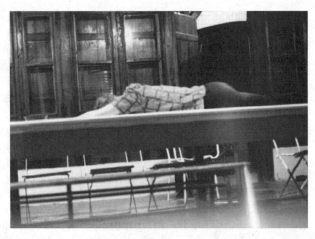

23.
Is This Really Me?

Gordon Spaeth wafted through the Fleshtones' camp infrequently after the Halloween calamity of 1988. He resurfaced in 1992 at a Full Time Men residency at Brownies, strolling in unannounced with two harmonicas stuffed in a back pocket. He was thinner, relatively well, and blew some mean harp with his old pals. He showed up a week later with a brand-new saxophone, and Peter made sure that he came to see his vanished pal. Near the end of the year the guys corralled Gordon to play sax on the languishing *Beautiful Light* recordings, and in 1995, much to Steve Albini's bafflement, flew him to Chicago to lay some raunchy sax solos onto "Nostradamus, Jr." and "I Don't Live Today." Peter acknowledges, "Albini wondered what the hell we were doing, bringing Gordon over, surrounded as we were by great horn players in Chicago." Friendship is a strong pull.

Mostly, Gordon Spaeth remained an apparition. Peter and Keith rarely knew how to get in touch with the Rooster after he'd left the band, and his sax, in pieces. Gordon would occasionally sit in with the Waldos (featuring Walter Lure from the original Heartbreakers) but mostly he'd disappear, sometimes to his parents' home in Queens, sometimes into the beds of women, mostly into itinerant flophouses. He eventually landed at the Broadway Hotel on Broadway and 101st Street, a continent away from his friends and old life in the East Village and a chancy neighborhood that he would call home for the bulk of the decade. The occasions when Gordon did venture downtown were exceptions to the rule: much of his life since 1988 would be marked by a stormy decline into drug abuse and mental illness. Like so many broken men before him, Gordon would use the urban camouflage of New York City to shake off his past as best he could, evanescing in and out of bars, flea bag hotels, and hospitals.

In 1990, Gordon's father died. The dysfunction of Gordon's adolescence flared up intensely, and he suffered a mental and physical breakdown, abetted in part by his numerous attempts to stave off drink. As the Fleshtones were gang-singing about being Living Legends, Gordon was spending months in psychiatric care at the Long Island Jewish Medical Center, where it was ultimately discovered that he was suffering from Hepatitis C. When he was deemed relatively fit for release, his physical condition still precarious, he had few options or friends and needed to run from old haunts. He checked into the Broadway Hotel with his hospital bracelet still dangling from his wrist, wearing his one and only suit (this from a man who once cherished his stylish retro wardrobe). In the lobby, cocaine and heroin dealers lurked and ancient men and women out of touch with reality sat staring into naught. Up in his dismal $400 room, Gordon propped open the one window with his tennis shoe and wearily sat down on a stained mattress. Paper hung from the wall, and a child-sized dresser sat wobbly before him. Gordon opened a drawer to find that the dresser was constructed entirely from cardboard, lined with contact paper.

"I'm in my Cardboard Years," he said aloud, bitterness seasoning his dreary revelation. Gordon sat back on his bed and began to weep, then he began to laugh, and then a gust of wind blew south down Broadway and snatched Gordon's tennis shoe from the window, launching it down the avenue. Gordon could only run downstairs and dash outside to chase his shoe, commencing the tragicomic drama that his life had become.

Gordon spent subsequent long days drying out, giving harmonica lessons, attending lectures at Columbia University, reading antique-instrument music books at the Barnes & Noble on Eighty-fourth Street, and chatting with various residents at the Broadway, notably an old black guitarist down the hall who played Bo Diddley all day. Quietly, Gordon enjoyed the hazardous neighborhood as best he could, buying coconut ices and idly watching neighboring Puerto Ricans play dominoes in the street.

Is This Really Me?

In the spring of 1995, Gordon's mother fell ill, and he briefly moved back to Queens to tend to her. He slipped and fell one afternoon, spraining his wrist; his mother offered him an MS-Contin pain pill, and by the end of the summer Gordon was addicted to morphine and Percocet. His ailing mother eventually sold her house; Gordon knew that it marked the end of an era. He moved back into the Broadway and his beloved Upper West Side. He had shrewdly parlayed the Fleshtones' appearances on *American Bandstand* and *Andy Warhol's Fifteen Minutes* into meager but lifetime financial support from Actors' Fund of America, and was also cashing in on Social Security and a mental illness custody grant from Music Cares, a West Coast organization, using the money to pay his rent. "No one knew me, and I could be anyone I wanted," he says.

Gaunt, nearly invisible, he'd repair to nearby Riverside Park with his saxophone and play scales and melodies into the lovely dusky night along the Hudson River, waving absently to passengers on the passing Circle Line. "It was very idyllic. I was very happy. I had no desire to be in a band. Every time I'd see a band I'd run the other way." Gordon's public performances were limited. He was issued a ticket for playing his harmonica on the subway, and then noticed an ad auditioning street performers at the South Street Seaport. "So I went down there and did some standup comedy, goofing on the mayor," says Gordon, always the ham, even in lean days. "I played some flashy crap and they went for it."

An uneasy balance of duress and leisure came to a crash in July of 2000, before Gordon would move to Gramercy near the heart of Tin Pan Alley into the Prince George Hotel, a notorious welfare inn refurbished as supportive housing for low-income and formerly homeless adults. Gordon had slipped, and though he wasn't drinking heavily, he'd started using heroin again, succumbing to his own aberration and to the uptown temptations. One evening ended in awful nirvana when Gordon overdosed in an apartment in East Harlem. The deadbeats with whom he was using panicked, dragged him down the stairs, and dumped him on the corner of 130th Street and Lennox Avenue. They called 911 and bolted.

Underneath the shadows and ironic succor of the House of Prayer Deliverance and New Hope Baptist churches, Gordon lay on the sidewalk, barely alive. The ambulance arrived, and the medics found Gordon splayed out near the wide avenue, inert and without vital signs. They defibrillated his body so intensely that his gray-white hair stood on end, and eventually they brought him back to stability. Gordon convalesced at Columbia-Presbyterian Medical Center, where the doctors told him that he was lucky to be alive. *We brought you back*, they said. Gordon eventually yanked out the IV tubes from his tracked-up arm and left on his own borderline power, disappearing back into the neighborhood.

The night that Gordon Russell Spaeth died for the first time came at the long end of a life's worth of tragedy, and the source of that tragedy was Leroy, Gordon's long-lost ghost of a friend from the Whitestone daze, who'd never stopped haunting him. "Lee and I had made a blood pact way back in the sixties, that we would both get high until the day we died," Gordon says. "And I'd always wondered what drove me." In the hospital bed Gordon said to himself: *I kept my promise. The war's over.*

He had come back from a long way off—his days spent lifting weights, writing short stories, and living simply and cleanly, his thick hair dyed red again. One of the ironies in Gordon's life involved the curious if alleged history of the Prince George Hotel, which in the 1950s allowed Pan American Airlines to dodge immigration laws and designate an entire floor as a "safe haven" for passengers flying from Europe to South America. The passengers were confined to their rooms during the brief layover, assured that they were, in fact, not officially in the country. "What if these laws were never taken off the books?" Gordon wondered. "Technically I don't reside in the United States. My alienation fantasies are complete! I'm beyond the law!" And he'd always felt like an outsider.

Perhaps the greatest irony in Gordon's life dawned the moment he recognized the street address of his current psychiatric counselor: 57 St. Mark's Place. Presently the Unitas St. Marks Place Institute for Mental Health, the building had housed Club 57 in its basement in the 1970s. Nearly a quarter century after Gordon spent late-night hours there blowing sax and harmonica and creating kicks with the Fleshtones, he was sitting in a chair one floor above that same basement, facing a psychiatric counselor and the devils he'd staved off those many years ago.

During one afternoon session at Unitas, Gordon's counselor invited him to make a list of all of the drugs and substances that Gordon had abused throughout his life. He went home that night and, in the sterile, pleasant cleanliness of his room at the Prince George, surrounded by his few books, his beloved radio/CD player, and an omnipresent cup of green tea, wrote in shaky hand on torn notebook paper a single-space list:

Is This Really Me?

History of Substance Abuse

1. Beer
2. Wine
3. Airplane Glue (Prince preferred over Testors)
4. Toluol (Industrial Strength)
5. Toluene (Industrial Strength)
6. Carbona
7. Marijuana
8. Hashish
9. Opiated Hashish
10. Opium
11. L. S. D.
12. Mescaline (synthetic)
13. Peyote (buttons)
14. Mushrooms (Fly Agaric)
15. Mushrooms (Amanita Muscaria)
16. Morning Glory Seeds (Heavenly Blues)
17. Morning Glory Seeds (Pearly Gates)
18. Hawaiin Baby Woodrose Seeds
19. Cough Medicine — Terpin Hydrate (Lemon Flavor)
20. ~~Cough Medicine - contained Codeine~~
20. Stokes Expectorant - contained tincture of Opium
21. Romilar - contained Dextro-Methorphan
23. Benzedrine (amphetamine)
24. Dexedrine (tablets & spansules)
   Dexamyl

26. Methamphetamine (capsule "Black Beauties")
27. Methamphetamine (pharmaceutical liquid)
28. Methamphetamine (powder, illegally manufactured)
29. Obetrol (a multiple-entity amphetamine)
30. Pre-Ludin
31. R. P.^{s} (amphetamine)
32. Nitrous Oxide (laughing gas)
33. Codeine tablets
34. Paragoric (tincture of opium courtesy of "Mrs. Tianovich")
35. Heroin (illicitly manufactured)
36. Heroin (Pharmaceutical from England)
37. Morphine Tablets (M.S. Contin)
38. Morphine Liquid
39. Demerol
40. Dilaudid
41. Tuinals
42. Seconals
43. Cibas
44. Chloryl Hydrate
45. Darvon
46. Perco-cet
47. Percodan
48. D.M.T
49. M.D.A
50. Extacy
51. Cocaine

52. Valiums
53. Libriums
54. Dalmanes
55. Crossroads (amphetamine)
56. T. H. C.
57. P. C. P.
58. Gin
59. Vodka
60. Amoretto
61. Belladonna
62. Stramonium Nitrate
63. Amyl. Nitrate
64. Didrex

Good Christ. An inventory of synthetic goodwill, the list nearly sub-sumed Gordon's memories and his present security. But remarkably, he'd survived, he'd survived, line after line after line until he reached the end.

Then he turned over the sheet on the desk, and he left it alone.

Meanwhile, the cold-water splash into fatherhood hadn't sobered Keith up, and he was still battling urges for his beloved *vodker.* Keith's road drinking, long a staple of the Fleshtones' lifestyle, was becoming more intense, and he'd taken to semihiding much of his daylight drinking from his bandmates. Keith's day would routinely begin with an agonizing hangover, followed by the shakes, followed by a beer to get him steady and allow him to consider rising and shaving. "I couldn't tell if the shakes were from the drinking, or if maybe I was detoxing from heroin," Keith admits. "I couldn't tell what I was detoxing from anymore." More and more he would main-tain his road discipline by getting bombed throughout each day, sus-taining the morning buzz during the long afternoons and letting himself go completely at night.

More upsetting and problematic for Keith and his family was the heroin use, which by the mid-nineties was cresting. Keith had shown a battle-tested tolerance for recreational drugs over the years, and he was usually able to balance his kicks with good sense. But deep demons would occasionaly rise to the surface: after a wasteful mid-eighties show in Pennsylvania during which he'd passed out mid-set, Keith gave in to a rare violent streak. After the show, doped-down on a hand-ful of forty-gram Valiums, he found the elemental force to fiercely lunge after a group of police officers outside of the club; luckily Marek and Peter were able to subdue Keith and toss him into the van.

He would never shoot up. He'd snort dope in a *faux* essay at staving off hardcore addiction (which he'd seen threaten many friends, including Marek), and maximize his use in three- or -four-day blow-offs in an effort to short-circuit a growing habit. "New York is a great place to be a heroin addict," Keith admits. "It's cheap, the quantity is good, you can get it anywhere." Every night at home Keith would drink at least a half a fifth of vodka and a half-dozen beers—"This was when I was behaved"—while his wife and daughter sat a few feet away in their tiny apartment. His drinking was spilling over into his visits to his father in Maine and to his in-laws in France, causing great domestic embarrassment and difficulty. For years, Anne had hit the bars and clubs with her husband, but much of that changed when Nascha was born. "It sort of turned into more of a lifestyle," Anne reflects. "It was getting to be too much at times, anyway, so it became a serious problem when it was no longer by choice. Eventually it all spiraled and backfired. Something had to give."

On a short tour of the South with like-spirited bands the Woggles and the Hatebombs in January of 1997, Keith faced his Waterloo. "I reached a point where I wasn't sober for one second of the day," Keith admits. "The first few shows of the trip I was playing very well because I could play drunk very well. I was becoming an expert at it after all of these years of being intoxicated, and whatever drugs I could put in me, it would be fine. But it had caught up to me. I was playing horribly." A tour of France had been scheduled following the southern circuit, and Keith knew in desperation that something had to change. "I had about ten days to get it together. Meanwhile, I'm out on the road with the guys, and they didn't know the problems that I was having at home. I was going to have to do something severe." Keith knew that he had to leave the tour without explanation, and that no accounting would satisfy the guys who were in the dark as to the severity of his problem. "I needed to be hospitalized. It wasn't like I needed a cold shower or I needed to stop drinking for six hours and I'd be okay."

In Birmingham, Alabama, Keith failed at scoring some heroin, and played a soundcheck blind drunk. Hunched over the bar, wild-eyed and miserable, he knew that he couldn't possibly play the show that night and *What? Another night of drinking a million Black Russians doing a show playing like shit. . . .*

"It was over."

Keith lurched for his Silver Gretsch, left his equipment, knowing that the bewildered guys would eventually take care of it, ordered a taxi, and went straight to the Birmingham airport. "I knew that if I told anybody, they would try to talk me out of it," Keith says. "I knew that if I called my wife she would try to talk me out of it; they would have thought that there was another way. But I knew there was no way that I could've done this." Keith arrived at the airport too late to catch a flight that night so he purchased a one-way ticket departing the next morning, nearly depleting his bank account. He bought eight cold beers, drove to a nearby cheap hotel, and stayed by himself in an anonymous room watching television, trembling, and fitfully sleeping. "When you're an alcoholic you never truly sleep well," Keith acknowledges. "It's all part of the sickness: you don't sleep, you blackout, then you wake up and you want to drink more and you blackout. It's a continuous, horrifying cycle. And that's the way I was for years."

Sweat

Keith woke up, his head splintered and echoing concerns he knew his old friends were vocalizing: *Where's Keith? Was he busted? Is he dead?* He drank some beer and found his way to the airport, in agony between fixes. He boarded the plane and eyed the approaching drink cart as if it were a chariot of salvation, ordering double screwdrivers and allowing himself a final settle into the lie of drink.

He arrived at La Guardia Airport, hopped into a cab still clutching his guitar, and immediately headed to the south side of Williamsburg, where he copped three bags of heroin and called Anne, who was frantic with worry. "I thought he was dead," Anne admits. "I get a call in the middle of the night from the guys asking me if I knew where Keith was." Keith had never been so much as late for a soundcheck, "so for him to not show up to an actual show at all. . . . There pretty much could only be one explanation. It was a very long night sitting up waiting, alone, watching our little girl sleeping, wondering if she still had a Daddy."

Knowing that he could only move gingerly one step at a time, Keith's plan was to avoid hard liquor cold-turkey but to use heroin for the next two days. Eventually he organized a band meeting in his apartment. Stoned, he explained everything in as emotionally honest a manner as he could muster in front of his old friends. "I'm telling the guys that I'm gonna stop drinking," Keith says. "They were thinking, *This is an impossi-fucking-bility!* But I was serious. It was beyond the band, it was everything. I knew that it was either that or I wasn't going to have a family and I'd wind up in a gutter." Keith's heroin supply eventually ran dry, and he commenced a few days of misery. He felt appalling, but likely not as putrid as if he'd quit everything at once.

The fierce, Prussian self-discipline that Keith had softened for so many years in a blur of vodka, drugs, and Pyramid freakiness was the same regimen that allowed him to arrange a semblance of order to his now-dry days. He managed to stay sober through the winter and spring, and began allowing himself a glass of wine at dinner and no more than two beers after shows, maintaining with strong will and determination relative sobriety, avoiding the private/public conscientiousness of counselors or Alcoholics Anonymous. Recognizing the alcoholic's penchant for lethal associations and clock-drinking—Keith would regulate his boozing before shows to maintain optimum if manageable intoxication onstage—he switched to Coca-Cola and water before shows and to herbal teas after, and began regaining his energy, sleeping and eating well, and enjoying himself more on- and offstage

than he had for years. "Something clicked inside and made Keith realize what he had to lose, what he had to live for," says Anne. She adds,
"I'm not sure what would have happened to him otherwise."

Keith wishes that he could have enjoyed the East Village without
having downed a nightly half-gallon of vodka, but those blurry
evenings are long behind him. Now he enjoys his songwriting, side
jobs as a borough moving man, and morning jogs in McCarren Park
past barbecuing families and sunbathing Polish girls, unburdened by
the dire decision to begin or to avert the obliviousness of drink with
the sunrise.

For Peter, he of sturdy stock, problematic drinking and hard drugs
weren't the issues. Social, gregarious, damned curious, he's a native
imbiber who rarely courts oblivion for the sake of oblivion, knows when
to pull up, and doesn't endure fractious domestic benders or ravaging
road trips. (Save for a grim Ash Wednesday, sometime in the mid-1980s:
leaving New Orleans with the band, Peter, wracked with a rare case of the
D.T.s, glanced down at his shaky arm and was convinced that his arm hair
had spelled out "God sucks.") Following Keith's scaling back in 1997, the
two friends began indulging a mutual interest in wine tasting and collecting, fostered by years of the band's visits to France and northern Italy.
Keith began to enjoy steeping himself in a bottle's relationship to its culture and regional history rather than to its mind-erasing potential.

Peter's problems and frustrations arose in a different guise. During the 1990s he watched with dismay as the Fleshtones' audience
diminished in size and clamor. The band was fighting rising tides of
irony and cynicism, as many younger fans who came of age post-Nir-
vana were often less interested in dancing and grinning than they
were in affecting an impassive but stubborn attitude. For twenty-
something American rock fans raised on David Letterman, Sub Pop,
and Lollapalooza, entertainment had devolved into a spectacle within quotation marks: when Kurt Cobain screamed "Entertain me!" in
"Smells Like Teen Spirit," he was echoing the disaffected, sardonic
posture of many of his fans. An anti-amusement attitude was nothing new—in the late seventies below Fourteenth Street it was accepted to sneer at anything remotely old-fashioned—and the Fleshtones
have been fighting it in one form or another for years.

In the spring of 1994 Weezer's "Buddy Holly" became a Top
Twenty hit, the mock-1950s video sailed into high-rotation on MTV,
and a contemptuous post-grunge stance was solidified: *Buddy Holly*
and *Mary Tyler Moore* were wry cultural figures to be affectionately
lampooned and coded in retro gear. The refrain to "Buddy Holly"

nearly dripped with sarcasm—that the lines and music were catchy only made the irony more fun. Against this alienation, the old-fashioned Fleshtones went trooping, trying to convince the few younger kids showing up at their shows that it was okay to look goofy and silly and have meaningless fun to catchy rock & roll, however traditional it might sound. Such an attitude seems largely absent among the Fleshtones' more rabid European fans. When they find something they like, they stick to it. What the band represented to them is something they can't find elsewhere.

There were some great shows in front of great crowds. On one occasion, the Fleshtones showed up at an underpublicized gig and played their longest show ever in front of only the owner and his wife and friend. In Munich, the guys prepared for a night's gig by visiting an old beer hall infamous for having been a Nazi meeting place. "It's a really wonderful, gorgeous place with schnitzel and brats on the menu, and all of the beers come in big steins," Bill remembers. The guys, without Ken, who stayed behind in the hotel, spent a long afternoon in the *Teutonic* sun, laughing and downing beer and korn, a very strong liquor in chilled glasses. "And by the time we came back to the club we were roaring," laughs Bill. "Thank god it was time to hit the stage. We had a great show. We felt bad because Ken was doing his usual good show but not in this euphoric state that we were in. In between songs we'd do the 'Vit the Bing, Vit the Bang, Vit the Boom!' bit from *The Producers*, and start the next song, trying to do our German accents! Honest to god, that was really super fun. I wish that that was recorded."

Suffering the decisions of booking agents—the band was slotted in such unlikely venues as the Hard Rock Café in Times Square and a kids' summer camp in upstate New York—the Fleshtones came face to face with their unhappy stock in the nineties and often found it hard to rise to the challenge. "We don't mind playing a club when it happens to not be a good turnout," Ken explains. "That happens. You have to play Monday, Tuesdays, Sundays somewhere. It's part of the game. The difference is when the booking is just *wrong*. You're put in a position of defeat right from the get-go." On one such occasion in Detroit, the Fleshtones endured a dismal scene straight out of *This Is Spinal Tap*. The guys were booked into Harpos Concert Theater, a famed, fifteen-hundred-seat heavy metal/hard rock club on the east side of the city that was, at best, a curious venue for the Fleshtones to be playing. Two men had been murdered the week before the Fleshtones arrived, and the guys drove their van warily through the streets upon arrival, sensing disappointment in the air. "Harpos' management were surprised when we pulled up with a van," Ken remembers. "They were looking around for an equipment truck. We were just dwarfed by the place." The waitresses, bummed by the low turnout, and the bouncers, openly laughing at the Fleshtones' puny amps, were surly and hostile.

The Fleshtones had no business being at Harpo's, Peter acknowledges of the demoralizing night that became a turning point for the band. "There was a handful of people in the orchestra pit. It was heartbreaking. I could barely pull myself through the songs. But we were doing it for the few people who were there." Dispirited, Peter scanned the mostly empty balcony seats and the top tiers, the few patrons there milling about and ignoring the Fleshtones. One skinny guy turned and faced the stage, his body language registering hostility. Peter remembers: "He comes down slowly, walking down the aisles, down the staircase, down the other aisle, down the other staircase, closer and closer. And he walks right down to the middle of the orchestra pit, stands there in front me, and gives me two middle fingers while he's mouthing the words, *You Guys Suck! You Guys Suck!*" Peter made some sharp remark to the guy, who eventually wandered off again, lost in the din and dark.

"That was the bottom," Peter admits.

The evening that ended up inspiring and reviving Peter came in the midst of similarly inauspicious circumstances. The Fleshtones had driven up from New York to play a weekend in Nova Scotia and New Brunswick, both decent performances in front of encouraging crowds. The next day, in a fiercely driving rain, they departed Monkton, New Brunswick, for Quebec City. "The rain turned into ice," Peter remembers. "Ice, ice, ice. And little by little that became snow. By the time we were heading across into Quebec, we were in the first really bad blizzard of the year. Somehow, we pushed through." Quebec City was a good, reliable place for the Fleshtones to play, a region where they had fans who dependably turned out for shows. The venue where they were playing was one of their favorites, a building dating to the eighteenth century that rubbed up against the old walls and cannons of the city.

But the snow accumulation was so heavy that everyone assumed the show would be canceled. "We showed up and played the show to, maybe, seven people. We had to. It was semi-heartbreaking. We had really battled through to get there, at times literally plowing through snow on the road, maniacs driving through this storm on roads that were solid ice. We made it to the show, and only a few friends showed up." Some kids informed the guys that the Fleshtones were playing at the wrong venue ("They always say that," laments Peter) and invited them to soothe their spirits at a friend's video club down the block. "We hung out there and the guy gave us whatever we wanted to drink. People were smoking hash oil, and normally I would not do that, but that night I felt, *What the hell.* So I'm smoking and drinking and watching video clips."

In the looped and blurry shenanigans of a night marked by sinking valor and rising sorrows, somebody at some point slid Elvis Presley's 1968 television "Comeback Special" into the VCR. "I hadn't watched that since the seventies," Peter says. With increasing attention, Peter and the small crowd watched the show, and by the end were glued to the set. "What struck me that night was a real revelation: Elvis was constantly able to transmit the rhythm of whatever song he was singing to the viewer. Always! He was a conduit. He was genius! He could *do* it. You didn't have to struggle to understand where the beat was because you were watching it and he was giving it to you, and he just wouldn't stop! It was amazing. He was really transmitting the 2 and the 4 to an audience which has trouble finding the 2 and the 4. It was infectious and wonderful."

Watching thirty-two-year-old Elvis find and translate the beat—watching Elvis find *himself* again after the calcified years in Hollywood singing appalling soundtrack songs—was nothing short of inspirational to Peter. Like so many before him, Peter had somehow forgotten about Elvis, had taken him and his mythic status for granted. Peter watched Elvis bathed in the red, mock-heroic E-L-V-I-S lights swing into a gospel number that built and built and built, Elvis trying to top himself with each sweaty measure, reaching an ecstatic point and then leaping on top of it, offering his hand to the crowd and leaping back into the thrill of performing. "Sometimes I find and transmit the beat, sometimes I don't, but watching Elvis made me feel so much better," Peter says passionately. "I had an epiphany that night. It gave me a renewed desire to sing and to be onstage. I've gotta *do* more, I've gotta *help* people, I've *gotta* be onstage. That night I'd been asking myself, *Why do this? It's so disappointing and I'm making a fool of myself.* It's hard not making any money and going home broke.

"During the drive back the next day, everyone was really down. I was very upbeat. *Guys,* I said, *We watched Elvis!*

"I was reenergized."

Peter had needed a visceral reminder of Why and How, and he got it, cutting through his own blues on a frigid night hundreds of miles away from home. The evening was buried deep in a glum era that was fated to end.

The simple but profound sight of Elvis Presley rediscovering the joy that had made music a spiritual and sexual force not only invigorated and fortified Peter, it helped to smooth out the contradictions that had been building inside of him. "Let contradictions prevail!" sang Walt Whitman. "Let one thing contradict another!" The bardic Whitman recognized that what make us complex and interesting as individuals are our contradictions, the mess of humanity worth singing about.

Self-centered and self-effacing. Controlling and reckless. Silly and smart. Bigheaded and humble. Difficult and generous. Intolerant and curious. Peter Michael Zaremba had amassed a hoard of tensions that motivated him as a man, a songwriter, and a performer. As the Fleshtones approached their twentieth anniversary, those tensions would continue to pull Peter and the band in interesting, sometimes maddening, directions. The Fleshtones were embarking on an era wherein they would make music that thrilled them, satisfied them, and energized them, but that threatened to make their already obscure status vanish entirely.

24.
Back to the Basement

"At times, the simpler the image, the vaster the dream."
—Gaston Bachelard

A round-faced, shaggy-haired scamp from the soggy Virginia coast-line arrived in New York City, swallowed hard, and thought, *Fuck*. He cackled a stoner's laugh, unpacked a four-track reel-to-reel tape machine, and commenced the exquisite baptism by fire of lower Manhattan. For months he surfed couches, snuck into production trucks on closed movie sets, and braved more than one ten-buck Bowery flophouse for a night or two of restless shuteye.

Paul Johnson was no stranger to rock & roll. From 1984 to 1991 he'd played in Waxing Poetics, a popular Norfolk, Virginia, band that released three albums, toured the Mid-Atlantic region, and built up a strong local reputation cashing in on the bourgeoning Eastern Seaboard indie and punk rock scenes of the mid-eighties. After Waxing Poetics imploded in 1992, Johnson made the move to New York City, on the lookout for like-minded musicians. His shaky confidence was buoyed by his cousin, a Manhattan building manager who'd heard promise in Johnson's lo-fi cassette recordings and who encouraged him to commit more fully to making music. One of Johnson's first gigs in the city was as a bicycle messenger, but he was sideswiped by brutal midtown traffic once too often. Bruised and bitter, he relievedly accepted his cousin's offer to sweep floors.

From there, Johnson moved fairly quickly into his own super's position in a building on West Fifteenth Street (coincidentally across the street from where Bill had been an on-again/off-again subletter for years) after the super there had lost his mind and began hiding from his tenants. To get the gig, Johnson had to lie his ass off in classic New York Hustle—*Man, fixin's my middle name!* he'd bullshit in his Tidewater drawl—and learn overnight how to mend a sagging building, but he got free rent, decent salary, full insurance, and the privilege of carrying an enormous ring of keys to four nearby buildings for which he ultimately became responsible as manager and general handyman.

Around this time, Peter had been in touch with Carol Taylor, who had managed Waxing Poetics and who was a big fan and supporter of the Fleshtones. Peter was waiting for the *Laboratory of Sound* sessions to begin, and was subsequently itching to demo some instrumentals with Euro-jazz and African accents that he felt weren't right for his band. Taylor knew that Johnson was struggling in one-off bands and trying to record music, and she recommended that Peter call him, sensing that the two men might become friends beyond being musicians playing together. In fact, Johnson and the Fleshtones had been friendly over the years. Waxing Poetics' albums were issued on Emergo, and the two bands played on the same bill several times in the 1980s (including a demented show at the 9:30 Club, after which a drunk Bill wrapped himself in toilet paper).

Peter gave Johnson a call. The two arranged to meet at Johnson's building, and Johnson was excited to meet Peter, as he'd always loved the Fleshtones' shows and records and was despairing of working with tattooed, opposite-minded musicians. When Peter arrived with his mini Casio keyboard inside a tattered canvas bag, Johnson was in the middle of a disaster—something had broken somewhere—but the two men were eventually able to repair to the building's basement. Peter initially intimidated Johnson with his overwhelming knowledge of music history, B-movies, restaurants, and New York City lore, but he eventually started dropping by every day. ("Paul learned to stop taking me seriously," jokes Peter.) The two would listen to records, watch movies, and talk at length about rock & roll. Reflects Johnson, "Peter was really enjoying having someone new to talk to about music."

Peter had been asked to contribute a song to a John Fogerty tribute compilation, and he wanted to record "Cross-Tie Walker" from

Credence Clearwater Revival's *Green River*. He'd really liked the analog warmth in Johnson's homemade four-track recordings, a palpable tone that Peter had felt was sorely lacking not only in the Fleshtones' recent recordings but in rock & roll generally. Johnson had been spending months setting up a tiny four-track recording studio in the basement of his building. A six-by-six, windowless cinderblock room behind an iron door, the setup was cobbled together on the cheap, literally a bargain-basement affair. "It was next to the room where the trash compactor was," Johnson remembers. "But the room was so small that if two people got in there, you couldn't breathe." Drawing on his perks as super and his growing ability to jury-rig, Johnson placed a small air conditioner in the compactor room, drilled a hole through the wall, and ran a vacuum cleaner hose up through and under the mixing console that could pipe in air from the compactor room. "It was this stinky shit, so I put perfume on the hose so that it wouldn't smell so bad," Johnson laughs. With guitars hanging from the ceiling and the floor crowded with amps and four-tracks, Johnson and Peter barely had enough room to sit on the couch and play. The low-budget room, dubbed Compactor, worked.

Peter had been apprenticing as an assistant engineer at Coyote Studios in Brooklyn as a way to make some pocket change when his band was idle and to indulge his love of recording. The experience piqued his interest, and in Johnson, who similarly detested modern production, he had found a kindred spirit. "The records that Peter loves—the same as me—are the records from the fifties and early sixties when they were still using four-track machines," says Johnson. "Peter had never heard the Fleshtones' records recorded in the way that the records that he admired were recorded." The basement version of "Cross-Tie Walker" is an exercise in homespun frugality. A raw take on Fogerty's tale of a rail-walking loner, the arrangement is deceptively simple, aired out in super-wide separation, creating a retro atmosphere that Peter adores and feels translates the pure essence of rock & roll. A lightly tapped drum (actually a plastic trashcan) and a plucked acoustic guitar rise in the left channel, a stepping bass and Peter's heavily filtered vocal emerge on the right, the simple blues tune augmented with harp from Peter, recorded in the building's laundry room, and crudely punched-in slide guitar work from Johnson. All of the instruments sound caked with dirt, warm, and eternal. Simple and affecting, the tune worked. "Cross-Tie Walker" appeared in 1996 on *John Fogerty: Wrote a Song for Everyone*.

Peter was turned on. Summer and fall passed, *Laboratory of Sound* was released, and he began dreaming of the next Fleshtones project involving Johnson, a batch of obscure old songs and stereo-separation so wide as to make *Meet the Beatles* sound as if it was recorded on a forty-eight-track. The Fleshtones had emerged from their Celebrity Producer Era relatively unscathed, and wiser: commercial hopes be forever damned, the guys just wanted to make old-fashioned rock & roll records.

The Fleshtones celebrated their twentieth anniversary in 1996, an auspicious year to be a bruised-but-alive New York band. In July, the Ramones observed their twentieth year making records by calling it quits, worn out from endless touring, infighting, and the frustration of never breaking into the big time.

The owners of Le Palace, the site of the Fleshtones' memorable appearance in 1982, invited the guys to play a show celebrating their two decades. On March 11 the band flew to Paris for a well-publicized and thoroughly entertaining evening hosted and emceed by "The King of Pigalle" Pierre Carré, a longtime, popular French cabaret singer as famed for his high pompadour as for his songs (and he was a personal favorite of Bill's). The Roadrunners opened the show, the end of their version of "American Beat" dissolving into the Fleshtones' opener, a driving take on Nick Lowe's "Truth Drug." The Fleshtones played with abandon and passion, a *Thank you* for years of Parisian support, and Peter's eyes were wild again in the face of hundreds of outstretched arms and ecstatic faces. The band pulled out old chestnuts and a handful of covers, many of which Peter had earmarked for the next album (among them, Keith's rousing version of the Animals' "Inside Looking Out" and Peter's stroll through Mickey Finn's "This Sporting Life"). The venue was sold out and raucous, the crowd carrying Peter aloft at several points, and parting to his Messianic harmonica blowing on the floor.

The respect and affection in the crowd was genuine and nearly overwhelming. The *Beautiful Losers* were received in all of their glory on this night. Says Ken, "Without sounding corny, I really felt loved. The people who put on the show did their best to not only put on a good show that'd be great for the audience, but to really surprise *us*, really make it fun for *us*. It was a great all-around night."

Ken's feeling of goodwill was deepened in June when he married his girlfriend, Jean Jewett, an auburn-haired hotel switchboard operator who hadn't heard or seen the Fleshtones before she met Ken. "I went to my first Fleshtones show alone," Jean remembers, "hoping that his band wouldn't suck like so many other of my friends' bands did back then. Most of my friends are musicians and it gets harder every time to keep an encouraging smile on your face while you're listening to real bad music." Happily, Jean found herself laughing out loud during the energetic show. "They were good, danceable, and very funny. But the very funny part had me nervous, thinking, *Are they serious or not?*" Afterward, Ken asked her how she'd liked the show and, wanting to be honest with her boyfriend, she said that it made her laugh. "He said that that's what they were going for," Jean smiles. "Thank god for that. Finally a band I could support with pride."

Ken and Jean tied the knot in a small garden ceremony in the East Village and celebrated at a cheap Chinese joint on Second Avenue. Together they share their tiny apartment in Williamsburg with a growing crowd of dinosaur toys, bootleg Slade videos, and rock & roll memorabilia. (A few of those monsters caught a whiff of fresh air and escaped up the Hudson River into Beacon, New York, where Ken and Jean were obliged to track them down and buy a larger house.)

Meanwhile, Peter kept busy touring with the "Wild Bunch," a band comprised of, among others, Pat DiNizio and Jim Babjak of the Smithereens, former Blondie drummer Clem Burke, Kathy Valentine from the Go-Go's, and Wayne Kramer. The Camel Cigarette company sponsored the shows, set lists of which were packed with everyone's favorites. At the New York show, Peter tore into "After Midnight" armed with a harmonica and a cowbell and dragged Keith on stage for a version of "American Beat," Burke aped vintage Keith Moon, and Noel Redding played on the old warhorse "Money." Audiences responded well to the fun-spirited, cobbled-together supergroup, and Peter, pleased to be asked along and grateful for the paychecks, would revisit the scene later.

After a swing through Italy, France, Switzerland, and Germany in the summer, the Fleshtones rested up, and in the fall turned their attention to recording and their backs to the industry. Paul Johnson had since bought and moved into a large Victorian fixer-upper in the Flatbush area of Brooklyn, and in the basement he re-created his reel-to-reel four-track studio in a larger room with better acoustics, a disco ball, and a wet bar. He put the word out in the city about his affordable studio, and in the course of the next several years many local bands would trek down his steps into analog heaven, the Fleshtones happily among them.

"I had a lot of ideas after working with Steve Albini," says Peter. "I met Paul Johnson and realized that there was someone with an incredible set of ears and a great four-track recorder. Sometimes you can't explain why, but a recorder is an instrument unto itself. Some of them have that magic, sweet tone that sounds like a record. Whatever you tape on it sounds like a record, as opposed to many studios you go into." Peter admired Johnson's engineering smarts and frugality, sensing that Johnson knew that no matter what a musician's using to do what he's doing, it's not the equipment, it's what he can get out of it. "Ninety-nine percent of people don't know that. People are so in love with all sorts of paraphernalia, and working like that has always been a big problem with me. They'll pipe your signal through a board, with all sorts of patched-in things and circuits, through miles of wire. And they'll say, *Well, that doesn't affect it*. But you *know* it affects it! Half the time I'd be more happy with just a playback of a tape without it going through any of the stuff."

With Johnson in tow, Peter dreamed up a loving attempt to get back to basics, to make a record without a producer or a label or the attendant intrusions, a record for the band and for their fans. Peter had recently read an interview with Lou Reed wherein Reed spoke of the early-sixties music that had inspired him to recreate a similarly raw, lo-fi simplicity in Velvet Underground (it was also the music that had influenced Reed's pre-Velvets Brill Building songwriting career that produced "Soul City," among other lowly gems). *Lou Reed's a creep*, Peter thought, *but he's right*. In February, Peter accepted an invitation from Dennis Diken of the Smithereens to appear at a sold-out Joe Meek tribute show at the Fez in downtown Manhattan. Charged by Reed's comments and by the ethereally junky genius of the "Alchemist of Pop" Meek—the English producer was fiercely independent and created his memorable records in a homemade, bedroom-sized studio—Peter borrowed bucks from his sister, old pal Freddie Patterson, Michael Rosenberg at Hollywood, and others in and out of the industry to make the new album happen, guaranteeing a twenty percent return on the money after six months.

Peter scoured his memory, his vast record collection, and boxes of old mix tapes brimming with songs that sounded ripe for a Super Rock treatment. By September, he had his haul, ranging from the unknown ("Dick Tracy" by the Chants, "I'm Crying" by Dave Davies, "If and When" by Chris Stamey and the dB's) to the lesser-known ("Keep Her Guessing" by Arthur Alexander, "Let's Get High" by Roscoe Gordon, "Rainbow" by Gene Chandler). The Fleshtones cut the songs quickly in Johnson's basement studio, Peter producing with Johnson engineering and mastering the delicate balance of four-track recording. Notable was a rerecording of Otis Williams'

"Panic," a rare rockabilly streak on Tarheel Slim's "Wild Cat Tamer," Champion Jack Dupree's "Let the Doorbell Ring" (with a blistering harmonica solo from Gordon), and Bill's first lead vocal, a hipster standup routine through Vern's "Mr. Custer," complete with corny sound effects. Peter's emphasis on a lo-fi sound dragged the band back to an early-sixties mood, if doing little to finesse the recording for wider consumption. "I have no idea what 'commercial-sounding' is," Peter admits. "Anyway, old-fashioned records are still selling millions."

At this point, the Fleshtones had virtually given up on commercial success and were eager to return to the bedrock sound and attitude that had inspired them twenty years earlier. Peter didn't care if fans or critics were turned off by the archaic sound he was pursuing now with nearly fetishistic passion. "Wide stereo separation gives a record an incredible amount of clarity," he insists. "It makes a record sound clear and beautiful, and with Paul we were working with primitive equipment, so it enhanced it." To the argument that a listener, not positioned strategically, might literally miss half or more of the recording while it's playing in a bar or a record store, Peter responds simply and stubbornly: "That's how stuff sounds good." The Fleshtones were challenging their audience to reevaluate how to listen to a rock & roll record. The guys were after purity and attitude now, clearly not marketable product.

Cracks Peter, "Too bad it took us twenty-five years to learn how to make a record."

Keith, Ken, and Bill were wary of Johnson, handpicked as he was by Peter and governed by his fixation. "I went in there thinking, *I'll see what this is like*," Keith remembers. "I was thinking that, at best, this was gonna be an interesting, lo-fi, demo/outtake situation available for fans." When Keith took the recordings home before the mixes, he was happy to hear that they sounded very good. "It goes beyond lo-fi, obviously. It sounds punchy and has its own sound because of the way it's being recorded. A lightbulb went off in my head. After *Laboratory of Sound*, there was no comparison." For his part, Johnson had promised the guys that he could only do so much. "I was freaking out," he admits. "I'd never really recorded a band before. Even though this project wasn't going to be on Ichiban, there was a lot of pressure for me to learn how to be an engineer. They came down, rehearsed for about a week, and I sat down there in the basement figuring out how to do it."

Exile on Flatbush Avenue it wasn't. The guys were more likely to be interrupted by the mailman than by a federal drug agent, to step over dozing cats than a dozen smacked-out wannabes or catering staffers. Johnson juggled his *learn-as-you-go* nerves inside of a young studio lacking soundproof rooms and state-of-the-art equipment. Proper mixing became a jittery process spread among the main room, a laundry room, a stairwell, and miles of tangled cord extensions, and Johnson quickly came face to face with Peter's pressure, inflexibility, and abrupt manner. "Peter can get quite hard to work for, to the point where we were actually yelling at each other," Johnson acknowledges. "I was getting pissed off because he can get quite derogatory. And I'm just trying to do my best down there." Coupled with the absurdly low rate that Johnson gave the Fleshtones ("They were basically paying the same, or less, than what they paid to rehearse"), Peter taxed Johnson's patience, and Johnson at one point considered pulling out of the arrangement altogether. "I got $300 for making that first record," he says. "If you break that down, it was probably like thirty cents an hour. I didn't realize that I was actually good at this!"

Johnson admits to his own bouts of flightiness—he accidentally erased wrong tracks and overdubs, and more than once the guys' headphones screamed painful feedback—but generally he and the Fleshtones would develop a friendly camaraderie built upon shared love of rock & roll, a sense of humor, and an independent DIY spirit. The Compactor Sessions would find the Fleshtones, with Paul Johnson as foot soldier, digging down to a basement to find the bare essentials of record-making. The five-year process would thoroughly revive the band.

In October, the guys got a bit of good news. "Let's Go" was selected to appear in a major Hollywood movie, *To Gillian on Her 37th Birthday*, starring Michelle Pfeiffer, a Brett Green licensing effort that would net Ken and the boys a pleasant bit of pocket change.

However, career moments withered under the very sad news that old friend Wendy Wild had died after a long battle with cancer. Keith took the news particularly hard, obviously, though he had been aware of his ex-girlfriend's deteriorating condition. With Wild's passing, New York City lost a true, kicky innovator and a very special friend to many, and the melancholy roll call of deceased Pyramid regulars continued. Peter posted a message on the band's Web site:

> It is with great sadness that I must announce that Wendy Wild died at home on October 25, 1996 after a long brave fight with cancer. It shouldn't be so difficult to find the right words for

Wendy, but she was so wonderfully original and this occasion so unhappy that this is not easy. She inspired and enriched the lives of all those around her, who in turn carried her humor and style to countless others. Fans around the world got a taste of a fraction of her talent through her recordings with the Wild Hyenas, The Mad Violets, Das Furlines, The Love Delegation and of course the Fleshtones, among others. We here in New York were lucky to count Wendy as a friend and witness her unstoppable torrent of energy and fun onstage and off. Wendy will always be missed and forever loved.

The new lo-fi album, titled *Fleshtones Favorites*, was pressed by the band and ready for sale at shows and via the Web site in January. (Todd Abramson would issue the album on vinyl on Telstar Records in early summer, and Imposible Records would add two tracks for a CD version for Europe; both labels retitled the album *Hitsburg USA*.) The album cover sported a shot of Peter's latest drumhead design—"Mr. Pro," a nattily dressed bartender offering the Perfect Pour—and inside were thirteen warmly recorded Compactor nuggets. Refreshed by basement basics and challenged by the absence of multiple takes, the band offered tight, playful arrangements of the fifties and sixties tunes, and Peter, filtered through cheap Shore microphones, sang with great confidence.

The guys swung up and down the Eastern Seaboard, and at the end of the month flew to France and Spain for two weeks' worth of gigs into February, hawking *Fleshtones Favorites* from a back table in every club. Keith tested his new relative sobriety on the road and, relieved of brutal hangovers and drooling, catatonic van rides, was playing with more energy and humor than he had in years. His days and weeks away from his little daughter were less burdensome now that drink and drugs were no longer exacerbating his guilt and sadness. Keith's life was slowly, and powerfully, coming into balance.

Before a tour of Italy in July, the Fleshtones flew to Detroit to play Gutterfest, a three-day garage rock festival, an early indicator of the band's rising profile among festival organizers and fans. The guys headlined the middle night, playing with pals Mt. McKinleys, the Hentchmen, and others. Later in the year they would fly to Denver for Treblefest, and then Atlanta for Fuzzfest, appearances that reestablished the Fleshtones as rightful "Garagefathers" while introducing them contextually with younger acts on the scene—the Makers, the Hatebombs, the Insomniacs, the Mooney Suzuki, the Woggles, the Swingin' Neckbreakers, *et al.*—bands associated with a garage rock revival spearheaded by labels such as Estrus, Crypt, Get Hip, In the Red, Telstar, and Sympathy for the Record Industry.

The Fleshtones felt as if they had something to be spirited and cocky about in front of the young turks. Inspired by their dash through an album's worth of oldies, Peter and Keith knew that their new songs were among the most alive and confident in years. Keith's newly discovered energy and life in morning light provided him with more impetus and time to write, and he took to regular composing on guitar and piano while in the country in western France visiting his in-laws. The guys liked that they could drop into Compactor needing relatively little advance warning for Johnson. In June, they settled into the basement for another brisk series of sessions, though their label of five years was in serious disarray. "Ichiban was starting to falter at this point," Keith acknowledges. The label would lay off half of its employees in early 1998, and as debts rose, would be unable to pay its recording artists, the smaller labels that it distributed, its vendors, or taxes; ultimately, John Abbey would be forced to use his personal credit card to pay debts. Keith remembers, "The Ichiban people came to me on the phone and said, *We know that your contract says you're supposed to get a bigger budget, but we quite honestly don't have that, and if we do another record together, it's gonna have to be for a really small budget of four grand.* Now, four grand is nothing! But I knew right away from working with Paul that four grand would cover it. If anything, we'd take home some money on the side!" Keith worked out a deal wherein the band agreed to record for the paltry sum as long as they would own the rights to licensing the record in Europe and the rest of the world.

Despite the Ichiban disorder, the summer of writing and recording at Compactor was, as Peter puts it, "idyllic." The new songs were short, catchy, and clever: Ken brought in the upbeat "Better Days" to test the guys' ragged harmonizing; Peter's "Anywhere You Go" and "Gentleman's Twist" were quirky pop tunes that could have been air-lifted from the *Hitsburg USA* sessions; "Bazooka Joe," "Dig In," and "Dance with the Ghoulman" flirted with the comic strip and B-movie-zombie worlds so dear to the guys' demented imaginations ("I'm more obsessed with 'Bazooka Joe' now than I was as a child," Peter admitted; "Ghoulman" dated to a number of songs earmarked for an original movie screenplay, a cheap horror-flick farce that he'd shopped around Hollywood in the early 1980s without success); Keith's "Smash Crash" cheekily rewrote an incident involving Marilla raining Peter's records down onto his head during a fight outside their apartment; "Blow Job" was a sleazy lounge instrumental with Gordon on sax and (an uncredited) Johnson on slide guitar; and "My Love Machine" was a noisy send-up of *Matt Helm* swinger ethos filtered through lesser Gamble and Huff soul bravado and Keith's Stooges-like riffing.

The guys barreled through a grab bag of covers at Compactor. "Don't Be a Dropout" was a ham-fisted take on 1967 James Brown; "Big Red Sunset," a muscular rendering of a Hank Ballard and the Midnighters single; "Laugh It Off," a breezy stroll through the Tams' B-side; "You Can Get Him Frankenstein," a Phil Spector–produced novelty tune by the Castle Kings that the guys were having fun opening shows with; and the rousing, Slade-like "Hand for the Band," a Mike Stoller/Jerry Lieber track from an infamous 1970 film, *The Phynx*, described by *Peep Show* as "a so-called musical-comedy about the U.S. government's attempt to rescue a slew of over-the-hill pop culture icons who've been kidnapped by an Albania dictator." In other words, a bizarre low-budget howler right up the Fleshtones' alley.

The strongest songs of the lot were, not surprisingly, autobiographical. Peter and Keith were now firmly planted in their forties and dealing with life's everyday challenges and disappointments. Keith's anthemic "I Wanna Feel Something Now" was a three-chord testament to his new sober lifestyle rededicated to rock & roll and family, and the brief "God Damn It" was a funny, concise, two-minute complaint about stoned hippies and woeful management decisions (specifically, Bruce Patron's ill-conceived 1982 U.K. tour). "My Kinda Lovin'/The Crossroads Are Coming" was a stirring medley of two tunes, Peter's fiery lament about prowling for someone who digs the world in the offbeat ways he does, and Keith's furious and honest account of having hit bottom and been forced to make a life-altering choice, the guys repeatedly chanting "I'm alive!" as the song hits the chorus.

With "I'm Not a Sissy," Peter wrote one of his strongest songs, an account of having grown up mocked because he couldn't play sports, and then having watched in respect at the end of the day as his father would arrive home, his inspiring working-class hands caked with dirt and dignity. Nearly twenty years earlier, Peter had written "The Way I Feel," and "I'm Not a Sissy," the guileless sing-along melody of which Peter had in his head since he was a kid, was a companion tune in directness and honesty:

I wanna know why children are so cruel.
I can recall being beat up after school, but that's all changed.

Back to the Basement

Now I can use all kinds of tools.
I don't care what you thought before, I'm not a sissy any more.

I couldn't catch, I couldn't tackle at football.
I heard them laugh every time I'd fall.
But now I know that that don't matter anymore.
I don't care what you thought before, I'm not a sissy anymore.

I never tried to understand my Daddy's dirty, greasy hands
when he finally got home.
But in the dirt for a wage I will earn my bread, until the day I'm dead.

Now I can walk into any hardware store,
Hey, there you! What you laughing for?
I'll make damn sure you never laugh no more!
I don't care what you thought before, I'm not a sissy anymore.

The Fleshtones spent the remainder of 1997 in relatively low-key style, hitting the road every six weeks or so for a handful of regionally centered shows, including a headline gig during a long, raucous day in Chapel Hill, North Carolina, at Sleazefest, another three-day garage rock extravaganza. There the guys enjoyed the southern sun, all-day barbecue, and hanging and drinking with their friends in Southern Culture on the Skids. In early December, the band flew to Italy for several shows, their third visit to the country in less than twelve months, and in between Peter was invited by old friend Jon Weiss to host the first annual Cavestomp! in New York City. Cavestomp! was high-profile event that would eventually include as an organizer Little Steven Van Zandt, Bruce Springsteen's guitarist, who would within three years expand the festival ambitiously, first into a series of New York area monthly shows, then into an Internet radio show and larger, national festivals and competitions.

More Than Skin Deep, the Fleshtones' fourteenth album and to Peter's ears the band's masterpiece, was released on January 13, 1998. The *Billboard* Top 200 must have looked like a roster from another galaxy at this point, starred as it was by the likes of Celine Dion, Chumbawamba, and the Backstreet Boys. On *Billboard*'s Modern Rock Tracks Chart, Green Day, Pearl Jam, Everclear, Matchbox 20, and Smashmouth muscled the Fleshtones away with ease. There were seismic rumblings undetected by the guys' oddly tuned ears: while they were recording *More Than Skin Deep*, a young married couple in Michigan changed their last names, picked color-coded outfits, and became the White Stripes, and within months a few private prep school kids would start jamming up on the Upper East Side of Manhattan and within a year dub themselves the Strokes. Aided and abetted by talent, hype, hard work, and connections (and, in the case of the Strokes, bucks) both bands would at the dawn of the next century launch a Neo Garage scene. The Fleshtones would be left hapless at the velvet rope.

"We were getting into a period where I felt personally affronted by the fact that we were the most forgotten band in the world, ignored, passed over, erased from history," Peter says. "The title, which some people didn't understand, states that our interest and our love and our involvement with this music is more than skin deep. It's not just nonsense that we're this garage band. We *love* this, and after twenty-five years, it was a way of life for us." Taking stock of younger and like-minded bands on the festival circuit and from the stages of Cavestomp!, Peter felt as if the Fleshtones were again being issued an enjoinder from a neglectful, capricious industry. "I looked at it as rising to a challenge," Peter acknowledges. Keith dedicated the record to Nascha (inaugurating a tradition on subsequent Fleshtones releases), and in a sly in-joke the guys wrote in the notes that "No LA-type session cats have been flown in to play the Fleshtones' instruments for them on this recording," a none-too-subtle reference to the 1980 *Up-Front* sessions. In the homemade spirit of the enterprise, Marilla posed for the album cover wearing only a wig and clutching a pair of maracas and a bottle of Jack Iron rum, the album's title projected onto her back in a Pop Art splash.

The thirty-two minutes of *More Than Skin Deep* (proudly presented in "Superpanoramasound") recaptured the nervous energy of young Fleshtones, and the album received positive reviews, many critics and fans comparing the album to *Roman Gods* and *Hexbreaker!* High-circulation glossy *Entertainment Weekly* wrote, "Leave it to those battle-scarred vets to make the most bitter party record of the year—and one of the most compelling," and MTV.com remarked that "Even after all these years, you couldn't ask for a better party record—basic, high-energy, sarcastic, and an all-around blast. Turn it up and have a beer." Writing in Consumable Online, Bill Holmes observed, "It's apparent that this record was not destined for widespread airplay. One listen to the opening track 'I'm Not a Sissy' and you know that's a GOOD thing. Cheesy keyboards, harmony vocals that don't quite align (but work anyway) and determined rhythm guitar frame the earnest vocals of Peter Zaremba, and if there were a better way to indoctrinate a newcomer to the beauty that is 'garage,' please tell me." *Maximum Ink*'s Claude Zacharly wrote that the record "is the best Fleshtones LP ever," that "over the course of their 20+ years together, these gray-hairs have evolved into a genre all their own." Concluded Zacharly: "This record is for real."

Not all notices were so splendid. Some listeners scratched their heads over the old-fashioned sound and wondered if the band wasn't simply recycling ideas. Writing on Allmusic, Stephen Thomas Erlewine was characteristic of the more even responses to *More Than Skin Deep*:

> The Fleshtones haven't changed at all in their 20 years together, which is both for better and for worse. On one hand, there's nobody—nobody—that delivers retro-garage raunch as consistently enjoyable as these guys. On the other hand, there isn't much stylistic variation between their albums, which means almost all of their records—especially the latter-day efforts, after the group's raw energy settled down a little bit—are interchangeable. A few of the songs are great, a few are terrible, many simply make the grade. If you've been following the group for any length of time, you won't be surprised and you won't be disappointed. If you haven't heard any of their other records, you may wonder what the fuss is about.

Peter had far more urgent matters on his mind than the reception for the new album. He and Marilla were closing in on their cherished adoption of an infant boy.

"We had put off having a child for so long, and we were in our forties," Peter says. "We were always one step behind the curve as far as how evasive we wanted to be." Stress, he adds knowingly, "really works against success." Peter and his wife resolved to look abroad, specifically to Russia, for adoption possibilities. "We wanted to do it the best way we possibly could. The American adoption laws at that time were going through a very strange, dubious, New Age phase where the laws were being challenged. We wanted the child to be *our* child, not have someone's grandmother come out of the woodwork and demand visiting rights." Also, Peter and Marilla were keen to avoid a situation "where someone would buy onto some poor pregnant girl, encourage her to have the baby, and then talk her into giving the baby up."

Peter and Marilla flew to wintry Moscow twice, in 1997 and 1998, the procedure blessedly relieved of red-tape delays. "Relatively it was no problem, but as you go through it it seems, of course, excruciatingly slow," says Peter, who with Marilla was required to face a Family Services–style interrogation in Russian court. "We were prosecuted in front of a judge. That was hard, even though I knew it was a formality." No boisterous party-animal ghosts leapt from Peter's closet, thankfully. "I was there as a *writer*. I wasn't a *rock & roller*," he smiles. "No one was showing pictures of me rolling around on the floor." Peter and Marilla brought one-year-old Sergei Zaremba home with them in March, enjoying their first spring together on the newly tender East Village sidewalks, at the swings in Tompkins Square Park, and in the renewed warmth of their Avenue A hearth. Daddy-O's life would only deepen and strengthen.

The Fleshtones were in no-man's land. Music reps had foggy notions that because the guys at one time associated with a major label and because Peter had been on MTV that the band made it. "We didn't make it!" Keith laughs. "People in the record industry were wary of us because they knew that we *didn't* make it, and people around us who don't truly know think that we *did* make it and didn't want to work with us because they thought we want too much money."

Following years of dubious booking agents, the band finally settled in with Dave Kaplan of Easy Action Booking. The San Francisco–based Kaplan was a true lover of rock & roll and very knowledgeable of the current scene and the Fleshtones' earned place. Through Kaplan's booking, the band's profile at festivals and appearances at proper venues paired with like-minded bands with good followings was secured (for the time being; in 2002 Kaplan left Easy Action, and the Fleshtones, to join the prestigious Agency Group in New York, booking the White Stripes and other buzz bands). Faced with diminishing returns on the road and taking stock of their private lives, the Fleshtones began an era of concentrated regional booking, flying to specifically selected areas of the country—the Midwest, the deep South, California, Texas, New England, etc.—renting a van, and playing a weekend's worth of shows in the area's larger cities. Drawing on dependable Friday and Saturday night crowds, and curtailing the number of demoralizing weekday off-nights, the band avoided oversaturation, lame-brain venues, and plain exhaustion. Keith's brainstorm, these limited jaunts allowed the guys to conserve their energies, pinpoint regions where the band was still popular, avoid having to arrive spent and dispirited after a two-hundred-mile drive, and minimize time spent away from family and friends.

With some exceptions—in Europe, namely, where visits by necessity often stretch to a week or more—these four-day swings would become the *modus operandi* for the Fleshtones, a band that manages to play a hundred or more shows a year to this day. "It's really hard to make ends meet, touring around the country for us," explains Bill. "Unless we get some action going with a hot new record, we're just not gonna make enough money to bust our ass for gas money. I would do it, to a point, because I'm not committed in any way. And I'd like to play more, because in New York it's so hard to practice." Ken, too, misses the longer forays and unbridled fun of extended touring, but Peter and Keith, fathers to small children, needed to reexamine their finances and their time away from home on the long, cumulative road.

1998 was satisfyingly bookended by two local residencies. Management at Nightingales, a small dive bar on Second Avenue where Patti Smith occasionally played, invited the Fleshtones for two monthlong Saturday night residencies in January and October. The guys grabbed a couple of horn players with them "onstage"—it was simply the floor, feet away from the crowded bar—and the loud, sweaty setup was reminiscent of the basement parties of yore. *Time Out* magazine sent Rob Kemp to cover the madness, and he called the Fleshtones "the most accessible classic rock & roll band currently working in New York," citing not only the Nightingales shows but an earlier gig at the Lakeside Lounge when the guys led a late-night conga line out onto Avenue B. "Places like Nightingales Bar are going to vanish soon," Kemp wrote presciently, "but until then, the Fleshtones can be relied upon to make it seem like the dive of all dives." (Ray Davies showed up at the October 3rd show, checking out the Kinks-worshipping Fleshtones from the end of the bar. "At least Ray didn't throw his beer over me," said Peter, suitably relieved.)

Invigorated by the new record, the guys hit the road in support. In April, they flew to Europe, highlighted by a show in Amsterdam with old labelmates the Cramps, and in July and August reprised the boozy mania at Sleazefest and Treblefest. In October the guys showed up at Cavestomp! again, with Peter as return host. Yet the band was again without a label. Ichiban had done their best, but the six-year association with the mid-major label was over, and the guys were going to have to hustle their recordings onto a dubious market. Keith's licensing deal with heavy-hitting Epitaph for the European distribution of *More Than Skin Deep* naturally aided that album's sales in the continent. (Epitaph also released a single, "Gentleman's Twist," pressed in five hundred copies, backed with "Red Sunset" and an alternate streak through the A-side with old pal Alan Vega on ghostly lead vocal.)

The end of the summer neared, and the guys began thinking about another covers album. They'd enjoyed recording *Fleshtones Favorites*, and Peter had scratched the surface of old and obscure tunes that he wanted to tackle. Freed from scheduling and budgeting concerns, the guys were able to drop into Compactor with relative ease. In August, following a show at the Lakeside Lounge previewing the new tunes, the guys stomped down to the basement for the their third extended visit in as many years. Highlights included Bill's first proper lead vocal on Annette Funicello's "Don't Stop Now," a rocking interpretation of the Stylistics' disco tune "Rockin' Roll Baby," Ken's blazing rip through Teenage Head's "You're Tearin' Me Apart," and a finger-snapping saunter through Mel Torme's Beat Generation–era "Comin' Home Baby." (A bizarre highlight was Peter's straight-faced read of Sammy Davis, Jr.'s "I'm over Twenty-five [But You Can Trust Me]," a solemn, kitschy Flower Power ode to closing the generation gap. Johnson was at first convinced that Peter was joking when he said he wanted to record a version.)

Near the end of the sessions, Peter brought in a quickly written tune that came to him so suddenly that he had to get arrangement assistance from Keith over the phone that very night. "Hitsburg USA" was a two-minute rip celebrating the guys' love of American music, a smoking performance from the band that captures the spirit and mayhem of rock & roll in breakneck fashion. Epitaph balked at releasing it as a single, so Peter happily tacked it onto the end of the new all-covers album.

In September, Bill turned fifty, an old man by rock & roll standards. The roustabout began living full-time in Peter's mother-in-law's house in the Brooklyn Heights neighborhood, acting as Amanda Palmer's general handyman and watchman as well as her "model and muse." (A painter and collage artist, Palmer told the *New York Times* that for twenty years she'd listened to the Fleshtones' music while she worked, but after Bill moved in with her, "You can't play a musician his own music." Added Palmer regretfully, "He won't play for me because he doesn't want to disturb the neighbors.") Onstage, Bill was playing more energetically and propulsively then ever, the occasional show begun white-faced and hungover ending in sweaty, beaming glory. He enjoyed living in Brooklyn and his daily visits to the Greenpoint Tavern, where he became a smiling regular, laughing with his hands around a giant Styrofoam mug of Budweiser, talking politics, watching the Mets, playing air drums to songs that only he heard. Between an OTB and a hard place, Lucky Bill hit his midcentury mark with style.

Back to the Basement

After a handful of American gigs and dates in Belgium and Holland, the Fleshtones closed out the year with a New Year's Eve show at Coney Island High with the Dictators. The response to *More Than Skin Deep* had been consistently positive and, although the guys no longer counted on sizable record sales, the glad word-of-mouth from critics and fans complemented the overall renewal that the guys enjoyed, self-producing and rediscovering the pleasure of making records.

In the early 1980s, the Fleshtones had been significant influences on younger bands such as R.E.M., Dream Syndicate, and Hoodoo Gurus—indeed, Super Rock sent the latter two bands into motion. Nearly two decades later, the Fleshtones were still having this effect on groups, with the Woggles and the Swingin' Neckbreakers, among others, loudly crowing about inspiring Fleshtones shows and records that acted as illuminating signposts on the long journey of rock & roll. Washington, D.C., band Hoover's G-String was so affected after seeing the Fleshtones play that they felt compelled to write a tribute tune called "Long Live the Fleshtones." "They are the *funnest* band I have ever seen live, plain and simple," explains G-String's Jeff Reinholz. "Our tune is just a short simple burst of a song that we hoped would express a bit of the Fleshtone Formula of Fun: rock out, keep it simple, put on a show, don't take your music too god damn serious."

For Reinholz, the fun factor is the essence of the Fleshtones. And fun, he laments, "has been slowly but surely stripped away from rock & roll."

25.
We Can't Change Our Luck,
but We Can Change Your Mind

In April of 1999, Ichiban International declared bankruptcy and folded. In an unfortunate twist, the label's substantial and diverse catalog was boxed away in a warehouse while associates dealt with bankruptcy issues that would remain unresolved for years. *Powerstance, Beautiful Light, Laboratory of Sound,* and *More Than Skin Deep* were, overnight, rendered out of print: Fleshtones Luck in full action. The strongest Hexbreaker couldn't remedy the band's recorded legacy, but deep down the guys knew that any attempt to understand them by listening only to their songs is like trying to understand a great party you didn't go to by looking at the photos the next morning.

The band flew to France in March and April for a two-week swing that included a live Internet-cast from the MCM Café, and at the end of April, following a show at venerable CBGB's, flew back over the Atlantic for a series of dates in Greece and Italy, where old pal Dave Faulkner met up with them in Athens for onstage blasts through select Hoodoo Gurus, Iggy Pop, and Screaming Tribesmen tunes. The bit was reprised in July in Boston. At Sleazefest in North Carolina, Peter and Keith ended a triumphant set by grabbing a guffawing Ken, flipping him on his side, and pile-driving him through the crowd and out the front door.

We Can't Change Our Luck, but We Can Change Your Mind

Hitsburg Revisited was released on Telstar Records in April. The Epitaph deal continued to pay dividends in Europe, where the album was well distributed on both CD and vinyl. For the cover, the guys posed in front of Bill's drum set, the head emblazoned with Peter's latest Day-Glo painting of mythical hit records flying about.

Although the Fleshtones' new DIY ethic was allowing the band to record regularly, Keith was looking to fill as much of his days and nights as he could with rock & roll, his first and truest love, and he was interested in reviving and recording Full Time Men. Keith had reactivated the outfit in the early nineties with Bill, Ken, and ex-Nashville Scorcher Andy York (original guitarist Rich Thomas had bolted to the Midwest, away from New York and his growing heroin habit). Full Time Men played play sporadic gigs around New York City, and one of Keith's goals *circa* 1999 was to finally wax the band with York in the lineup.

Keith wasn't finished—"It's funny what you can do when you have energy and a clear head," he quips—and he wanted to work with Andy Shernoff again. "Andy's a brilliant songwriter," enthuses Keith. "One of the best in the U.S., an icon, almost. And I wanted to be around that." Keith brought Paul Johnson into the mix, and when an initial drummer didn't cut it he invited Bill who, as always, was happy to make some rock & roll. The guys dubbed themselves the Master Plan and very quickly became Keith's new part-time men. The two groups would duck in and out of Compactor over the next couple of years, and the Master Plan eventually cut enough material for a full-length album. Keith struck up a deal with a small indie label out of Oregon to release an EP split between Full Time Men and the Master Plan. Each lineup contributed two tracks to *The Fabulous Sounds of Coney Island*, which featured on the cover a sepia-tinted photograph by Anne of the guys roaring down the Cyclone roller coaster at Coney Island. The EP was a solid representation of Keith's work ethic and his quenchless drive to make music.

While the band was inactive the guys had to hustle to find means of support, and Peter's energy was often directed in critical efforts to earn money for his new family. His pockets nearly empty, and he and Marilla sensing that they would need a larger (read: frightfully more expensive) house in which to raise their son, Peter relied on Paul Johnson to hook him up with various oddball jobs to keep him in some green. They hooked up with a crazy Alabama transplant who scoured industrial sites for work and had Peter and Paul on major manual-labor details across the boroughs; the fellas hauled seventy-ton, heavy-duty, grease-soaked equipment out of apartment basements among other glamorous work. Meanwhile, Ken was happily watching his one-man contractor work expand across Brooklyn and into upstate, and he was able to stay in pocket money renovating apartments and houses, while Keith was socking it away with his Man-With-Van moving business, hauling everything from apartment furniture to local bands' gear all over Manhattan and Brooklyn. Bill managed to slide along rent-free and pick up small change here and there with local handyman and moving projects. The guys all commenced together on one occassion to assemble ecologically friendly "Green clocks" in a Brooklyn warehouse. Blessedly short-lived, the gig was notorious enough among local New York bands that it became memorialized in a song by the Cuccumbers. In "Musicians I Know," the Hoboken band cheerfully sings, "The guys in the Fleshtones, they make clocks"—not quite the sexy name-check a rock & roll band desires.

Wearying of dispiriting days of manual labor, Peter concentrated more on parlaying his interest in writing. With help from friends and connections in the magazine and newspaper industry, Peter began freelancing, a side job that paid well and that he maintains continually. His biggest splash came with a June 1999 article on "Rock & Roll Hair" in *GQ*, in which he outed a certain Ramone for wearing a hair piece, but most of his attention is devoted to travel writing for the *New York Daily News* and pieces for various Condé Naste glossies such as *Jane*, *Lucky*, and even *Modern Bride*. Though hounded by deadlines on the road, Peter managed to enliven the pieces with his unique voice and his considerable knowledge of the New York City area. On good assignments Peter will be flown, sometimes with family in tow, to exotic Caribbean or Mexican locations to report on food and cultural festivals, and to advise the would-be traveler on resorts and attractions. The well-paying pick up in work was a very glad distraction.

In April, Peter reluctantly made the move out of Manhattan. He and Marilla found a roomy if banged-up row house in the largely Polish working-class area of Greenpoint in Brooklyn, a mile-walk away from Keith and Ken. With much-needed financial help from in-laws, they bought the house and renovated where necessary, moving into a community that was fiercely divided between two waves of Polish immigration. McCarren Park and plenty of friendly taverns are nearby, and though Peter and Marilla missed living in an artists' community, they left the crack bags and escalating rents of the East Village behind happily.

The guys spent the summer, Ken's tenth in the band, ducking in and out of Compactor laying new tracks for the next album. In November, Peter reprised his emcee role at Cavestomp! to good times, and the guys played a well-attended four-weekend residency at Manitoba's—but everyone received a scare when Bill hit a bit of trouble. He'd spent a long night drinking at his favorite bar in Troy during Christmas when he took a backward tumble off of his stool and hit his head on a cigarette machine; a week later at a New Year's Eve show he banged his head on a low-hanging pipe downstairs at the Mercury Lounge. Woozy, Bill played the show with a crippling headache—and before long he was in the hospital. A battery of tests revealed nothing terribly serious. There would be more scares, stress tests, EKGs, and brain scans in the coming years, but a recipe for a scaled-back lifestyle didn't appeal much to Lucky Bill, who was back at the Greenpoint Tavern happily drinking through his road wages.

The graying Fleshtones warily shouldered their responsibility as Elder Statesmen to the New Garage Scene. The Mooney Suzuki, the D4, the Vines, the Hives, and other shaggy-haired bands were assaulting stages small and large, mining source material that the Fleshtones had stood knees-deep in for decades. Most journalists and reviewers were quick to toss the Fleshtones props while writing wide-eyed about the scene's new energy and momentum, even as some of the bands tagged with the garage label (the Strokes and the White Stripes, especially) bore little resemblance to the Fleshtones, save for sweat and loud guitars.

But here and there the guys were shakily propped up as influences. A reviewer in the *Washington Post* described the White Stripes' hit "Fell in Love with a Girl" as "Fleshtones-like." And another *Post* reviewer offered an interesting historical take: "Want to know what the Strokes will sound like in 25 years? The Fleshtones show . . . might give you an idea. . . . But the Strokes comparison probably isn't a fair one as the Fleshtones certainly have a lot more fun on their albums and in live performances." To most garage bands rocking in the twenty-first century, the Fleshtones were has-beens from budget bins, grainy 1980s-era MTV relics whose entire catalog was out of print. When asked about the Fleshtones as an influence, Sammy James of the Mooney Suzuki shrugs his shoulders. "I am thoroughly unfamiliar with them," he admits. "I don't have any of their records and couldn't name a song of theirs. None of us ever really listened to the Fleshtones."

What did the Fleshtones launch into the New Garage scene of 2001? A record that sounded as if it were built on the cheap in a hobby shop. Cobbled together from visits to Compactor and a one-off session in Paris, *Solid Gold Sound* is the most democratic Fleshtones record—every band member sings lead at least once—but despite Rodney Mills' mastering job and the aural Band-Aids applied by Johnson, the overall thin sound destined the album to be tossed in Peter's "Best Laid Plans" file, which was now bulging. Sounding a bit like *More Than Skin Deep* after a shower and a change of shirt, the album energetically wears different styles, from Latino-esque funk ("Line Check") and generic Elvis-travelogue ("Baja Weekend") to a lonesome cowboy paean to fatherhood ("Daddy-O") and a gospel-inflected rave-up ("Love's in the Grave"). Strewn throughout was self-affirming gang-singing ("Sound Check 2001") and yet another tribute to Bazooka Joe. In "Whatever It Takes," the guys fantasized about Casablanca Records chairman Neil Bogart being President of the United States, but they were all too mindful of reality.

The title track, considered by Peter one of the best songs he's written, is a midpaced dance-groove paying testament to an adolescence of record stores and a lifetime of rock & roll's saving grace. ("When I crank it up," he barks at his critics, "I can't hear what you say!") Held aloft with a ringing guitar line, the celebratory song always quickened up onstage, a grinning Peter hopping atop his galloping love for feel-good music. The gaudy seeds sown in that tune burst into fruity flower in "Good Good Crack," the first pure disco song that Peter has written. A full-on floor thumper, the tune leaps between tribute and kitsch, the super-tight rhythm section and exciting R&B changes grooving beneath Paul Johnson's inept attempts at imitating Chuck Berry's jive-voice. In a perfect world, the thinly recorded tune would've been remixed in High Gloss and sent on spec to Manhattan's nightclubs, but the guys had gotten used to peering in their pockets for small change and couldn't have financed a remix.

Well-trained Fleshtones fans may have recognized the campy falsetto in the chorus of "Solid Gold Sound": Marek Pakuski was back in the fold, invited down to Compactor by his old friend Keith. Marek had sobered up and quit heroin in 1988 during Robert Warren's final days with the Fleshtones, and endured some lean years staving off temptations by driving limos and doing sound at clubs, salving his wounds after a busted-up marriage. By the end of the 1990s he'd found himself strong and clean, working in the soaring computer/Internet industry and spending his weekends skiing or surfing. He lived for years in a roomy apartment on Fourteenth Street, peering over that fabled boundary into the recklessness and chaos of the East Village, fitting for a man who was always more of a looker than a doer. (He still loves music, though he eyes his guitars more often than he plays them.) He and Keith slowly renewed their friendship, warmed by regular rooftop barbecues. Before long, Marek found himself in front of a microphone in a cramped borough basement with Keith and Peter, rubbing his eyes to chase away the Whitestone hallucinations.

Solid Gold Sound was released in February (a month that saw the ageless *Blast Off!* sessions released yet again, on vinyl, in the U.S. and Spain). Telstar, holding their nose at the sound, had rejected *Solid Gold Sound*, as did several other small labels, so Keith financed a modest distribution deal with Blood Red, which released the album on vinyl and CD. Reviews in major trade magazines were unsurprisingly scarce, but fans and critics on the Web weighed in, Allmusic's notice being fairly typical: "The Fleshtones have struck gold with many fans of punk-infused retro-rock, and the meat of this disc will do nothing to dissuade them." Listeners losing patience with Peter's stereo-separation fixation were unaware that *Solid Gold Sound* would be the last Fleshtones release so-recorded: Paul Johnson was finished with Compactor. He'd made the decision to move back down south to be nearer to family, and he had begun taking apart his loving basement studio the previous fall as the guys were finishing up the album. By the end of 2000, the Compactor Era was officially over, the boxes of junky tubes and reel-to-reels on their way back to Tidewater.

The Silver Jubilee Tour. . . .

The summer of 2001 was darkened by an especially sad loss, the death of Joey Ramone in April. The guys bowed their heads, opened a beer, and added Joey to the lengthening roll call of departed friends.

Meanwhile, the Fleshtones were aware that their own golden anniversary was approaching. Numb expectations and financial duress made any kind of major celebrating out of the question, and Paris wasn't gonna throw them a party this time around. In between long days of odd-jobs and ordinary living, the guys trusted that Dave Kaplan would secure them dependable weekend jaunts, whatever milestone celebrations there'd be coming in the ordinary ways: through long van rides, road food, and half-filled clubs and bars. In June, the Fleshtones embarked on a modest five-city tour. They met in front of Keith's apartment, kissed their wives goodbye, pooled their gas money, loaded up their gear in the rented van, and squeezed in a box or two of merchandise. They headed north to Buffalo, and then west to Detroit, Chicago, Cleveland, and Columbus. Each city promised a reliable draw, and the mood in the van was good. With Keith doing much of the driving, the guys settled in to their road routine *circa* the twenty-first century: hours of talk radio, pit-stops for Tim Hortons donuts, and quiet consumption of *Conservative Chronicle* and Jesse Ventura's latest tome, each of which was passed around. Ken, fiercely apolitical, declined, plugging up his ears while trying to lose himself in *National Geographic* or *Natural History*. Idle talk drifted to the energy crunch, to Timothy McVeigh, to California deregulation . . . the days of long, wild drunken drives steadied by a tour driver long behind the fellas, their livers and mental states all the better.

Hotel rooms weren't standard luxuries anymore: more often than not, the guys gratefully crashed at the homes of promoters or club owners, and were by now used to the routine of waking up hungover and disoriented on someone else's floor. When a cheap hotel room was available, they slept two to a bed, bad news for whomever bunked with lanky Bill. Waking up to porn on a grainy TV, anonymous stains on bed sheets, unrecognizable glop dripping from bathroom ceilings: Happy Anniversary, Fleshtones.

. . . The Mohawk Place in Buffalo was semifilled and energetic. The guys broke out tight versions of the Music Explosion's "Jack in the Box" and Elvis' "Spinout" and surrounded them with a handful of well-received tunes from *Solid Gold Sound*. . . . In a self-effacing bit of rewriting, Keith sang the line "I think this record will be a smash!" from "Whatever It Takes" as "Even if this record's not a smash." . . . In Chicago, they played in front of a good-sized Friday crowd at the Empty Bottle on the city's west side, the only downer coming from overzealous fans in the front who repeatedly knocked Peter's mike stand back into his mouth during the encores. Midtune, Peter grabbed one of the offenders by his sweaty shirt and screamed at him over the din to cut it out: "I got no medical plan!" . . . The guys ended the show by ducking out of the club through the front door, still playing their wireless guitars, hopping into the van parked across the street, and peeling away down Western Avenue smiling and waving through the windows while a crowd outside hooted. . . . In Cleveland, the guys began the night with beers at a blue-collar Slovenian bar where Peter opened a card he'd been carrying, a Father's Day note from four-year-old Sergei. . . . At the Beachland Ballroom, Peter had a dozen sweaty people, including Ken and Keith, lying prone on the floor during "The Way I Feel" while he hollered and testified and later, atop the bar, he noticed a couple of shrugging people leaving the club during the show; stung, Peter pointed at the closing door and, half-grinning and half-embarrassed, said to the remaining crowd: "They think we're making fun of rock & roll! We *are* rock & roll! And so are *you*! The losers just left!" Cheers all around. . . . At the end of the set Bill spotted a vacuum cleaner in the backstage kitchen area, grabbed it, spun on his heels, and proceeded to vacuum the area in front of the stage while Peter followed him with a piercing drill-whistle and the crowd hooted at the clean-up boys. . . . In Columbus the show ended with push-ups on the floor by Keith and Ken and a challenge to any fan to top 'em (no one tried) and in a final sweaty flourish an impromptu Flamenco dance by the two guitarists on top of the bar while the final notes faded and a few fans rolled their eyes or guffawed and merchandise flew out the door. . . .

Amidst all of the goofy shenanigans, the loud rock & roll, the local friends offering food and shelter, and the hungover bleariness, the show in Detroit at the Magic Stick stood out as both the nadir and the peak of this brief Midwest tour, and as such is a barometer of the fate that has been dealt the hard-working Fleshtones. They arrived in the Motor City following a brief holdup with Canadian customs at the Niagara Falls border where Ken, absent his green card, inspired officials to pull the van over and search the gear, much to Keith's irritation. Luckily for all concerned Bill wasn't hiding any beer bottles in his drum kit this time around. In Detroit they gave a brief three-song performance and an interview on WDET radio. A few hours later they met for dinner at the restaurant attached to the club where they were asked to make a guest list for the show. Peter sat and stared at the blank sheet of paper for several minutes. As the guys ordered, he began to idly doodle an oversized foot with little faces for toes. Keith glanced at the sheet deficient of friends' names, sighing at Peter's childlike drawing.

"This is what we have to show for twenty-five years?" he asked no one in particular.

A few hours later, Peter recognized the dread growing in his belly: he stood in a venue nearly empty with an hour left before show time, an all too familiar scene. His mood darkened visibly, and he disappeared backstage after a perfunctory soundcheck. "This is Peter's career, after all," says Ken. "And let's face it: he likes being the center of attention." Peter was going to have to drag himself through another show in front of a handful of people, tough circumstances to stomach for any frontman, and word circulated that a trendy and more popular band was playing across town at a sold-out venue. Indeed, it felt as if the Fleshtones were shouting particularly hoarsely into the wind on this night in June of 2001: in a couple of weeks the White Stripes would release their career-defining *White Blood Cells* album, and in retrospect that Detroit duo's imminence was stealing the spotlight from the garage-rocking Fleshtones, who were once again forced to create fire in a damp cell.

They hit the stage at ten o'clock with a sprightly "Solid Gold Sound" and there was literally no one in front. A sparse crowd had congregated near the back bar, and the cavernous Magic Stick felt empty. The Fleshtones might as well have been at rehearsal. For the first half-dozen songs, they played to no one.

Halfway through the set, his eyes glinting with desperation, Peter halted proceedings. Waving at his band, laboring to disguise how pissed off and humiliated he was feeling, intuiting the need to shake things up if only to shake things up, he turned to the small knot of people near the back. "Hey! C'mon up!" He waved at them. "C'mon up." Then he barked: "I'll give you the intimate fucking evening that you want!"

He turned to Ken. "Kenny, play your tune, play that folk song of yours," he said sarcastically. "That must be what they want!" Peter was referring to "Dreaming About Work," Ken's midpaced, poppy lament of the working class. Fucking folk song.

Ken rushed to the mike, unprepared, and the band lurched into the tune. Smiling, Peter jumped into the barren pit and started moving, dancing, glad-handing the couple of people who'd answered his invite.

Something jelled. Within a song or two, Bill's and Keith's smiles looked less forced, the guys started to play with a confident, looser feeling. Song by song more people moved toward the stage, though in hipster stubbornness most refused to come too close. The second half of the Fleshtones' show was essentially played off of the stage, as Ken and Keith roamed the floor and Peter hopped up onto the top of the back bar. *If you can't beat 'em. . . .* There was no encore on this night, though the show dissolved with grins on everyone's faces and Peter standing on the bar indulging in a sweaty discourse with a few passionate fans about the merits of Motown and the grimy charms of Detroit. The last notes faded and, alone on the stage, Bill stood up from his drums, grabbed a white towel, mopped his brow, Keith headed back to dismantle the gear, Ken rushed to the merchandise table. . . . Across town, some group was whipping up a packed house in a frenzy. At the Magic Stick, the heroic Fleshtones were testifying and anointing a small crowd.

A night that began with no one in front of the stage ended with the Fleshtones' merchandise table surrounded by beaming, dollar-waving fans. *We can't change our luck, but we can change your mind. . . .*

Back home in New York, Peter, Keith, Bill, and Ken settled back into their domestic routines, spreading the tour's lean guarantees among themselves. The rest of the summer and fall was uneventful but for a late-July treat when the Fleshtones played the Greatest Bar on Earth at Windows on the World, atop the World Trade Center. They played two sets on a "Spi-Fi Friday," most notable for a couple of songs featuring a harmonica-blowing Gordon Spaeth on the cusp of his fiftieth birthday. It took awhile for the crowd to get into the show, but by the end of the night the Fleshtones handed a group generally ignorant of Super Rock a bar- and table-treading good time, silliness high above the East River and a glittering Manhattan. Forty-six days later, Windows on the World was gone. The Fleshtones were one of the last bands to play at the World Trade Center.

26.
Fun, Truth, and Tradition:
Forever Fleshtones

"We have no plans to change, that's for sure.
What would be the point?"

—Peter Zaremba

Following a New year's Eve gig at Manitoba's, the Fleshtones laid low for a quiet year. 2002 saw the boys mostly at home, writing songs and leaving New York for the occasional five-city weekend, the new shows featuring Keith and Ken playing each other's guitar during "The Dreg" and rotating together like some Coney Island sideshow attraction.

In June, Keith corralled Rick Miller after a Southern Culture on the Skids show at Maxwell's, and, in a late-night chat that would pay dividends, interested him in producing the next Fleshtones record. In the fall Keith swung a record deal with Yep Roc, a North Carolina indie label that was building a strong reputation. Formed in 1997 by childhood pals Glen Dicker and Tor Hansen, the label grew out of Redeye, a distributor, and now bulges with a roster including, as well as many new acts, artists like Nick Lowe, Jason and the Scorchers, Paul Weller, and Robyn Hitchcock, who hint at Dicker and Hansen's affection for the seventies and eighties.

"Tor and I were both in bands growing up and we opened a few shows here and there for the Fleshtones," says Dicker, whose love for Super Rock was ignited in the mid-eighties as a student at Gettysburg College. Dicker had made a roadtrip with friends to Washington, D.C., to catch a predictably wild Fleshtones show at the 9:30 Club and, shortly thereafter, with the devil-may-care ingenuity typical of a college kid, had a brainstorm. "We'd secured some funds from our college radio station to throw a party at a fraternity house I was in," he remembers. "And we decided to hire the Fleshtones as a special event. They came and put on an incredible show. A couple times the house blew a fuse so the lights went out, and of course all of their equipment. But the band somehow managed to keep rocking through this and everyone was completely into it. It was light out before anyone actually went to sleep. I think one of the guys actually slept in the creek behind the house."

Peter remembers the frat party as so infamous "that it went down in local history as the 'Gettysburg Address' of the Fleshtones," he laughs. "The one great frat party that we ever played. We were in the living room and they locked the doors because the police were trying to get in to unplug us—and the police came in through the windows right behind us as we were playing." Dicker was impressed at the amount of imbibing that went on before, during, and after the long, fun night for the boys of *ATO* House, and at the crackerjack, near-chaotic show that resulted. The next day he said to the guys, "When I get out of school I'm gonna start a record label so I can sign the Fleshtones!" Two decades later, he did just that. His love for the Fleshtones had never waned, and he was happy to ink them to a deal. The Yep Roc alliance rescued the band from having to hustle low-budget labels and provided them with a solid team of publicists and media folk, a support system that they'd been lacking for years. After signing with Yep Roc, the Fleshtones' visibility increased and their shows generally drew larger crowds.

In January, the Fleshtones headed down south to Rick Miller's studio in North Carolina, Miller providing vintage gear and equipment, a place to crash, and copious servings of Southern barbecue. There they swiftly recorded an album's worth of material, including "Destination, Greenpoint," Peter's loving ode to his new neighborhood. Other highlight's were Keith's rousing "Are You Ready for the Mountain"; Peter's sardonic and politically incorrect send-up of trendy feminism, "Right on, Woman"; rips through the Searchers' "Alright" and Led Zeppelin's "Communication Breakdown"; and "Do You Swing?," the latest in a decades-long string of party invitations. Yep Roc released *Do You Swing?* in April. Included in the media package was a handwritten note from Peter challenging any band to top the Fleshtones' live act, which these days included an all-out, old-school push-up competition in front of the stage at the end of sweaty encores. All comers were welcomed; the Iron Men were usually victorious.

Reviews were nearly unanimous in their praise for the album and especially for the Fleshtones' longevity in the face of a fair-weather recording industry. Jeff Clark in *Stomp and Stammer* magazine wrote, "I've long held fast in my conviction that the Fleshtones are one of rock 'n' roll's all-time greatest bands," ending the review by calling the Fleshtones "a national treasure." *Billboard* also weighed in with an effusive notice:

> You have to love this band. After some 25 years, these hard-lovin', apparently hard-drinkin' guys from Queens, N.Y., are still bangin' out vintage, backbeat-driven, gang-vocal-laden guitar rock recalling the Cramps and a blusier, mainstream-leaning Iggy. It's the kind of stuff that makes you want to get sloppy drunk and dance your ass off. And, really, what else can you ask for from a rock'n'roll record?

By the end of the year, "Destination, Greenpoint" had made the "Hot List" in *Rolling Stone*, was named "Best New York Song" by *Slate*, was rotating on Little Steven's Garage radio/Internet show, and was rocking the blue-collar Polish laborers and twenty-something hipsters at the Greenpoint Tavern in Williamsburg. *Do You Swing?* was named on Jim DeRogatis' *Chicago Sun-Times* Best of 2003 list, and even scored two votes on *Village Voice*'s Pazz & Jop 03.

The kudos were certainly appreciated by Yep Roc, even if the album's sales didn't threaten the Top 40. ("The Fleshtones have always delivered on record for us and we've been happy with what we've accomplished sales-wise with the band," says Dicker. "I'd always want to sell more of something, but we are realistic about what can be done.") The guys supported the new album with the usual regional tours, a highlight being a show at the Virgin Megastore in Manhattan at Union Square, a block—and a lifetime—away from Peter's 1970s art-school loft. In August, Ken injured his playing hand at a construction site, and Peter's house flooded biblically; shows were cancelled, and in this ignominious way the Fleshtones closed out a productive year, but not before a December gig with the Dictators at CBGB's celebrating that storied club's thirtieth anniversary. The show was packed, and thick snow fell outside, making for an idyllic winter cityscape along the now-restored and gentrified Bowery.

Snow had fallen the night Peter first ventured in CBGB's more than a quarter century before, a long evening of fun and noise ending with Peter tobogganing down a considerably riskier avenue. A quiet bookend to an odyssey twenty-five years young.

In January, Bill's father died after a long illness. Grieving, and soberly reassessing his living situation, Bill moved back up to Troy, where he now lives in the house in which he was born and raised. The cut-rate beds and showers in the Greenpoint YMCA are a short bus ride away when touring calls, and Bill found himself at the check-in desk often in 2004: the Fleshtones played Europe on no less than four occasions, spreading the word and hawking *Do You Swing?* from every table. In February the guys headed to Scandinavia for the first time in a generation, hitting the stage in Norway in memorable fashion: "Guess what?" Peter barked. "We're back, baby!" In March they visited Spain for an eight-city tour, avoiding the international chaos of the Madrid terrorist bombings that killed over two hundred people; the Fleshtones were three hours south in Gijon, and they hightailed it out of there. They screwed their courage up to head back to Greece in April for a whirlwind weekend with the Seeds, and then to France in May for a nine-city tour.

In August, a few weeks before Peter turned fifty, the Fleshtones were invited to join nearly forty bands, including Bo Diddley, Iggy and the Stooges, and the Strokes, to play at Little Steven's Underground Garage Festival at Randall's Island in Manhattan. The behemoth event was widely publicized and well-covered in newspapers, magazines, Internet sites, and blogs across the country. The Fleshtones played early in the day; each group (save for the big-name acts at the end of the day) was allowed three songs and afforded a rotating stage. The guys tore through "Right on, Woman," "Destination, Greenpoint," and, as a surprise, the Hoodoo Gurus' "Like Wow— Wipeout" with an invited Dave Faulkner singing lead. The daylong event was a tornado of hectic preparations and execution and, due to their early appearance, the Fleshtones suffered from a low-profile as well as an improperly working stage. But the guys were happy to have been invited by the scene-making Little Steven (who would continue to slot the Fleshtones on his garage rock multiband revues) and they dug hanging out in the East River sunshine and in the tents with old friends—and sticking around as darkness fell to see the Stooges put on a devastating show.

The renewed Fleshtones rode out the year touring and writing and arranging songs. In January they headed down to Rick Miller's studio for another week of recording, and in April west to Detroit to record with Jim Diamond at Ghetto Recordings. The dual-studio approach paid off nicely, and by the spring the guys had a new album in the can.

An event in between those two sessions, however, cast a pall and a long shadow. On March 8, 2005, on a wintry, blizzardy night, Gordon Spaeth committed suicide. He suffered a psychotic episode at the Prince George Hotel, destroying his room and his possessions, and leapt to his death after onsite EMS, in response to calls from neighbors, knocked down his door. In a tragic twist to an oft-repeated tale, Gordon had placed himself out of reach of the kind of help that—in this case—might literally have saved his life.

The unfriendly elements outside of his apartment window had likely mirrored the storm inside of him. Gordon had, at fifty-three, settled into a comfortable routine. He was living near his beloved Tin Pan Alley, avoiding drugs and alcohol, lifting weights, writing short stories and reading them at the YMCA, and occasionally giving harmonica lessons and sitting in on saxophone with the Fleshtones and the Waldos. But the lifetime strain of mental illness and addictions proved wearing for Gordon, who wore his after-hours, mock-scowling, smirking second-banana *noir* too well. He'd last played with his old friends in 2001, last recorded with them in 1998—and now he lives on eternally in alcohol-soaked memories of a social misfit who dressed and acted the part of the sincere, aging JD with a heart of gold, in memories of his wicked sense of humor, his razor-sharp asides, his personal generosity, and, above all, his love for retro fashion, R&B, and rock & roll.

Peter, Keith, Bill, and Ken, with their wives, attended Gordon's wake on the fourteenth. Also paying their respects were Marek, Andy Shernoff, Phast Phreddie Patterson, and Walter Lure, as well as other fans, friends, and family members. Gordon was laid to rest in Queens.

Though deeply saddened and in grief following Gordon's suicide, the guys steadied themselves for the April sessions with Diamond. The road called as always, and in June they flew to Stockholm for the popular and well-attended Gearfest Festival. Yep Roc released *Beachhead* in August (among the promotional pushes was a special feature at Budweiser's Web site, certainly a career zenith for Lucky Bill). Highlights on the record included "Pretty Pretty Pretty," Keith's anthemic ode to the street-walking beauties outside his apartment, and a few statements of purpose, "Bigger and Better," "I Am What I Am," and the self-explanatory "Serious (About Not Being Serious)."

Within the year the guys' past would revisit them in pleasant ways: Sanctuary Records reissued *Marty Thau Presents 2X5* on CD, and Rhino selected "The Girl from Baltimore" and "The World Has Changed" for inclusion on the mammoth *Children of Nuggets: Original Artyfacts from the Second Psychedelic Era 1976–1995* box set, a nice B-day present for Keith's fiftieth. The following spring saw the release of a DVD, *Back in the Day: Live from Hurrah's New York City*, a multiband compilation featuring the guys at their sweaty, late-seventies best, onstage with Action Combo in manic perpetuity. Meanwhile, reviews for *Beachead* were glorious. Ken Tucker spoke highly of the album on National Public Radio's *Fresh Air*, and in *Entertainment Weekly* Tom Sinclair raved, "Man, what fortitude: These guys started out in '76 as a proudly retro, party-hearty garage band and have yet to alter their philosophy or approach one whit. Their single-mindedness pays off once again on this stompingly satisfying set."

In the *Chicago Sun-Times*, loyal supporter Jim DeRogatis said simply: "A case can be made that The Fleshtones are the greatest garage band in history."

The Push-Up Men continued to write, plug in, hustle, grin, and grimace around the world in 2006, marking their thirtieth anniversary in May as the only band from the mid-seventies New York City punk/New Wave scene without an inactive year. The Fleshtones even outlasted CBGB's, which closed its epochal grimy front door in October.

Onstage, a perennial highlight was Ken's "I Want the Answers" from *Beachhead*, a tune that succinctly sums up the Fleshtones' careerlong joys and frustrations as well as any song that the band's recorded. Against a bopping pop beat the guys sing, with Peter hoarsely out in front:

I wanna know why money doesn't just fall down from the trees
I wanna know why fame doesn't just blow in with the breeze
Why do the bad things feel so good
when the good things find another neighborhood?
Why does the upside always bring me down
while the downside finds me lifting off the ground?

I wanna know why if I'm so good I didn't die young

Sweat

I wanna know why, maybe then I'd have me a Number One
Why does everybody wanna steal my act?
And then I waste all these years, I'll never get 'em back
Why does everybody wanna bow at my feet
When I can't earn enough just to make ends meet?

Gimme, c'mon and gimme the proof
Gimme, c'mon and gimme the truth

I want the answers,
just give me the answers,
I want 'em right now.

In 1984, on the *Cutting Edge* MTV program, Peter spoke about what drove him to lead his band. He surprised himself with his own honesty, discussing what drives him to this day as a man, as well as a performer. "I try to do something I've never done before," he said. "I try not to be afraid of anything, not be afraid to jump anywhere, to do anything, to ask anyone to do something. I guess I'm just trying to make up for the first twenty years of my life when I was always embarrassed, when I had no friends. Onstage, I don't want to ever have to be embarrassed again. I don't want anyone in the audience to ever have to be embarrassed again."

The Fleshtones' long career—what Peter himself has half-jokingly, half-bitterly called an Odyssey to Nowheresville—has been a worldwide campaign waged on large and small stages before large and small crowds to reclaim for everyone that embarrassment from the wrenching days of adolescence, to reclaim moving for the sake of moving, grinning for the sake of grinning, sweating for the sake of sweating. Fun for the sake of fun. They're probably on the road now.

Epilogue

Here are a couple more stories.

It's 1985 or 1986 in Washington, D.C. I'm driving the short distance from George Washington University to the 9:30 Club with my then-girlfriend and a couple of buddies, Rob and Gary. We'd left a little earlier than usual to get to get tickets: down Pennsylvania Avenue past the White House (back in the days when you could drive past) and the Old Executive Building. In my lousy '72 Datsun we're blasting *Hexbreaker!* in the tape deck and trying to figure out the lyrics: *It's a nude disco, baby??* As we pass the famous, long-gone Old Ebbitt's Grill on E Street we recognize a silhouette in the front door: it's Keith Streng, glancing down the street.

Very drunk and having fun, I swing the car over a lane. I don't know what I'm going to do; I figure we'll just yell out the window and drive on. Gary chimes in that we ought to at least offer him a ride to the club, which is a couple of blocks away. We pull up, and Rob—by far the most gregarious of the three of us—jumps out of the car before I've stopped it and runs straight up to Keith. Rob cuts a tall, imposing figure, and Keith must have no idea what's happening, some car screeching up and a stranger hopping out and running toward you in the middle of the night.

Keith's response? A shudder? An involuntary lurch for protection? Hardly: a huge grin—bigger than ours—that floors us. He immediately steps into the street before Rob offers him a lift, hops into the car, and squeezes into the backseat next to Gary. He cocks an ear to the speakers (at that moment playing "BRAINSTORM,"), snorts, wrinkles his face, and says, "Shit, I don't want to hear that!" I turn down the tape and the four of us exchange drunken small-talk and before I know it we're at the club.

"Thanks, guys," Keith says as he hopped out. "Hey, you know you're on the guest list!"

The Fleshtones once played Ritchie Coliseum at the University of Maryland with Gang of Four. I'd thought that that was a bit of a curious bill—I had records by both bands but listening to one rarely inspired the playing of another. At any rate, there was no question who was opening up for whom at this college gig. I wasn't at the show, but my brother was; I hadn't seen the Fleshtones yet, though I was starting to dig their records on local WHFS. The Fleshtones hit the stage and played a great gig, spirited and just beyond explanation. As the show was lifting to its anthemic close, Zaremba jumped onto the Gang of Four's considerable (and, I'm guessing, considerably expensive) speaker stacks and started duck-walking and shimmying and dancing and hollering. The crowd loved it, but something bothered the Gang's roadies and soundmen, who tried desperately to put an end to this spontaneity by catching any Fleshtones eye and giving a none too subtle, across-the-throat "cut" signal.

No Fleshtone responded, or noticed. Within seconds the sound was off, the lights were up, Zaremba was alone on the stacks. The band grumbled, echoing the larger anger buzzing from the confused if titillated crowd, Peter hopped down, and they slowly left the stage. My brother ended up leaving before the Gang of Four even got onstage, and he and his friends found their way to a McDonald's on Route 1, a good mile or so from the Coliseum. There was no real reason he should have noticed five Fleshtones standing there in line—they looked like regular guys ordering burgers and Cokes. They were digging into their pockets for change; it was maybe an hour after the gig was truncated. "Hey, man," my brother hesitantly offered to Zaremba. "What a drag. What just happened." Zaremba just smiled, and shrugged.

For the Fleshtones it's never been about money or fame or the Message or egos or compromises or selling out. Perhaps to a fault, they've remained fiercely true to their self-proclaimed motto of "Fun,

Truth, and Tradition." It's always been about simply spreading a good time to anyone who wants it—record sales, half-filled clubs, embarrassment, beat-up livers, and the occasional poor spirits be damned. But how long can a party last?

The Fleshtones manifest how great, timeless rock & roll really works from the inside out; it gets into your heart and your bone marrow first and sticks there for good, and whatever trappings there may be on the outside—trendy haircuts, petulant pouts, narrow ties, or flannel shirts—don't matter. The Fleshtones certainly never bothered with altering their style for mass-marketability. For them what mattered was the sweat, the American beat, the tom-drum dragged out and pounded on the beery floor, the on-mike and off-mike gang chants that anyone who's drunk more than they usually would can holler along with.

I began writing this book in 2000. I was visiting New York in July for the first of many extended visits, and I was on the roof of Keith's apartment on Bedford Avenue in Brooklyn, where the Fleshtones were gathered for an impromptu photo shoot orchestrated by Keith's wife, Anne. I was asking him what kept the band together in the face of towering odds, bad luck, hopeless trends, and self-induced body-taxing behavior. "We're all just really good friends," he said to me. "And we love to make rock & roll together." The mood was a bit subdued; something bittersweet hung in the air, and one or more of the guys was nursing a hangover. As the band variously posed against the Manhattan skyline, the Strengs' six-and-a-half-year-old daughter, Nascha, ran underfoot, careful to avoid the muck and the tar. The guys were hoping to get a good photo for *Solid Gold Sound*, which was coming out in a few months, but the midsummer light was fading fast. Anne managed to shoot one roll of film. As the sun retreated rapidly behind the Empire State Building, she gamely packed her camera and gathered up her daughter. Keith, Peter, Bill, and Ken left the roof discussing rehearsals, dinner plans, and an upcoming mini-tour in the South, enduring uncooperative daylight like it was any other roadblock in a long rock & roll story.

Peter Zaremba once remarked to *New York* magazine, "Sometimes I say, 'Lord, how long can this go on?'" Stubbornness, fickle, ever-evolving rock scenes, glossy magazines, yawning MTV or VH1, major label contracts, befuddled PR guys, hipsters and rock critics who would never be seen smiling or laughing at a rock show, Internet downloading—none of this has stopped the Fleshtones. Long after the spotlight swung off of them, long after the crowds grew sparse over lengthy, lean years, long after the backstage bacchanals thinned out and the scenesters stopped hanging around regularly, long after the next New Buzz Band began selling out venues across town, the Fleshtones kept on, as from their beginnings in that smoky Queens basement. It's been noted often that they give a hundred percent at every show, whether they're playing in front of five hundred or five. I've witnessed this firsthand, in the mid-1980s at sold-out venues, and on the road with them twenty years later when some nights they'd hit the stage and play to no one.

The Fleshtones have a new album scheduled for release in January of 2008, another grab-bag of crazed fun and loud guitars. The only thing now, it seems, that will get in the way of the Fleshtones is their collective body, graying and lined and a half-step slower, punished by decades of 4 AM epiphanies, brutal sunrises, plates of toxic road food and garbage cans of Blue Whale, by lumpy mattresses and hardwood floors. But they've got Herculean energy. And as long as Peter, Keith, Bill, and Ken strike the Powerstance and grin, they'll be plugging in.

Zaremba once told me that all people really want is for the Fleshtones to go away. He said simply: "But we're not going to."

Joe Bonomo
Autumn 2007

Appendix One
The Fleshtones Discography

Albums

Roman Gods LP/cassette (I.R.S.) 1982 CD [limited] (Eur. I.R.S.) 1990

Blast Off! cassette (ROIR) 1982 CD (ROIR) 1990 CD (ROIR/Fr. Danceteria) 1993 CD (Red Star) 1997 LP (Sp. Munster) 2001 LP (Get Hip) 2002

Hexbreaker! LP/cassette (I.R.S.) 1983

Speed Connection LP (Fr. I.R.S.) 1985

Speed Connection II: The Final Chapter LP/cassette (I.R.S.) 1985

Fleshtones vs. Reality LP/cassette/CD (Emergo) 1987

The Fleshtones: Living Legends Series CD (I.R.S.) 1989

Soul Madrid LP (Sp. Imposible) 1989

Powerstance! CD/LP/cassette (Aus. Trafalgar) 1991 CD/LP/cassette (U.K. Big Beat) 1991 CD (Naked Language/Ichiban) 1992 download (Ichiban) 2006

Forever Fleshtones LP (Gr. Hitch Hyke) 1993

Beautiful Light CD (Naked Language/Ichiban) 1994 download (Ichiban) 2006

Angry Years 1984–1986 CD (Sp. Imposible) 1994 CD (Amsterdamned) 1997

Laboratory of Sound CD (Ichiban International) 1995 LP (Gr. Hitch Hyke) 1996 download (Ichiban) 2006

Fleshtones Favorites CD (Flesh) 1997

Hitsburg USA! LP (Telstar) 1997 CD (Sp. Imposible) 1997

More Than Skin Deep CD (Ichiban International) 1998 LP (Telstar) 1998 CD/LP (Eur. Epitaph) 1999 download (Ichiban) 2006

Hitsburg Revisited CD (Telstar) 1999 CD/LP (Eur. Epitaph) 1999

Solid Gold Sound CD/LP (Blood Red) 2001 CD (Fr. Fantastika) 2001

Sweat

Do You Swing? CD/LP (Yep Roc) 2003
Beachhead CD/LP (Yep Roc) 2005

EPs

Up-Front twelve-inch (I.R.S.) 1980
"American Beat '84" + "Hall of Fame" b/w "Mean Ole' Lonesome Train" + "Super Hexbreaker" twelve-inch (Fr. I.R.S.) 1984
Live in Europe CD (Fr. Alliance Optique) 1997 [limited]

Seven-inch Singles

"American Beat" b/w "Critical List" (Red Star) 1979
"The Girl from Baltimore" b/w "Feel the Heat" (I.R.S.) 1980
"Shadow Line" b/w "F-f-fascination" (UK Criminal) 1980
"The World Has Changed" b/w " Around the World" (I.R.S.) 1981
"Shadow Line" b/w "All Around the World" (UK I.R.S.) 1981
"Chinese Kitchen" b/w "The Dreg" (Fleshtone-77) (Eur. Illegal) 1981
"Ride Your Pony" b/w "Roman Gods" (I.R.S.) 1982
"Screamin' Skull" b/w "Burning Hell" (Eur. I.R.S.) 1983
"Right Side of a Good Thing" b/w "Legend of a Wheelman" (Eur. I.R.S.) 1983
"American Beat '84" b/w "Hall of Fame" (I.R.S.) 1984
"Panic" b/w "San Francisco Girls" (UK The Next Big Thing) 1986
"Armed and Dangerous" b/w "Let It Rip" (U.K. Big Beat) 1991
"Take a Walk with the Fleshtones" b/w "One of Us" (Naked Language/ Ichiban) 1994
"Gentleman's Twist" b/w "Red Sunset" + "Gentleman's Twist" [alt] (Eur. Epitaph) 1998
"Soul Struttin'" [alt vers] + "Cara-Lin" [alt vers] b/w "Rockin' This Joint Tonight" [alt vers] + "Soul Struttin'" [alt vers] seven-inch EP (Get Hip) 2002

Twelve-inch Singles

"Roman Gods" [Dance Remix] b/w "Ride Your Pony" + "Chinese Kitchen" (I.R.S.) 1982
"Armed and Dangerous" b/w "Let It Rip" + "The Electric Mouse" (UK Big Beat) 1991 CD (UK Big Beat) 1991

CD Singles

"Armed and Dangerous" + "Let It Rip" + "The Electric Mouse" CD (Aus. Trafalgar) 1991
"Beautiful Light" + "Beautiful Light" [Big Mix] CD (Naked Language/ Ichiban) 1994
"Beautiful Light" + "Treat Me Like a Man" + "Mushroom Cloud" CD (Fr. Danceteria) 1994
"Let's Go!" CD (Ichiban International) 1995
"High on Drugs" + "Nostradamus, Jr." CD (Fr. Music Disc) 1995
"One Less Step" + "Accelerated Emotion" + "Sands of Our Lives" CD (Ichiban International) 1996

Appendix One: The Fleshtones Discography

Compilations

"Shadow Line" + "F-f-fascination," *Marty Thau Presents 2X5* LP (Red Star) 1980
CD (Sanctuary) 2005

"Cold, Cold Shoes," *I.R.S. Greatest Hits, Vols. 2 and 3* LP (I.R.S.) 1981

"Shadow Line," *URGH! A Music War* LP (A&M Records) 1981

"Wail, Baby, Wail" + "Big Man" (Calling Dr. Cranklin), *Start Swimming* LP (Stiff America) 1981

"American Beat '84," *Bachelor Party* soundtrack LP/cassette (CBS/I.R.S.) 1984
CD (Superfecta) 2003

"Hall of Fame," *Just What the Doctor Ordered* LP (CBS Europe/I.R.S.) 1985

"Return of the Leather Kings" + "Inner Groove," *688 Presents* LP (688) 1986

"I Was a Teenage Zombie," *I Was a Teenage Zombie* soundtrack LP (Enigma) 1987

"I Was a Teenage Zombie," "In My Eyes You're Dead," "I Forget How to Talk," "She Turned My Head Around" + "Sonnet XX" [with Ian McKellen], *Time Bomb: Fleshtones Present the Big Bang Theory* LP/cassette (Skyclad) 1988 LP (Fr. New Rose) 1988 LP (Gr. Hitch Hyke) 1988

"5 New Fleshtones" [incorrectly titled demo of "Hall of Fame"], *The BOB* seven-inch flexidisc EP 1988

"It's Too Late" + "Too Much on My Mind," *Shangri-La: A Tribute to the Kinks* LP/cassette/CD (UK Imaginary) 1989

"Watch Junior Go," *New York Rockers: Manhattan's Original Rock Underground* cassette (ROIR) 1989

"American Beat," *Ten ROIR Years* cassette (ROIR) 1990

"Shadow Line" + "F-f-fascination," *The Groups of Wrath: Songs of the Naked City* CD (TVT) 1991

"Told Me a Lie" + "Well, Alright," *Abus Dangereux* mini-CD EP (Fr. Abus Dangereux) 1992

"Told Me a Lie," *Abus Dangereux* CD (Fr. Abus Dangereux) 1993

"Take a Walk with the Fleshtones" + "Whistling Past the Grave," *Tense It Up* CD (Sky) 1994

"Medicine Man," *Turban Renewal: A Tribute to Sam the Sham & the Pharaohs* CD/LP (Norton) 1994

"Ride Your Pony," *Just Can't Get Enough: New Wave Hits of the 80s, Vol. 7* CD (Rhino) 1994

"High on Drugs," *Huh CD15* CD (Huh) 1995

"New York, New York," *Dictators Forever Forever Dictators: A Tribute to the Dictators, Vol. 1* CD (Sp. Roto) 1996

"American Woman," *New Sound: Rock Therapy* CD (Gr. Pop & Rock) 1997

"God Damn It" + "My Love Machine," *Roadkill* CD (Eur. Epitaph) 1998

"You Can Get Him Frankenstein," *Flaming Burnout* CD (Man's Ruin) 1998

"Don't Be a Dropout," *Super Bad @ 65: A Tribute to James Brown* CD (Zero Hour) 1998

"The Friends of Bazooka Joe," *Blood Red Battle Royal* CD (Blood Red) 1998

"Time Zone," *Mondo Beat Vol. 1* CD (It. Sony International) 1999

"Soundcheck 2000," *Larsen 17* seven-inch EP (Fr. Larsen) 2001

"Ride Your Pony," *Under the Covers: Modern Rock* CD (Time-Life) 2002

"Keep Her Guessing," *A Tribute to Arthur Alexander* CD (Fr. Larsen) 2002

"One Less Step" + "God Damn It," *Sk8erboy Rock! Vol. 1* CD (Critique) 2003

Medley: "My Kinda Lovin'"/"The Crossroads Are Coming," "Fading Away" + "Dig In," *Sk8erboy Rock! Vol. 2* CD (Critique) 2003

Sweat

"Soul Train," *Guitar Ace: Tribute to Link Wray* CD (MuSick) 2003

"The Girl from Baltimore" + "The World Has Changed," *Children of Nuggets: Original Artyfacts from the Second Psychedelic Era 1976–1995* CD box set (Rhino) 2005

"Time Zone," *Stomp! Shout! Scream!* soundtrack CD (Chicken Ranch) 2006

"Ghoulman Confidential," *Rockin' Bones: A Halloween Sampler* online CD (Yep Roc) 2006

Video

"Right Side of a Good Thing," *The Beast of I.R.S. Video Vol. 1* VHS (I.R.S. Home Video) 1984

"F-f-fascination," *Back in the Day: Live at Hurrah's New York City* DVD (WEA) 2006

The Fleshtones: Brooklyn à Paris! Live at La Maroquinerie DVD (Big Enough) 2006

Tribute

Vindicated! A Tribute to the Fleshtones CD (UK Dirty Water) 2007   LP (Fr. Larsen) 2007

Selected Side Projects

Peter Zaremba's Love Delegation

Spread the Word LP (Moving Target) 1986 CD (Amsterdamned) 1997

"I'm Gonna Knock You Out" [twelve-inch Remix] b/w "Love Delegation" [seven-inch Remix] twelve-inch (Moving Target) 1986

"Through the Night," *Time Bomb: Fleshtones Present the Big Bang Theory* LP/cassette (Skyclad) 1988 LP (Fr. New Rose) 1988 LP (Gr. Hitch Hyke) 1988

Delegation Time LP/CD (Fr. Accord Musidisc) 1989

Full Time Men

Fast Is My Name EP (Coyote) 1985

"High on Drugs," *Time Bomb: Fleshtones Present the Big Bang Theory* LP/cassette (Skyclad) 1988 LP (Fr. New Rose) 1988 LP (Gr. Hitch Hyke) 1988

Your Face My Fist LP (Coyote) 1988

The Fabulous Sounds of Coney Island seven-inch EP [w/the Master Plan] (Blood Red) 1999

The Master Plan

The Fabulous Sounds of Coney Island seven-inch EP [w/Full Time Men] (Blood Red) 1999

Colossus of Destiny CD (Sp. Imposible) 2002 LP (Bel. Demolition Derby) 2003 CD (Total Energy) 2004

Appendix Two
The Cover Songs

When the Fleshtones formed in a basement in 1976, they didn't have the nerve to write their own material. Since cobbling together a version of Eddie Cochran's "Nervous Breakdown," they've made a point of covering songs, most of them willfully obscure, some outright surprising.

The artists listed here aren't necessarily those who recorded or released the songs first, but whose versions the Fleshtones dug. Rufus Thomas cut "Jump Back" for Stax Records in 1964, but the Small Faces' radical deconstruction for a 1965 BBC radio session caught the Fleshtones' attention. The same was true with the Rolling Stones' live rave-up of Hank Snow's "I'm Movin' On," Edwin Starr's funky-frat update of Titus Turner's "All Around the World," and Screamin' Jay Hawkins' tear through Fats Domino's "Please Don't Leave Me." What follows is a party among scratchy flip-sides, long-forgotten album tracks, and obscure movie soundtracks, a motley crew of rock & rollers, wanna-bes, and one-offs.

Some songs have been lost in the memory-swiping vapors of the last thirty years, but by next week the Fleshtones are bound to add to the list. (Thanks to Peter Zaremba, Keith Streng, and Ken Fox, Steve Coleman, Jean-Marc Rimette, Jean-Pierre Soulignac, Anne Streng, Eric Fusco, Jon Quin, Billy Miller and Miriam Linna at Norton Records, and the folks at Searching the Shakes and Fuzz Acid & Flowers Web sites.)

Sweat

Tune	Artist
Abigail Beecher	Freddie "Boom Boom" Cannon
Action Woman	The Litter
After Midnight	J.J. Cale
Ain't That Loving You Baby	Elvis Presley
All Around the World	Edwin Starr
All Hung Up	The Flies
Alright	The Searchers
American Woman	The Guess Who
Anarchy in the U.K.	The Sex Pistols
Around and Around	Chuck Berry
Baby, Don't You Do It	Marvin Gaye
Baby-Get It On	Ike and Tina Turner
Beg, Borrow and Steal	Ohio Express
Big Bird	Eddie Floyd
Big Red Sunset	Hank Ballard and the Midnighters
Bittersweet	Hoodoo Gurus
Bony Maronie	Larry Williams
Boom Boom	John Lee Hooker
Boss Hoss	The Sonics
Bossa Nova Baby	Elvis Presley
The Boys in the Band	The Phynx
[aka Hand for the Band]	
Brown Paper Sack	The Gentrys
Burning Hell	John Lee Hooker
Burning Love	Elvis Presley
Can't Get Enough of Your Love	The Dantes
Cara-Lin	The Strangeloves
Chain Gang	Sam Cooke
Cheating	The Animals
Chicken Wah Wah	Bobby Marchan
Come On Let's Go	Richie Valens
Come on Up	The Rascals
Comin' Home Baby	Mel Torme
Communication Breakdown	Led Zeppelin
Concentration Baby	The Dave Clark Five
Cotton Candy	Lenny Capello and the Dots
Cross Fire	Johnny and the Hurricanes
Cruisin' in the Lincoln	Eddie and the Hot Rods
Crystal Liaison	The Fugs
Dance with Me	The Blendells
Dancin' All Around the World	Little Richard
Theme from *The Defenders*	Leonard Rosenman

Appendix Two: The Cover Songs

Dick Tracy	The Chants
Did You See Her Eyes?	The Illusion
Diddy Wah Diddy	Bo Diddley
Dinner with Drac	John Zacherle
Do the Mouse	Soupy Sales
Do You Wanna Funk?	Sylvester
Doctor Rhythm	The Dave Clark Five
Don't Be a Dropout	James Brown
Don't Stop Now	Annette Funicello and the Afterbeats
Down on Me	Big Brother and the Holding Company
The Eel	The Barons
"8" Teen	? and the Mysterians
Endless Sleep	Jody Reynolds
Endless Tunnel	Serpent Power
Everlovin' Man	The Loved Ones
Every Day and Every Night	The Trolls
Everybody But Me	Gene Allison
Everybody Needs Somebody to Love	Solomon Burke
Faster than the Speed of Life	Steppenwolf
Feelings	The Grass Roots
Feels Like a Woman	The Troggs
Find Somebody	The Rascals
Fingertips Pt. 2	Little Stevie Wonder
Fire Engine	Thirteenth Floor Elevators
5-4-3-2-1	Manfred Mann
The Float	Hank Ballard and the Midnighters
Foxey Lady	The Jimi Hendrix Experience
Function at the Junction	Little Richard
Funtime	Iggy Pop
Get Down with It	Bobby Marchan
Get Off My Cloud	The Rolling Stones
Gimme Gimme Good Lovin'	Crazy Elephant
Girl (You Captivate Me)	? and the Mysterians
Girl, You Don't Know	SOS Unlimited
Gloria	Them
Go Away	[unknown]
Going Down to Tiujana	Andre Williams
Gonna Make You	The Troggs
Guybo	Eddie Cochran
Hang Up	The Wailers
H.A.P.P.Y. Radio	Edwin Starr

Sweat

Haunted Castle	The Kingsmen
Have Love, Will Travel	The Sonics
Hey Hey Hey Hey	Little Richard
Hey Joe	Wilson Pickett
Hey Little Girl	Dee Clark
Hey Sah-Lo-Ney	Micky Lee Lane
Hey You, the Wind, and the Rain	The "You-Know-Who" Group
Hide & Seek	The Sheep
High on Drugs	The Titanics
How Does It Feel to Feel?	The Creation
I	Knight Riders
I Ain't Done Wrong	The Yardbirds
I Ain't Got You	The Yardbirds
I Betcha Gonna Like It	Jeb Stuart
I Don't Know Why I Love You	Desi Young
I Don't Live Today	The Jimi Hendrix Experience
I Get So Excited	The Equals
I Got a Line on You	Spirit
I Hate You All	Los Dudes
I See the Light	The Music Explosion
I Took My Baby Home	The Kinks
I Want More	The Tropics
I Want You	The Troggs
I Wish You Would	The Yardbirds
If and When	Chris Stamey and the dB's
Igloo	Screaming Tribesmen
I'm a Little Airplane	Jonathan Richman
I'm Alive	Johnny Thunder
I'm Crying	Dave Davies
I'm Fed Up	Ike and Tina Turner
I'm Five Years Ahead of My Time	The Third Bardo
I'm Movin' On	The Rolling Stones
I'm Not Like Everybody Else	The Kinks
I'm over 25 (But You Can Trust Me)	Sammy Davis, Jr.
Imagination	The Saints
In Need of Love	[unknown]
Inside Looking Out	The Animals
It'll Be Me	Jerry Lee Lewis
It's a Hang Up	The Capitals
It's Love, Come What May	The Bobby Fuller Four
It's Too Late	The Kinks
Jack in the Box	The Music Explosion
Jeannie, Jeannie, Jeannie	Eddie Cochran
Judge Baby, I'm Back	Cliff Nobles

Appendix Two: The Cover Songs

Jump and Dance	The Carnabys
Jump Back	The Small Faces
Jump, Jive, and Harmonize	Thee Midniters
Keelee's Twist	Joey Dee and the Starliters
Keep Her Guessing	Arthur Alexander
Keep on Dancin'	The Gentrys
King of the Surf	The Trashmen
Kitty Kitty	Floyd Dakil Four
La La La La La	The Blendells
Land of 1000 Dances	Otis Redding
The Last Time	The Rolling Stones
Laugh It Off	The Tams
Leaving Here	Eddie Holland
Leilani	Hoodoo Gurus
Let It Rock	Chuck Berry
Let the Doorbell Ring	Champion Jack Dupree
Let's Get High	Rosco Gordon
Let's Go in '69	The Customs Five
Let's Stick Together	Wilbert Harrison
Like Wow-Wipeout	Hoodoo Gurus
Little Girl	Syndicate of Sound
Little Latin Lupe Lu	Mitch Ryder and the Detroit Wheels
Little Lu	Eddie Cochran
Lonely Bull	Herb Albert and the Tijuana Brass
Long Green	The Kingsmen
Loretta	Nervous Eaters
Lost Girl	The Troggs
Theme from *Lost in Space*	Johnny Williams
The Magic Touch	The Bobby Fuller Four
Mama Weer All Crazee Now	Slade
Margio	The Rob Hoeke Rhythm and Blues Group
Mean 'Ole Lonesome Train	Lightnin' Slim
Medicine Man	Sam the Sham and the Pharaohs
Midnight Hour	? and the Mysterians
Mighty Idy	D.M.Z.
Miss Freelove '69	Hoodoo Gurus
Moon Dawg	The Challengers
Morgus the Magnificent	Morgue and the Ghouls
Motorhead	Motorhead
Move It on Over	Del Shannon
Mr. Custer	Larry Verne
My Pledge of Love	The Joe Jeffrey Group

Sweat

My Wife	The Who
Nervous Breakdown	Eddie Cochran
New Orleans	Gary "U.S." Bonds
New York, New York	The Dictators
Next Time	Richard Berry
Night of the Long Grass	The Troggs
No Stopping	The Dave Clark Five
La Novia de Mi Mejor Amigo	Los Crazy Boys
Off the Hook	The Rolling Stones
On the Road Again	The Lovin' Spoonful
Outcast	The Animals
Panic	Otis Williams and His Charms
The Party Starts Now!!	Manitoba's Wild Kingdom
People Sure Act Funny	Titus Turner
Play with Fire	The Rolling Stones
Playboy	The "You-Know-Who" Group
Please Don't Leave Me	Screamin' Jay Hawkins
Pleasure	Iggy Pop
Theme from *The Powerpuff Girls*	Bis
Psycho	The Sonics
Rainbow	Gene Chandler
Ramblin' Gamblin' Man	Bob Seger System
Rats in My Kitchen	Sleepy John Estes
Reggae Reggae	Real Kids
Rich with Nothin'	Split Ends
Ride Your Pony	Lee Dorsey
Rock & Roll, Pt. 2	Gary Glitter
Rocket U.S.A.	Suicide
Rockin' Behind the Iron Curtain	Bobby Marchan and the Clowns
Rockin' Roll Baby	The Stylistics
Rockin' This Joint Tonight	Kid Thomas
Roll on Big Wheel	Benny Spellman
Rooster Blues	Lightnin' Slim
Roses Are Red My Love	Bobby Vinton
Roses Are Red My Love	The "You-Know-Who" Group
Ruler of My Heart	Irma Thomas
Salade de Fruits	Bourvil
San Francisco Girls	The Fever Tree
Shake	The Shadows of Knight
She's a Lady	Tom Jones
She's My Baby	Johnny O'Keefe
Sitting on My Sofa	The Kinks

Appendix Two: The Cover Songs

Slow Death	The Flamin' Groovies
Smokes	? and the Mysterians
Smokestack Lighting	Howlin' Wolf
Somebody's Been Sleeping in My Bed	100 Proof (Aged in Soul)
Sometimes Good Guys Don't Wear White	The Standells
Soul City	The Hi-Lifes
Soul Struttin'	1910 Fruitgum Co.
Soul Train	Link Wray
Speedy Gonzales	Trini Lopez
Spinout	Elvis Presley
Spread It Around	The Bags
Steam Engine 99	The Monkees
Stoned	The Rolling Stones
Stupidity	Solomon Burke
S-w-i-m	Bobby Freeman
Switch-A-Roo	Hank Ballard and the Midnighters
Take My Love (I Want to Give It All to You)	Little Willie John
Tallahassee Lassie	Freddie "Boom Boom" Cannon
Tear for Tear	Gene Chandler
Temptation Eyes	The Grass Roots
That's Your Problem	The Outsiders
There's Something on Your Mind	Bobby Marchan
They Took My Money	Chris Kenner
Thinkin' of You Baby	The Dave Clark Five
This Sporting Life	Mickey Finn
Tiger Man	Elvis Presley
'Till the End of the Day	The Kinks
Time Has Come Today	The Chambers Brothers
Time Will Tell	Michel Polnareff
Tired of Trying, Bored with Lying, Scared of Dying	Manfred Mann
Too Much on My Mind	The Kinks
Train of Thought	Cher
Treat Her Like a Lady	Cornelius Brothers and Sister Rose
Trouble	The Kingsmen
Truth Drug	Nick Lowe
The Turn-On Song	Don and the Goodtimes
Try It	The Standells
Twelve Months Later	The Sheep
25 Miles	Edwin Starr
2000 Man	The Rolling Stones
The 2,000 Pound Bee, Pt. 2	The Ventures

Sweat

Up and Down	John Fred and the Playboys
Voodoo Voodoo	LaVern Baker
Wail Baby Wail	Kid Thomas
Wave Your Flag and Stop the Train	The Move
We Gotta Go	The Shy Guys
Well . . . Alright	Buddy Holly
What'd I Say?	Ray Charles
When the Night Falls	The Eyes
Who'll Be the Next in Line	The Kinks
Wild Cat Tamer	Tarheel Slim
Wild Weekend	Rockin' Rebels
Wind Out	R.E.M.
Word Up	Cameo
The World Keeps Going 'Round	The Kinks
You Can Get Him Frankenstein	The Castle Kings
You Can't Sit Down	Phil Upchurch Combo
You Can't Win	The Kinks
You Just Ain't Good Enough	The Titanics
You Told a Lie [aka Told Me a Lie]	Frantic Freddie and His Reflections
You're Holding Me Down	The Buzz
You're Lookin' Fine	The Kinks
You're Tearin' Me Apart	Teenage Head

Appendix Three
Set Lists

Whether scribbled in inspiration or dispiritedly scrawled after a lonesome soundcheck, Fleshtones set lists change from night to night—somethimes song to song—but the goal's always the same: string together the right tunes that maintain pace and pleasure. "What we noticed long before there were even any Fleshtones was that the performances we liked built on excitement," says Peter. "We look for a strong intro, maybe a 'change of pace' in the middle for folks to catch their breath and realize what's happening to them, then a steady build to the climax. If we notice that people don't react to certain songs, we drop them, no matter how much we might like them ourselves." Duct-taped to a stage monitor, any sheet of paper will do, whether it's the back of another band's flier or directions to the last night's gig. Grabbed by a sweaty fan, a set list acts as the next day's indelibe proof of notes and chants fading in ringing ears.

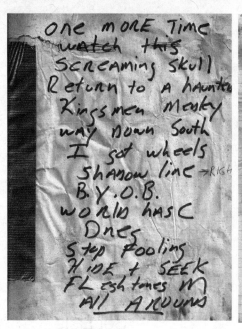

One more Time
watch this
Screaming Skull
Return to a haunte
Kingsmen Monky
Way Down South
I got wheels
Shadow line →Right
B.Y.O.B.
World has C
Dreg
Step Pooling
Hide + Seek
Fleshtones M
All Arounds

1984

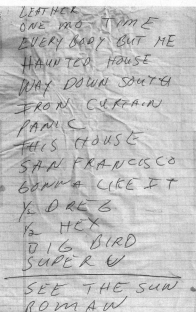

LEATHER
ONE MO TIME
EVERY BODY BUT ME
HAUNTED HOUSE
WAY DOWN SOUTH
IRON CURTAIN
PANIC
THIS HOUSE
SAN FRANCISCO
GONNA LIKE IT
½ DREG
½ HEX
BIG BIRD
SUPER V

SEE THE SUN
ROMAN

1987

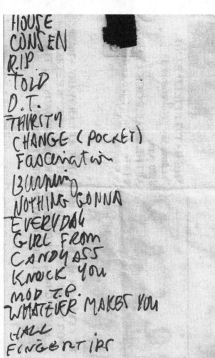

HOUSE
CONSEN
R.IP.
TOLD
D.T.
THIRSTY
CHANGE (POCKET)
Fascination
Burning
NOTHING GONNA
EVERYDAY
GIRL FROM
CANDYASS
KNOCK YOU
MOD T.P.
WHATEVER MAKES YOU

HALL
FINGERTIPS

1992

SGS
I AM WHAT I AM
SERIOUS
SWING
ANSWERS
PRETTY
WANT
DOUBLE DIP
OPUS
DREG → V
TROGGS
PICKIN PICKIN
PUSH UP
HTSBURG
B4G ONE BETTER

GRAND MIX
TOUR/CONFIG - 11 APRIL 2007

2007

Sources

Interviews

Albini, Steve. Phone interview with the author. June 4, 2004
Aldredge, Leslie. Phone interview with the author. July 23, 2003
Alexander, Betsy. Phone interview the author. May 20, 2003
Ball, Jim. Interview with the author. New York, NY, July 3, 2001
Barken, Miles. Interview with the author. New York, NY, July 2, 2003
Boberg, Jay. E-mail to the author. July 4, 2001
Bruce, John. Interview with the author. Brooklyn, NY, July 12, 2003
Buck, Peter. Phone interview with the author. November 7, 2002
Butterick, Brian. Interview with the author. New York, NY, July 7, 2003
Calderon, Lenny. Phone interview with the author. January 16, 2003
Case, Peter. Phone interview with the author. May 5, 2003
Coleman, Steve. E-mail to the author. August 27, 2002
____. November 9, 2003
Costello, Mike. Letter to the author. June 20, 2001
Descant, Jimmy. E-mail to the author. ca. 2000
Destri Jimmy. E-mail to the author. November 27, 2003
Dicker, Glen. E-mail to the author. July 30, 2006
DuBose, George. E-mail to the author. May 25, 2003
Everson, Karen. E-mail to the author. February 17, 2003
Farber, Dia. Interview with the author. New York, NY, July 18, 2002
Faulkner, Dave. Phone interview with the author. August 18, 2003
____. Comment to the author. Brooklyn, NY, July 12, 2004

Fox, Ken. Interview with the author. Brooklyn, NY, July 11, 2001
___. July 12, 13, 2004
Fox, Jean. E-mail to the author. November 25, 2006
Gilbert, Daniel. Phone interview with the author. February 22, 2003
Gilmore, George. Interview with the author. New York, NY, July 20, 2004
Gottehrer, Richard. Interview with the author. New York, NY, July 16, 2002
Grasso, Carlos. Phone interview with the author. January 27, 2003
Green, Brett. Phone interview with the author. July 23, 2003
Guarnieri, John. Phone interview with the author. May 4, 2003
James, Sam. E-mail to the author. August 19, 2004
Johnson, Paul. Interview with the author. New York, NY, July 12, 2002
Jones, M. Henry. Interview with the author. New York, NY, July 10, 2001
Jones, Nick. E-mail to the author. August 12, 2002
Kristal, Hilly. Interview with the author. New York, NY, July 3, 2002
Lahana, Alain. E-mail to the author. August 19, 2002
Lebreton, Max. E-mail to the author. May 29, 2003
Linna, Miriam. Interview with the author. Brooklyn, NY, July 6, 2000
Manitoba, Richard. Interview with the author. New York, NY, July 4, 2000
Marshall, Jim. Interview with the author. New York, NY, July 8, 2003
Mazda, Richard. Phone interview with the author. January 2, 2003
McNeil, Legs. E-mail to the author. April 23, 2003
Milhizer, Bill. Interview with the author. Brooklyn, NY, July 3, 2000
___. June 25, 2001
___. July 17, 2002
___. Comment to the author. Brooklyn, NY, July 4, 2001
___. ca. summer 2002
Miller, Billy. Interview with the author. Brooklyn, NY, July 6, 2000
Nemeth, Cathy. E-mail to the author. June 19, 2004
Pakulski, Marek. Interview with the author. New York, NY, June 28, July 5, 2000
___. July 5, 12, 21, 2001
___. July 15, 2004
Palmeri, April. Interview with the author. Brooklyn, NY, July 8, 2001
Patron, Bruce. Interview with the author. New York, NY, July 12, 2001
Patterson, Freddie. Interview with the author. New York, NY, June 27, 2001
Quinn, Jon. Interview with the author. New York, NY, June 25, 2001
Reinholz, Jeff. E-mail to the author. April 29, 2004
Rev, Martin. E-mail to the author. February 16, 2004
Ringenberg, Jason. E-mail to the author. June 4, 2004
Robbins, Ira. Interview with the author. New York, NY, July 3, 2001
Roinell, Jules. Phone interview with the author, notes. July 12, 2004
Saade, Kim. Phone interview with the author. June 10, 2004
Sadd, Randy. E-mail to the author. June 10, 2004
Schwartz, Andy. Interview with the author. New York, NY, July 10, 2003
Shernoff, Andy. Interview with the author. Brooklyn, NY, June 30, 2000
Shoor, Rick. E-mail to the author. February 19, 2004
Singerman, Robert. E-mail to the author. August 12, 2002
___. May 31, 2003

Sources

Smith, Fred. Interview with the author. New York, NY, June 30, 2003

Spaeth, Brian. Interview with the author. New York, NY, June 26, 2001

Spaeth, Gordon. Interview with the author. New York, NY, July 2, 9, 2001
____. July 5, 2003

Streng, Keith. Interview with the author. Brooklyn, NY, June 27-28, 2000
____. June 22, 26, July 7, 2001
____. June 27-28, July 10, 2003
____. July 8, 2004

Streng, Anne. E-mail to the author. November 28, 2006
____. November 30, 2006

Thau, Marty. Interview with the author. Brooklyn, NY, October 19, 2000
____. E-mail to the author. February 20, 2003
____. Phone interview with the author. May 13, 2003

Trakin, Roy. Phone interview with the author. February 5, 2003

Warren, Robert Burke. Interview with the author. New York, NY, June 29, 2001
____. E-mail to the author. May 9, 2004

Weisbard, Eric. E-mail to the author. September 1, 2004

Weiss, Jon. Interview with the author. New York, NY, July 11, 2001

Wexler, Paul. Phone interview with the author. June 3, 2003

Wrigley, Rick. E-mail to Fleshtones Hall of Fame web site, May 12, 2004.

Wynn, Steve. Interview with the author. New York, NY, July 21, 2004

Zaremba, Peter. Interview with the author. Brooklyn, NY, October 18, 2000
____. July 7, 2001
____. Chicago IL, August 6, 2002
____. Brooklyn, NY, July 8, 2003
____. July 20, 2004
____. Interview notes. Brooklyn, NY, July 17, 2002
____. E-mail to the author. May 28, December 1, 2003
____. December 16, 2003
____. July 31, 2006
____. November 14, 2006

Books

Andriote, John-Manuel. *Hot Stuff: A Brief History of Disco* (Perennial Currents, 2001), 24

Antonia, Nina. *The New York Dolls: Too Much Too Soon* (Omnibus, 1998), 43

Bachelard, Gaston. *The Poetics of Space* (Beacon, 1969), 137

Ellis, Bret Easton. *Less Than Zero* (Penguin, 1987)

Gimarc, George. *Post Punk Diary: 1980-1982* (St. Martins Griffin, 1987), 132

Haden-Guest, Anthony. *The Last Party: Studio 54, Disco, and the Culture of the Night* (William Morrow, 1997), 122

Kozak, Roman. *This Ain't No Disco: The Story of CBGB* (Faber & Faber, 1988), chapters 4, 5, 6

Nite, Norm N. *Rock on Almanac: The First Four Decades of Rock 'n' Roll* (Harper Reesource, 1997), 350-51

Sandler, Irving. *Art of the Postmodern Era: From the Late 1960s to the Early 1990s* (Westview, 1997), 513

Seawall-Ruskin, Yvonne. *High on Rebellion: Inside the Underground at Max's Kansas City* (Thunder's Mouth, 1998), 245

Swenson, John. *Headliners: The Who* (Tempo, 1979), 9

Whitman, Walt. "Poem of the Proposition of Nakedness," *The Essential Whitman* (Ecco, 1987), 106

Young, Jon. *The Trouser Press Record Guide*, fourth ed. Ed. I. Robbins (Collier, 1991), 662

Articles: Magazine, newspaper, and fanzine

Abramson, Todd. "The American Sound of The Fleshtones," *Young, Fast, & Scientific* #2, 1979, np

Rafael Alvarez, "Ten Years of 'Trash'," *Baltimore Sun*, April 4, 1986, np

Mark Anderson, "Fleshtones," *Newsreal*, December 11, 1981–January 14, 1982, 7

Anonymous. *The Aquarian*, February 23–March 2, 1977, np

Anonymous. *Billboard*, December 13, 1980, 77

____. *Billboard*, March 13, 1982, np

____. *Billboard*, March 20, 1982, 27

____. *Billboard*, June 25, 1983, np

____. *Billboard*, April 4, 1987, 78

____. "Albums," *Billboard*, July 2, 1994, np

____. "Singles," *Billboard*, October 7, 1995, 103

____. *Billboard*. May 3, 2003

Anonymous. *Blue Lunch* #1, December 1980, np

Anonymous. *Cash Box*, June 25, 1983, np

____. "East Coastings," *Cash Box*, June 13, 1987, np

Anonymous. *CMJ New Music Report*, April 10, 1987, np

Anonymous. "'Give 'em the Powerstance!'," *The Drum Media*, # 15, 1991, np

Anonymous. *New York Post*, June 20, 1980, np

Anonymous. *New York Rocker*, February/March, 1977, np

____. "NY News: A Finger in Every Pie," *New York Rocker*, January 1981, np

Anonymous. Record reviews, *Pulse*, June 1993, # 115, 89; qtd. in Santa Fe newspaper, name/date unknown, ca. 1993

Anonymous. *Punk*, May/June 1979, np

Anonymous. "Single Picks," *Record World*, August 1, 1981, 20

Anonymous. "Fleshtones: Palace: 15.4.82," *Rock 'n' Folk*, May 1982, np

Anonymous. "Random Notes," *Rolling Stone*, February 1991, np

Anonymous. *Slash* #8, September 1979, np

Anonymous. "The Fleshtones: On the Right Side of a Good Thing!", *Tiger Beat Star*, January 1984, 50

Anonymous. *US Weekly*, March 3, 1981, 51

Anonymous. *Village Voice*, February 28, 1984, 36

Anonymous. *Zig Zag* #111, March 1981, np

Barber, Lynden. "Great American Disaster," *Melody Maker*, February 28, 1981, 38

Barnes, Ken. "Stranger in Town," *New York Rocker*, October 1981, 46

Baumgardner, Lisa. *Film News Magazine*, 1979, np

Becker, Elisa. "Talking Garage Music and . . . 'Super Rock!'," *First Cut*, September 23, 1984, np; emphasis mine

Sources

Beeson, Frank. "American Beat," *The BOB*, February–March 1988, 26

Berg, Scott. *Deseret News*, September 6, 1984, np

Bernard, Jami. "'Teenage Zombie': the pits, with zits," *New York Post*, July 10, 1987, np

Betrock, Alan. *New York Rocker*, November/December, 1977, np

Buckley, John. "Celluloid Heroes," *Soho News*, September 3, 1980, 42

____. "Fleshtones File Late Returns," *Soho News*, October 27, 1981, 66

Carlton, Bill. "A Clear, Smooth Complexion," *Daily News*, December 8, 1980. np

____. "Christmas Platters," *Daily News,* December 21, 1980, 20

Carson, Tom. "You Burn Some, You Rust Some: New York New Wave Takes on the Heartland," *Village Voice*, October 22, 1979, 41

____. *Rolling Stone*, April 29, 1982, 55

Christgau, Georgia. "Don't Be Denied: The Econmics of a New York Rock Band," *Village Voice*, October 10, 1977, 42

Christgau, Robert. *Village Voice*, February 27, 1979, np

____. "The Fleshtones," *Village Voice*, March 12, 1979, 68

____. "Licks: Dance this Mess Around," *Village Voice*, December 31, 1980–January 6, 1981

Clark, Jeff. *Stomp and Stammer*, April 4, 2003, np

Coast, Jud. *Magnet*, October/November 1995, np

Cohen, Eliot. *The Aquarian*, December 8-15, 1976

Considine, J.D. "Fleshtones vs. Reality," *Rolling Stone*, 1987, np

Cullman, Brian. *Musician*, February 1984, np

De Filippo, Roberto. "Fleshtones. Un'esplosione," *Il Gazzettino*, July 20, 1990, np

DeMuir, Harold. "The Way of All Fleshtones," Night Owl. *Supplement of the Aquarian*, No. 501, December 14, 1983, 48

DeRogatis, Jim. "Secure in 'Obscurity,'" *Chicago Sun-Times*, June 13, 2003, W5.

Farrell, "Marathon 8: Wave On!" *Sweet Potato*, October 1979, 14

Flaherty, Mike. *Entertainment Weekly*. April 8, 1994, np

Flatte, Bea. "A Touch of Village Green at Crisco Disco," *The Aquarian*, August 9–August 16, 1978, np

Francos, Robert. "The Fleshtones," *Ffanzeen* #3, Winter-Spring 1978–79, 6

Geiger, Barry and Dan Cohen. "Fleshtones: Too Good to Be Ignored," *3rd Wave*, 1978, 24

Gelfand, Michael. "Working Musician: Under Cover," *Musician*, November 1997, 16–17

Goldberg, Michael. "The Fleshtones: Primal Rock," *Creem*, May 1982, 18

Goldstein, Toby. *Trouser Press*, September 1980, np

Grabel, Richard. "The Pleasures of the Flesh: Could the Fleshtones Be America's Next Big Thing and If Not, Why Not?," *New Musical Express*, September 6, 1980, 29

____. *New Musical Express*, December 12, 1981, 25

____. "The Fleshtones: New Blood Meets Old Beat at the Heart of Parties," *New Musical Express*, April 3, 1982, 13

Hammond, Stefan. "Three Perspectives on Marathon '80," *Minnesota Daily*, September 28, 1979, 16AE

Harrington, Richard. "The 9:30 Club, Just in Time; Ten Years Later, Still Catching the Next Wave," *Washington Post*, May 27, 1990, g01

Harrison, Don. "Hard Rockin' Fleshtones Have a Good Time," *Daily Break*, ca. 1986, np

Hibbert, Tom. "On Stage," *London Trax*, nd, np

Hoekstra, Dave. "Revved-up Rock By Garage Bands," *Chicago Sun-Times*, November 8, 1985, 7

Hoskyns, Barney. "Singles," *New Musical Express*, March 20, 1982, 16

Hurr, Gary. *Record Mirror*, April 7, 1982, np

Hutton, Lindsay. "Zaremba Speaks (A Chat with an American in Paris)," *Watch This*, August/September 1985, np

Kaplan, Ira. "Soho a-Go-Go," *The Soho News*, August 27, 1980

Karp, Marjorie. "Confessions of a Fleshtones Fan," *Village Voice*, January 20-26, 1982, 66

Kirb. *Variety*, October 6, 1976, np

Koepp, David. *New York Rocker* #12, 1978, np

Leland, John. "Also Around Town," *New York Newsday*, January 5, 1990, 12

Linna, Miriam. *New York Rocker*, February/March, 1977, np

Lloyd, Robert. "The Great American Fleshtones," *L.A. Weekly*, February 26-March 4, 1982, 21, 22

Marshall, Brian. "The Fleshtones," *Noises from the Garage* #9, 1999

Marts, "Fleshtones," *Zig Zag* #112, April 1981, 45

Masley, Ed. "Frontman Says Fleshtones Still Fresh," *Pittsburgh Post-Gazette*, May 30, 2003, 25

McCormick. "The Fleshtones' French Connection," *Mix*, November 1985, np

McKenna, Dave. "White Stripes, Without a Bass of Support," *Washington Post*, Apr 3, 2002, C3

McLennan, Scott. "Fleshtones Maintain Their Fresh Sound with Little Effort," *Telegram & Gazette*, June 11, 1998, C5

Morris, Chris. "The Fleshtones' 'Super Rock,'" *Rolling Stone*, October 27, 1983, 92

———. "Speed Connection II," *Musician*, November 1985, np

Morse, Steve. "Fleshtones Look Faded," *Boston Globe*, February 2, 1982, 12

Mortifoglio, Richard. "Fleshtones Beat," *Village Voice*, July 16, 1979, 56

Oaten, Brett. "In the Flesh," *The Drum Media*, October 15, 1991

O'Halloran, Dave. "The Fleshtones," *What Wave* #10, 1986, 18

O'Neil, Jr., Lou. "The Scene," *New York Post*, February 23, 1979, np

Palmer, Robert. "The Pop Life," *New York Times*, December 5, 1980, np

———. "New York Rock Bands Excite London," *New York Times*, February 20, 1981, C17

———. "The Pop Life: 3 Bands Find New in the Past," *New York Times*, January 13, 1982, np

———. "Fleshtones' 'Hexbreaker!' Is a Surprise," *New York Times*, August 3, 1983, C20

———. "Four Pop Albums: From Irish Defiance to Urban Drone," *New York Times*, July 12, 1987, Sec. II, 23

Panebianco, Julie. "Love Is All Around," *SPIN*, October 1986, np

Peanuts. *Alternative Press*, November 1995, np

Pratt, Tim. "Loopy, Unpredictable, Upbeat 'Tones Put on Show Anyone Would Appreciate," *Grand Rapids Press*, b7, 27 May 1994

Puterbaugh, Parke. *Rolling Stone*, September 15, 1983, 60

Sources

Pye, Ian. *Melody Maker*, March 13, 1982, 17

____. "Hexbreaker!," *Melody Maker*, August 20, 1983, 24

Rambali, Paul. *New Musical Express*, September 6, 1980, 39

Ressner, Jeffrey. "Coast to Coast," *Cash Box*, April 9, 1983, np

Righi, Len. "Fleshtones: Rock 'n' Roll the American Way," *The Morning Call*, ca. 1983, np

Robbins, Ira. *Trouser Press*, September 1983, np

Salkind, Michael. "It's the Fleshtones," *Unicorn Times*, September 1983, 19

Sasfy, Joe. "Pop in the Age of Punk," *Washington Post*, May 13, 1982, C4

Schulz, Curt. "Mighty Mighty Fleshtones of Garage Rock," *Portland Oregonian*, January 29, 1999, 38

Schwartz, Andy. "The 'American Sound' of the Fleshtones," *New York Rocker*, 1978, np

____. *New York Rocker*, 1979, np

Shore, Michael. "Dancing in the Streets: Dance Band of the Month," *Soho Weekly News*, March 1, 1979, np

____. "Music Picks, *Soho News*, May 7, 1980, np

Smart, Vickeye. "Marty Thau Presents," *East Village Eye*, summer 1980, np

Sommer, Tim. "Hot Spots," *Trouser Press*, September 1980, 64

Strauss, Neil. "Recalling a Genius of British Pop," *New York Times*, February 6, 1996, C14

Sullivan, Jim. "Here Come the Police, with Hits—and Misses," *Boston Globe*, November 29, 1980, 13

Wadsley, Pat. *Soho Weekly News*, September 7, 1978, np

Wynbrandt, James. *Good Times*, December 14-27, 1976, np

Zeiler, Dave. "Leaving the Garage Door Open," *The Choice*, December 1985, 13

Zimmer, William. "Now Playing, in Studios Near You," *New York Times*, November 19, 2000, 26

Web sites

All Music Guide. "Soundsville!" Accessed January 17, 2004 <http://www.all music.com/cg/amg.dll?p=amg&uid=UI-CASS 70311061907571302&sql=A7gdnvwxla9xk>

____. Bush, John. "Steve Albini." Accessed June 5, 2004 <http://www.allmusic .com/cg/amg.dll>

____. Dougan, John. "New Wave." Accessed September 7, 2003 <http://www.all music.com/cg/amg.dll?p=amg&uid=MISS70308202104&sql=J128>

____. Erlewine, Stephen Thomas. "Nevermind-Review." Accessed May 29, 2003 <http://www.allmusic.com/cg/amg.dll?p=amg&uid=UID-CASS70311061907571302&sql=A3mcyxdybjols >

____. "More Than Skin Deep-Review." Accessed July 31, 2004 <http://www.all-music.com/cg/amg.dll?p=amg&token=ADFEAEE4781FDB4AA97720CE85 3D4BC7946AF301D14CB48D112D5653D0B02240990278FD0BBADAC-CAEF875B47DE3FB24A45805D2C3FE3681&sql=10:eqf6zf0oehpk~T1>

Anonymous. "Marilla Palmer Is Bride of Peter M. Zaremba." *New York Times*, May 26, 1985. Archives. Accessed November 30, 2006 <http://query.nytimes.com/gst/fullpage.html?res=9904E6DB1639F935A1 5756C0A96394826>

Anonymous. "Freaks Come Out at Night," *Time Out New York*, October 2–9

2003 Accessed August 6, 2004 <http://www.timeoutny.com/clubs/418/418.clubs.freaks.box.html>

Arrow 93—This Day in Rock & Roll History. Accessed April 25, August 27, 2004 <http://www.arrowfm.com/cgi/history.pl>

Australian Radio Interview 1991. Transcript. Accessed May 27, 2003 <http://www.garage.clara.net/fleshtones/aussie.htm>

Avenue A/Essex: New York Songlines. Accessed March 6, 2004 <http://home.nyc.rr.com/jkn/nysonglines/ava.htm#14st>

"Blast Off—The Fleshtones." Accessed July 31, 2004 <http://www.limbos.org/fleshtones/fleshtonesa.htm>

Bonomo, Joe and S. Coleman. "Adventures in the Musical Glue Factory with Robert Burke Warren." Fleshtones Hall of Fame. Accessed August 5, 2003 < http://www.garage.clara.net/fleshtones/rbw.htm >

Ceneclear Journal Archives. Accessed June 1, 2003 <http://www.32 brinkster.com/ceneclearchives>

CM, Mojo. "The Fleshtones Archive." Accessed June 7, 2004 <http://www.garage.clara.net/fleshtones/laborat.htm>

Coleman, S. "A Hand for the Band," The Fleshtones Archive, circa 1998 Accessed August 3, 2004 <http://www.garage.clara.net/fleshtones/ mtsd.htm>

____. "Hexbreaking with 'Count Zaremba.'" Accessed August 6, 2003 <http://www.garage.clara.net/fleshtones/cranklin.htm >

Coleman, Zach. "Ichiban Sings the Blues as Deals Sour, Debts Rise," *Atlanta Business Chronicle*, June 21, 1999. Accessed August 6, 2004 <http://www.bizjournals.com/atlanta/stories/1999/06/21/story6.html>

Darzin, Daina. MTV.com-News-More Than Skin Deep. Accessed July 31, 2004 <http://www.mtv.com/news/articles/1440121/20010223/fleshtones.jhtml>

"Deadendkid," forum posting, December 14, 2003, Fleshtones Hall of Fame. Accessed May 23, 2004 < http://fleshtones.org/index.asp?inc=forum-read&article=164>

Design album discography, Part 4. Accessed January 17, 2004 <http://www.bsnpubs.com/pickwick/stereospectrum.html>

DM Records. "Ichiban Records Profile." Accessed May 30, 2004 <http://www.dmrecords.com/companyprofile.html>

Widows on the World: Greatest Bar on Earth, Entertainment and Events Schedule, July 2001. Cached.

Hagelston, John. "We See Better with Hair in Our Eyes: A Place for Contemporary Psychedelic Rock." Rhino.com. Accessed January 20, 2007 <http://www.rhino.com/rzine/StoryKeeper.lasso?StoryID=704>

Heim, Joe. "Soundcheck: This Week in Music," WashingtonPost.com. May 21, 2003

Holmes, Bill. "More Than Skin Deep," Consumable Online. Accessed July 31, 2004 <http://www.westnet.com/consumable/1998/05.12/revflesh. html>

Hoskyns, B. "Trash on Delivery," New Musical Express, ca. 1983. Accessed July 24, 2004 <http://www.garage.clara.net/fleshtones/nme.htm>

I.R.S. Records. < http://www.irsrecordscorner.com >

Kemp, Rob. "Nightingales Bar," *Time Out*, circa 1998. Accessed August 3, 2004 <http://www.garage.clara.net/fleshtones/night.htm>

"La Mama Theater." Accessed February 10, 2003 <http://www.lamama. org>

Lou Reed: A pre-VU discography. Accessed February 5, 2003 <http://www.olandem,chez.tiscali.fr/loureed/lrprevu.html#albums>

Magnuson, Ann. "ArtForum: The East Village 1979-1989 A Chronology: Ann

Sources

Magnuson on Club 57." Accessed February 10, 2003. <http://www.findarticles.com/m0268/2_38/57475770/p1/article.jhtml>

O'Neill, John. "In the Flesh: NYC's Fleshtones Return to Hitsburg," *Worcester Phoenix*, July 16–23, 1999. Accessed June 24, 2004 <http://www.worcester phoenix.com/archive/music/99/07/16/ON_THE_ROCKS.html>

"The Phnyx (1970)," phoenixnewtimes.com. Accessed August 3, 2004 <http://www.phoenixnewtimes.com/extra/dewey/peep/movie177.html>

Pollstar Artist Tour History Report: The Fleshtones. Accessed May 15, 2003

Rhino Records <http://www.rhino.com/rzine/StoryKeeper.lasso?StoryID=704>

Robert Christgau: Dean of American Rock Critics. Accessed June 20, 2004 <http://www.robertchristgau.com/get_artist.php?id=1933&name=Fleshtones>

Roberts, Jamie. "The Fleshtones-Laboratory of Sound," Consumable Online. Accessed June 7, 2004 <http://westnet.com/consumable/1995/09.22/revflesh.html>

Robinson, Charlotte. "Hitting the Beachhead and Coming on Strong: An Interview with the Fleshtones' Peter Zaremba." PopMatters. September 2, 2005 <popmatters.com/music/interviews/fleshtones-050902. shtml>

RockCritics.com. Accessed June 3, 2004 <http://www.rockcritics.com/ topfive/proudowner_v.html>

"Set List Information," Steve's Tape and MiniDisc Exchange. Accessed July 31, 2004 < http://www2.cruzio.com/~stever/BootListSetList.html >

Sinclair, Tom. "Short Takes: EW reviews four hot new albums—We take a closer look at new releases by the Fleshtones, Mobius Band, Holopaw, and Minotaur Shock." *Entertainment Weekly*. August 5, 2005 <http://www.ew.com /ew/report/0,6115,1090040_4_0_,00.html>

Skwire, Brendan. "World Trade Center—27 July 2001." The Fleshtones Archive, Fleshtones Hall of Fame. Accessed November 30, 2006 <http://garage .brinkster.net/wtc.htm>

"Steve Albini Dissects his Music," *The Daily Cardinal*, April 3, 2003. Accessed June 5, 2004 <http://www.dailycardinal.com/news/ 2003/04/03/Arts/Steve.Albini.Dissects.His.Music-408532.shtml>

Thau, M. "The Legend of the Lipstick Killers," blogcritics.org. Accessed May 4, 2004 <http://blogcritics.org/archives/2003/03/23/161845.php>

Tucker, Ken. "CD Reviews: '80s Punk Rocks On." National Public Radio. Audio. August 9, 2005 <http://www.npr.org/templates/story/story.php?storyId=4792548>

Young, J. and I. Robbins. TrouserPress.com. Accessed June 7, 2004; July 31, 2004 <http://www.trouserpress.com/entry_90s.php?a=fleshtones>

Zacharly, Claude. "Hi Fi Report," Maximum Ink. Accessed July 31, 2004 <http://www.maximum- ink.com/archive/98/aug/html/cd-02.html>

Advertisement

Advertisement, *Village Voice*, 4/17/78, np

Press release

The American Federation of Arts, "New Release: SOUL CITY," May, 1979

Sweat

Memorandums

CBS Disques France, memorandum, April 12, 1982

I.R.S. internal memorandum to Richard Mazda, from Jay Boberg, Carl Grasso and Michael O'Brien, January 19, 1983

Mailings

The Fleshtones' Hall of Fame, March 1992

____. November 1992

____. 1993

____. 1996

____. February 1999

Liner notes

Quaglieri, Al. *I Want Candy: The Best of the Strangeloves* (Legacy/Epic, 1995)

Schwartz, Andy. *Blast Off!* cassette (ROIR, 1982)

Zaremba, P. *Fleshtones vs. Reality* (Emergo, 1987)

____. *Angry Years 84–86* CD (Sp. Imposible, 1993)

Radio, television interviews

Zaremba, P. "The Fleshtones: Interview," *Cutting Edge*, MTV, ca. 1983

____. Radio interview, Atlanta, GA, February 20, 1988

Unpublished

Zaremba, P. "Addition to Manifesto: Handbook," ca. 1978

____. memoirs. Used by permission

Index

Index

Index

Index